NOTES

ON

UNCLE TOM'S CABIN:

BEING

A LOGICAL ANSWER

TO ITS

ALLEGATIONS AND INFERENCES

AGAINST

SLAVERY AS AN INSTITUTION.

WITH A SUPPLEMENTARY NOTE ON THE KEY, AND AN APPENDIX OF AUTHORITIES.

BY THE

REV. E. J. STEARNS, A.M.

LATE PROFESSOR IN ST. JOHN'S COLLEGE, ANNAPOLIS, MD.

"Libertate opus est: non hac quam ut quisque Velina
Publius emeruit, scabiosum tesserula far
Possidet. Heu! steriles veri! Quibus una Quiritem
Vertigo facit!" PERSIUS, SAT. 5. l. 73.

"Men are always seeking to begin their reforms with the *outward* and *physical*. Christ begins his in the heart."—KEY TO UNCLE TOM'S CABIN, p. 33.

PHILADELPHIA:
LIPPINCOTT, GRAMBO & CO.
No. 14 NORTH FOURTH STREET.
1853.

SLOTE & MOONEY,
Stereotypers.

CONTENTS.

APPENDIX.

PREFATORY.

The Work to which this is in reply has called forth already a good many answers *in kind*,* but none of them, I believe, occupying the ground I have here taken. Throughout the preparation of these Notes, I have kept the promise of my Title Page constantly in view, and have endeavoured to fulfil it; how successfully, must be left to others to determine. For myself, I can only say that, so far as the logic of the work is concerned, I can see no flaw in it. As to the style, should any be disposed to censure in it an occasional departure from the gravity they might think befitting such a theme, my answer is, That in this I have but followed the example set me by the author of the original work, and that her lucubrations and argumentations have, at times, been irresistible provocatives to it. I have throughout endeavoured to treat her with the respect due to a woman, but I confess that I have occasionally found it hard work, especially in the Note on the Key, and where her course in England has come under review. If she would but consider where she stood, and where "the Professors of Lane Seminary" stood, twenty years ago, (and if she cannot remember so far back, Mr. Stanton and his fellow-students could give her memory a jog,) she would be more chary of her reflections upon others who stand where she stood then—where they have always stood, and who are, therefore, *probably*,

* Among these is one entitled, "The Planter: or, Thirteen Years in the South. By a Northern Man. Philadelphia, H. Hooker & Co.," which, I am surprised to learn, has had, as yet, a comparatively limited circulation. It is one of the most readable books I have met with on the subject.

A*

as good as she, seeing they have had the grace to preserve their consistency.

In the course of the following Notes I have had frequent occasion to refer, in no very flattering terms, to a class of Abolition leaders. In this class are *not* included such men as Charles Sumner and Salmon P. Chase, each of whom, in spite of his position on this subject, is every inch a gentleman. In this class *are* included such *epicene* characters as Garrison, Abby Folsom, Theodore Parker, Lucy Stone, Henry C. Wright, Abby Kelly Foster, and, last, not least, Horace Mann, *Vir gregis*, who, "like the bulls of Borrowdale, run mad with their own bellowing." They may be "very estimable characters in private life," for aught I know; some of them, I am told, are: but it is as public characters that I have to do with them, and, as such, *feeling* no respect for them, I have accordingly expressed none.

In conclusion, as I have had to follow the obliquities and sinuosities of the original work, treading in the footsteps and on the heels of "my illustrious predecessor," and have, therefore, been unable to make my work a systematic one, I have to request the reader, after going through the Introduction, to turn to pages 110, 111, 122–125, and 139, and read them carefully before commencing the work in course: he will then understand the ground I occupy, and will come, I think, to the conclusion, before he gets through, that it is the only tenable one.

PRELIMINARY.

A Kentuckian, dining at the Astor House in New York, took up the "Bill of Fare," and began devouring its contents, but falling foul of such jaw-breakers as "*Huitres au gratin*," "*Pâté de foie gras*," "*Pieds de cochon de lait*," &c., &c., he at last gave up in despair, and called out, "Here! waiter! give me some bacon and greens! I'll go back to first principles."

If the author of "Uncle Tom's Cabin" had followed the Kentuckian's example, and, when she found herself getting beyond her depth, gone back to first principles, she would have saved herself the trouble of writing the book, and me that of refuting it. To be sure, she might have been some twenty, or thirty, or perhaps fifty thousand dollars poorer for it, but her loss would have been the country's gain. I do not mean merely that the purchasers of the book would have saved their half-dollar, or dollar, or dollar-and-a-half, as the case might be; this would have been a small consideration: they would have saved much more than this; they would have saved themselves so lavish an expenditure of "righteous indignation," and the country a great deal of useless, nay, mischievous excitement.

The object of the following "Notes," is to answer a question that has been put to me *ad nauseam*. During my last summer's annual trip to the North, wherever I went, the first question was, How do you do? and the second,

What do you think of Uncle Tom's Cabin? and this latter question asked, too, more than once, with an air of triumph, as though the book were, to use its author's expressive epithet, a "settler." For my part, I think it is a *riler:* it has stirred up more bad bile in twelve months, than can be settled in as many years.

It is evidently a *live* book. This is proved by the *run* it has had. Several months ago, its circulation had reached 100,000 in this country, and 150,000 in England, in which latter country an Abridgment has also been issued for children, (!) entitled, "A Peep into Uncle Tom's Cabin." (See London Guardian, of Jan. 26.) Moreover, it has been translated into several modern languages, French, German, Danish, and even Welsh; the latter, under the euphonious title of "Caban F' Ewythr Twm!" The next thing will be to translate it into Grebo, for the benefit of Quashy at home, to show him how much better a Christian his cannibal master in Africa is, than his brother Quashy's Christian master in America!

To crown the whole, the *story* (her story, not history, as some one has very aptly remarked,) has been dramatized and brought out on the London boards; and in Paris, on the night of the 18th of January, it was produced *in eight acts* (!) to an overflowing house, who "didn't go home till" *after* "morning," sitting it out till *half past one, A. M.* Shades of the Puritans! A descendant of yours, the daughter of one Theological Professor, and wife of another, catering for the Parisian Theatre, and "taking the shine off (*deslustrer*) of" Moliere and Eugene Scribe! Verily, truth *is* strange—stranger than fiction; than any other fiction, that is, than Uncle Tom's Cabin.

The book, then, is a *live* one. But in what does its life reside? Not in its plot, for it has none; probably for the same reason that Coleridge gave for women having no souls:* it is itself a plot;—a plot against the peace of society. (I am speaking of the character of the work, not of the author's motives.) I say, it is a plot against the peace of society. But of this more hereafter. My present business with it is, as a work of art; and viewing it as such, I must say, that of all the works of fiction I remember to have met with, it, so far as unity of action is concerned, is the most slovenly put together: its only bond of unity is an external one—the thread and paste of the binder.

The life of the work, then, is not in its organism: we must seek it elsewhere. Luckily, we have not far to seek. Like an old cheese, its life is in its *dramatis personæ*. Such characters as Topsy, Miss Ophelia, and Black Sam, might carry on their backs all the *lead* of all the novels of the present generation, with a fair prospect, still, of floating down to posterity. Of all the characters in the book, there is but one that is a *failure;* and the reason is, that in that one, the author had no original to draw from: Legree is neither man nor devil, but a *tertium quid*, and such as none but a *quidnunc* could swallow.

In one respect, Uncle Tom's Cabin is like General Harrison's: its *proprietor* has left the "latch-string out," in sign of invitation; or rather, she has left the Cabin itself *open*, and she must not, therefore, take it ill, if, in Western parlance, I "walk into it."

But first, while standing on the threshold, or rather, before the threshold, (*præ limen*,) I wish to "define my position," that there may be no mistake about it.

I start, then, with the Christian doctrine of human brotherhood. I say, the Christian doctrine, for I am writing

* Nay, dearest Anna, why so grave?
I said you have no soul, 'tis true;
For what you *are*, you cannot *have*:—
'Tis *I* that have one, since I first have you.

for Christians, not for Theodore Parker and his coterie: they cannot appreciate the argument; it takes common sense and common honesty to do that.

I start, then, with the Christian doctrine of human brotherhood; and by brotherhood, I mean what any plain man would understand me to mean; not mere resemblance, but *relationship;* in other words, identity of origin.

For instance, I claim relationship with the new-found Bourbon's reputed brothers, the descendants of Eunice Williams: I trace my pedigree through five generations, and hers through two, and find them meeting in one and the same person, Samuel Williams, son of Robert, freeman of Roxbury, Mass., 1638.

Again, I *admit* (not *claim*) relationship with the *coterie* above-mentioned, through our common ancestor, Noah: a rather remote relationship, to be sure, but near enough *for practical purposes.* Of the two relationships, I consider myself infinitely more honoured by the former than by the latter.

I trust, I have made clear what I mean by human brotherhood. I mean by it what Holy Scripture means. St. Paul declares that God "hath made of one blood all nations of men, for to dwell on all the face of the earth," (Acts xvii. 26,) and I believe it *because* he has declared it. Even if he had not declared it explicitly, I should still believe it, for it is implied in the doctrine of the incarnation, the cardinal doctrine of Christianity. Certainly, they who have no relation to the first Adam, have none to the second; and if there *are* any such, then Christ did not die for the whole world, and will not by his death draw all men unto him. Thus the doctrine of certain modern *savans*, that the brotherhood of the human races is one of resemblance, and not of relationship, is a doctrine that strikes at the foundation of Christianity, and no Christian, therefore, can have any sympathy with it.

Having thus laid down, as my starting point, the doctrine of human brotherhood, I join to it that other Scripture doctrine, that, under certain circumstances, we are our brother's keeper, and from the two I draw the inference that, under certain circumstances, it is not only justifiable, but *our bounden duty*, to hold our brother in bondage.

Of course, the *coterie* will cry out against this, and "curse up hill and down," as St. Clare has it, (vol. 2, p. 12,) spite of "Northern folks" being "coldblooded,"—spite of their being "cool in every thing."

St. Clare never made a greater mistake, so far as "cursing up hill and down," is concerned, as I can testify from personal knowledge. The Southern fanatics "can't *begin* to curse" like the Northern ones; partly, probably, because they have not the talent for it, (for it requires talent of a peculiar order,) and partly, because there are not enough of them to keep each other in countenance.

Well, let the railers rail on: truth can afford to be railed at; better, at least, than they can afford to rail at her, as they may one day find to their cost. Leaving them to rail it out, I address myself to quite a different class of people,—to the truth-loving men of the North, and especially to the honest rank and file of the Free-Soil Party, whose only fault is, that they have let their heart run away with their head; in which, as in many other points, they are the reverse of their leaders, who have let their head run away with their heart, if, indeed, they ever had one.

To come back to my subject. We hear a great deal about "slavery in the abstract," and Mrs. Stowe makes St. Clare say, (vol. 2, p. 10,) "On this abstract question of slavery, there can, as I think, be but one opinion." On this abstract question of slavery, there can, as *I* think, be no opinion at all, simply because the abstract question is no question at all. Slavery in the abstract, (admitting for the sake of the argument that there can be such a thing,) means slavery considered in its essence, irrespective of its accidents, just as the abstract triangle signifies a figure with three sides and three angles, irrespective of the comparative magnitude of those sides and those angles. But what is true of the abstract triangle, is true of all triangles, and in the same manner what is true of slavery in the abstract, (admitting that there is such a thing,) is true of all slavery. To say, therefore, that slavery in the abstract is wrong, and slavery in the concrete, right, is to talk nonsense. The truth is, slavery in the abstract is a non-entity, and nothing, therefore, can be predicated of it, or inferred from it :

"Nothing can come of nothing; speak again!"

Slavery, then, is right or wrong, according to circumstances. Slavery, as a means, may be right ; slavery, as an end, is always and everywhere wrong ; slavery, as a transition state (of a race), may be right ; slavery, as a permanent condition (of a race), is wrong ; the subjection of an inferior race to a superior one, may be right ; the subjection of a superior to an inferior, is always wrong.

The simple test of the right or wrong of its continuance, in any given case, is its effect upon both races : if its continuance would elevate the subject race in the scale of being, then it is not only right, but the duty of the superior race, to continue them in bondage ; if, on the contrary, the discontinuance of servitude would elevate the subject race, without depressing the dominant one, then it ought to be discontinued at once. These are the principles with which I start, and they are such, I think, as must commend themselves to every unbiassed mind. With these preliminary observations, I proceed at once to the examination of the work.

NOTES

ON

UNCLE TOM'S CABIN.

NOTE 1.—OBJECT OF UNCLE TOM'S CABIN.

THIS shall be given in the author's own words: "The object of these sketches is to awaken sympathy and feeling for the African race, as they exist among us; to show their wrongs and sorrows, under a system so necessarily cruel and unjust as to defeat and do away the good effects of all that can be attempted for them, by their best friends, under it." (Preface, p. 6.) Such is the author's declaration of her object, and we are bound to believe it; but had she avowed her object to be to awaken in the North antipathy to the Southern people, as a people, to show their cold-blooded indifference to, nay, positive sanction of, a system of heartless and mercenary oppression, we should have said the whole internal evidence of the book was in accordance with such an avowal.

But let us take her declaration as we have it, and let us examine into it a little. Had it occurred as an incidental observation in some exciting part of the narrative, we might have considered it as rhetorical exaggeration; but standing, as it does, in the preface, (which is expected to be a plain, unvarnished, matter-of-fact sort of thing,) and being, as it is, a declaration of the author's object, where, if anywhere, we should expect that she would weigh her words, I see not how I can give it any other than a literal interpretation.

And yet, in doing this, I am puzzled by the very next paragraph, in which the author tells us that she "can sincerely disclaim any invidious feeling towards those individuals who, often without any fault of their own, are involved in the trials and embarrassments of the legal relations of slavery. Experience has shown her that some of the noblest of minds and hearts are often thus involved;" for how "some of the noblest of minds and hearts can often be," (i. e. continue, for that is the meaning here of the verb "be,") involved in "a system so necessarily cruel and unjust as to defeat and do away the good effects of all that can be attempted for them," (the negroes,) "by their best friends, under it," passes my comprehension. They cannot thus continue, ignorantly, for if the system be, what it is here represented to be, a system of *necessary* cruelty and injustice, *always* and *everywhere*, without *one* redeeming trait, so that, in point of fact, they have never, in any instance in which they have attempted it, succeeded in doing *any* good to *any* of their slaves, but have, always, and under all circumstances, done them evil and only evil, (for such is the literal meaning of the author's language); I say, if all this be so, they cannot but know it, and knowing it, and still continuing connected with the system, they can be neither "noble minds," nor "noble hearts."

Before God, as I am a Christian, nay, as I am a man, if I believed the system were what, in the literal meaning of the language, it is here represented to be, I would renounce, at once and forever, all social intercourse with the people of the South; nay, I would not even preach the gospel to them, for the gospel is for *men*, and not devils, and none but a devil incarnate could uphold such a system, or have anything to do with it, except to execrate it, and to spurn it from God's earth, which it pollutes and dishonours.

But, as I said, I am in doubt about the meaning of the

paragraph. If it stood by itself, I should have no difficulty with it; but, as it is, I know not whether it is to be taken as a literal statement of fact, or as a rhetorical exaggeration. One or the other it must be. I would be glad if our author would tell us which.

If she says it is to be taken as a literal statement of fact, then she ought to expunge the two paragraphs that follow it. Nay, more, she ought to join at once the crusade of Garrison, and Philips, and Wright, against the slaveholder, as a monster to be hunted from the face of the earth. (*See Appendix, A.*)

If, on the other hand, she says that it is to be taken as rhetorical exaggeration, then all I have to say is, if such be the exaggeration of the sober preface, what are we to look for in the body of the work? What but a tissue of exaggeration from beginning to end? And such (so far as the evils of slavery are concerned,) we shall actually find it to be when we get to it.

NOTE 2.—BLEEDING AFRICA.

But I have not yet done with the preface. Here is another rhetorical specimen: "In this general movement, unhappy Africa at last is remembered; Africa, who began the race of civilization and human progress in the dim, gray dawn of early time, but who, for centuries, has lain bound and bleeding at the foot of civilized and Christianized humanity, imploring compassion in vain." (p. 6.)

Now if this means anything to the purpose, it means that *that* Africa, which "began the race of civilization and human progress in the dim, gray dawn of early time," "has for centuries lain bound and bleeding at the foot of civilized and Christianized humanity." But history tells us that *that*

Africa is Northern and Eastern Africa; and the same history tells us that *that* Africa has "for centuries lain" (whether "bound and bleeding," or otherwise,) at the foot, not of "civilized and Christianized humanity," but of fanatical, Mussulman barbarism. And the same history tells us further, that the only Africa that has anything to do with Uncle Tom's Cabin is that Africa which for the last three or four centuries has furnished America with slaves, and that *that* Africa, so far from having been reduced to its present degraded condition by European and American Christendom, (which is what the author means, if she means anything to the purpose,) is, to say the least, no lower in the scale of degradation now, than when discovered by the Portuguese four centuries ago.

But perhaps the Africa of our author is, not the Africa beyond the ocean, but the African race here; for she tells us (vol. 2, p. 302,) that they "have *more* (the italics are her own) than the rights of common men" here; that they "have the claim of an injured race for reparation." And again (p. 318,) she puts the question, "Does not every American Christian owe to the African race some effort at reparation for the wrongs that the American nation has brought upon them?" And again, she says, (p. 321,) "If this persecuted race," &c.

Well, let it be so. But, observe, it is *Africa*, not here and there an African,—it is "this persecuted *race*," not here and there a persecuted *individual;* for one hundred, or one thousand, or even ten thousand, bleeding negroes, do not make "bleeding Africa," any more than one swallow makes a summer.

According to our author, then, the African has been deteriorated by his bondage here. She means this, or her language is mere declamation.

But is this so? Let us look into it a little. Are there

any Uncle Tom's in Africa, or even any Black Sam's? Are there any B——'s, (see vol. 2, p. 320,) or C——'s, or K——'s, or G——'s, or W——'s, or G. D——'s, there? Nay, rather, are not ninety-nine in every one hundred of the negroes here, ages in advance of ninety-nine in every one hundred there, in the onward march of humanity. (See Appendix, B.)

And to what is all this owing? To what but to American slavery, and to the humanizing influences with which, as a *race*, they have been brought into contact under it? But for American slavery, they had been now as degraded as "the African in his native ranges," or had not been at all.

Say I this of myself? Nay, our author says the very same. "When an enlightened and Christianized community shall have, on the shores of Africa, laws, language and literature, drawn from among us, may then the scenes of the house of bondage be to them like the remembrance of Egypt to the Israelite,—a motive of thankfulness to Him who hath redeemed them!" (Preface, p. 8.)

This is genuine good sense, and it is refreshing to meet with it; but then it puzzles me about the other paragraph, for it follows from it that the Africa of the preface is not the African race here. What, then, in the name of wonder, is it? I cannot tell. Reader, can you? Nay, can the author herself?—And this, too, is in the *sober* preface!

NOTE. 3.—THE SLAVE-TRADE.

But I have not yet done with the preface. Here is another choice bit of rhetoric: "Thanks be to God, the world has at last outlived the slave-trade."

I would to God that this thanksgiving were not premature; but when I see, by almost every arrival from the African coast, that the accursed traffic is still carried on, as vigorously almost as ever, and under circumstances of even greater cruelty, I cannot join our author in her rejoicing.

The truth is, all the efforts of France and England to suppress the trade have only aggravated it. Their intervention was prompted, I am willing to believe, by a good motive, but it has been a signal and notorious failure, from the beginning.

As far back as 1826, in the ninth report of the American Colonization Society, (p. 23,) I find the following: "The extent and atrocity of the slave-trade remains, it is believed, undiminished, and in more than one instance during the year, has the flag of our country been seen to wave over vessels employed beyond all doubt in this traffic."

In the following year, Mr. Clay, in a speech before the society at its annual meeting, uses this language: "Notwithstanding the vigilance of the powers now engaged to suppress the slave-trade, I have received information that in a single year, in the single island of Cuba, slaves equal in amount to one half of the above number of 52,000, have been illicitly introduced."

How it was with the other great slave-market on this side of the Atlantic, we learn from Mr. Walsh's notices of Brazil in 1828-9: "It should appear, then," says he, "that notwithstanding the benevolent and persevering exertions of England, this horrid traffic in human flesh is nearly as extensively carried on as ever, and under circumstances, perhaps, of a more revolting character." He then adds, that from June, 1819, to July, 1828, only 13,281 Africans were recaptured from the slavers by the British cruisers, being an average of less than 1500 annually, while the annual shipments, during that period, were 100,000, and from 15 to 20 per cent of these were lost or thrown overboard, *to elude those cruisers;* being a far greater annual sacrifice of life than had ever before accompanied the traffic.

In 1833 came West-India Emancipation, giving a fresh stimulus to the trade in Cuba, to make up for the falling off in the other West-India islands; large numbers being imported into it annually, notwithstanding the Spanish treaty, and the importation winked at, it is said, by the local authorities, *for a consideration.*

This trade is still going on. Even while I write, the Post brings information of the arrival of the Baltic, with Liverpool dates to the 17th inst., (November,) and the very first paragraph of English intelligence is the following:

"In the House of Lords, on the 16th, Lord Brougham presented a petition from Jamaica, praying for more active measures on the part of Government for the suppression of the slave trade. Lord Palmerston moved to demand a return of the slaves imported to Cuba and Brazil. Mr. Hume complained of the infraction of the slave treaty by Spain and Portugal."

And yet we are told, in the face of all this, that the world has outlived the slave-trade. If so, then it has outlived slavery also, and "Uncle Tom" is a work of supererogation. (See Appendix, C.)

But enough of the preface: let us come to the body of the work.

NOTE 4.—THE SLAVE CODE;—WHAT SLAVERY IS.

This is not the first subject in the order of the narrative, but it is the first in logical order, in the body of the work, and so I take it up first. Here is our author's view of what slavery is: "This cursed business, accursed of God and man, what is it? Strip it of all its ornament, run it down to the root and nucleus of the whole, and what is it? Why, because my brother Quashy is ignorant and weak, and I am intelligent and strong,—because I know how, and *can* do it,—therefore, I may steal all he has, keep it, and give him only such and so much as suits my fancy. Whatever is too hard, too dirty, too disagreeable for me, I may set Quashy to doing. Because I don't like work, Quashy shall work. Because the sun burns me, Quashy shall stay in the sun. Quashy shall earn the money, and I will spend it. Quashy shall lie down in every puddle, that I may walk over dry-shod. Quashy shall do my will, and not his, all the days of his mortal life, and have such chance of getting to heaven, at last, as I find convenient. This I take to be about what slavery *is*. I defy anybody on earth to read our slave-code, as it stands in our law-books, and make anything else of it." (Vol. ii. p. 11.)

Well, if this be so, then I have two observations to make; first, that slavery is not confined to the Southern States, but is coextensive with Christendom, not to say Heathendom; and second, that if this be "about what slavery *is*," then it is not so very bad, after all.

No doubt it strikes at the opening paragraph of the Declaration of Independence; but then, it is because that paragraph strikes at common sense, and common observavation; unless, indeed, it be considered a rhetorical flourish; in either of which cases, it is sadly out of place, the American Revolution needing no such false philosophy to justify it. Men are *not* born free and equal in any practical sense of the terms; neither have they any such inalienable rights as are here asserted. No man has an inalienable right to life, or to liberty, (for men may, and often do, forfeit them both,) or even to the pursuit of happiness, except so far as it is involved in the pursuit of virtue. No. Man's inalienable rights, (for inalienable rights he has,) are of an altogether different class; as, for instance: Every man has an inalienable right to love the Lord, his God, with all his heart, and soul, and mind, and strength, and his neighbour as himself. Every man has an inalienable right to do justly, love mercy, and walk humbly with his God. Every man has an inalienable right to keep himself unspotted from the world. Every man has an inalienable right to love his enemies, to bless them that curse him, to do good to them that hate him, and to pray for them that despitefully use him and persecute him. These, and such as these, are man's inalienable rights, and if every man would assert them, by acting upon them, the world would be a great deal better than it is. These, and such as these, I say, are man's inalienable rights; if there is any inalienable right of another class, it is that so ably set forth by Carlyle,—the right of every man to be compelled to do what he is fit for, if he won't do it voluntarily; and this brings us back to Quashy, who *is* doing here in the United States, just what Quashy is fit for—Quashy himself being judge. But on this point, Aunt Chloe shall speak for us:

"Yer mind dat ar great chicken pie I made when we guv de dinner to General Knox? I and Missis, we come pretty near quarreling about dat ar crust. What does get into ladies sometimes, I don't know; but, sometimes, when a body has de heaviest kind o' 'sponsibility on 'em, as ye may say, and is all kinder '*seris*' and taken up, dey takes dat ar time to be hangin' round and kinder interferin'! Now, Missis, she wanted me to do dis way, and she wanted me to do dat way; and, finally, I got kinder sarcy, and, says I, "Now, Misses, do jist look at dem beautiful white hands o' yourn, with long fingers, and all a sparkling with rings, like my white lilies when de dew's on 'em; and look at my great black stumpin hands. Now, don't ye think dat de Lord must have meant *me* to make de pie-crust, and you to stay in de parlour? Dar! I was jist so sarcy, Mas'r George." (Vol. i. p. 45.) And if Auguste St. Clare, in the passage before us, had been "jist so" sensible, he would have given us a little less rhetoric, and a good deal more logic.

Aunt Chloe evidently understands Quashy's capabilities. She sees clearly his inferiority to his white brother, and she speaks out what she sees. Witness her observation on "Mas'r George," (vol. ii. p. 41): "How easy white folks al'us does things!" And again, (vol. ii. p. 58): "I wouldn't hear to Missis givin' lessons nor nothin'. Mas'r's quite right in dat ar; 'twouldn't do, no ways. I hope none our family ever be brought to dat ar, while I's got hands." Witness also the way she addresses her own sable offspring, (vol. i. p. 42): "Here you Mose and Pete! get out de way, you niggers!"—a mode of address, not, by any means, peculiar to her; for we have it again, with an additional epithet, in Andy's address to black Sam, (vol. i. p. 71): "'So she would,' said Andy; 'but can't ye see through a ladder, ye black nigger?'" And any one who is familiar with the negroes at the South, knows that their standing compellation of disparagement is, "you nigger!" and, when they would be particularly disparaging, "you black nigger;" showing thereby their own sense of their inferiority to the whites, and of their adaptedness to the work that is put upon them. And in this I have no doubt that they are in the right of it.

Certain it is that there is a good deal of "hard," and "dirty," and "disagreeable" work to be done, and that *somebody* must do it; and certain it is, too, that there is a good deal of work that is neither hard, nor dirty, nor disagreeable, and that somebody must do *it*. Now it so happens that the work that is hard, and dirty, and disagreeable, requires little skill and less brains; and it so happens, too, (unfortunately for Quashy,) that the work which is neither hard, nor dirty, nor disagreeable, requires a modicum of both.

Now, then, comes the question: Shall Quashy be set, or rather, set himself, to do the work which requires brains, and for which he has no brains, and Quashy's master have to throw away *his* brains upon the work that has no need of brains, and which Quashy could do just as well as he, and, it may be, a little better?

But perhaps it may be said, If Quashy has no brains, then go to work and give him brains. Well, this is just what we are doing, and have been doing for the last two hundred years, and with encouraging indications, too, of eventual success. Quashy is already, as I said above, (Note 2,) undeniably several generations in advance of his black brother in Africa, but he is, no less undeniably, several generations behind his white brother in Europe and America; and, therefore, he must not think to put himself on a level with him, but must e'en content himself with being in process of melioration, however slow the process be. Even should it take four hundred years in all, as did the disciplining of the Israelites in Egypt, it will be time well spent.

Meanwhile, so long as so many of Quashy's white brethren in America, and so many more in Europe, have to do work, to the full, *as* hard, and *as* dirty, and *as* disagreeable, as Quashy himself, I do not see that Quashy's case calls for any *peculiar* sympathy, so far as the *hardness*, and the *dirtiness*, and the *disagreeableness* of his work is concerned; and therefore, all about the said hardness, and dirtiness, and disagreeableness, in the paragraph aforesaid, may go for so much rhetoric, thrown in for effect upon the undiscriminating, who, unhappily, in those cases where the sympathies are enlisted, form the majority even of educated people.

So much for the hardness, and the dirtiness, and the disagreeableness, of Quashy's work; at least, for the present; I shall have more to say on it, by and by, when we come to the subject of the European labouring classes.

But there is another assertion in the paragraph quoted at the commencement of this note, that requires notice:

"Because my brother Quashy is ignorant and weak, and I am intelligent and strong,—because I know how and *can* do it,—therefore, I may steal all he has, keep it, and give him only such and so much as suits my fancy."

This, if true, is a very serious matter; neither more nor less than a deliberate and wanton violation of the eighth commandment. But *is* it true? Is it a fact that Quashy does not receive a fair return for his labour? Let us make a calculation. For the first fourteen years of his life, Quashy is a bill of expense to his master, costing him, on the average, here in Maryland, twenty-five dollars a year, which, for fourteen years, amounts to three hundred and fifty dollars. To this must be added the average interest, which would be six per cent. for seven years, if the earlier years of the fourteen were as expensive as the latter; but as they are not, we will put it at six per cent for five years, or one hundred and five dollars in all; which added to the three hundred and fifty makes four hundred and fifty-five dollars for the cost of Quashy to his master, at fourteen years of age. From fourteen to twenty-one, he barely pays his keeping, so that to his cost at fourteen must be added seven years' compound interest at six per cent, making his cost to his master, at twenty-one, omitting fractions, six hundred and eighty-four dollars. This is supposing him to live till twenty-one; but as, according to the census returns for 1850, thirty in every one hundred die before that age, and the average time of their death is at seven years old, the expense of raising thirty for seven years, or, which is the same, say twelve for fourteen years, (it would be, fifteen for fourteen years, if the expense of the last seven years were no greater than the first seven,) must be added to the cost of seventy in every one-hundred; that is to say, to the above six-hundred and eighty-four dollars must be added twelve-seventieths of itself, to get at the actual cost of Quashy to his master, at twenty-one; which gives, in round numbers, eight-hundred dollars.

Now, if Quashy is not to be a bill of expense to his master, he must pay six per cent. interest on his cost, and an additional one and three-quarters per cent. life-insurance; in all, seven and three-quarters per cent., or sixty-two dollars per annum, which is a little over five dollars a month. This, then, is Quashy's wages, already paid him, in advance, in the shape of food and clothing, &c., during his minority.*

If now we add to this, (what every New-Englander who has lived at the South *knows*,) that Quashy does not do more than one-third, or, at the very utmost, one-half as much work as an able-bodied labourer on a farm at the North, (see Note 15,) and that for this he receives, besides the five dollars above mentioned, his food, clothing and shelter, with medical attendance and nursing when sick, and no deduction for lost time, even though he should be sick for years, while the "farm-hand" at the North gets only ten or twelve dollars, and has to clothe himself out of it, and pay his own doctor's and nurse's bill in sickness, to say nothing of lost time, I think we shall come to the conclusion that if there has been stealing anywhere, it has not been from Quashy.

But it will be said, Quashy's master gets rich on Quashy's labour. Well! what is the inference from this?—that Quashy's master is a thief? If so, then Jonathan is a bigger thief, for he gets rich faster on the labour of his "hired man." For my part, I do not think that either of them is a thief, though Jonathan certainly comes the nearer to it of the two.

* Should it be said that the free labourer at the North does not pay his father for the expense he has been at in rearing him in childhood, and therefore Quashy ought not to be required to pay interest on that item, I answer, He does pay him, though in a different way; he pays him in rearing his own children,—an expense that Quashy is free from.

There is one other thing in the quotation requiring notice:—"Quashy shall do my will, and not his, all the days of his mortal life, and have such chance of getting to heaven, at last, as I find convenient." Now, if it were true that slavery diminished Quashy's chance of getting to heaven, that, of itself, would be sufficient to condemn it. But the truth is, Quashy's chance is better in slavery, than it would be out of it; just as a poor orphan boy's chance of getting to heaven would be better as an apprentice, even under an exacting master, than as a truant and a vagabond; for a truant and a vagabond, out of slavery, Quashy would be. He cannot take care of himself; he has never been used to it. In his native land, he was uncared for, and ran wild; here, he has been taken good care of, and has improved; but he must improve a good deal more, before he will be capable of self-government, either socially or individually.

To use an expressive epithet of Miss Ophelia's, Quashy is a *shiftless* creature;—shiftless, in the figurative sense of the term, and would be so, very soon, in the literal, if left to himself. He *is* so, in his native land; he is very nearly so, in Jamaica, and the other British dependencies in that quarter, as I shall show in a subsequent note. (See Note 9.)

But that Quashy's chance for heaven, in slavery, is not quite so hopeless, after all, is shown by the fact that about one-tenth of the Methodist communicants in the United States, are slaves, which is almost the proportion of the slaves to the whites throughout the whole country. (See Appendix, D.) But even if the proportion of the negro communicants to the whites were not one-half, or even one-fourth, as large as it is, it would still have to be shown, (which it never could be,) that it would be larger, were they set free, before Quashy's chance for getting to heaven could be said to be diminished by slavery.

NOTE 5.—THE SLAVE-CODE—ABUSES OF SLAVERY.

"Talk of the *abuses* of slavery! Humbug! The *thing itself* is the essence of all abuse! And the only reason why the land don't sink under it, like Sodom and Gomorrah, is because it is *used* in a way infinitely better than it is. For pity's sake, for shame's sake, because we are men born of women, and not savage beasts, many of us do not and dare not,—we would *scorn* to use the full power which our savage laws put into our hands. And he who goes the furthest, and does the worst, only uses within limits, the power that the law gives him." (Vol. ii. p. 11.)

In our author's eye, the slave-code is evidently a raw-head and bloody-bones—a monster of injustice,—and she can hardly say enough against it. I will here set down what she does say, and then, after some general observations on the subject, take up each point in detail. The quotations that follow, are in the order of the narrative.

(1.) "Whoever visits some estates there," (in Kentucky,) "and witnesses the good-humoured indulgence of some masters and mistresses, and the affectionate loyalty of some slaves, might be tempted to dream the oft-fabled poetic legend of a patriarchal institution, and all that; but over and above the scene there broods a portentous shadow—the shadow of *law*. So long as the law considers all these human beings, with beating hearts and living affections, only as so many *things* belonging to a master,—so long as the failure, or misfortune, or imprudence, or death of the kindest owner, may cause them any day to exchange a life of kind protection and indulgence for one of hopeless misery and toil,—so long it is impossible to make anything beautiful or desirable in the best regulated administration of slavery." (Vol. i. p. 23.)

(2.) "Nevertheless, as this young man was, in the eye of the law, not a man, but a thing, all these superior qualifications were subject to the control of a vulgar, narrow-minded, tyrannical master." (p. 28.)

(3.) "It's a free country, sir; the man's *mine*, and I do what I please with him,—that's it!" (p. 31.)

(4.) "Don't you know a slave can't be married? There is no law in this country for that; I can't hold you for my wife, if he chooses to part us." (p. 36.)

(5.) "And she was whipped, sir, for wanting to live a decent Christian life, such as your laws give no slave girl a right to live." (p. 166.)

(6.) "But now what? Why, now comes my master, takes me right away from my work, and my friends, and all I like, and grinds me down into the very dirt! And why? Because, he says, I forgot who I was; he says, to teach me that I am only a nigger! After all, and last of all, he comes between me and my wife, and says I shall give her up, and live with another woman. And all this your laws give him power to do in spite of God or man." (p. 166.)

(7.) "Kind families get in debt, and the laws of *our* country allow them to sell the child out of its mother's bosom to pay its master's debts." (p. 167.)

(8.) "The feeling, living, bleeding, yet immortal *thing*, which American State law coolly classes with the bundles, and bales, and boxes, among which she is lying." (p. 191.)

(9.) "It is commonly supposed that the *property* interest is a sufficient guard in these cases." (Vol. ii. p. 7.)

(10.) "Here is a whole class,—debased, uneducated, indolent, provoking,—put, without any sort of terms or conditions, entirely into the hands of such people as the majority in our world are; people who have neither consideration nor self-control, who have n't even an enlightened regard to their own interest,—for that's the case with the largest half of mankind." (p. 7.)

(11.) "All government includes some necessary hardness. General rules will bear hard on particular cases. This last maxim my father seemed to consider a settler in most alleged cases of cruelty." (p. 17.)

(12.) "Miss Ophelia well knew that it was the universal custom to send women and young girls to whipping-houses, to the hands of the lowest of men,—men vile enough to make this their profession,—there to be subjected to brutal exposure and shameful correction." (p. 147.)

(13.) "And that soul immortal, once bought with blood and anguish by the Son of God, * * * can be sold, leased, mortgaged, exchanged for groceries or dry goods, to suit the phases of trade, or the fancy of the purchaser." (154.)

(14.) "Here, a worn old negress, whose thin arms and callous fingers tell of hard toil, waiting to be sold to-morrow, as a cast-off article, for what can be got for her." (p. 158.)

(15.) "'You must not take that fellow to be any specimen of Southern planters,' said he. 'I should hope not,' said the young gentleman, with emphasis. 'He is a mean, low, brutal fellow,' said the other. 'And yet your laws allow him to hold any number of human beings subject to his absolute will, without even a shadow of protection; and, low as he is, you cannot say that there are not many such.'" (p. 173.)

(16.) "Ye say that the *interest* of the master is a sufficient safe-guard for the slave. In the fury of man's mad will, he will wittingly, and with open eye, sell his own soul to the devil to gain his ends; and will he be more careful of his neighbour's body?" (p. 269.)

(17.) "'Do!' said Legree, snapping his fingers scornfully. 'I'd like to see you doing it. Where you going to get witnesses? How you going to prove it? Come now!' George saw at once the force of this defiance." (p. 282.)

(18.) "That the tragical fate of Tom, also, has too many times had its parallel, there are living witnesses, all over our land, to testify. Let it be remembered that in all Southern States it is a principle of jurisprudence that no person of colored lineage can testify in a suit against a white, and it will be easy to see that such a case may occur, whereever there is a man whose passions outweigh his interests, and a slave who has manhood or principle enough to resist his will. There is, actually, nothing to protect the slave's life, but the *character* of the master. Facts too shocking to be contemplated occasionally force their way to the public ear, and the comment that one often hears made on them is more shocking than the thing itself. It is said, 'Very likely such cases may now and then occur, but they are no sample of general practice.' If the laws of New England were so arranged that a master could *now and then* torture an apprentice to death, without a possibility of being brought to justice, would it be received with equal composure? Would it be said, 'These cases are rare, and no samples of general practice?' This injustice is an *inherent* one in the slave system. It cannot exist without it." (p. 311.)

(19.) "I beseech you, pity the mother who has all your affections, and not one legal right to protect, guide or educate the child of her bosom!" (p. 316.)

A formidable array of charges, but evincing on the part of our author a strange forgetfulness of the very nature and object of human law. Verily, if laws are to be held responsible for the wrongs which they *passively* permit, the slave-code will find plenty of other codes to keep it company, even in the Northern States, to say nothing of European Christendom. Nay, under the scalpel of our author, the Mosaic code itself will not escape. Witness the following enactments: "If a man smite his servant, or his maid, with a rod, and he die under his hand, he shall be surely punished. Notwithstanding, if he continue a day or two, he shall not be punished: for he is his money." (Exod. xxi. 20, 21.)

Now, what is the inference from this enactment? Recollect that the Mosaic law, viewed even as a national code, is from God. I know this is denied by some, but I am speaking to Christians. The Mosaic law, I say, viewed even as a national code, is from God, and its provisions, therefore, the very best that the nature of such a code will admit of; in other words, perfect adaptations of means to ends, and, as such, applicable not only to the Jewish people, but, in analogous circumstances, to every other people.

What, then, I say, is the inference from the above enactment? Not that a man may flog his slave to within an ace of his life, and still be a good man. God forbid! But that the prohibition of his doing it, by legal enactment, would, under the circumstances, all things considered, be a greater evil than the *passive* permission of it.

Here we have the vindication of the slave-code in a nutshell; nine-tenths, if not ninety nine-hundredths of its provisions—those of them, I mean, that are more usually objected to—will come under a similar category. They may seem to bear hard, in individual instances, but their operation *as a whole* is benignant. Even the slave himself, to say nothing of the rest of the community, is, all things considered, better off for them, and would be worse off for their repeal, or material modification.

This consideration seems to be entirely lost sight of by those who are so horrified at the enactments of the slave-code. Our author herself, loses sight of it; or rather, she gives it an implied denial in one of the foregoing quotations, (11): "General rules will bear hard on particular cases. This last maxim my father seemed to consider a settler in most alleged cases of cruelty." This maxim our author, it would seem, does *not* consider a settler; and yet the common sense of mankind has embodied it in a proverb:—

Summum jus, summa injuria:

The rigor of the law is the extreme of injustice. And that this is really so, might easily be shown in instances almost innumerable. To mention but one or two: The laws of most civilized nations recognize the principle of prescription;—that where, for instance, a man has been in undisputed possession, for a certain number of years, (twenty is the usual number,) of a piece of land, the law will not disturb his possession; and the provision is a wise one, for it operates to quiet titles and prevent litigation. But suppose a landed proprietor, who is wallowing in wealth, takes advantage of the provision to keep possession of a few acres which he knows belong in justice to his poor neighbour, who has been prevented by some cause beyond his control, (shipwreck, for instance, and detention in an enemy's territory, or among a barbarous people,) from asserting his title within the limited time, would not every honourable man cry out against such conduct as worthy of universal execration?

Or again; take the statute of limitations, which is designed as a safeguard against fraudulent claims, trumped up against a man, when, from lapse of time, he could not easily find testimony to disprove them, and suppose a just debt, by some fault or mischance of the creditor, barred, or, as the popular term is, *outlawed*, by the statute; if the debtor takes any other advantage of the fact than to keep himself out of the clutches of the law till he can obtain the means to pay the debt, he can lay no claim to the character of an honest man.

The law of bankruptcy is another instance in point; and I might go on to mention several others, but as many of them will come in more appropriately when I come to take up the author's specific charges, already quoted, I shall defer them till then.

A word upon the police regulations of the slave-code. Our author has said little or nothing about them, either because she considered them of little consequence, or because she thought they were, on the whole, neither oppressive nor unjust.

These regulations are founded in necessity, and are therefore the more rigorous in the more southern of the slaveholding States. No doubt they are often irksome to the slave, but so are parental restraints often *very* irksome to the child; and yet parental restraint, properly applied, is a good thing; and so are the police restraints of the slave-code.

At any rate, that they are necessary, we may fairly infer from the fact that the masters, by enacting them, subject themselves, in most cases, to great trouble and inconvenience, which they certainly would not be disposed to do unnecessarily; and the same may be said of most of the other provisions of the slave-code. Indeed, our author herself, not only admits, but even maintains their necessity to the continuance of the system, and that, too, in some cases where, in fact, they are not necessary; but instead of drawing from this fact the inference of their justice, she draws from it the inference of the injustice of the system which requires such enactments. This inference I shall have occasion to controvert in the sequel; I might, therefore, fairly pass over the specific objections before-mentioned: but as some of them are palpable misrepresentations of fact, and others lie with equal weight against recognised laws and customs in all free civilized communities, I prefer to take them up, and dispose of them one by one.

In the Appendix will be found a collection of extracts from the statutes and decisions of several of the slaveholding States. I would not be understood as maintaining that they are all to be found in the code of each State: I do not say this, for it is not true; but I do say that I see no reason why they should not all be introduced into each State, and that if they were, they would, it seems to me, leave little to be desired in the way either of alteration or of addition.

Be that, however, as it may, the extracts are to my purpose, as much as though their provisions were, each and all of them, to be found in the code of every slave State. For I am not undertaking, be it observed, to defend every provision of the slave-code in every State: the nature and design of the work I am sifting does not require it of me. The object of Mrs. Stowe in writing Uncle Tom's Cabin was not to bring about the melioration of the slave-code, by showing that several of its provisions, some in one State, and some in another, bore unnecessarily hard upon the slave, and ought therefore to be repealed or modified. Had that been her object, many of her allegations against the slave-code would have been in point, and I, certainly, should not have controverted her application of them. But her object was quite a different one. It was, as is clear from her declaration of it in the preface, and from the whole tenor of the narrative, to strike at the *system* of slavery, by showing its *necessary* cruelty and injustice, and therefore no provision of the slave-code, however "cruel" and "unjust," that is not *inseparable* from the system, in other words, that is not found on the statute-book of *every* slave State, has any business in Uncle Tom's Cabin.

Now, leave out all these unnecessary provisions, which, if they prove anything, prove, not that the *system* is wrong, but that in the code of Kentucky, for instance, as also in that of several of the other States, there is room for improvement, which, I presume, no Kentuckian would deny,—I say, leave out all these unnecessary provisions, and the parts of the story founded upon them,—leave out, also, all those provisions which, though necessary, are not peculiar to the slave system, being found, substantially, on the statute books of the free States,—leave out, further, all those portions of the book that are inconsistent with themselves, and with each other,—finally, leave out all the false premises, and all the inconsequent conclusions, all the sequences turned into consequences, and the rhetoric turned into logic, with all, in the story, that is built upon them, and what would be left of Uncle Tom's Cabin might be put in a nutshell, "ay, and leave room for the kernel."

So much by way of general observation; I now proceed to take up each point in detail. The figures in parenthesis refer to the same figures on pages 27 to 30.

The first charge of our author against the slave-code is, that it makes the slave a thing and not a person. This seems to be a favourite accusation with her, to judge from the frequency with which she introduces it, for it is found, either express or implied, in (1,) (2,) (3,) (8,) (10,) and (13.) And yet, if the reader will turn to Appendix, E. 1, and the passages in *italics* in E. 2, he will see that the charge has no foundation in fact, but is the creature of the author's teeming fancy. Undoubtedly the slave is a chattel *for certain purposes;* but *as* undoubtedly, for certain *other* purposes, he is *not* a chattel. A chattel is a thing which its owner may use as he pleases, so he do not injure his neighbour, or society, in the using of it. A farmer's sheep, for instance, are chattels, and he may shear them when he pleases, and as often as he pleases; and when he has *done* shearing them, he may kill them, and cut them up for mutton. But can the planter serve his slave "such scurvy sauce?" When he can, and shall, with the sanction of the law, then Mrs. Stowe shall be welcome to call the slave a mere chattel, for a chattel, then, he will indeed be, with a vengeance. Such a chattel he was in ancient Rome, prior to the civil law; such a chattel he *is* in modern Africa; his negro master may work him when he pleases, and kill and eat him when he pleases; and he does it, too. (See Appendix, B.) The old Roman did not *directly* eat his slave, but he fed his *lampreys* on him, and ate them, and so ate him *at second hand.* But, as Judge

Henderson says, (STATE VS. REED, Appendix, E. 2,) "these are not the laws of our country, nor the model from which they are taken."

As to the other allegation in quotation (1,) I answer it by a slight change of language, the substituted words being put in *italics:* "So long as the failure, or misfortune, or imprudence, or death of the kindest *husband and father*, may cause *his wife and children*, any day, to exchange a life of kind protection and indulgence for one of hopeless misery and toil, so long it is impossible to make anything beautiful or desirable in the best regulated administration of *the social system*."

If the argument is good in the one case, it is in the other. Indeed in the latter, it is the stronger of the two; for, in exchanging masters, the slave may get as good a one, or he may get a better one, or he may get a worse one; and therefore, on the doctrine of chances, not more than one time in three will he get a worse one; and as even in this case, the new master may be only a little worse, or, considerably worse, or, a good deal worse in every shade and degree of comparison, the chances of his getting a *very* bad one, are *very* small; whereas, in nine cases out of ten, if not in ninety-nine out of a hundred, the husband and father who dies bankrupt, leaves his wife and children an inheritance of "misery and toil." And yet the present social system has continued for some time past, and seems likely to continue for some time to come, spite of the evils incident to it.

Should it be said that the reference, in the case of the "misery" spoken of in the quotation, is not to the change of masters, but to the breaking up of slave families, then I answer, that these separations are very rare, and that the aggregate of suffering from this source in free families left destitute, is incomparably greater than that aggregate in slave families. But of this, more by and by.

"Nevertheless, as this young man," &c. (2.)

Let us make a slight change in the sentence:—"Nevertheless, as this young man was, in the eye of the law, not a man, but *an infant*,* all these superior qualifications were subject to the control of a vulgar, narrow-minded, tyrannical *father*."

That there *are* such fathers, cannot be denied; and that they are far more numerous in proportion to the whole number, than are the masters of the like character, will be readily believed, when we consider that the master is necessarily a man of some property, and therefore, presumably, of some standing in the community, and consequently, with a *character* to maintain among his fellow masters, and with his neighbours in general; while large numbers of fathers are of the offscourings of society. Yet no one proposes to take the child from the father,—even the "vulgar, narrow-minded, tyrannical" father,—except in cases of cruelty; and the cruelty must be manifest and marked, for the law will not weigh the conduct of the father, any more than that of the master, "in golden scales." (See Appendix, E. 2, STATE VS. REED. *Marginal note.*) Should it be said that the father has the control of the child only till he is twenty-one, while the master, ordinarily, has the perpetual control of the slave, I answer, He who shapes the character of the child, during the first twenty-one years of his life, shapes, nine times out of ten, his after destiny. The child of a "vulgar, narrow-minded, tyrannical" father, *may* grow up to be a good citizen, but, ten to one, he will be worse than his father before him.

"It 's a free country, sir; the man's *mine*, and I do what I please with him,—that's it!" (3.)

Well, then, suppose you kill him and eat him, as the master does his slave in Africa. In that case, I rather

* In law, a man is an *infant*, so long as he is under twenty-one years of age.

think we should soon see whether "that's it." As, however, you are not likely to do that in a hurry, if the reader will turn meanwhile to Appendix, E. 2, and read the authorities there cited, he will find that there is a limit to your authority, and a pretty definite limit, too; that, while, on the one hand, your slave is yours *for certain purposes*, viz., to labour for you, "not with eye service, as a man-pleaser, but in singleness of heart, fearing God;" and, on the other hand, you are his, for certain *other* purposes, viz., to supply his physical and moral necessities, yet, aside from these purposes, neither he has any claim upon you, nor you upon him, but that you are, both of you, the servants of a higher Master, and the subjects of a higher law. (See Note 11.)

"Don't you know a slave can't be married? There is no law in this country for that; I can't hold you for my wife if he chooses to part us." (4.)

Here are two assertions, the first of which is untrue, if Maryland and Louisiana are a part of "this country," for in the former, the marriage of slaves is expressly recognized by statute, (see Appendix, E. 7,) and the courts of the latter have decided in regard to slaves, (GIROD vs. LEWIS, 6 Martin's Rep. 559,) that, "With the consent of their master, they may marry, and their moral power to agree to such a contract or connection as that of marriage, cannot be doubted; but whilst in a state of slavery, it cannot produce any civil effect, because slaves are deprived of all *civil* rights. Emancipation gives to the slave his civil rights; and a contract of marriage, *legal and valid*, by the consent of the master, and *moral* assent of the slave, from the moment of freedom, although dormant during the slavery, produces all the effects which result from such contract among free persons."

There is, moreover, a law of Maryland, (1777, chap. xii. sec. 11,) and I suppose, of course, though I have not examined, that there is a similar law in all the slave-holding States, prohibiting any minister from celebrating the marriage of a slave, without leave of the master or mistress, on penalty of fifty pounds, a prohibition which would be ridiculous, did the marriage produce no legal effect upon the *status* of the slave.

The other assertion, "I can't hold you for my wife, if he chooses to part us," is true, if by "hold" be meant "live with;" but then the pauper in Massachusetts is in the same predicament, or was, twenty years ago, (see Appendix, F., BOSTON and ROXBURY,) and I presume is still. He was so in Cambridge, some years after this, to my certain knowledge; and I have no reason to suppose that there has been any change since. And the separation in this latter case is worse than in the former, because more tantalizing, and because it comes at a time when the man can least nerve himself to bear it,—at a time when he is suffering under that affliction, to a freeman the most trying of all, the helplessness of utter poverty.

But "two wrongs do not make a right," and I do not, therefore, bring forward the latter to justify the former—it must be justified, if it all, on very different grounds. That it can be justified, occasionally, I have no doubt; but that the occasions are *very* rare, I have just as little. The law of the land separates husband and wife on the conviction of either party for crime, and if the crime be a very heinous one, it separates them for life. Now the greatest crime that a slave, *as such*, can be guilty of, is insurrection, and next to it, and hardly less heinous, is that of continued insubordination. Of the former of these, the law of the land takes cognizance; the latter is left, wisely, I think, to the discretion of the master; and if, when milder means have failed, he sells the slave, at length, into a more rigorous bondage, what law of God or man shall say him nay?

Will it be said that the master has no right to the labour of the slave, and that therefore the slave is not to be blamed for his insubordination ? I answer, That is the very point in dispute, and it must not be so quietly assumed. I affirm that the system of slavery in this country is right; and I am endeavouring to show it by taking up and answering, one by one, the strongest objections that have been, or can be, brought against it. It will not do, then, to say that slavery is wrong because it separates husband and wife, and then turn round and say that husband and wife must not be separated for insubordination because slavery is wrong, and insubordination, therefore, no crime. If you say that husband and wife are sometimes separated without any fault of their own, then I answer that, in the first place, it is very rarely done, and, in the second place, when it is done, it is ordinarily the fault, not of the system, but of the individual slave-holder.

I say, it is very rarely done: I have a right to infer this from the fact that during a ten years' residence in Maryland, (a State in which slavery is fast becoming unprofitable, and from which, therefore, large numbers are annually "sold south,") the first instance has never come to my personal knowledge. I have a right to infer it, also, from the fact, that, as a general thing, husband and wife sell better together than apart. This we might suppose beforehand, for where there is anything like a strong attachment between them, they will be more effective if kept together, than if separated; it is not in human nature to render as faithful service, where the ties of affection have been rudely snapt in twain, as where those ties have been recognized and respected. It is clear, then, that in this matter, interest and humanity usually work together, and where that is the case, they may be safely trusted to carry the day: men will not ordinarily be cruel even gratuitously, still less when it is against their own interest.

But suppose worse comes to worst, and husband and wife are separated without any fault of either party. Whose fault is it? Not, ordinarily, that of the system, whose ever else it may be. True, the law permits it, but then it is as it permits so many other things that still ought not, ordinarily, to be done,—because, namely, the prohibition would bring with it another and a greater evil. That such would be the case in the present instance, needs little argument to show.

It is well known that it is a common thing for the slaves of adjoining plantations to intermarry, and it is a benefit to them in more ways than one. It benefits the individual, and it benefits the race. It benefits the individual by enlarging the sphere of his associations and his sympathies, and giving him more of a character to support: it benefits the race by invigorating it physically and mentally, it being a well-established physiological law, that where families and petty clans marry "in and in," for several generations, they are deteriorated, sinking rapidly into imbecility, physical and mental,—an imbecility issuing often in insanity, oftener still in drivelling idiocy.

Now, suppose the separation of husband and wife, under any and all circumstances, prohibited by law, how many of these intermarriages, think you, would take place? How many masters would consent thus to tie their own hands? for a tying of them it would be, since where the husband and wife belonged to different estates, neither owner could sell, except within definite limits, without the co-operation of the other; and these limits, to be of any practical effect, must be very narrow; for a separation of fifty miles would, in most cases, be as effective a separation, practically, as one of five hundred, or five thousand. The restriction of the sale, therefore, would have to be to the neighbouring plantations, some eight or ten at the outside, and thus the number of competitors being limited, the marketable value of the slave would be lowered; for though, as I said above, husband and wife sell better, *as a general thing*, where they are to be kept together, than when they are to be parted, in the case supposed, the restricted competition would have a preponderating effect the other way. Besides, it might well happen, that, of the eight or ten, not one would be both able and willing to purchase; and, in that case, the sale would be impossible.

I ask again, then, Would the master be willing thus to tie his own hands? I trow not. On the contrary, though having no intention of selling his slaves, but designing and expecting to keep them, I think he would still be very apt to say with the Irishman in the play, "I won't be forced to do as I've a mind to." The consequence would be, a total cessation of the intermarriages referred to. But, as love is not confined within plantation limits, there would still be as many instances as ever of mutual attachment between slaves of neighbouring estates, with this difference, that the attachment could not find its natural termination in marriage; and the aggregate of suffering from this source would, I verily believe, be tenfold greater than the aggregate of suffering from the few, the *very* few, separations that take place under the present system.

But it will be said, The master *ought not* to withhold his consent to an intermarriage of a slave of his with a slave from a neighbouring estate, for any such reasons as those above referred to. I answer, That may be, or it may not be. It is a point that I am not called upon to determine, for it is aside from the question at issue, which is, not what men ought to be, but what they are; for the law has to do with men as they are: men as they ought to be need no law, being a law unto themselves.

I think I have, then, clearly proved that the prohibition

in question would occasion more suffering than it would prevent, and that, therefore, the law is right in not enacting it.

But it is said, the law not only does not prohibit it, but actually does, itself, the very thing; as, for instance, in sales under execution, or for the division of an estate; well, if it does, it is very bad; almost as bad as the law that separates husband and wife for being unfortunately in debt, and without the means to pay, and leaves the wife and children to starve,—an outrage against justice which, I am happy to say, has been wiped from the statute book of Maryland, but which still lingers, and I fear will continue to linger for some time to come, in that of several of the free States, the "Model Commonwealth" included. I say *almost* as bad; but if the goodness or badness of laws is to be measured by the *aggregate* of human suffering occasioned or prevented by them, it is *not* almost as bad, and does not come nigh being so. It is true we have not the statistics, but if they could be got at, I have no doubt they would show that there are one hundred separations of husband and wife for debt in the free States, to one under execution or other civil process in the slave States; for custom requires, and law sometimes, as in Alabama, (see Appendix, E. 8,) sanctions the requisition, that in sales under civil process, they shall be offered, and, if practicable, sold in families; and it only needs now that the law should be made imperative in all such cases, as I am satisfied it might safely be; for I agree with the author of "Slavery in the Southern States, by a Carolinian," (understood to be Mr. Pringle):—"In slavery we know that it, [the destruction of family ties,] exists as yet more than is necessary to the system." But, as he adds in the next period, "Every day, however, greater efforts are made among us to lessen the evil," and if the North would only mind its own business, and let the South alone, I have no doubt the melioration would go on much more rapidly. Let Northern men consider this, and act accordingly.

"Kind families get in debt, and the laws of *our* country allow them to sell the child out of its mother's bosom to pay its master's debts." (7).

This accusation does not come next in the order of the narrative, but I take it up next because of its connection with the foregoing. I am sorry to say that in most of the slave States it is too true; and I am sorry, too, to be obliged to add, that it is equally true that such works as Uncle Tom's Cabin, do more than all other causes put together, to perpetuate the wrong. Moreover, its admission into the work is gratuitous, for the object of the work is, as I have before remarked, to show the *necessary* cruelty and injustice of the *system* of slavery, and this has no *necessary* connection with the system, as is proved by the fact that it has been prohibited in Lousiana for more than twenty years, under the severest penalties, and that in the other States, the Courts of Equity will not countenance it. (See Appendix, E. 8.)

"And she was whipped, sir, for wanting to live a decent Christian life, such as your laws give no slave girl a right to live." (5.)

If this means that the law does not prohibit the crime referred to, it is untrue. (See Appendix, E. 9.) But if it means that the law is not omniscient and omnipresent, and therefore not omnipotent, that is an imperfection which it labours under, in common with all things human. Besides, the proper question is, not whether certain things happen (in spite of the laws) under the system of slavery, but whether they would cease to happen, or happen less frequently in a state of freedom; and this question has heen answered for us in Jamaica (see Appendix, G. 1,) and recollect that the statement there given is made by one of the Editors of the New York Evening Post, a thorough-going Free-Soil paper,) and the answer applies not only to the paragraph quoted above, but to what is said elsewhere about the sale of "beautiful Quadroon girls," and it is a *full* answer to it.

"But now what? Why, now comes my master, takes me right away from my work, and my friends, and all I like, and grinds me down into the very dirt! And why? Because, he says, I forgot who I was; he says, to teach me that I am only a nigger! After all, and last of all, he comes between me and my wife, and says I shall give her up, and live with another woman. And all this your laws give him power to do in spite of God or man." (6.)

As to the first part of this charge, if the cruelty is of a definite and tangible kind, the laws of Kentucky, as well as the other slave States, provide a remedy, (see Appendix, E. 4;) and if it is not, it comes under the remarks on extract (2). As to the last charge, it is simply untrue: the laws in question give the master no such power.

"The feeling, living, bleeding, yet immortal *thing*, which American State law coolly classes with the bundles, and bales, and boxes, among which she is lying." (8.)

If this means that the classification is, in the eye of the law, an exhaustive one, in other words, that this is the only category under which the law puts the slave, it is not true, and if it does not mean this, it is aside from the purpose. Let us make a slight change in the language:—"The feeling, living, immortal *things* which the Northern farmer coolly classes with the implements they wield, calling them his *hands*." Does he mean thereby that they have no souls, and no heads? So our author's logic (!) would infer; but so does not the logic of common sense. For certain purposes, man is a thing, as really as for certain other purposes, he is a person: the powers of nature,—fire and frost, the ocean and the tempest treat him as a thing, "coolly classing him with the bundles, and bales, and boxes among which he is lying;"

they pay no respect to his personal endowments. The law treats him as a person and as a thing, classing him under both categories; but were he not a thing, were there no exchangeable value in him, the law might call him one, all day, it would not make him one. "Father," said one of the rising generation to his paternal progenitor, "if I should call this cow's tail a leg, how many legs would she have?" "Why five, to be sure." "Why, no, father; would *calling* it a leg *make* it one?"

Apropos of names, one of our author's French translators calls her "Madame *Stove*;" probably because he thought there was *more heat than light* in Uncle Tom's Cabin.

"It is commonly supposed that the *property* interest is a sufficient guard in these cases." (9.)

Change the position of the adverb in this sentence, so that it shall come after the second "is," and it will *then* assert a truth: it *is* not only supposed, but *known* that the property interest is *commonly* a sufficient guard in these cases. As to the *exceptions*, I will notice them under (18.)

"Here is a whole class,—debased, uneducated, indolent, provoking,—put, without any sort of terms or conditions, entirely into the hands of such people as the majority in our world are; people who have neither consideration nor self-control, who haven't even an enlightened regard to their own interest,—for that's the case with the largest half of mankind." (10.)

Our author here asserts that *all* the slave-holders are "such people as the majority in our world are," and then tells us that that majority are without "consideration or self-control, or *even* an enlightened regard to their own interest;" and yet in her preface she puts *some* slaveholders in a very different category. I am therefore bound, in charity to her, to suppose, that she has here misrepresented herself, and that she meant to say that the *majority* of slave-holders are such people as the majority of the world at large, in regard to consideration and self control, &c. But even this is not true; for the slave-holders generally are the *elite* of society,—the picked men; and if I may judge of them from a pretty extensive acquaintance with them in Maryland, and a more limited one in Virginia, during a two years' residence there, I should say that three-fourths at least, if not seven-eighths of them are far, very far, in advance of "the majority in our world," in both "consideration" and "self-control." As to "an enlightened regard to their own interest," if by that is meant, minding the main chance, i. e. looking out for the greatest good of the greatest number, meaning thereby, as Thelwell has it, "number *one*," I am very much afraid that they would have to yield the palm to us Yankees; I say, *us* Yankees, because being a Yankee by birth, and a Southerner by residence, I put myself in either class, as occasion requires.

There is another assertion, that the slaves are all "put, without any sort of terms or conditions, into the hands of such people as," &c. It would seem from this, that in the absence of any acquaintance with the facts, our author had given *carte blanche* to her imagination. How wide of the mark she is, may be seen by turning to Appendix, E. 2.

There is yet one other thing requiring notice, and that is the admission of our author that the slaves as a class are "debased, uneducated, indolent, provoking." I wish the reader to note this admission, as I shall have occasion to make use of it by and by.

"Miss Ophelia well knew that it was the universal custom to send women and young girls to whipping-houses, to the hands of the lowest of men,—men vile enough to make this their profession,—there to be subjected to brutal exposure and shameful correction." (12.)

A universal custom is one that is followed by all, and a

general custom is one that is followed by most; and the custom in question is neither universal nor general. My opinion is, (and it ought to be worth as much as Mrs. Stowe's, considering our respective means of forming one,) my opinion is, that not one in ten of slave men, and not one in one hundred of slave women, are ever thus punished, and when they are, it is for crimes and misdemeanors, such as are punished in the free States by fine or imprisonment, or both; but to fine a slave would be absurd, and to imprison him, would be wholly ineffective, while it would be a great inconvenience and loss to the master. Whipping, then, seems to be the only thing left. If Mrs. Stowe knows of any other equally effective and less unpleasant mode of discipline, and will make it known, I will answer for it, every Southern Legislature will adopt it at once. Men do not whip for the mere love of whipping; I have heard of amateur hangmen, but of an amateur whipper, never. It is as a necessary punishment that it is resorted to. Mrs. Stowe admits its necessity, or, at any rate, its utility, in the training of children, for she tells us that it made part of that training in New England one hundred years ago, and that "it is an undisputed fact that our grandmothers raised some tolerably fair men and women under this regime." (Vol. ii. p. 38.) In this she is undoubtedly right, and I am glad to see that she does not set herself up, like so many at the present day, for a wiser than Solomon. The truth is, they who make such an outcry against whipping are novices not only in theology, but in physiology. When a child is angry, whipping acts as a counter irritation, and thus as a sedative, soothing the nerves, and allaying the excitement of the passions. I have known many a boy who could not be made to listen to reason, till you had given him a sound whipping, and then he would be as rational as you could wish.

But, it will be said, the objection is to the whipping of

adults, not of children. Well, if the adult in body, is a child in mind, with passions dominant, and reason undeveloped, why should not the same mode of discipline be appropriate to him? And such in the present instance is the fact; what the poet says of men in general, is *literally* true of the slaves of the South—they are but children of a larger growth, with all the faults and many of the excellencies of childhood, and requiring a similar discipline. To attempt to govern them as you would the whites would be absurd; and yet even the whites cannot always be controlled without the lash. It is but yesterday that flogging was abolished in the navy and the commercial marine, and already a movement is making to restore it; and that not merely by the officers, but by the men. They never sought its abolition, and it was anything but popular with them. They know that if the bad may shirk with impunity, the good will have to do double duty, and they do not relish the prospect. If indeed the crews of our vessels were composed of picked men, or even of the average of labouring men on shore, it might do; but made up, as they are, to a very great extent, of the riff-raff of society,—men of all nations, and no character,—to talk of managing them without flogging, may sound very fine in theory, but won't do in practice; this is not merely my opinion, but that of one whose sound judgment and freedom from prejudice Mrs. Stowe, at least, will not question. (See Appendix, H.)

But in the paragraph under consideration, it is the whipping of females that is objected to. Well, if they will unsex themselves, they must expect to be treated accordingly. I am not aware that the free States make any distinction in the punishment of a male and female thief or murderer. If any distinction *were* made, it ought to be in favour of the former, for on the principle, *Corruptio optimi pessima*, women when they *are* bad, *are* bad: they are

"Like Jeremiah's figs,
The good are very good, the bad
Too sour to give the pigs."

As to the alleged *custom* of sending women and *young* girls to whipping-houses for slight faults, they who know most of slavery will give least credence to the allegation. That the thing is *sometimes* done is as true, probably, as that good children are sometimes treated cruelly by bad parents,—as true, and no truer. Indeed, the instances of the latter are, probably, far more numerous than of the former, for Tom, Dick, and Harry may be parents, but Tom, Dick, and Harry cannot be slaveholders. Now and then a vulgar man who has amassed wealth may become one; but it must be recollected that there are ten vulgar rich men at the North to one at the South; ordinarily, in the slave States, wealth and refinement go together; ordinarily, therefore, the slaveholder must be, as I have before remarked, a man of character and standing in society.

"And that soul immortal, once bought with blood and anguish by the Son of God, * * * can be sold, leased, mortgaged, exchanged for groceries or dry goods, to suit the phases of trade, or the fancy of the purchaser." (13.)

This is a roundabout way, the author has, of saying, (what might be much better said in plain and simple language,) that the *labour* of the slave can be sold, leased, mortgaged, &c. This I take to be her meaning, for I have too much charity for her intellect to suppose that she could have intended, for one moment, that her language should be taken literally. If she means that the master has a tremendous influence over the soul of the slave, she is right; but then so has the parent over the soul of the child. If she means anything more than this, she is wrong: so far is the soul of the slave from being purchased, that not even the body can be; you cannot, when your slave is past labour, cut him up for beef, as you can your ox, or flay him, and sell his hide for leather, as you can your horse's, or your mule's. His wool (luckily for him) is too coarse to find a market, or I would not be certain that his *Yankee* owner would not shear him, for there is no statute, so far as I am aware, against it, any more than against shearing the wolf, and the common law would hardly furnish an analogy to settle the point.

It is the *labour* of the slave, then, that is purchased; and what there is so wonderful in this, I cannot comprehend, for labour is a marketable commodity the world over,—the labour of the freeman, as well as of the slave; the only difference being that the labour of the free man commands a higher price, as being more productive. If there is anything else the master purchases, beside the labour of the slave, it is the means of enforcing it; and this is what the Northern master equally does, in taking an apprentice, and the means *known to the law* are the same in the two cases, and the legal remedy for abuse of power the same, with the single exception of testimony, which shall be considered in its place.

Of course, I do not maintain that there is no difference between the condition of the slave and that of the apprentice: but what I do say is this:—that so far as the simple selling, apart from its adjuncts and accompaniments, is concerned, they are on a par; and it is this simple selling, leasing, &c., that Mrs. Stowe, in the paragraph before us, seems so shocked at, as though it were, *in itself*, a degradation. Elsewhere, it is true, she speaks of its accompaniments; "actually buying a man up like a horse,—looking at his teeth, cracking his joints, (what that means, I, not being versed in the horse-jockey dialect, do not exactly understand,) trying his paces, and then paying down for him." (Vol ii. p. 21.) In another place (p. 165) she tells us that

Legree "seized Tom by the jaw, and pulled open his mouth to inspect his teeth; made him strip up his sleeve, to show his muscle; turned him round, made him jump and spring, to show his paces;" i. e., I suppose, how he could trot, rack, canter, and gallop. Now, if he had wanted Tom for a race-horse, or even for a saddle-horse, I can imagine how he should want to "put him through his paces;" but what those same "paces" had to do with his capacity for labour, I can't exactly make out. As to the other part of the examination, it is not peculiar to the condition of slavery. Every candidate for admission to the U. S. Military Academy at West Point, or the U. S. Naval Academy at Annapolis, is subjected to a minute personal examination, being required to submit himself, stark naked, to the inspection of the Medical Board. The object is the same in both cases, viz. to ascertain the capacity of the several subjects of it, for the service that will be required of them; and if there is nothing degrading in the one case, (as most certainly there is not,) why should there be in the other? Undoubtedly, the examination of young girls, as described p. 165, if it exist, and so far as it exists, is an evil, but is it a greater evil, nay, is it anything like as great an evil, as "to live with a white person on any terms, rather than be married to a negro," which is the case with the Quadroons of Jamaica, (see Appendix, G. 1,) and would be the case with the Quadroons of the South, were slavery abolished.

"Here, a worn old negress, whose thin arms and callous fingers tell of hard toil, waiting to be sold to-morrow, as a cast-off article, for what can be got for her." (14.)

And who, I pray, is going to buy her. A cast-off garment may find a purchaser, for it costs nothing to keep it; but a cast-off slave will eat as much as a hale and hearty one,—often more; and who, I ask again, is going to buy such an one? Why, the allegation is absurd on the face of it! and the wonder is that the author did not see its absurdity; but her perceptions were too much obfuscated by her eagerness to fasten one more charge upon the South. No! if you would see this sort of cast-off article set up to sale, you must go North,—to the good old commonwealth of Massachusetts, for instance. There you may see (at least, you might twenty years ago, and I have no doubt you may still,) worn-out men and women sold at auction, not to the highest, but to the *lowest* bidder,—i. e. to the one who will feed and clothe them for the lowest sum,—of course, therefore, ordinarily, to the one who will feed and clothe them worst; and it is stated that in one instance at least, (see Appendix, F., WEST-SPRINGFIELD,) they were neither well clothed nor well fed. How could they be at such starvation prices?

But you see nothing of all this at the South. Nine out of every ten, aye, ninety-nine out of every hundred, of the "worn old negresses," spend the evening of their life in quiet, on the estate where they have grown old, nursed in sickness, and kindly cared for, often by the mistress in person, always by some of the family. The few whose masters become unable to support them, are cared for at the public expense,—kindly cared for, not set to sale to the *lowest* bidder.

"'You must not take that fellow to be any specimen of Southern planters,' said he.

"'I should hope not,' said the young gentleman, with emphasis.

"'He is a mean, low, brutal fellow,' said the other.

"'And yet your laws allow him to hold any number of human beings subject to his absolute will, without even a shadow of protection; and, low as he is, you cannot say that there are not many such.'" (15.)

There is nothing here but what has been already remarked

upon under (1.) or will be under (18.), with the single exception of the last sentence, "Low as he is, you cannot say that there are not many such."

Yes! That is just what I *can* say: there certainly are not many such; were it not that I did not like to contradict a lady, I should say there was not one such; as it is, I suppose I must admit the existence of one, though I think that one has about as much to do with "flesh and blood," as the "*chimera bombinans in vacuo*" of the Schoolmen. But more of Legree, by and by. (See Note 17.)

"Ye say that the *interest* of the master is a sufficient safeguard for the slave. In the fury of man's mad will, he will wittingly, and with open eye, sell his own soul to the devil to gain his ends; and will he be more careful of his neighbour's body?" (16.)

What was said under (9.) will apply here. I will merely add that if a farmer will not ordinarily pay one hundred dollars for a horse or a yoke of oxen and then turn round and beat them to death, *a fortiori* will not a planter, ordinarily, pay one thousand dollars for a slave, and then destroy his own property. I say, *ordinarily:* the extraordinary cases the law takes care of, to the extent of its power.

"'Do!" said Legree, snapping his fingers scornfully. 'I'd like to see you doing it. Where you going to get witnesses?—how you going to prove it?—Come now!' George saw at once the force of this defiance." (17.)

Then George must have had a very short memory, for Legree had just before confessed the deed to him: "I gave him the cussedest flogging I ever gave nigger yet. I believe he's trying to die; but I don't know as he'll make it out." (P. 278.) Now if Mrs. Stowe does not know it, I will inform her that George had only to testify to this confession of Legree's and to the condition in which he found Uncle Tom, and any Southern jury would have brought in a verdict of *Guilty*, so far as testimony was concerned, almost without leaving the jury-box; for Southern juries, in these cases, bring in a verdict according to the law and evidence, as they are sworn to do: I wish I could say as much for *all* Northern juries.

"That the tragical fate of Tom, also, has too many times had its parallel, there are living witnesses, all over our land, to testify." (18.)

If it has "had its parallel" *once*, it has been "too many times;" but the author evidently means that there have been a good many instances, for she says that "there are living witnesses, *all over our land*, to testify." Why, then, has she not brought them forward? She has brought forward a witness to prove the business capabilities of the colored people of Cincinnati, the city of her former residence, and where, therefore, she might be supposed to have some *personal* knowledge of the matter; but, here is a large number of alleged facts of which she pretends to no personal knowledge; and yet she has not attempted to substantiate them by testimony, though she tells us "there are living witnesses all over the land" to prove them. Are we, then, to understand that the fact that *six* colored people in Cincinnati, (see p. 320. vol. ii.) have made themselves comparatively rich by their own energy, is so incredible *in itself*, that the author must bring forward a witness,—and that, too, a theological professor,—to back it, while these other alleged facts are, *in themselves*, so credible, that though she pretends to no personal knowledge of them, she may safely rest them on her *ipse*—I beg her pardon,—*ipsa dixit?* If so, then, it speaks poorly for the fitness of the colored people, generally, for freedom.

No! let us have the witnesses; let her give the particulars,—the time and the place. Possibly she may be able to produce half a dozen instances, on the outskirts of civili zation, (*not* "all over our land,") though I doubt it; but, with the same file of Newspapers before me, I think I might venture to produce, for every instance she brought forward, of cruelty to blacks, two instances at least, if not three, of equal or greater cruelty to whites. But, then, as has been well remarked, a black skin is a great blessing in this nineteenth century: it creates a world of sympathy.

"Let it be remembered that in all Southern States it is a principle of jurisprudence that no person of colored lineage can testify in a suit against a white, and it will be easy," &c. (18.)

This principle, as usual, is stated too broadly, as will be seen by turning to Appendix, E. 10. It is not true that no person of colored lineage can testify in a suit against a white, if by persons of colored lineage be meant a person some one of whose ancestors, near or remote, was a negro. The disqualification attaches, not to the lineage, but to the visible admixture of negro blood; and this is a question to be determined by the jury by ocular inspection. Where there is not this visible admixture, the clearest and most undoubted proof of pedigree will not disqualify.

In the Spanish and French West-Indies, a more definite rule obtains, the following grades being distinguished. "The first grade is that of the mulattoes, which is the intermixture of a white person with a negro; the second are the *tercerones*, which are the production of a white person and a mulatto; the third grade are the *quarterones*, being the issue of a white person and a tercerone; and the last one the *quinterones*, being the issue of a white person and a quarterone. Beyond this there is no degradation of colour, [they] not being distinguishable from white persons, either by color or feature. Edwards, W. I. B. 4, ch. 1. Stephens' Sl. of the W. I. Colonies Delineated, p. 27." Wheeler's Law of Slavery, p. 5. Still the general rule is as our author has stated it.

She goes on: "Facts too shocking to be contemplated occasionally force their way to the public ear, and the comment that one often hears made on them is more shocking than the thing itself. It is said, 'Very likely such cases may now and then occur, but they are no sample of general practice.' If the laws of New England were so arranged that a master could *now and then* torture an apprentice to death, without a possibility of being brought to justice, would it be received with equal composure?" (18.) From this it appears that the author is ignorant of the laws of the very State she resides in, let alone those of the slave States. Her allegation against the latter is, that they are so arranged that a master can, now and then, torture a slave to death without a possibility of being brought to justice. This allegation has exclusive reference to the disqualification of witnesses, and so far as that is concerned, it is true; but then, so far as that is concerned, it is true, also, of the laws of New England. They *are* so arranged that a master can *now and then* torture an apprentice to death without the possibility, so far as testimony is concerned, of being brought to justice. He may do it in the presence of an infidel. It is but a few days ago that "the trial of Loring Prince, of Douglass, charged with the manslaughter of John L. Howard, was suddenly terminated at Worcester, Mass., by the ruling out of the dying declarations of the deceased, on the ground that he was an infidel." (See Appendix, I.) In Massachusetts the dying declaration of the infidel is ruled out, not because he may not tell the truth, but because he belongs to a class whose testimony it is not safe to trust. *For precisely the same reason*, in Louisiana, the dying declaration of Uncle Tom is ruled out.

But the infidel is not the only one in whose presence the master may torture his apprentice to death without a possibility of being brought to justice; he may do it in the presence of the convict who has served out his time in the penitentiary, of which class of persons, I take it, there are *some* in New England. Nay more; he may do it in the presence of his own wife; she can testify neither for him nor against him.

I remember being present at a lecture delivered before the Lyceum in Billerica, Massachusetts, some fifteen years ago, by John C. Park, Esq., of Boston, in which, speaking on this subject, he brought forward a supposed case, by way of illustration. A man had been murdered, and two brothers, A. and B. were arrested on the charge and brought to trial. The evidence, which was circumstantial, was very strong against them, but they undertook to prove an *alibi.* A. had been married but the week before, and B. was to be married the week after, to a sister of A's wife. B's betrothed was brought into court, and testified that on the evening in question B. was with her at her house, and he was accordingly acquitted. A's *wife* was ready to testify similarly in behalf of her husband, but her testimony could not be received, and as there was no other rebutting evidence, he was convicted and executed.

Here was a hard case, resulting from the bad working, in a particular instance, of a general rule, which the experience of ages and the collective wisdom of all Christendom have pronounced good. Yet I have not heard that any effort has been made to banish it from New England jurisprudence.

I have said that the wife can testify neither for her husband, nor against him. It is the same with the colored man; he can no more testify *for* the white man than against him. One white man may murder another in the presence of any number of colored men, provided there be no white man present, without the possibility, so far as the testimony of eye-witnesses is concerned, of being brought to justice. The rule, therefore, operating not unfrequently to the prejudice of the whites, we cannot for a moment suppose that it would have been adopted but on the most undoubting conviction of its necessity.

But suppose the rule were repealed and the testimony of the colored man admitted against the white; what weight would it have, think you, with the jury? What weight has the testimony of seamen with a Northern jury? Read the remarks on this subject in Appendix, H., and compare the sailor with the colored man, and the shipmaster in the merchant service with the slave-holder, and then say whether the repeal of the rule would be of any service to the negro? I trow not.

"I beseech you, pity the mother who has all your affections, and not one legal right to protect, guide, or educate the child of her bosom!" (19.)

Yes, pity her, but remember that in pitying her, you are pitying Mrs. Stowe, for *she* "has all your affections, and not one *legal* right to protect, guide, or educate the child of her bosom. Her husband has the power, by law, and if he were the man to do it,—I beg his pardon for the supposition, for I *know* him, and there is not a kinder-hearted man living. But if he were the man to do it, he might take from her the child of her bosom and send it away where she would never see it again, at least while he was living; he has the *legal* right to do it, and it is the *legal* right that we are considering. As to the *moral* right, no one claims it on either side, that I am aware of, except in those cases where the mother is manifestly incompetent, from insanity, or other equally incapacitating cause, to have the charge of it.

I have now, I believe, gone through the whole list of the author's objections to the slave-code; I have taken up her allegations, one by one, and have shown that some of them have no foundation in fact; that others are against enactments which prevent more suffering than they cause; and that the rest, with one exception, lie with equal weight against established laws and recognized principles of jurisprudence in the freest and most enlightened communities;—laws and principles objected to by none but the most ultra radical reformers,—the Garrisons, and Wrights, and Theodore Parkers, *et id omne genus*.

I say, with one exception. I refer to the separation of families; in regard to which I have, as I have already remarked, the authority of Mr. Pringle for saying that "it exists as yet more than is necessary to the system." (Slavery in the Southern States by a Carolinian, p. 32.) I know not whether he would agree with me, but, for my own part, I am fully convinced—and I have thought a good deal on the subject, and endeavoured to consider it in all its bearings,—I say, I am fully convinced that, while for reasons already stated, (4.) the law should not prohibit the owner of slave families from separating them, except, as in Louisiana, in the case of mother and young child, still it ought not itself, by its own act, to separate them, except for crime; for there is a wide difference between doing the thing itself, and *passively* permitting it to be done, on the ground that interfering to prevent it would do more harm than good.

In Alabama, the law already requires, (see Appendix, E. 8,) that in all sales of slaves under civil process, they shall be "offered, and, if practicable, sold, in families; unless," &c. Now, the "if practicable" and the "unless," &c., should be left out, and the sale in families, (so far as the members belonged to the same owner,) be made imperative, including in the term "family," father and mother, unmarried sons under twenty-one years of age, and *all* unmarried daughters. If this were done by all the slave-holding States, as I am persuaded it might be, without any more serious inconvenience resulting from it, in the long run, than from the homestead-exemption law,—a law which has its inconveniences, but which is nevertheless demanded by humanity and sound policy, and is fast getting to be universal,—I say, if this were done by all the slave-holding States, it would take off the odium of the unjust separation of families from the law, and leave it, (where it ought to rest,) on the shoulders of the individual slave-holder, who would in that case, soon find it a burden too heavy for him comfortably to bear.

Note 6.—The Scripture Doctrine of Slavery.

Mrs. Stowe brings forward but two passages, I believe, that have, or are supposed by her to have, any bearing on the subject. The one, "Cursed be Canaan," &c., which she puts into the mouth of a *pro-slavery clergyman*, whom she represents as saying, (vol. i. p. 181,) "It is undoubtedly the intention of Providence that the African race should be servants," &c. But as I do not rest my justification of slavery on that passage, I do not feel called on to make any observations upon it. The other passage is, "All things whatsoever ye would that men should do to you, do ye even so to them;" and this passage she puts into the mouth of an anti-slavery clergyman: but what it has to do with the subject I can't exactly make out. Most men would like to be let off without punishment, if they had committed a crime; does it follow, therefore, that they should let off others? Such an interpretation of the text would strike at the foundation of all law. The passage, then, is not to be taken without limits, but is to have a common-sense application; and thus applied, I find a great deal in it against bad masters, (as against other bad men,) but nothing at all against masters simply so considered.

And it is the same with the entire New Testament. Not

a hint can be found in it, from beginning to end, that the Master was wrong in holding his slave in bondage,—that such holding was incompatible with the Christian character; on the contrary, its compatibility is expressly recognized, as we shall presently see; and yet our Saviour and his Apostles came continually in contact with slavery in its most aggravated form. In proof of this, if proof is needed, read the following *admissions* of the Rev. Albert Barnes, in his work against slavery, (p. 250.)

"All that the argument does require, whatever conclusion we may reach as to the manner in which the apostles treated the subject, is, the admission of the *fact* that slavery *everywhere* abounded; that it existed in forms of great severity and cruelty; that it involved all the essential claims that are now made by masters to the services or persons of slaves; that it was protected by civil laws; that the master had the right of transferring his slaves by sale, donation, or testament; that in general he had every right which was supposed to be necessary to perpetuate the system; and that it was impossible that the early preachers of Christianity should not encounter this system, and be constrained to adopt principles in regard to the proper treatment of it."

And, again, page 251: "It is fair that the advocates of this system should have all the advantage which can be derived from the fact, that the apostles found it *in its most odious forms, and in such circumstances as to make it proper that they should regard, and treat it as an evil, if Christianity regards it as such at all.*"

And, again, pages 259, 260: "I am persuaded that nothing can be gained to the cause of anti-slavery by attempting to deny that the apostles found slavery in existence in the regions where they founded churches, and that those sustaining the relation of master and slave *were admitted to the churches*, if they gave real evidence of regeneration, *and were regarded by the apostles as entitled to the common participation of the privileges of Christianity.*" (Rev. Albert Barnes, as quoted in Fletcher's Studies on Slavery, pp. 117, 118.)

With these facts staring us in the face, the *silence* of Holy Scripture, so far as any expression of disapprobation of the *system* of slavery is concerned, is very *expressive.* This silence is usually attempted to be got over by the allegation (see Paley's Moral Philosophy, Bk. 3, Pt. 2, ch. 3,) that "Christianity, soliciting admission into all nations of the world, abstained, as behooved it, from intermeddling with the civil institutions of any." But, with all due deference to Dr. Paley, there was no need of interfering with civil institutions. In the time of our Saviour, polygamy was a civil institution, and yet Christianity prohibited it to its converts; nor did it thereby come in collision with the civil government; for the civil government did not compel the practice of polygamy, it only allowed it.* Just so with slavery. Had it been incompatible with Christianity for Christians to hold slaves, they could have been prohibited from it, without any conflict with the civil government; for the holding of slaves was *optional* with the citizen; there was no compulsion about it. Quakerism *does* prohibit slavery; in this, as in so many other points, wiser than God: the Quakers in Alexandria, Virginia, will not hold slaves, and yet, though formerly a resident in that city, I never heard that they were looked upon as thereby coming into conflict with the civil power. Quakerism thus does what Christianity did not do: if, then, Paley and his followers be right, Christianity has less moral courage than Quakerism. But is it indeed so? God forbid that it should be. The silence of Holy Scripture, then, as to the

* Had it compelled it, Christianity would undoubtedly have thrown down the gauntlet to it, for its Founder was no temporizer.

incompatibility of slaveholding with Christianity, is an expressive one. But its silence is not all: there is an express recognition of the compatibility of slaveholding with Christianity:. "Let as many servants as are under the yoke count their own masters worthy of all honour, that the name of God and his doctrine be not blasphemed. And they that have believing masters, let them not despise them, because they are brethren; but rather do them service, because they are faithful and beloved, partakers of the benefit." (1 Tim. vi. 1, 2.)

The word here rendered servant means, literally, slave; it is never used for a *hired* servant. It is sometimes, however, employed metaphorically: thus bad men are called servants (δοῦλοι) of the devil, and good men, servants (δοῦλοι) of God; but in both these cases it is an *absolute* service that is designated. So St. Paul calls himself a servant (δοῦλος) of Jesus Christ, and some men, not having the fear of rhetoric before their eyes, have inferred from this that the word, even in its literal application, could not always mean a slave; but this is a palpable *non sequitur*, as I will show by two unexceptionable witnesses, Mr. Senator Sumner and Mrs. Stowe herself.

Mr. Sumner, in his speech in the United States Senate last August, (a copy of which he was so *benevolent* as to send me under his official *frank*, and for which I am much obliged to him, as it has furnished me with this illustration,) holds the following language:—"Sir, I have never been a politician. The *slave* of principles, I call no party master" (p. 5); and Mrs. Stowe tells us, (vol. i. p. 230,) that "Miss Ophelia was the *absolute bond-slave* of the 'ought'." Now if Mr. Senator Sumner could be the slave of principles, and Miss Ophelia the slave of duty, I see not why St. Paul could not be the slave of Him who is the incarnation and embodiment of both.

But even if there could be any doubt about the meaning of the word, the apostle himself has explained it: "Let as many servants *as are under the yoke* count their own masters worthy of all honour." Now I challenge any one to find a single instance in the whole range of Greek literature in which the phrase "servants under the yoke" means hired servants, or any other servants than slaves.

And these servants are here exhorted to count their own masters worthy of all honour, that the name of God and his doctrine be not blasphemed.

But it will be said, This is an inculcation of duty on the slaves, and it does not follow that their masters are right in holding them in bondage, any more than it follows from the command to us, if any man smite us on the one cheek, to turn to him the other, that he is right in smiting us.

Granted, *for the argument's sake;* but what says the next verse? "And they that have believing masters, let them not despise them, because they are brethren; but rather do them service, because they are faithful and beloved, partakers of the benefit."

There were, then, at the time the apostle wrote these words, Christians who were "faithful and beloved," and who, yet, held even their Christian brethren in bondage.

But, it will be said, these Christians were, as yet, imperfectly instructed in their duties, or they would not have done such a deed. Let us see how this is. The epistle from which the passage before us is taken, is addressed by St. Paul to St. Timothy, the first bishop of Ephesus,—made so by the laying on of the apostle's own hands,—and the Christians here referred to were members of the church of Ephesus. Now this church was favoured beyond all others with the apostle's personal presence and ministrations. This we learn from his farewell address to them at Miletus, (Acts xx. 17–38):—"Ye know from the first day that I came into

Asia, after what manner I have *been with you at all seasons.* * * * And how I *kept back nothing that was profitable unto you*, but have showed you, and have taught you publicly, *and from house to house.* * * * * And now, behold, I know that ye all, among whom I have gone preaching the kingdom of God, shall see my face no more. Wherefore I take you to record this day *that I am pure from the blood of all men.* For I have *not shunned* to declare unto you *all the counsel of God.* * * * Therefore watch, and remember that by the space of three years I ceased not to warn *every one night and day with tears.* * * * * *I have showed you all things, how that so laboring ye ought to support the weak;* and to remember the words of the Lord Jesus, how he said, *It is more blessed to give than to receive.*"

This address of the apostle was *five* years earlier, be it observed, than his first epistle to St. Timothy. *Four* years after this address, and *one* year prior, therefore, to the first epistle to Timothy, he addressed an epistle to the Ephesian Christians themselves, and though with all the other churches to whom he wrote epistles he has some fault to find, with the church of Ephesus, he has none. Among the Romans, there were those that "caused divisions and offences contrary to the doctrine they had learned, and served not the Lord Jesus Christ, but their own belly;" (Rom. xvi. 17, 18.) The Corinthians were "carnal," and "incestuous;" (1. Cor. iii. 1, and v. 1.) Of the Galatians the apostle "stood in doubt;" (Gal. iv. 20.) The Colossians, though professing to be "dead to the world," were still, "as though living in the world, subject to ordinances," "after the commandments and doctrines of men;" (Col. ii. 20–23.) Among the Thessalonians, there were those that walked disorderly, working not at all, but being busy-bodies; (2 Thess. iii. 11.) The Cretans (who, to be sure, were not directly addressed by St. Paul, but only indirectly, through St. Titus, their first bishop,) were "always liars, evil beasts, slow bellies;" (Tit. i. 12, 13.) Even to the Philippians, the apostle speaks of their "lack of service" to him; (Phil. ii. 30.) But with the Ephesian Christians, slaveholders as some of them were, he finds no fault at all. Nay he even gives them directions how to exercise their authority over their slaves, without even once hinting that the *having* authority over them was wrong.

So much for the apostle's teaching in the passage before us; I have dwelt the longer upon it, because one passage, clearly understood, is as good as a hundred. I close this note with two inferences.

First: When the apostle exhorts the Colossian masters to give unto their servants "that which is just and equal," (Col. iv. 1,) he means what any man of plain common sense would suppose him to mean,—that they should treat them kindly and endeavour to promote their welfare; and he does *not* mean, what none but drowning men that catch at straws, and the shadows of straws, would ever suppose him to mean,—that they should set them at liberty.

Second: If the apostle could preach to the Ephesians "publicly and from house to house," "night and day with tears," teaching them all the while to "*support the weak*," and they, notwithstanding continue slaveholders, and five years after, be recognized by him as "faithful and beloved," and he could still "take them to record" that he was "pure from the blood of all men," having "not shunned to declare unto them the *whole* counsel of God," then, if the ministers of Christ at the South cannot take *their* people to record that *they* are pure from the blood of all men, it will be because they have not been equally faithful with the apostle to the spiritual interests of master and servant, and *not* because they have not denounced the master as a man-stealer, but have maintained that it was his right, and, under the circumstances, *his bounden duty*, to keep his brother in bondage.

NOTE 7.—EFFECTS OF SLAVERY ON THE NEGRO.

I have already remarked, in the introduction, that the simple test of the right or wrong of the continuance of slavery, in any given case, is, its effect upon both parties. It becomes important, therefore, to inquire what has been, thus far, its effect, here in the United States, upon the negro. I have already alluded to the subject, (Note 2,) but something more than an allusion is needed, especially as the matter is very generally misapprehended.

Mrs. Stowe charges slavery with having " barbarized" the negro: " To fill up Liberia with an ignorant, inexperienced, *half-barbarized* race, just escaped from the chains of slavery, would be only to prolong, for ages, the period of struggle and conflict which attends the inception of new enterprises." (Vol. ii. p. 318.) And again: " On the shores of our free States are emerging the poor, shattered, broken remnants of families,—men and women, escaped, by miraculous providences, from the surges of slavery,—feeble in knowledge, and, in many cases, infirm in moral constitution, from a system which confounds and confuses every principle of Christianity and morality." (p. 317.)

And the London Examiner, in a review of her work, chimes in with her: " We are for our own parts disposed to regard as the chief evil the fact which is sometimes adduced in extenuation of the whole crime against human rights—that under the slave system the negroes have been plunged into such depths of ignorance and brutishness, that they have acquired not only the brute's vices, but in a great measure even the brute's habit of unquestioning content with his position. * * * Not more than two negroes in five thousand yearly have the spirit to attempt to escape. They go to their cabins as the oxen to their stalls. And that by deliberate denial of education, by a long course of debasing treatment, human beings should have been reduced to this—is in our opinion a more horrible result of slavery than even the tearing of the child from the slave parent, or the selling of a husband by auction out of his wife's arms." And again: "The complete acceptance of the slave's position indicated by Aunt Chloe in this last extract, the contempt of their own skin which negroes *acquire* from the habitual tone adopted by their white oppressors, that element of degradation upon which we have already dwelt, is happily touched in many portions of the book." (See Littell's Living Age, No. 439, pp. 102 and 105.)

The charge here is, that American Slavery has caused the negro to degenerate. In refutation of this charge, I appeal "from Philip drunk, to Philip sober," from Mrs. Stowe the Advocate, seeking to bolster up a bad cause with worse argument, to Mrs. Stowe the Judge, giving, in the person of George Harris, an *obiter* (and, therefore, unprejudiced) *dictum:*

"The desire and yearning of my soul is for an African *nationality*. I want a people that shall have a tangible, separate existence of its own; and where am I to look for it? Not in Hayti; for in Hayti they had nothing to start with. A stream cannot rise above its fountain. The race that formed the character of the Haytiens was a worn-out, effeminate one; and, of course, the subject race will be centuries in rising to anything.

"Where, then, shall I look? On the shores of Africa I see a republic,—a republic formed of picked men, who, by energy and self-educating force, have, in many cases, individually, raised themselves above a condition of slavery." (Vol. ii. p. 300.)

Now the meaning of all this is very plain; it means that as the feeble character of the Haytiens was formed in slavery to a "worn-out, effeminate race," so the energetic character of the "picked men" on the shores of Liberia was formed in slavery to a race composed of "stern, inflexible, energetic elements," to which had "been entrusted the destinies of the world, during its pioneer period of struggle and conflict." (p. 302.) And this is undoubtedly true. Yet it is a truth entirely lost sight of by the opponents of slavery, if, indeed, they were ever aware of it. They speak of the poor African as

"Forced from home and all its pleasures,"

just as if he ever had a home, or even the *idea* of one. They seem to look on Africa as a paradise, with the golden age of pastoral innocence and simplicity still lingering among its inhabitants, though long since gone from the rest of the earth. If the reader has heretofore indulged in such a dream, let him turn to Appendix, B., and he will there find what will dissipate it forever.

Hobbes, in his Leviathan, (Pt. i. ch. 18,) thus describes the condition of Europe in the Middle Ages:—"No arts, no letters, no society,—and which is worst of all, continual fear and danger of violent death, and the life of man solitary, poor, nasty, brutish and short." And it must be owned that there is too much truth in the description. Yet Europe in the Middle Ages was paradise, compared with Western Africa in *all* ages that we have any knowledge of her, the present included. She is the darkest of those "dark places of the earth" which, the Psalmist tells us, "are full of the habitations of cruelty."

I have spoken of the slave traffic as an *accursed* traffic, (Note 3,) but it is because of the cruelty with which it is carried on. To stow human beings "in a sitting posture, wedged in between each others' legs, in a space between decks only three feet and a quarter high, with no air but what is admitted through the grated hatchways, through which their food is passed to them," and to keep them thus cramped up for weeks, and even months, together, is a deed that one would suppose none but a devil would be guilty of; and they who do it, deserve the same treatment in return: hanging is too good for them. Why! even the Guinea pigs are not thus stowed away; if they were, they would die on the voyage.

But if the slave traffic were carried on without cruelty,—if the negroes were as comfortably accommodated on board the slave ships, as the Irish and the Germans are in our emigrant vessels, then the slave traffic, so far from being accursed, would be a positive blessing *to them.** The slave, thus brought under the control of a Christian master, would be as much better off than he was under his savage master in Africa, as the German or Irish peasant in this country is better off than he was in his native land. Nay, taking into consideration his own improvement and that of his posterity,—their gradual civilization and Christianization,—and he would be far the greater gainer of the two.

As to the slave trade severing family ties, it is all, to use St. Clare's expression, "humbug:" there are no family ties, among the Western Africans, that are at all regarded by themselves. Parents sell their own children, and husbands their wives, without compunction. (See Appendix, B.) Indeed, properly speaking, there are no husbands and wives; the marriage relation, as we understand it, is unknown among them: its place is supplied by a temporary concubinage; the man can put away the woman at any time, for any reason, or for no reason at all.

As to the slave trade *reducing* free men to slavery, ordinarily, it is not true; most of the natives of Africa are born

* Or rather, it *would be* a blessing to them, but for the fact that where there is a fresh supply from Africa *at a low rate*, the owner can afford to work up his hands, and, *in some cases*, does actually work them up.

in slavery;* and even where they are free, their freedom is a curse to them, and not a blessing. Those slaves at the South who belong to the *hardest* masters, and are *most rigorously* treated, are far better off than the freest native inhabitants of Western Africa; and the *average* condition of the Southern slaves is infinitely preferable to the average condition of the West-African negro, bond or free.

All this, no doubt, will sound very strange to Northern ears: it would have sounded so to mine twenty years ago. It is not the teaching of New England school-books. The children there grow up under the *impression* that the slaves at the South go regularly to their work under the lash, with every nerve of endurance strained to its utmost tension. They have read the words of Cowper,—what schoolboy has not read them?—those glowing words:—

> "Thus man devotes his brother, and destroys;
> And worse than all, and most to be deplored
> As human nature's broadest, foulest blot,
> Chains him, and tasks him, and exacts his sweat
> With stripes, that mercy, with a bleeding heart,
> Weeps when she sees inflicted on a beast:"—

and they have taken them for gospel, and thought them literally applicable to the southern slaveholder. True, they have learned better as they have grown up, but their early *impression* still clings to them and exercises a powerful influence over them. It is with them very much as it was with a class-mate of mine whom I recollect to have met in Virginia, the year after we graduated. "Why," said he, "when I was at Cambridge, I always felt as though the Unitarians were the majority, not only there, but everywhere. True, when I reflected, I knew it was not so, but, then, I did not realize it. And now, I have come here in

* Of the fifty millions that inhabit that continent, forty millions are slaves to the other ten.

Virginia, and they hardly think a Unitarian a human being." This shows how early impressions tyrannize over us, even when we know them to be false. The Northern people know that their early impression of the physical condition of the negro is unfounded, and yet they can't rid themselves of it. I say, they know it is unfounded. Now and then, some greenhorn revives some old exploded fable, but only they believe it who are as green as he. The anti-slavery orators have dropped the physical condition of the negro from their list of topics: it no longer makes up the staple of their harangues. They know, if they know anything about the matter, that the negro is, as a general thing, far better off, physically, than the English day-labourer;—that he works less, is fed better, and has more relaxation. Mr. Senator Sumner, in the speech already quoted, speaks of slavery (p. 7,) as a power, "which, amidst a *plausible physical comfort*, degrades man, created in the divine image, to the level of a beast."

Mr. Horace Mann, in his speech before the House of Representatives last August, when asked by Mr. Mason, (p. 7,) Are not our slaves better off, both mentally and physically, than any three millions of negroes ever were in Africa? instead of speaking out *like a man*, squirms and wriggles through a whole column of circumlocution, because he *could* not answer the question in the negative, and *would* not answer it in the affirmative.

The London Times, of September 1st, with commendable straight-forwardness, speaks thus upon the point: "The efforts made in the South to improve the condition of the slave show at least that humanity is not dead in the bosoms of the proprietors. Mrs. Stowe has certainly not done justice to this branch of the subject. Horrors in connection with slavery —itself a horror—unquestionably exist; but all accounts— save her own, and those of writers actuated by her extreme views—concur in describing the general condition of the Southern slave as one of comparative happiness and comfort, such as many a free man in the United Kingdom might regard with envy. One authority on this point is too important to be overlooked. In the year 1842 a Scotch weaver, named William Thomson, travelled through the Southern States. He supported himself on the way by manual labour; he mixed with the humblest classes, black and white, and on his return home he published an account of his journeyings. He had quitted Scotland a sworn hater of slave proprietors, but he confessed that experience had modified his views on this subject to a considerable degree. He had witnessed slavery in most of the slaveholding States, he had lived for weeks among negroes in cotton plantations, and he asserted that he had never beheld one-fifth of the real suffering that he had seen among the labouring poor in England. Nay more, he declared—

"'That the members of the same family of negroes are not so much scattered as are those of working men in Scotland, whose necessities compel them to separate at an age when the American slave is running about gathering health and strength.'

"Ten years have not increased the hardships of the Southern slave. During that period colonization has come to his relief—education has, legally or illegally, found its way to his cabin, and Christianity has added spiritual consolations to his allowed, admitted physical enjoyments."

Such are the admissions of the opponents of slavery. But it is said the negroes on the sugar estates are exceptions, especially in the "sugar season;" that they are then worked beyond their strength without regard to consequences.

Now so far is this from being the case, that the negroes themselves look forward to the time with pleasurable anticipation; it is to them a harvest-home, a frolic, like our

Northern "huskings." True the work goes on through the whole twenty-four hours; it must or the sugar could not be made, but the negroes work by *relays*, and so far are they from being overworked, that they come out from it, at the end of the season, "fat and well-liking."

The truth is, this story is of a piece with a good many others invented by the Abolitionists, and which they have told so long that they have at last come to believe them without stopping to consider how incredible they might be: *Credo, quia impossibile est*, being apparently their motto. Let one example serve for all:

"The following amusing scene," says the Holly Springs, Miss., correspondent of the Memphis Eagle and Inquirer, "actually occurred last summer between a citizen of our town and a Yankee on board one of the Northern steam-boats:—

"Our Southern friend discovered a disposition in a very gentle looking man on board the boat to open a chat with him, and nothing loth to hear what his friend wished to say, indicated by his manner that he was approachable, whereupon the following dialogue ensued:

"*Yankee.*—Well, sir, I wish to ask you a question; I hope it will be no offence.

"*Southerner.*—Certainly not; I will hear you with pleasure.

"*Yankee.*—Well, sir, is it true, that they work negroes in the plough at the South?

"*Southerner.*—I will answer you in the favourite method of your own countrymen, by asking you a question or two.

"*Yankee.*—I admit the right, sir.

"*Southerner.*—How many negro fellows do you suppose it would require to draw a good large one-horse plough?

"*Yankee.*—Well, I suppose six or seven—say seven.

"*Southerner.*—What are they worth per head?

"*Yankee.*—Well, I suppose $800.

"*Southerner.*—That would be $5,600. Now what would one large, strong horse cost?

"*Yankee.*—I guess about $100.

"Upon this the Southerner looked a little quizzically at his neighbour, who, without waiting to hear the conclusion, stuttered and stammered—

"Well, I–I–I knew it was a d——d lie!"

The physical comfort of the negro, then, is admitted. How is it with his intellect? Has slavery deteriorated it, or has it improved it? Let those who have seen the Guinea negro side by side with the descendants of the original stock imported into this country two-hundred years ago, answer the question; they will all answer it one way, for it admits of but one answer.

The same may be said of their moral condition, only here the contrast is still more striking. Of all the inhabitants of the earth, I suppose it would be difficult to find any others so low in the scale of morality as the West African negroes. Certainly none lower can be found, for they are at the *bottom* of the scale. Says Mr. Fletcher in his "Studies on Slavery," (a work that should be read by all who would thoroughly understand the subject,) in answer to the allegation of Dr. Wayland that slavery "tends to abolish all moral distinctions in the slave, and fosters in him lying, deceit, hypocrisy," &c. If the doctor had seen the native African and slave in the wild, frantic joy of his savage worship, tendered to his chief idol-god, the embodiment of concupiscence; if he had seen all the power of the Christian master centered to effect the eradication of this heathen belief, and the habits it engendered; had he witnessed the anxiety of the master for the substitution of the precepts of Christianity; if he had seen the untiring efforts of the masters, sometimes for several generations, before this great object could be accomplished, and the absolute necessity of its accomplishment before the labour of the slave could ordinarily become to him an article of full and desirable profit,—he would probably never have written the paragraph we have quoted!" (p. 26.) And again; "The African negro has no idea of marriage as a sacred ordinance of God. Many of the tribes worship a *Fetish*, which is a personification of their gross notions of procreation; but it inculcates no idea like that of marriage; and we have known the posterity of that people, four or five generations removed from the African native, as firmly attached to those strange habits as if they had been constitutional." (p. 38.) Of course, the moral elevation of such a people must be more than ordinarily an uphill work; yet slavery has effected it to a considerable degree. Of the three millions of slaves in this country, there are, I suppose, at least one hundred thousand exemplary Christians. These stand at the head of the scale. At the foot of it, is, of course, a very different class; yet take ten thousand of the dregs of the slave population, and place them alongside of ten thousand of the *elite* of West-African negroes, and the comparison will be greatly to the advantage of the former. But take the *average* moral condition of the American and the African negro, and the former will be found incomparably superior to the latter in every element of moral worth.

Say I this, of myself? Nay, every one that has the means of forming an opinion says the same; he cannot say otherwise.

But it will be said, admitting that it is so,—admitting that slavery has elevated the negro, freedom would have elevated him still more. This allegation requires consideration. Before considering it, however, and as a help to the solution of the problem involved in it, let us glance at the condition of the laboring classes at the North and in Europe. In a subsequent note I will recur to this subject.

Note 8.—The Labouring Classes.

On this subject, my remarks will be confined principally to the laboring classes of England, both because it is to them, chiefly, that Mrs. Stowe alludes, and because I have not equal means of information in regard to the European continent. As to our own country, it is too new, as yet, to groan under so heavy a burden of social evils as the old world; though we shall see, before we get through, that even it has its full share, ay, and more than its share, considering its extent of territory and comparatively recent settlement.

I shall confine myself, I say, principally to the laboring classes of England. I wish it, however, to be distinctly understood, that what I have to say, is not said by way of recrimination; there has been enough of that already. Besides, I do not think it Christian; if I did, I could easily find plenty of provocation to it, and that not merely in the English partizan press, but in other quarters, where least it would be looked for. Only a few days ago, I purchsed of a travelling book-vender a stray copy of a little volume entitled, "The Clouds and Peace of Aristophanes, translated into English prose, by a graduate of the University of Oxford. Oxford: Henry Slatter, 1840," and on cutting the leaves I found on the first page of the translation, on the passage, "Out upon you, O war! on account of many evils, and because you prohibit me from chastising my servants," the following note: "For the alleviation of evil which the Peloponnesian war brought to the Grecian slaves, (see Mitford, v. 9.) In a modern Republic, which exhibits all the vices, cruelty, and tyranny of the Athenians, without one particle of their genius or refinement, it is to be hoped that war, if it should again occur, may enforce the lesson which humanity has failed to inculcate; and that the Transatlantic

Strepsiades will be taught, to his amazement, that he can no longer 'flog his nigger' with impunity."

Now as to the "genius" of the "modern Republic," I shall not stop to argue the question, though I think it might easily be shown that we are not altogether destitute of the commodity; but on the score of "refinement," if the above note is to be taken as a fair specimen of what passes under the name, at the most ancient and venerable seat of learning in England, sure I am, that our scholars,—and we have some,—some whose scholarship England herself is ready enough to appropriate, with or without credit, though she does not always make the best selection, at least, in the classical line,—I say, if the above note is to be taken as a fair specimen of what passes for refinement among the graduates of the University aforesaid, sure I am that our scholars will not envy them the possession of it.

Seriously, the above note is a disgrace to the Republic of Letters, and the only apology I can frame for its author is, that he was a tyro, and had not yet cut his wisdom teeth. The translation is a very respectable one; not, however, above the capacity of the better half of our undergraduates of two years standing; and as to the Notes,—the few of them, I mean, that are original,—there is not one that might not have been written by the aforesaid undergraduates,—the above-quoted note about the "genius," the "refinement," &c., of course, always excepted: not one of our undergraduates, certainly not one of our *scholars*, could have written such a note: he would have felt the burning blush of conscious degradation tingling his cheek while writing it, and would have stopped short in mid-way, for very shame.

And such is the state of feeling towards us in the quiet cloisters of England's oldest University! What then must it be in the nation at large! And can we wonder that such malignant and wanton abuse should provoke the bitterest recrimination? No! it is human nature, and however much we may regret it, we cannot wonder at it. Says An American in London, (said to be Col. Mayne Reid,) in a Letter to the Editor of the Times, under date of Dec. 14, 1852, and first published in the New York Journal of Commerce, the Times having refused to publish it: "Travel where he will, an American finds but abuse of his country on the most frivolous grounds, in all journals. I left it in England, to find it fresh where I was so inconsiderate as not to expect it, in the petty press of Germany; I have come back, and the first thing that greets me is not a welcome from those I still like, still esteem, still love, though they do everything to make me dislike, disesteem, and hate them—not a welcome—no, not a welcome—witness your columns of this day! * * * If we do not grow fonder of the country of our ancestors and our commercial competition, we can point to such writings as this latter, and say she will not let us. * * * If I have written warmly—and I do not deny it, for I have felt warmly—it is from that indignant sense of wrong which Americans are everywhere made to feel on subjects that concern their country, sometimes (as in the case of a young Carolinian whom I met with recently,) without a grain of that liking which, with me, where England is concerned, must, even despite myself, always qualify its bitterness." And he adds in a note, "This gentleman (the Carolinian) carried his resentment so far as to be indignant that I should say anything in favor of your countrymen, while his ardent aspiration, though he was really a man of sense, well informed, well educated, and who had the advantages of foreign travel, was for another war with England! 'but one more!' which he significantly said 'would be the last.' I mention this for the benefit of the Times, whose Philippics have helped to make such cordial haters, not less perhaps than has the dishonest meddling with other men's property, of the anti-slavery propagandists, who put their hands without scruple into the pockets of the planters, and sow without remorse the seed of dissensions that have nearly fructified with a harvest of blood between *brothers*. For myself, I hope that, if this writing should meet the eyes of the young Southerner above alluded to, he will now believe, though he may not even yet comprehend 'how it can be,' that I *can* 'reconcile' my love and esteem for what is English, with my sense of duty and a paramount affection for my own country."

To all that the writer says, in the above, of attachment to "what is English," I say, Amen, with all my heart. I love England, as the land of my fathers,—the noblest land, *that* side the water, that the sun ever shone upon, spite of social evils and abuses: I love her Church,—the Pillar and the Ground of the Truth,—the fairest representative, in the Old World, of the Virgin Spouse of Christ, spite of certain practices that have an ugly look of simony,—spite of certain excrescences and accretions, that her truest sons must, I think, find it hard to submit to. And shall I seek to foment discord and ill-will between my countrymen and such a people? When I do it, may I forfeit all the untold blessings which I have inherited from her glorious free Constitution and her more glorious Church!

In bringing forward the condition of the English labouring classes, then, I do it from no vile motive of recrimination. I do it, because the subject is introduced into the work I am commenting on, and because my *argument* requires it.

The author of "Friends in Council" in his "Letter upon Uncle Tom's Cabin," takes exception to its representations of the labouring classes of England, and in place of them gives us a *creation* of his own, a genuine Arcadian picture of rural content; fine *poetry*, no doubt, but contrasting oddly with the prose reality, as exhibited in the extracts I have given in Appendix, K., from Parliamentary and other documents, and the police reports of the newspaper press. Most of these extracts speak for themselves, and little need therefore be said upon them.

The first is from the Rejoinder of the American ladies to the Stafford House Remonstrance against slavery in America. I give it as I find it in the London Guardian of January 19th, 1853. On another page of that paper is the following comment:

"'The Women of America,' we with confusion admit, are more than a match in fluent and pugnacious rhetoric for 'the women of England.' Crushed under a prodigious rejoinder, which seems to have been hurled across the Atlantic by some strong-minded coterie at Boston, lies the crow-quill 'appeal' from Stafford House. Possibly it deserved its fate—certainly it provoked it; yet the reply, we submit, is a parody rather than a retort. No real parallel can be drawn between a bad institution, which is defended and upheld, and the ignorance, misery, and vice which grow up in every old and densely peopled country, and which, if we do not our very best to conquer them, we at least unanimously deplore. To the allegation that the law in Virginia makes the marriage of slaves a kind of concubinage, and permits women to be sold openly for the purpose of prostitution, it is no answer to say that there is a great deal of vice in London streets. There is plenty of it also in the streets of New York. Show us how to eradicate it, and we will try. No, this is no answer; yet it may help us to lay more seriously to heart the things we are reproached with—to be more earnest with ourselves (and O, what resolution it needs to realize the duty to its full extent!) in making the society we live in more like a Christian community than it is."

Now in answer to the above, I have one or two remarks to make. In the first place, I challenge the Guardian to bring forward the "law in Virginia," or any other slave State of the American Union, that "makes the marriage of slaves a kind of concubinage," or "permits women to be sold openly for the purpose of prostitution." On the contrary, against this latter, here in Maryland, there is, and has been for more than one hundred years, a stringent enactment (see Appendix, E. 9); and everywhere in the slave States, public opinion frowns upon it. Can as much be said in regard to the whites and the quadroons of Jamaica? (See Appendix, G. 1.) In the second place, that "no real parallel can be drawn between a bad institution," or *any* INSTITUTION, and "ignorance, misery, and vice," I grant, for an "institution" and "ignorance, misery, and vice," differ in *kind*, and things that differ in kind do not admit of comparison: but between the *consequences* of one institution and the consequences of another institution a real parallel *may* be drawn; and that is what I propose doing. The editor of the Guardian seems, somehow or other, to have got the idea that the "ignorance, misery, and vice" of the slave States are the results of an institution, but that the "ignorance, misery, and vice" of England are *not* the results of an institution; and Punch, in his Poetical Epistle to Mrs. ex-President Tyler, has the same notion. Can it be that the editor of the Guardian writes for Punch? or did Punch borrow the idea from him? Surely, two *sane* men could not have chanced, independently of each other, on so original an idea.

The editor of the London Times understands this matter better. In his paper of December 1st, 1852, in an article on the "Stafford House Appeal," he has the following:— "We will not anticipate the American rejoinders on the mere question of slavery itself, its physical distresses, and moral degradation. These must have occurred to the aristocratic and not less philanthropic circle at Stafford-house, who know too well the fragile materials of *their own social system* not to fear the damaging reply they are bringing on themselves."

The "social system," I take it, is an "institution," *wherever* existing; certainly, the *English* social system. What though it be the product of circumstances, and you can find no law establishing it? So is the institution of slavery. Let the editor of the Guardian look into the books, and examine for himself: laws recognizing the institution and regulating its working, he will find in abundance, just as he will, laws recognizing the social system and regulating *its* working; but any law *establishing* either, he will look in vain for. I know the Judges in England and in this country,—some, even in the slave States,—tell us that slavery is the creature of positive law; but they speak without book. Slavery existed in "the colonies," years before any statute-law even *regulating* it, much less *establishing* it. Why, it is only the other day, as it were, that Maryland enacted the following law:—

"An Act declaring Domestic Slavery to be lawful in this State. 1839. chap. 338.

"*Whereas*, the courts in some of the non-slaveholding States require the owners of fugitive slaves to prove that slavery exists in this State, and it is right to provide a convenient mode of enabling such owners to procure a certified copy of a law, proving that slavery exists by law in this State; therefore,

"Be it enacted by the General Assembly of Maryland, That negroes and mulattoes have been held in slavery in this State as the property of their owners from the earliest settlement of this State, and are, and may be hereafter held in slavery as the property of their owners, and that every owner of such negro or mulatto is entitled to the service and labour of such negro or mulatto for the life of such negro or mulatto, except in cases where such negro or mulatto can show, that by the grant or devise of the owner or some former owner of such negro or mulatto, or his or her maternal ancestor, a shorter period of service has been prescribed."

Slavery, then, in the United States, is an institution, in the same sense that the social system in England is an institution, and in no other sense.

"Ay, but slavery is a *bad* institution."

Nay, Mr. Guardian ! not so fast. How do you know it is a bad institution ?

"Because it produces bad results."

So does the social system of England.

"Not so ! the ignorance, misery, and vice which exist in England, are such as grow up in every old and densely peopled country."

Aye, but the question is, not what they grow up *in*, but what they grow up *from*. A dense population is only the soil in which they thrive : the social system, as it exists in England,—the competitive, or demand-and-supply system,—is the seed from which they spring. *

"That ignorance, misery, and vice, if we do not our very best to conquer, we at least unanimously deplore."

So do we, the comparatively trifling amount of misery and vice resulting from slavery. As to the ignorance, I have a few words to say in explanation. I have not the statistics of Europe at hand, but in the little island of Sardinia, I learn from official sources, that of the 548,000, and

* If the editor of the Guardian wants further proof of this, I will refer him to "The Slave Trade Domestic and Foreign, by H. C. Carey, Philadelphia," published since the above was written, in which he will find my position *demonstrated.*

odd, of its inhabitants, over 512,000 are unable either to read or write. I doubt if anything like that proportion could have been found among the slaves of the last generation. With the present generation it is different; as a general thing, they are not permitted to be taught to read. That it should be so, we "unanimously deplore," but there is no help for it: a hard necessity is upon us;—a necessity, of life and death. Let the abolitionists cease to flood the South with incendiary publications reeking with the fires of hell,—let the inculcation of such devilish doctrines be given over forever, and let the South be *assured* of this, and, my word for it, our Legislatures will repeal forthwith the laws against the education of the slaves.

But, it will be said, the very fact that such laws are necessary, proves that the institution of slavery is a *bad* one. Nay, it proves no such thing: it only proves that plausible falsehood is dangerous to those who receive it for gospel. If all the slaves could be made to see, (as some fugitives *have* seen, and gone back to tell their masters,) how much better off they are than the free negroes at the North,—nay, how much better off they are than the great majority of the European peasantry,—abolitionists might come among us, and preach insurrection, to their heart's content, and no harm come of it: so far from the negroes being excited to bloodshed by it, they would be content with their condition, and heartily thank God for having called them to such a "state of salvation" from the miseries of the peasantry of Europe.

A real parallel, then, with the Guardian's leave, *can* be drawn, *not* between "a bad institution" and "ignorance, misery, and vice;" but between the results of two institutions good or bad; and this is what I propose doing, or rather, setting the reader to do for himself; for if he will turn to Appendix, K., and read the documents there cited, he will need few words of mine, in the way of comment.

What would be said, if the statements there made (and they are only a *specimen* of what might be made,) could be made, with equal truth, of the slaves of the South? The "laboring classes" working for less than one dollar and three quarters a week, (see Appendix, K., 2, [5],) and out of that, feeding and clothing a family, and paying for fuel and rent, and unable to get constant employment, even at that! *One hundred thousand* persons, in the city of London alone, "rising in the morning without the certainty of a meal during the day!" "prowling about the thoroughfares," existing "partly by petty pilfering," and lodging at night, "seventy or eighty persons huddled together, in a small eight-roomed house in a fœtid alley, built up close at the back, so that the circulation of even the smallest current of air is rendered impossible!" (Appendix, K., 2, [1].) Misery so abject that, in the words of the London Morning Herald, (see Appendix, K., 2, [2],) "we may venture *to set against all the degradation of human nature that prevails over ten thousand square miles of the most savage district upon earth, the utter abasement of our fellow-creatures, which is, at the very hour when we write, contained within the limits of the metropolis of great and Christian England!*" "White slaves," in the words of the London Times, (Appendix, K., 2, [3],) "of a sex and age least qualified to struggle with the hardships of their lot—young women, for the most part, between sixteen and thirty years of age, *worked in gangs* in ill-ventilated rooms, or rooms that are not ventilated at all," lest particles of soot and smoke, coming in with the air, should soil and damage the work on which they are employed; sewing "from morning till night, *and night till morning*—stitch, stitch, without pause—without speech—without a smile—*without a sigh!*"

At work "in the gray of the morning," with "a quarter of an hour allowed for breaking their fast;" their food "scanty and miserable enough." "From six o'clock till eleven," "stitch, stitch;" "at eleven, a small piece of dry bread," compelled still to "stitch on;" "at one, twenty minutes for dinner—a slice of meat and a potatoe, with a glass of toast and water;" "then again to work—stitch, stitch—until five;" "fifteen minutes" "for tea;" "once more, stitch, stitch, until nine;" "fifteen minutes" "for supper—a piece of dry bread and cheese, and a glass of beer." "From nine o'clock at night until one, two, and three o'clock in the morning, stitch, stitch; the only break in this long period being a minute or two—just time enough to swallow a cup of strong tea, which is supplied lest the young people should 'feel sleepy.' At three o'clock, A. M., to bed; at six o'clock, A. M., out of it again to resume the duties of the following day." Even this, not all! "During the few hours allotted to sleep"—"rather say, to a feverish cessation from toil"—no relief from their miseries; "*cooped up in sleeping-pens*, ten in a room which would perhaps be sufficient for the accommodation of *two* persons." "Not a word of remonstrance allowed, or possible." The only alternative, "prostitution," or "starvation"!!! Why, the cotton-picking on Legree's plantation,—caricature, ay, *outrageous* caricature, as it is, (see vol. ii. p. 183,) is a paradise in the comparison.

And who are they who, in their refinement of cruelty, thus shame the devil himself? Who, indeed? "The milliners and dressmakers of the metropolis," who "will not employ hands enough to do the work;" who "*increase their profits* from the blood and life of the wretched creatures in their employ."

And have these "milliners and dressmakers" no souls, that they thus fatten on the miseries of their fellow-creatures? Souls! To be sure they have. Why, they claim to be Christians! But will Christ own them for his?—will he allow any such to pass the narrow gate? No, never! His words to all such, individually, will be, "Remember,"—and a bitter memory it will be,—"Remember that thou, *in thy life-time*, receivedst thy good things, and likewise, thy poor workwomen evil things; but now, they are comforted, and thou art tormented." Eternal punishment seems to some too terrible to be true; but I confess, I can conceive of no punishment too severe, or too long-continued, for those who thus drain out the life-blood of their fellow-creatures, to pamper their own pride or avarice. One would almost feel towards them what I once heard one man say of another: "I wish I could be devil for one half-hour, to have the handling of him;" and that, not from any feeling of vengeance,—certainly not, in the bad sense of the term,—but from a sentiment of simple justice. The human mind is so constituted that it *aches* at injustice: it feels that the fitness of things is outraged when the guilty are suffered to go clear; and though with man, as with God, mercy rejoiceth against judgment, there are cases when mercy has exhausted itself, and can plead no longer: "He shall have judgment without mercy, that hath showed no mercy," is the voice of God, and it is a voice that finds an echo in every unsophisticated human breast.

And these things are done in "*merry* England!" Ay, and not these alone. The milliners and dressmakers are not the only ones who thrive on the miseries of their fellows; the keepers of "furnishing" shops are in the same category,—witness the "song of the shirt;" and so are the "fashionable tailors," as many an Alton Locke could testify. Nor are the employers *generally*, altogether clear in this matter; they are, almost all of them, more or less guilty of their brother's blood.

Nor is this misery confined to England, though it is more aggravated there: there is plenty of it in New York, (see Appendix, K. 6. (1.), (2.) and (3.),) and in all our Northern cities.

But worst of all, is the frequent inability to procure work at all, even at the starvation prices; see Appendix, K. 2. (2.) and (4.), and 6. (3.),). If any one can read the "Lay of the Laborer" and the comments immediately following it, (Appendix, K. 2. (4.),), with a dry eye, I do not envy him his feelings.

And this state of things is working out, or rather, has already worked out, its legitimate results in the moral and intellectual condition of the people. I say, its *legitimate* results: the author of the letter to the London Times, of Dec. 14th, 1852, before referred to, speaks of "those creature comforts, which, after all the stuff that is uttered by such dirty birds* as Mrs. Beecher Stowe, and such wholesale libellers as Mr. Charles Dickens, are the mainsprings not only of human happiness, but of human order and of the commonest morality;" and the editor of the London Guardian, (Appendix, K. 2. (1.),) tells us,—and tells us *truly*,—that "although, unfortunately, moral improvement does not necessarily keep pace with physical comforts, one thing is certain, that if any set of human beings be lodged and treated materially as beasts, or worse than beasts, their moral and intellectual natures will soon undergo an analogous degradation."

And such is actually the case with large numbers of the laboring classes of England:—"Poor pale-looking creatures, wearing out their existence in the cellars of damp ware-

* Alluding, no doubt, to the proverb, "It's an ill bird that fouls its own nest,"—a proverb which has had a fresh exemplification, in the speech of Prof. Stowe at Liverpool two or three weeks since. (See Appendix, L.)

houses, with bleached cheeks and sunken eyes, and sharp pointed red noses, chuckling to themselves—laugh they cannot; they have forgotten how to do it; they used to laugh when they were children, but that was a long time ago, and there have been many changes since;" (Appendix, K. 3. (1.),)—"More than twenty instances, occurring within two months, in London alone, of the most foul and savage attacks, committed mostly by men, on women and defenceless children. *The old chivalry of common life, which held it base to lift a hand against a woman, seeming to be extinct,*" (Appendix, K. 3. (2.),). Children of less than seven years old, trained by their fathers as pickpockets, that they may be imprisoned and *maintained at the public charge,* (Appendix, K. 3. (3.),). Of the "couples living together," among the costermongers, only one in ten, (Appendix, K. 1.), and among the chimney-sweepers, only one in fifty, (Appendix, K. 3. (5.),), married; the sin of impurity "no less unhappily prevalent among the *country population* than in the manufacturing districts," (Appendix, K. 3. (6.),); and as the consequence, in part, of this, and in part, of abject poverty, *infanticide,* frightfully prevalent, (Appendix, K. 3. (7.),). To sum up all, according to a statement in the National Temperance Chronicle, (rather a suspicious authority, by the way; for these "papers of one idea" are prone to exaggeration,) sixteen thousand children, in London, trained to crime; five thousand persons, receivers of stolen goods; fifteen thousand gamblers by profession; twenty-five thousand beggars; thirty thousand drunkards; one hundred and eighty thousand habitual drinkers (to excess?); one hundred and fifty thousand persons subsisting on profligacy; fifty thousand thieves; making a grand total of crime, of four hundred and seventy-one thousand, or *one in every five* of the entire population, in the city of London alone!

And such is the moral condition of the English laboring classes!

After this we are prepared for the following statement of their intellectual condition:—More than two-thirds of the *entire population*, (see Appendix, K. 1.,) and of course, therefore, more than three-fourths of the laboring classes, with no "education" at all, or, the little they have, gained at the Sunday School, and by its meagerness forcibly exemplifying the truth of the remark of Mrs. Stowe, (vol. ii. p. 22,) that "a mind stupefied and animalized by every bad influence from the hour of birth, spending the whole of every week-day in unreflecting toil, cannot be done much with by a few hours on Sunday." If "reading and writing" be necessary to salvation, as one would imagine from the outcry that is made against a certain *modern* provision of the slave-code, (considered a few pages back,) alas for the laboring classes of England! How few of them will ever find the strait gate, and the narrow way! Even of the few who are "educated," *how* few are the better for it! In very many cases, their education serves only to make them clever devils.*

After all this, what becomes of the fancy sketch contained in the following paragraph from the "letter," before adverted to, by the author of "Friends in Council?" "There is, however, *even in our poorest districts and in the worst of times*," "between the condition of the English laborer and that of the American slave," "all the difference that exists between humanity and barbarism; between the dignified suffering of a man oppressed by untoward circumstances and the abject wretchedness of another driven about like a beast;—in short, between manhood and brutehood."

"Dignified suffering," forsooth! There must be a good deal of *dignity* in living, as do "a very large number" of

* If the *Yankee* reader cannot see how a devil *can* be clever, let him go to the Dictionary, and get his eyes open.

the "agricultural population" of England, (see Appendix, K. 1.), "in filthy and crowded cottages, where the sexes are in close and perilous contact night and day, where decency is difficult and comfort impossible; the effect of which is to break down the barriers of morality, to obliterate all the sweet and saving attractions of a home, to weaken and desecrate all domestic ties, and to brutalise the manners and debase every natural feeling;" with the "tone of morality" so "low," as to draw from the *North British Review*, of May, 1852, the following; (see Appendix, K. 1.):—"There are few things more remarkable in the sight of observant residents in many *country villages* than the small number of marriages solemnised in the course of the year. Among these few things, we are afraid, must be mentioned the number of *illegitimate children* that are born into the world. *In some villages, indeed, these events are of such frequent occurrence as to excite neither surprise nor indignation.* * * * *. There is something in this kind of *insensibility* which is very chilling and disheartening. This obtuseness of the moral senses, this *deadness to shame*, makes one almost despair over it. *When the standard of public opinion is so low, there is little hope of practical improvement.*" VERY "dignified" this!

"Oppressed by untoward circumstances." Untoward circumstances? Ay, a *very* untoward "circumstance" is the remorseless "Demand-and-Supply System" of modern Civilization,—the system of "unregulated, stimulated, and universal competition,"—the "keep-what-you've-got-and-get-what-you-can" system, which the Guardian would have us believe is not an "institution." Let him beat that into the heads of the laboring classes if he can. I think he will have hard work, judging from the following, which I take from "The Address of the Metropolitan Trades' Delegates to their Fellow-Countrymen, on the Interests and Present

Position of the Laboring Classes of the Empire;" "Signed on behalf of the Delegates,—John Segrave, President; Augustus E. Delaforce, Secretary, 10, North Square, Portman-place, Globe-road Mile-end. Committee-room, St. Andrew's Coffee-House, 82, High Holborn, London, April 11th, 1850:"—"We have it thus announced to us that it is under the operation of unregulated, stimulated, and universal competition, we are henceforth to live. Cheapness is proclaimed to be the one great and desirable attainment. * * * * Bad and appalling, however, as is the existing condition of so many whose only means of supporting themselves and their families is the exercise of their daily labour, yet we maintain that the prospect before us is still more dark and gloomy. We declare to you our conviction, that a far greater degree of suffering and of destitution impends over the laboring class and their families, both of this and of all other nations, unless the falseness of the free or competitive system be thoroughly penetrated. * * * * The predominating influence and power of aristocratic government having prevailed for a lengthened period, are now passed away. The aristocratic part having raised the structure of its government upon the ancient constitutional principles, departed from these principles, introduced corruption, and is now deposed. The predominating influence and power of the middle classes of the nation are acknowledged and accepted at the present time. This party having introduced, *as principles of general social action*, the meanest incentives and motives that can animate the human mind, namely, *the free and full action of unenlightened self-interest*—the unqualified love of wealth and the gratification of this love—the accumulative principle of social action instead of the distributive—their political philosophy being of a character wholly mercantile—is now impaired and degraded by the conflicting operation of those courses which it sets in motion and stimulates."

So say the "Trades' Delegates." What the London Times says, I have already given, but it may not be amiss to repeat it: "We will not anticipate the American rejoinders on the mere question of slavery itself, its physical distresses, and moral degradations. These must have occurred to the aristocratic and not less philanthropic circle at Stafford-house, who know too well *the fragile materials of their own social system*, not to fear the damaging reply they are bringing on themselves." (Appendix, K. 7.)

So much for the Times. And what says the London Morning Herald? Read the following:—"Let men prate as they will about our progress, we do not believe that scenes like these existed in the olden time. Discomfort there may have been—distress, and hard and pinching times—but we do not believe that any generation but our own has ever witnessed *so hideous a congregation of squalid, abject, and hopeless destitution* as is to be found in these loathsome receptacles to which *our busy civilization* drives its cast-off and rejected victims to rot." (Appendix, K. 2, (2),).

"Our busy civilization!" Pregnant words, as its "cast-off and rejected victims" can testify.

And what are to be the results of this "stimulated and universal competition?" What *have* been those results already? We have seen no small number of them, physical, moral, and intellectual; but there is one that I have not yet adverted to, and a frightful one it is, as witness the following from the London Guardian of Feb. 9th, 1853:—

"The *Lancet* states that insanity is on the increase among the working classes in the parish of St. Marylebone, and that none but those whose duties bring them in contact with the sufferers can form an idea of its fearful spread. There are no less than *four hundred and ninety-four* chargeable to the parish. In St. Pancras, insanity also prevails to an unusual amount, especially among the humbler classes." Can we wonder at it?

And this is the condition to which the Abolitionists would *reduce* the slave of the South! Well may the latter say, "Save me from my friends, and I will take care of my enemies!"

There is another point that remains to be adverted to. In the Appendix (K. 3, (7),) are two instances of cruelty to young children, and here is another instance, of oppression of a "poor girl;" I give it as I find it in the London Guardian, of Jan. 26th, 1853:—

"The National Guardian Institution for Hiring Servants, at 40, Bedford-row, has obtained a bad name from circumstances mentioned by a poor girl, named Green, at the Clerkenwell Police-office last week. Having applied for the purpose of becoming a member, her name was taken down, and she paid 5s. Her mistress was applied to for a character, and she forwarded a letter to the institution speaking highly of her. She, (applicant,) however, procured a situation herself at Hanwell, and, on applying to the institution for her character, they refused to give it to her, and the lady declining to write another, she lost the situation. Mr. Tyrwhitt, the magistrate, sent an officer to the institution, but all to no purpose, and the magistrate was obliged to content himself by saying that the 'National Guardian Institution' exhibited anything but a respectacle figure in the affair. He would bear it in mind. The young woman left the court convulsed with grief."

Now, if I were to say that these instances of cruelty and oppression were the natural and legitimate results of the English Social System, I should think I was telling a lie; yet I should only be doing as Mrs. Stowe and her English endorsers do, in the case of the instances of cruelty and oppression which "*now and then* occur," (vol. ii. p. 311), in which Southern slaves are the victims.

Having said thus much of the social evils of England, it is fair to say further that the English people are awaking, at length, to the necessity of doing something, and that *something* has already been done; witness the "Model Lodging-Houses" lately erected in London: but having made this admission, candor compels me to add that what has yet been accomplished by the English employer for the benefit of the working-man, is but as a drop in the bucket compared with what the Southern Planter has done and is doing for the comfort and improvement of the slave, physical and moral. (See Appendix, M.)

Here, then, there is ample room and verge for generous national rivalry; and if all Christian nations, instead of intermeddling with each other's domestic arrangements, would enter heartily into this noble competition who should do most to mitigate the evils incident to *all* social systems, and peculiar to *none*, humanity would be largely the gainer by it.

NOTE 9.—EMANCIPATION—ITS RESULTS.

In the foregoing Note, I stated that in bringing forward certain facts in regard to the condition of the laboring classes of England, I did it, not for the sake of recrimination, but because my *argument* required it. The bearing those facts have on the argument, I now proceed to point out.

I take it for granted, in the first place, that the slaves ought not to be emancipated, unless their condition, as a class, would be thereby improved, or, at any rate, not deteriorated. I say, I take it for granted, for it seems to me an axiom of common sense. And yet, I am not sure that the Abolition orators will grant it; for to do so would be fatal to their argument. They seem to have a wonderful fancy for the *name* of freedom, forgetting that names are not always things, and that calling a man a freeman, will not make him one.

> " He is the freeman whom the truth makes free,
> And all are slaves beside." COWPER.

> " The sensual and the dark rebel in vain :—
> Slaves by their own compulsion, in mad game
> They burst their manacles, to wear the *name*
> Of freedom, graven on a heavier chain." COLERIDGE.

Strange that men should be so fascinated with a name! They should read the motto on my title page, and, indeed, the whole satire from which it is taken, and which contains more good sense on this subject than all the Abolition speeches and writings I have ever fallen in with ;—and they are not few. (see Appendix, N.)

But to come to the subject in hand. If the negroes of the South are to be emancipated *on the soil*, (which is what the Abolitionists are seeking,) one of two things must follow:—either they must remain in the condition of the free negroes, (see Appendix, M,) north and south, scattered about among the white population, and in competition with them for their daily bread, *or* they must become, as in Hayti and Jamaica, lords of the soil, to the dispossession of the present owners.

Let us consider the first alternative,—that of unrestricted competition of labor for daily bread.

How is the negro to "hoe his row" with the Anglo-Saxon, or the Celt ? We have seen, in the preceding Note, how the Anglo-Saxon hoes *his* row with his brother Anglo-Saxon, and the Celt, with his brother Celt, and each with the other ; and a hard hoeing they have of it,—and a short row, when it is hoed ; but the negro would have a harder and a shorter : he cannot do more than one-third, or, at the outside, one-half, as much work as the Yankee, or the Irishman, and under the system of competition he would soon, therefore, have to give place to his betters. As it is, he has a monopoly of labor, and is *certain*, therefore, of a comfortable support; *positively* comfortable, in most cases; *comparatively* so, in all; comparatively, I mean, with the laboring poor of England.

It may be thought that the *climate* will protect the negro from competition; but this is a mistake: the tobacco and grain-growing region of the South, containing one-third of the entire colored population, is as inhabitable for the white laborer as the black; the whole colored population, therefore, would be crowded into the cotton-growing States; and even here, they would be wanted only as plantation hands; the in-door work could be done as well, and much more economically, by the whites. One-half the negroes would thus be thrown out of employment, and the wages of the other half brought down to ruinous rates. Then would be re-enacted here, that scene so familiar to England and Ireland,—a universal scramble for a bare subsistence: those *in* employment would work harder and fare worse than they do now as slaves; and those out of it, betaking themselves to the swamps, (see Note 19,) would live on the spontaneous productions of the earth, *and by plunder*, till the whites, driven to it by a hard necessity, should turn out *en masse* and exterminate them.

And is this what the Abolitionists are seeking to bring on their colored brethren? Probably not. There is another alternative—that of their becoming lords of the soil to the dispossession of the present owners.

And what would be the consequences of such a change? It would not, I think, be hard to conjecture them: but with the Abolitionists, our conjectures would go for nothing. Luckily we have something more tangible and trustworthy. The experiment has been tried,—tried more than once,—

and the results are before us, and in a shape that Abolitionists themselves will find it hard to get round.

In Hayti, for half a century, the negroes have been lords of the soil. And how have they exercised their lordship? Read the official correspondence of Mr. Walsh, in the Appendix (G. 2,), and the following comments upon it in the Washington Union of Dec. 21st, 1852:—

"HAYTI.—NEGRO GOVERNMENT.—The recent encroachments of the French on a portion of this island have awakened throughout the country a lively interest respecting its political and social condition. Indeed, this interest prevailed to a considerable extent before the usurpations of the French arrested the attention of the country.

"Of that cluster of islands which repose in the mingled waters of the Mexican gulf, the Caribbean sea, and the Atlantic ocean, to which early navigators gave the name of the West Indies, Hayti is most remarkable for the fertility and beauty of its natural resources. When the adventurous followers of Columbus first beheld it, clothed in the wild luxuriance of that virgin beauty which has since been so sadly desecrated by the passions of man, they fancied they had discovered the lovely Atlantis of ancient fable. Columbus was so attracted by its beauty that he gave it the name of Española, (little Spain,) and made it the scene of the first experiment in European colonization in the New World. By the treaty of Ryswick, 1691, Spain ceded to France the western half of the island; which, after the introduction of African slaves, 1688, first began to be successfully cultivated. The period of most signal prosperity in the island, extended from 1776 to 1789. Its productions were immense and valuable, and its commerce in the most flourishing state. Sugar-cane, cotton, cocoa, indigo, the plantain, vanilla, potatoe, manioc, mahogany, satin-wood, iron-wood, and every variety of fruit and vegetable, were produced in the greatest abundance, and almost by spontaneous growth. Its population exceeded 600,000. Its export of coffee was 68,151,180 lbs.; of sugar, 163,405,220 lbs. Owing to the inequalities of its surface, the climate varied from the intense heat of the plains to the refreshing coolness of the mountain summits, and the sea-beaten coasts. An abundance of pure water was found in every portion of the island; and it was exempt, comparatively, from those terrific hurricanes which desolated the other Antilles.

"Such was the condition of the island of Hayti, when in 1791 the doctrines and machinations of the apostles of *Liberté*, *Egalité*, and *Fraternité* incited the negroes to insurrections. From that time to 1804, the island was ravaged by that most terrible curse, a servile revolt. The scenes and acts of the bloody tragedy of St. Domingo, are unfolded with transcendent power of description in the pages of Allison's History of Europe. At last, exhausted and devastated by all the horrors of civil and servile strife, the island found the relief and repose of slumber under the despotism of Dessalines. The whites were subjugated or expelled; the African race was undisputed master of at least the principal portion of Hayti. Then began that experiment in the result of which the civilized world is so much concerned—then was presented to the eye of philosophy a new phase of social development. In full possession of a civilization imparted to him by a superior race, with the *éclat* of successful prowess and triumphant patriotism, in the bright morning of the nineteenth century, and standing in the great highway of the commerce of the world, the negro began the untried experiment of freedom and self-government. As the theatre of this unexampled and momentous experiment, Hayti became an object of additional interest. The ethnographer, puzzled with questions touching the equality of races; the philanthropist, doubting the practicability of his benevolent purposes; the man of science, the politician, and the moralist all looked to Hayti for lessons of wisdom.

The result of the experiment of negro freedom and negro government in the island of Hayti has long since been ascertained. Whether we look to its social, industrial, or political condition, we find the same evidences of degradation and degeneracy. The dominion of the African is a blight under which religion, commerce, liberty, and law, wither and perish. No longer elevated and guided by the influences of a superior race, and compelled to work out their own destiny, the negroes of Hayti have relapsed from the semi-civilized condition of 1800 into a state of comparative barbarism. The mild subjection of slavery has been succeeded by the wild riot and unbridled license of savage passion; enlightenment has been quenched in ignorance; religion has degenerated into superstition; poverty and want reign where once were only abundance and contentment. In a word, the experiment of freedom and self-government among the negroes of Hayti has been a signal and disastrous failure."

But "in Hayti they had nothing to start with. A stream cannot rise above its fountain. The race that formed the character of the Haytiens was a worn-out, effeminate one; and, of course, the subject race will be centuries in rising to anything." (Vol. ii. p. 300.)

Well, then, let us take the other experiment,—that of a people trained under very different auspices,—a people whose character was formed by the Anglo-Saxon race,—that race of "stern, inflexible, energetic elements," to which "has been entrusted the destinies of the world, during its pioneer period of struggle and conflict." (Vol. ii. p. 302.)

For nearly twenty years, the negroes of Jamaica have been "free;" and how have they used that freedom? Read the statements in the Appendix (G. 1), and recollect that they are made by a Free-Soiler, one of the editors of the New York Evening Post,—and then read the following from the London Times of December 1st, 1852, (Appendix, K. 7):—"At the present moment, indeed, if there is one thing in the world that the British public do not like to talk about, *or even to think about*, it is the condition of the race for whom this great effort was made." And the following, from the same paper, as copied by the Washington Union, of December 23d, 1852:—

"THE BLACKS IN THE WEST INDIES.—In an article in the London Times, we find the following passage relating to the result of emancipation in the English West Indies. The picture drawn is indeed a distressing one, but its correctness is confirmed by accounts from various quarters:

"'Our legislation has been dictated by the presumed necessities of the African slave. After the emancipation act, a large charge was assessed upon the colony in aid of civil and religious institutions for the benefit of the enfranchised negro, and it was hoped that these colored subjects of the British Crown would soon be assimilated to their fellow-citizens. From all the information which reaches us, no less than from the visible probabilities of the case, we are constrained to believe that these hopes have been falsified. The negro has not acquired with his freedom any habits of industry or morality. His independence is little better than that of an uncaptured brute. Having accepted few of the restraints of civilization, he is amenable to few of its necessities; and the wants of his nature so easily satisfied, that at the current rate of wages he is called upon for nothing but fitful and desultory exertion. The blacks, therefore, instead of becoming intelligent husbandmen, have become vagrants and squatters, and it is now apprehended that with the failure of cultivation in the island, will come the failure of its resources for instructing or controlling its population. So imminent does this consummation appear that memorials have been signed by classes of colonial society hitherto standing aloof from politics, and not only the bench and the bar, but the bishop, clergy, and ministers of all denominations in the island, without exception, have recorded their conviction that, in absence of timely relief, the religious and educational institutions of the island must be abandoned, and the masses of the population retrograde to barbarism.' "

No wonder the *Reverend* Theodore Parker said, in his speech at Framingham Grove, last summer, "In America, we have been steadfastly kept from knowing the truth of emancipation in the West Indies by our newspapers, [*Abolition* newspapers, he means, of course,] which have taken great pains to conceal the real facts. Even the people of New England are but illy informed of the actual condition of those islands." (See his speech, in the Weekly Commonwealth of August 7th, 1852.)

And yet, in the face of all this, Garrison, Parker, & Co., keep up their annual powow over West-India emancipation, and go frantic over its results, as if the negro had actually been benefitted, and not ruined by it.

At the "celebration," last August, Mr. Parker, in the speech above referred to, said:—"It might be, as was often asserted, that there was not so great an exportation of products as before the act of emancipation. The circumstance of the condition of the workers might account for such a variation. If but two hours' labor per day were necessary for the support of each colored man, he knew not why he should toil longer."

In a similar strain spoke Charles C. Burleigh:—"He would not argue whether the planters of the West-India islands exported the same quantity of sugar or rum as before the liberation; it was sufficient for him to know that beasts had been turned into men. How many barrels of sugar, he would like to know, were the equivalent for the freedom of a single immortal being? Let those who were disposed enter upon the statistics of the products of those islands before and since the act of emancipation. It was enough for him to know that thousands had been set free, raised from degradation, made glad in the light of liberty, and compared with such a fact, no calculation of mercantile success weighed the least iota."

So, Mr. Parker, you don't see why the colored man should work more than two hours a day, if that amount of labor is sufficient for his support. So I suppose: that is just what I should expect of a "baptized infidel." (See Appendix, P.) But you will excuse me if I prefer St. Paul's teaching to yours:—

"Ye yourselves know, that *these hands* have ministered unto my necessities, *and to them that were with me.* I have showed you all things, how that *so labouring ye ought to support the weak;* and to remember the words of the Lord Jesus, how he said, It is more blessed to give than to receive." (Acts xx. 34, 35.) "Let him that stole steal no more; but rather let him *labour, working with his hands the thing which is good, that he may have to give to him that needeth.* (Eph. iv. 28.)

There! there is something manly there: no shirking in that!

But you do not feel "at all bound to believe what the church says is true, nor what any writer in the Old or New Testament declares true." (See Littell's Living Age, No. 459, p. 437.) Well, then! Listen to Dr. Channing: you used to believe *him:*

"I have faith in labor, and I see the goodness of God in placing us in a world where labor alone can keep us alive. I would not change, if I could, our subjection to physical laws, our exposure to hunger and cold, and the necessity of constant conflicts with the material world. I would not, if I could, so temper the elements that they should infuse into us only grateful sensations; that they should make vegetation so exuberant as to anticipate every want, and the minerals so ductile as to offer no resistance to our strength and skill. *Such a world would make a contemptible race.* Man owes his growth, his energy, chiefly to that striving of the will, that conflict with difficulty, which we call effort. Easy, pleasant work does not make robust minds, does not give men a consciousness of their powers, does not train them to endurance, to perseverance, to steady force of will, that force without which all other acquisitions avail nothing. Manual labor is a school in which men are placed to get energy of purpose and character, *a vastly more important endowment than all the learning of all other schools.* They are placed, indeed, under hard masters,—physical sufferings and want, the power of fearful elements, and the vicissitudes of all human things; but these stern teachers do a work which no compassionate, indulgent friend could do for us, *and true wisdom will bless Providence for their sharp ministry.* I have great faith in hard work. The material world does much for the mind by its beauty and order; but it does more for our minds by the pains it inflicts, by its obstinate resistance, which nothing but patient toil can overcome, by its vast forces, which nothing but unremitting skill and effort can turn to our use, by its perils, which demand continual vigilance, and by its tendencies to decay. I believe that difficulties are more important to the human mind than what we call assistances. *Work we all must, if we mean to bring out and perfect our nature.*" Dr. Channing as quoted by "A Carolinian;" "Slavery in the Southern States;" (pp. 51, 52.)

There! there is good sense in that, *though* it comes from an emancipationist. *O si sic omnia!*

But what do *you* care whether the negro "brings out and perfects his nature," or "relapses into barbarism," so you can "curse up hill and down," (you must have sat to Mrs. Stowe for *that* portrait,) and spit "the venom of your spleen" on Christians and Christianity. It is lucky for you that you live in a country where you *can* spit it out, for if you were obliged to "digest" it, it would certainly "split you."

And you, Mr. Burleigh! you will not argue whether West-India exports have fallen off: it is enough for you to know that "beasts have been turned into men." So? It is a pity that *some* of the *Abolition Leaders* could not be *emancipated*, then.—You "would like to know how many barrels of sugar are the equivalent for the freedom of a single immortal being?" "Freedom," say you? The freedom of the savage in his native wilds: a *vagabond* freedom that no man has a right to, on God's earth.—You *sneer* at any "calculation of mercantile success;" and you are not alone in this: your brother abolitionists—the leaders, I mean,—have, all of them, an ugly trick of doing the same thing. You forget that commerce is the great civilizer, and that without the cultivation of the soil there can be no commerce, and, consequently, no civilization. I wonder you were not ashamed of such twaddle. I should have thought you would have felt, as Miss Lucy (Lucius?) Stone, who preceded you, did, "like sinking into the remotest corner." Why *did n't* you do it? It would have been more to your credit.

As to Miss Stone, that remark of hers shows that there is hope of her: if she could only be got out of "bad company," she might be made a woman of yet. Bear that in mind, and *don't* "take your time, Miss Lucy," or you may be too late.

But to return from the West-Indies to the Southern

States. We have seen the results of negro domination in Hayti: we have seen the results of negro domination in Jamaica. Reader, do you wish to see them *here?* Have you reflected what they would be? First and foremost a falling off in the cotton crop: for just so sure as the coffee crop, in Jamaica, fell off to one-fourth, and the sugar crop to less than one-third, and just so sure as like causes produce like effects, just so sure would the cotton crop fall off from 3,000,000 bales to less than 1,000,000. And what would be the consequences of this falling off? According to the last census returns, the number of hands employed in the cotton manufacture in the United States for the year ending the 1st of June, 1850, was 92,286, of whom 61,893, —more than two-thirds,—were employed in the New-England States: the amount of cotton consumed in the same period was 641,240 bales, (averaging 400 pounds each,) of which 430,603 bales,—more than two-thirds,—were consumed in New-England, and 223,607, or more than one-third, in the single State of Massachusetts. This was when the whole cotton crop of the Southern States was 2,484,531 bales. Last year the crop was over 3,000,000 bales, of which, if I recollect right,* (for I have not the authority at hand,) a trifle over 2,000,000 were exported to England. More than 500,000 annually are exported to other countries.

According to De Bow's Review, as quoted by the Baltimore Sun of May 14th, 1852, "In the year 1849 there were, in Great Britain, Europe, and the United States, 3,323,365 bales of cotton consumed, and 873,634 operatives

* According to the New York Weekly Times of April 30th, the exports, to Great Britain, of the present crop, have been, thus far, 1,266,000 bales, and they are still going on, at the rate of nearly 50,000 bales a week.

employed, and $671,000,000 invested in the manufacture of cotton." This was four years ago: at the present time, the number of "operatives" must be at least 900,000. Of these, at least two-thirds, or 600,000, by the falling off in the cotton crops consequent upon emancipation, would be thrown out of employment; and if we take into the account those dependent upon them for their daily bread, we shall have, at the lowest calculation, 3,000,000 human beings reduced to destitution. To these must be added the brokers, factors, commercial agents, ship owners, seamen, &c., with their families and dependents, that would be affected by the change. Besides this, there would be a revulsion in the trade of Christendom, to which that of 1837 was but "a circumstance,"—a revulsion, bringing with it untold misery to hundreds of thousands. To crown the whole, millions upon millions of human beings, whose only clothing is the fabric manufactured from this cotton, would be left without a rag to cover their nakedness. (See Appendix, Q.)

And all this for what? To give the negro freedom. Freedom! Ay, a vagabond freedom;—the freedom of a savage;—a freedom which, as sure as God's law makes degradation, physical and moral, consequent upon idleness, would fast hurry him back to his original barbarism.

Out upon such philanthropy, and those who teach it! In this category, are *not* included the rank and file of the Free-Soil party, who have been led away by their *feelings*, not having investigated the subject, and, as a general thing, not having had the means of investigating it. In this category *are* included the Abolition Orators who figure at Emancipation Powows on the first of August. These men *know* what they are doing: they do it with their eyes open, and with the most unblushing hypocrisy. If any one is so "verdant" as to suppose that they are sincere, he must have a comfortable share of the commodity.

But to come back to the negro. Is there no redemption for him? Must he toil on in hopeless bondage? No! thank God! a brighter destiny awaits him; but it is in a distant land, and in the *distant* future. And he must *work it out*, too, for himself: it cannot be worked out for him.

He must work it out for himself, under the leadings of God's providence, and in accordance with the laws that govern the moral world: gradually, therefore, and slowly. He will be wanted here for several generations to come, to clear up, and subdue the soil, and make it healthy where now it is unhealthy, thus serving as the pioneer of the white laborer. At the same time his own melioration will be going on *pari passu* with that of the soil, so that by the time the latter is ready for the white laborer, he (the negro) will be ready for his exodus.

Meanwhile, that exodus is preparing. "On the shores of Africa I see a republic,—a republic formed of picked men, who, by energy and self-educating force, have, in many cases, individually, raised themselves above a condition of slavery." (Vol. ii. p. 300.) These are the men to lay the foundations of a great empire.

That there are such men, I know, for I have seen them. I could mention three such, at least, in Annapolis,—two of them jet black; and they are to be found *scattered* "all over our land." But they are not common; not more than one in a thousand.

If Liberia has been filled up with such, (and I have reason to believe it has been, in a good degree,) it is to be ascribed to an interposition of Providence.

Twenty years ago, the American Colonization Society was in the full tide of successful experiment: money was pouring into its treasury, and emigrants were offering themselves in great numbers. God saw that there was danger that those who were sent out would not all be "picked men," and that it was necessary, therefore, that a temporary check should be put to the emigration. Accordingly, He raised up Garrison, as he had raised up Pharaoh before him, to work out *unconsciously* His purposes, and as He raised up Theodore Parker after him, to bring about a revulsion of feeling, which he is fast doing in the breasts of all the honest men of the party. I say, He raised up Garrison for this very purpose, and well did *he* "do his dirty work," as Pharaoh had done *his* before him. He knew not what he was doing: he meant it for evil, but God meant it for good: He makes the wrath of man praise Him, and the remainder thereof,—that is, all that will not praise Him,—He restrains. Why do the infidels so furiously rage together? Why do they imagine a vain thing? He that sitteth in the heavens shall laugh: the Lord shall have them in derision.

To come back to Liberia. I said, I had reason to believe that it had been filled up, in a good degree, with "picked men;" time will show whether this is so, and it will also show the success or the failure of the Liberian experiment. If it succeeds, as I firmly believe it will, then the colored man is provided for.

As to the alleged impossibility of transporting him to Africa, it is all moonshine: the race may go on multiplying at their present rate of increase, till the year 1900, at which time they would number about 13,500,000, and then an annual transportation, less than double the actual emigration from Ireland last year, would carry them all over, long before the year 2000; and when Liberia shall have become a great commercial empire, as it will in less than fifty years, if it succeeds, such a transportation, with the improved means of conveyance that will then be in common use, will be a mere *bagatelle.* Let the negro, then, toil on, in faith, and thankfulness, and hope :—in faith that he is fulfilling his mission, and preparing the way of the Lord; in thankfulness that he has been taken from the lowest deep of degradation,—a degradation to be found nowhere out of Africa,—and placed in a condition which has elevated him, *and is still elevating him*, in the scale of being; in hope that a brighter destiny is in store, if not for him, for his posterity.

NOTE 10.—THE INTERNAL SLAVE-TRADE.

On this subject Mrs. Stowe has expended, as usual, abundance of rhetoric and very little logic. She sees the evils of the traffic,—who doesn't see them?—and she resolves that it must be abolished, without stopping to ask (she never *does* stop to ask,) whether its abolition would not bring with it greater evils: she is *in* the frying pan, and she determines to jump *out*, without looking to see whether or not it is into the fire that she is jumping. There is an old saying, and it used to be thought a wise one, Look before you leap. What would be the consequences of abolishing the trade? A repletion of the slave population and consequent glut in the labor market in the more Northern slave States, which in less than ten years would render slavery, not only unprofitable, but, so ruinous to the master that, from sheer inability to support his slaves, he would have to turn them loose, to shift for themselves,—in other words, to emancipate them. Then would be realized the first alternative spoken of in the preceding Note,—that of universal and unrestricted competition between black and white for daily bread; a struggle in which the former would be remorselessly trampled under the iron heel of the latter, by the inevitable operation of the "demand-and-supply-principle;" —and the "horrors" and the "heart-break" of *that* struggle, who can tell? Why the horrors and the heart-break of the domestic slave-trade, are joy and gladness in the comparison.

NOTE 11.—THE FUGITIVE LAW AND THE HIGHER LAW.

On this subject Mrs. Stowe makes a most astounding confession. She tells us that after "the passage of the legislative act of 1850," she "heard with perfect surprise and consternation, Christian and humane people actually recommending the remanding escaped fugitives into slavery, as a duty binding on good citizens." (Vol. ii. p. 314.) And yet "Christian and humane people" had been not only "actually recommending" it, but actually doing it, under the act of 1793, for nearly fifty years, and during the last ten of them, at least, she *knew* that they were doing it, and knew it, too, without any surprise or consternation. How comes it, then, that the act of 1850 has so frightened her from her propriety?

The truth is, but for the doings of the Abolitionists, that act would never have been needed: the act of 1793 would have been sufficient. In the words of Mr. Webster, speaking of this latter, "It was thought wise at the time to leave the execution of that law pretty much in the hands of State tribunals; State magistrates, and officers, and judges were authorized to execute that law. It was so administered for fifty years, and nobody complained of it. Things went on until this new excitement of the slavery question, this abolition question, was brought up, and then some of the States, Massachusetts, Ohio, and others, enacted laws making it penal to execute this law of Congress.

"Then the statute became a dead letter in this part of it; when, of course, it became a matter of necessity to provide for the execution of this Constitutional enactment by the authority of the Government of the United States, or give it up altogether. Well, I made no question myself, that if we meant to fulfil the contract of the statute, *if we meant to be honest*, it was our duty to make a provision, which, by the authority of the Government itself, should carry into execution the provisions of the Constitution. And that is the origin of the present Fugitive Slave Law." (Speech at Syracuse, May, 1851, p. 30.)

Now what are the provisions of the Constitution? They are the following:—"No person held to service or labor in one State, under the laws thereof, escaping into another, shall, in consequence of any law or regulation therein, be discharged from such service or labor, but shall be delivered up on claim of the party to whom such service or labor may be due." (Article 4. Sec. 2.) All this would seem very plain. And yet Mr. Senator Sumner tells us, in his speech before referred to, that the act of 1793 and the act of 1850 are both unconstitutional, and that for two reasons: first and foremost, because the clause in the Constitution is a "naked compact" between the several States, without any grant of power to Congress, and that therefore Congress have nothing to do with it. (p. 19.) And yet he admits (p. 17.) that in the case of Prigg vs. Pennsylvania, before the Supreme Court, (16 Peters, 539.)—Mr. Justice Story delivering the opinion,—"the power of Congress over this matter is asserted." This concludes the question, so far as the citizen, or the United States executive officer in his executive capacity, or judicial officer in his judicial capacity, is concerned: they have no right to go behind it. With the legislator, it is of course, different, and Mr. Sumner is right in the position he takes, and President Jackson, whom he quotes, (p. 18.) is right also, though the passage from him in *italics* is unguardedly expressed, and is liable to be, and has in fact been, misunderstood: the two sentences, however, that follow it, make his meaning plain.

I come now to Mr. Sumner's other reason why the act is unconstitutional, viz., its denial of trial by jury. (p. 21.) And here he cites two provisions of the Constitution, one, that "No *person* shall be deprived of life, *liberty*, or property, *without due process of law*;" (the *italics* are his own;) the other, that "In suits at common law, where the value in controversy shall exceed twenty dollars, the right of trial by jury shall be preserved." He then goes on to argue that the "claim for a fugitive" is a "suit at common law," whereas, it is not a suit at all. The case of Cohens vs. Virginia, (6 Wheaton, 407.) cited by him, does not show that it is. In that case, "the court say: 'What is a suit? We understand it to be the prosecution of some *claim*, demand, or request.' Of course, then," says Mr. Sumner, "the 'claim' for a fugitive must be 'a suit.'" The court say, A suit is the prosecution of a claim; Mr. Sumner says, *Therefore* the prosecution of a claim is a suit. In the same way he might prove that as a mare is a horse, *therefore*, a horse is a mare.

His second citation, then, will not serve him. How is it with his first? "No *person* shall be deprived of life, *liberty*, or property, *without due process of law*;" "that is," says Mr. Sumner, "without due proceedings at law, with trial by jury." But, to be deprived of liberty, a person must first be in possession of it; and to be deprived of liberty, within the meaning of the above clause of the Constitution, he must be in the *lawful* possession of it;—that is to say, in possession of it *in accordance with the law of the land*: if he is in the unlawful possession of it, he may be deprived of it "in a summary way." For instance, if a convicted pirate, or mail-robber, escapes from prison in a Southern State, and flees into New York or Massachusetts, the Marshal, or his deputy, may seize him and take him back, *summarily*; even Mr. Sumner himself would consider a trial by jury in such a case absurd. And why? Because he was not in the *lawful* possession of his liberty, and therefore is not "deprived of" it, within the meaning of the Constitution.

Just so with the fugitive slave: he is not in the *lawful* possession of his liberty. Mr. Sumner admits that he is not, for he says, (p. 29.) that by the provisions of the Constitution, "the States are prohibited from any 'law or regulation' by which the fugitive may be discharged," and unless lawfully discharged, he is unlawfully at liberty, and therefore the clause of the Constitution in question does not apply to him.

Another objection of Mr. Sumner's to the Constitutionality of the law is, that it takes away the privilege of the writ of *habeas corpus;* but this is a mistake: the law does no such thing. The writ may be issued and served; and if served, a "return" must be made to it, just as in any other case. The law only provides what shall be a *sufficient* return, viz., the production of the judge's or commissioner's "certificate;" and this is *properly* made sufficient, for the object of the writ being to ascertain, not whether the person in whose behalf it is issued, is rightfully (in a moral point of view,) in custody, but whether he is *legally* so, as soon as this has been shown, by the production of the certificate, the writ has exhausted itself.

Mr. Mann, in his speech of August, 17th, (p. 16.) objects that, under the law, a freeman may be sent into slavery; and he says, (p. 15.) that it has actually been done in four cases. He specifies, however, but one instance, (the only one, of course, that he *could* specify,) that of Adam Gibson. And what was the result? Why, to use Mr. Mann's own words, "When the claimant's agent brought Gibson to him, he refused to receive him; for he knew, *and he knew that all his household and neighbors would know*, that Gibson had never been his slave." The first of these reasons is the true and sufficient one; the second (in *italics*,) is, therefore, supererogative, and is, moreover, a mean fling at the character of the claimant, such as none but Horace Mann, and his *fellows*, would indulge in; they are common with him, and they are as contemptible as the littleness from which they spring.

Again, Mr. Mann objects that the law decides "*conclusively* (the *italics* are his,) the question of a man's liberty, in what is to him a foreign State, and before what is to him a foreign tribunal, without the possibility of his appearing there to confront witnesses," &c. Now Mr. Mann *knew* when he said this, that the law does no such thing;—that no law of Congress *can* decide conclusively the question of the liberty of a fugitive from a slave State. The law in question simply sends the fugitive back to the State from which he fled, to have the trial of the question (if he claims one,) where alone it can be tried, and the decision of it by the laws by which alone it can be decided. And in this, there is no more hardship than in the case of the fugitive from justice, who, charged with the commission of crime in one State, and escaping into another, is arrested and sent back to take his trial where the crime is alleged to have been committed; and the one fugitive is as certain of a fair trial, and a decision according to law and evidence,* as the other. Since my residence in Maryland, there have been repeated trials of "petitions for freedom," and almost always resulting in favor of the petitioner.

Another of Mr. Mann's objections to the law is, "its fabrication of such a code of evidence as was never before placed on the statute-book of any civilized nation." (p. 16.) Now if the reader will turn to Appendix, E. 11, he will find an abstract of the law, taken from the American Almanac for 1851, and I am willing "any civilized nation" should

* For a specimen of the kind of evidence required in suits for freedom, (see Appendix, E. 10.,) particularly the cases, "*Delphine vs. Deveze*," "*Oatfield vs. Waring*," "*Metayer vs. Metayer*," and "*Mahoney vs. Ashton*."

read it, and then say whether the code above described is a provision of the law, or the *fabrication* of the *Hon.* Horace Mann.

But Mr. Senator Sumner objects to the law that "it authorizes judgment on *exparte* evidence, by affidavits, without the sanction of cross-examination." Ay, but affidavits to what? Why, to the fact that Cuffy or Sambo has escaped from service in Virginia, for instance, and fled into New York. And where is this affidavit made? Not in New York, where he who makes it is unknown, and where it might therefore go for nothing, but in Virginia, in the State and County of his residence, where he is well known, and where the escape of his servant is well known too. And how is this affidavit authenticated? By the certificate of the County Clerk, *under his official seal.* This the law expressly requires.

And now I would like to know of Mr. Sumner how such an affidavit is to be any other than *exparte*? Is the fugitive to go back, to cross-examine witnesses?—or send on counsel, to do it for him? Really, it is hard to believe that a man of Mr. Sumner's intelligence can be serious in such an objection.

But to proceed:—Fortified with this affidavit the claimant goes to New York, arrests the alleged fugitive, and takes him before the judge or commissioner. And who are these commissioners? "Petty magistrates," says Mr. Sumner. If by this he means they are subordinate to United States' judges, he is right; if he means anything more than this, he is wrong. So far are they from being, as he would seem to imply, irresponsible men, they are, as is well known, men of high standing in their profession (the legal) and in the community. Their office is not a new one: it was in existence years before the passage of the present fugitive law. It was created for an entirely different purpose,—to hear, in the vacation of the courts, cases arising on the high seas, in order to prevent the necessity of detaining seamen in jail, for months, as witnesses. No one objected to them, then, as "petty magistrates," and the objection comes with an ill grace from the Free-Soilers now.

Well, the commissioner examines the affidavit, and finding it properly drawn and vouched, admits it in evidence, as he is bound to do by the Law and the Constitution, the latter of which expressly declares (Article 4. Sect. 1.) that "Full faith and credit shall be given in each State to the public acts, records, and judicial proceedings of every other State. *And the Congress may by general laws prescribe the manner in which such acts, records, and proceedings shall be proved, and the effect thereof.*" I say he receives it in evidence. But to prove what? Why that Sambo has run away. But now comes the question, Is *the* Sambo in custody, the *run-away* Sambo? And *this* question is investigated, not on *exparte* evidence, but by counsel on both sides, with cross-examination and rebutting testimony, if any can be procured. The commissioner then decides the question. If in his opinion, the identity is not made out, he discharges the prisoner: if, on the contrary, he considers it made out, he delivers a certificate to that effect to the claimant, in virtue of which certificate, he (the claimant,) takes the prisoner back to the State and County of his residence, there, (as I said before,) to have the trial (if he claims one,) of his title to liberty; just as fugitives from justice are taken back, almost every day, to the State from which they escaped, there to take their trial for the offence with which they stand charged.

And this is the famous Fugitive Slave Law, which Mrs. Stowe has heard of "with perfect surprise and consternation!"

"——the head and front of its offending
Hath this extent,—no more."

No more? I beg pardon. Mr. Sumner does bring forward two other objections, but he surely cannot expect a serious answer to them;—one, that the law "sends the fugitive back *at the public expense*," and the other, that it "*bribes* the commissioner" to "pronounce against freedom," by giving him a fee of *five* dollars for making out the "certificate"! This last objection is unworthy of Mr. Sumner: he should have left it to Horace Mann, who would bring it forward with a relish; for detraction is his "fifth element:" he enters into it, *con amore*, as if he had received from "Protestant Jesuitism" an "indulgence" to break the ninth commandment, *ad libitum*.

I have now, I believe, noticed all the objections that have been brought forward, except one, and this one lies, not merely against the law, but against the *sending back the fugitive in any case*. Here we come at once on the domain of the "Higher Law."

And what *is* this "higher law"? A "law," says Mr. Webster, "that exists somewhere between us and the third heaven, I never knew exactly where." (Speech at Albany, May, 1851, p. 43.)—I can tell him where:—*in nubibus*. Sambo would say, not so high as *that*. Sambo met Cuffy one day, in front of the seven-story "pagoda," (corner of Washington and State streets, Boston,) then just completed, and the cock-loft of which was to be the office of the "Commonwealth" newspaper, the organ of the Free-Soilers. I say, Sambo, says Cuffy, after having gazed for some time in wonderment at the aforesaid cock-loft, what *be* dat ar? Why, Cuffy! you no know dat, says Sambo; I's 'stonished you so ignorant; you be more ob a *nig*noramus dan de white niggers! (meaning the abolitionists.) Dat ar? dat be Mas'r Sumner's *Higher-Law office*. The "higher law," then mounts only to the seventh *story*, not to the seventh heaven.

Mr. Horace Mann charges Mr. Webster and others with saying that there is no higher law than the Constitution; yet he *knows* that they say no such thing, but only that *the* "higher law" is not higher than the Constitution.* They admit,—they maintain,—that the law of God is higher than the Constitution,—than *all* Constitutions; but the practical question is, Does the Constitution *conflict* with that law? This question was put to Mr. Mann, in the course of the speech before referred to:—

"Mr. SUTHERLAND. I ask the gentleman if every American citizen does not obey the higher law of God when he obeys every part of the Constitution? And can any good result come from discussing these immaterial abstractions? Is not the spirit of the Constitution in accordance with the higher law? Can you point to a clause in the Constitution which, when fulfilling to the best of my ability, would make me violate the higher law of God?

"Mr. MANN. That is not to the point." (p. 11.)

Here we have him at his old tricks again; wriggling and squirming, in order to shirk the question, because he *dare* not answer it, either way: if he should say the Constitution was against the law of God, then he would convict himself

* It may be well to place the three laws side by side:—

HIGH LAW.—"No person held to service or labor in one State, under the laws thereof, escaping into another, shall in consequence of any law or regulation therein, be discharged from such service or labor, but shall be delivered up on claim of the party to whom such service or labor may be due."—*U. S. Constitution, Article IV., Section* 2.

"HIGHER LAW."—"Block the locomotives!—Tear up the rails!—Law or no law, Constitution or no Constitution, resolve that this law shall not be enforced."—*Wendell Philips's Anti-Slavery Oration.*

HIGHEST LAW.—"The powers that be are ordained of God. Whosoever, therefore, resisteth the power, resisteth the ordinance of God: and they that resist shall receive to themselves damnation."—*Holy Writ.*

of perjury in having taken a solemn oath to support it; if he should say it was in accordance with that law, then his occupation's gone. What honest man can have any patience with such a shuffler?

But the "higher law"—what is it? Ay, sure enough! what *is* it? The law of each man's conscience, healthy or diseased, enlightened or unenlightened,—that persecutes the Church, and verily thinks with itself it is doing God service,—that sets itself up above the teaching of the Bible, and the practice of the holy Apostle! And is this *religion*, "which can bend and turn," and be one thing here, and another thing there, and therefore, nothing everywhere? "No! When I look for a religion, I must look for something above me, and not something" merely within: (vol. ii. p. 265.) I must have an objective reality, and not the shifting fancies of this, that and the other individual!

But is a man to go counter to his own conscience? Of course, not. But then, the gist of the matter lies here:— a man in a Christian land has no business to *have* such a conscience, and he will be held accountable *for* having it.

How, then, are we to ascertain our duty? I answer, By the teaching of Holy Scripture. But how are we to get at that teaching? One man interprets a passage this way, another, that: which is right? Probably neither. Most men go to work the wrong way to get at the truth. That "Spirit of Truth," which is given to men to lead them into *all* truth, is given to them only in the Church, and he who is without its pale has no right to be confident in his own interpretation of an obscure passage; and by the Church, I mean, not this, that, or the other sect claiming that appellation, but that which *is* the Church. Here, then, we get rid of ninety-nine out of every hundred of the higher-law men: they are without the pale of the Church, and therefore though they *may* interpret a difficult and obscure passage correctly, the chances are against them.

But the passages involved in the present inquiry are neither obscure nor difficult: there are some passages where the meaning lies so on the face of Holy Scripture, that no one *need* mistake it; and these are of the number.

To come, at once, to the point:—It cannot be denied that St. Paul did send back a converted runaway slave to his Christian master, for we have the Epistle that he sent with him: there was, therefore, nothing *wrong* in his sending him back; it may not have been *obligatory;* I do not touch that point; it *certainly* was not wrong. But further: Holy Scripture requires servants (δουλοὺς) to be subject to their masters, not only to the believing ones, but to the unbelieving,—not only to the good and gentle, but to the froward; (1 Tim. vi. 1; 1 Pet. ii. 18.) It follows, therefore, that they who run away even from unbelieving and froward masters, sin against God; that sin they are bound, at once, to repent of; and as repentance is good for nothing, unless it brings forth fruits meet for repentance, they are equally bound to return, at once, and submit themselves to their masters. Now if it is their duty to return, it cannot be *wrong* in us to put them in the way of duty,—that is, to send them back: moreover, whatever the laws of our country require us to do *that is not wrong*, we are bound to do: it follows, therefore, that we are bound to send them back.

But here we are met with a passage from the Old Testament; for the Abolitionists, so many of whom dislike that "antiquated" volume, are very ready to quote it when they find, or think they find, it on their side. The passage is as follows:—"Thou shalt not deliver unto his master the servant which is escaped from his master unto thee: He shall dwell with thee, even among you, in that place which he shall choose in one of thy gates, where it liketh him best: thou shalt not oppress him." (Deut. xxiii. 15, 16.) This passage is quoted by Rev. Albert Barnes, and on it he says, (page 140):—"I am willing to admit that the command *probably* relates only to the slaves which escaped to the country of the Hebrews from surrounding nations; and that in form it did not contemplate the runaway slaves of the Hebrews in their own land." (See Fletcher's Studies on Slavery, p. 119.)

Now what Mr. Barnes is ready to admit as the *probable* interpretation, we may safely assume to be the *true* one; especially when, as in the present case, the whole connection, and, indeed, the language itself, shows it to be so. For, it will be observed, the language is, "the servant which is escaped from his master unto *thee;* he shall dwell with *thee*, even among *you*, * * * * in one of *thy* gates." All the pronouns I have *italicised*, refer not to one tribe, but to the *whole nation* of Israel, as will be seen by the preceding verses; the master, therefore, *from* whom the slave escaped to the *nation* of Israel, must have been himself *outside that nation;* in other words, a foreigner and a *heathen;* this last circumstance was the reason why the slave was not to be delivered up. But *exceptio probat regulam*, and the very exception, therefore, in the present case, shows that *in all other cases*, he *was* to be delivered up.

The direct argument from Holy Scripture having thus failed the Abolitionists, they have recourse to the indirect: they quote the passage, Whatsoever ye would that men should do to you, &c., and try to work on our sympathies: "Folks don't run away," they tell us, "when they are happy." Of course, they don't, unless, indeed, they are *enticed* off. But "folks" are not always happy when they ought to be: children are sometimes unhappy under the benignant restraint of kind parents; apprentices are sometimes unhappy under the benignant restraint of kind employers; idlers and vagabonds are sometimes unhappy under the benignant restraint of kind laws; and in the same way, slaves are sometimes unhappy under the benignant restraint of kind masters. The truth is, some "folks" don't like work of any kind, and are never happy when they are compelled to it.

But, there are, no doubt, now and then cases,—possibly one in ten, more probably, not one in twenty,*—where slaves have run away on account of cruel treatment. What are we to say of such cases?

I think I could answer this question very easily; luckily, however, the Commonwealth, of May 2, 1853, has saved me the trouble by answering it for me. The Post and the Courier, it seems, had been advising the Free-Soilers instead of wasting their resources in the Quixotic attempt to abolish slavery, to apply those resources to the redemption of individual slaves. Thereupon, the Commonwealth thus discourseth:—"Following up this scheme, the very men who have shown that they would favor the indefinite spread and perpetuation of slavery, coolly bring subscription papers to Abolitionists to ransom slaves, and evidently consider the measure of our liberality as the test of sincerity in the anti-slavery cause. It is time such hypocrisy was properly met.

"In the first place it is time for the *Courier*, *Post*, and people of that sort, to understand that we do not recognize the right of man to hold property in man. And unless a very strong case is made out, it is by no means a duty to

* Is one in twenty of the cases of runaway apprentices, that we frequently see advertised in the newspapers, under the heading, "A basket of chips reward!" "One cent reward, and no charges paid!" a case of running away from cruel treatment? God help Northern masters, if it is!

contribute for the purchase of slaves; beneficence to one family *may*, and probably *does*, hinder the final exodus of the race.

* * * * * *

"But if we are to break over this rather hard, though just rule, and contribute to the relief of individual cases, we further desire to choose for ourselves as to the objects of our charity.

* * * * * * *

"It is from no lack of *objects* of philanthropy that we do so little. The difficulty is not in beginning; the question is where shall we end? But when we are conscious that with our present means we could not ransom half the natural inevitable *increase* of the slaves, and further, that such occasional emancipations and removals only prune and invigorate the old Upas tree—giving it a new lease of life, is it not enough to make us turn away—however sorrowfully—and strike at the root of the whole system, trusting that God in his good time will aid in its overthrow?"

Now for the *application* of the above "rather hard, *though just* rule:" "Unless a very strong case is made out, it is by no means a duty" to help off the fugitive; "beneficence to one" may be, and probably, nay, *certainly*, is, cruelty to a hundred that remain behind on the same plantation, and who are *necessarily* subjected to greater restraints and deprived of many of the indulgences to which they have been accustomed, and which, but for the runaway, they might still be enjoying. And "when we are conscious that" a case, strong *enough*, cannot be "made out," but that, on the contrary, every time we help off one, we only draw the chains the tighter on a hundred others, "is it not enough to make us turn away—however sorrowfully"—from the fugitive, and bend all our efforts to humanize and

Christianize those masters that need humanizing and Christianizing, so that there may be no fugitives, but of the idle and vicious? (See Note 16.) So much for the appeal to our sympathies, *and the Commonwealth's answer to it.*

We arrive at the conclusion, then, that the Fugitive Slave Act is not repugnant to the Constitution, nor to the law of God, and that, consequently, the outcry against it has no foundation in justice or equity.

NOTE 12.—PATRIOTS AND POLITICIANS.

These constitute a class for which Mrs. Stowe seems to have very little respect, if we may judge from her repeated flings at them: as, for instance, (vol. i. p. 190.) "The trader, who, considering his advantages, was almost as humane as some of our politicians," &c.; and again, (p. 95.) "So spoke this poor, heathenish Kentuckian, who had not been instructed in his constitutional relations, and consequently was betrayed into acting in a sort of Christianized manner, which, if he had been better situated and more enlightened, he would not have been left to do." (See, also, pp. 8, 70, 71, and 121; and vol. ii. pp. 10, and 17.)

All these observations seem general, but they are meant to have a particular application. Mrs. Stowe mentions no names, indeed, but every one understands the mark she aims at,—"one gray, Titanic head." That head is now low in the dust,—hastened there by the fiendish malice of Horace Mann, *and followed there* by the hyæna, Theodore Parker, who having no reverence for his God, (see Appendix, P.) cannot be expected to have any respect for his fellow man.

And what are the charges that they thus bring against one as much their superior in every element of intellectual and moral worth, as he was in those physical qualities that "give the world assurance of a man?" I say, what are those charges? Some of them are contained in the following extract from a Review in the London Guardian, of Jan. 26., of two works,—one, Lanman's Life of Daniel Webster, and the other, Theodore Parker's Address on the same subject:—" That Webster may have appeared to Mr. Lanman all that he would have others believe him is very likely, but when his biography is written there will be blacker shades and more discreditable passages in the history than any of which the secretary has even suggested the existence.

" These darker lines are abundantly supplied by the honest, hearty eloquence of Mr. Parker. His 'Address' is a very remarkable paper, and strikes us as the best and fairest estimate we have ever met of the whole character of Mr. Webster. Full justice is done to his great qualities: hearty admiration is rendered to the intellect and eloquence which so often swayed the assemblies of his country. Yet the truth is told. His unprincipled conduct on the Fugitive Slave Law, is handled with a force and severity, all the more telling because it is employed with evident reluctance, and in the exercise only of judicial honesty. His want of the higher qualities of the statesman is not concealed. His loose, lax morality is fairly admitted. 'No living man,' says Mr. Parker, 'has done so much to debauch the conscience of the nation, to debauch the press, the pulpit, the forum, and the bar.' And again—'He contracted debts and did not settle; borrowed, and rendered not again. Private money sometimes clove to his hands. I wish the charges brought against his public administration may be disproved, whereof the stain rests on him to this day.' "

Such are the charges. Perhaps the Editor of the Guardian would have been slow to receive them on such authority, had he been aware that Theodore Parker is an *Infidel*, and that his testimony, therefore, would not be received on oath in any Court of Justice in his native Commonwealth.

(See Appendix, P., and also the remarks on testimony, near the end of Note 5.)

Were Theodore Parker the only authority for these charges, I should pass them by with silent contempt; but they have been endorsed by better men, and may, therefore, claim a passing notice.

The last two sentences in the above extract are obscurely worded, but I suppose they are designed as a repetition of the charge that Mr. Webster received a bribe to accept the post of Secretary of State, under President Fillmore, and that his independence was thereby compromited. This charge has been disproved by Mr. Franklin Haven, the very man through whom the "bargain" was alleged to have been proposed by Mr. Webster, and who, in the concluding paragraph of his letter to the Editor of the Boston Transcript, under date of May 17, 1851, thus disposes of the whole matter:—"The gift so honorably offered by men of high sense of honor in Boston to Mr. Webster, was not offered to him until many weeks after he had become Secretary of State. Not more than two of the persons who offered it to him could, in any way, be regarded as of the class of bankers, or concerned in banking; and so far from his 'position of independence' being affected by it, as Mr. Dana declares it was and is, I have good reason to believe, that Mr. Webster does not to this day know the name or position of one of the individuals, who have thus nobly and unostentatiously expressed to him their gratitude for his patriotic services."

The charge next preceding is in these words:—"He contracted debts, and did not settle; borrowed, and rendered not again."

This charge has been well replied to by the Hon. Geo. T. Davis, in his speech in Congress, Jan. 34, 1852, on the Mexican Indemnity Bill:—"It is an inevitable incident to greatness, that its pangs and struggles are as bare to the public eye as its energies and achievements. There is not a man who does not know that the great statesman of the country is as indifferent to money as he is devoted to the higher cares of the public weal. There is not a man, perhaps, (except my colleague, and some of those who think with him,) who does not wish that the order which reigns in that vast understanding, and reduces to their elements the most complicated national questions, were equally exemplified in every detail of his personal expenditure. But it is not so. His devotion to the public has left him neither time nor disposition to take care of himself; and this well-known fact leaves the question simply whether the public, in exigent crises, shall be deprived of his services, or whether friends shall aid him. Nor is this case, however sad, a rare one. If the views of my colleague could prevail, neither Burke, nor Pitt, nor Canning, in the Old World, nor I think Jefferson, or Madison, or Monroe, in the New, but would have been disqualified by their poverty, *and that very unthrift which devotion to great thoughts produces*, from lending their great powers to their country's service. * * * * If there is anything in my colleague's position, it is this: that the fact that Mr. Webster has been embarrassed in his pecuniary affairs, and has received pecuniary favors, would disqualify him from serving his country as a statesman. Has my colleague been so much more fortunate than most other men as to have utterly escaped such embarrassments? Has the black ox never trode on his foot? If so, I congratulate him that that bitterest drop has never been added to his cup of misery.

"But if it should be true, of which I know nothing, that he, too, like perhaps the majority of mankind, has known the agonies of the proud man subjected to the calls of the imperious creditor—if he too has 'served for a term in that leprous armada' of debt, entanglement, and evasion—and if in happier and more prosperous hours he forgets the sufferings of earlier years, and is prompt to urge against others a state of embarrassment as a reason of disqualification—why, what then? It is but a modern illustration of the savage line of the Roman annalist, *eo immitior quia toleraverat*, 'all the more pitiless because he, too, had suffered,' and all that need be said is, that the people among whom he lives have dealt and will deal with him more sparingly and kindly than he is inclined to deal with others." (pp. 3 and 5.) I may add, that this is the last charge that should be brought against another by such men as were assembled at the late "Hale dinner," one of whom, at least, and that one still high in the confidence of the rest, has notoriously "served" for more than one "term in that leprous armada of debt, entanglement and evasion."

Another charge sometimes made, and probably meant to be included in the phrase "loose, lax morality," above quoted, refers to Mr. Webster's personal habits; but when it is recollected that most of those who bring this charge profess to think it a sin to take a glass of wine on a festive occasion, (and ought, therefore for consistency's sake, to turn Mahometans at once, instead of claiming to be Christians, and at the same time reflecting on the character of Christ himself,) and that they belong to a party who, but a few days ago, gave a public dinner to the Hon. John P. Hale, late U. S. Senator from New-Hampshire, the accusation may be safely left to pass for what it is worth.

The truth is, not one of these charges would have been heard of but for the speech of March 7, 1850. And what was there in that speech to call down such a storm of obloquy on his devoted head? Nothing,—absolutely nothing. In that speech, Mr. Webster is where he always was, (and, I may add, where he continued to his death,) and Mr. Mann *knew* it, too, at the time he charged him with apostasy. And on what did he ground the charge? What were his "irrefragable and conclusive" proofs of it? Read the following, from his speech of Aug. 17, before referred to:—

"The Buffalo Convention of 1848, proclaimed its determination to 'maintain the rights of free labor against the aggressions of the slave power, and to secure free soil for a free people.'

"It declared its 'independence of the slave power, and its fixed determination to rescue the Federal Government from its control.'

"It declared that the proviso of Jefferson, to prohibit slavery in all the territories, and the ordinance of 1787, excluding slavery from the North-Western Territory, 'clearly show that it was the settled policy of the nation, not to *extend, nationalize*, or *encourage*, but to *limit, localize, and discourage* slavery; and to this policy, which should never have been departed from, the government ought to return.'

"It declared 'that it is the duty of the Federal Government to relieve itself from all responsibility for the existence or continuance of slavery wherever that Government possesses constitutional authority to legislate on that subject, and is thus responsible for its existence.'

"It declared 'that the only safe means of preventing the extension of slavery into territory now free, is to prohibit its existence in all such territory by an act of Congress.'

"It declared 'that we accept the issue which the slave power has forced upon us, and to their demand for more slave territories, our calm but final answer is, no more slave States—no more slave territory.'

"And what did Mr. Webster say of this platform, within one month after it had been adopted? This is his language:—

'I have said, gentlemen, that in this Buffalo platform,

this collect of the new school, there is nothing new. There is nothing in it that all the Whigs of the Northern and Middle States may not adopt. Gentlemen, it is well known that there is nothing in this Buffalo platform which, in general, does not meet the approbation of all the Whigs of the Middle and Northern States. Suppose, now, that all of us who are Whigs should go and join the Free Soil party, what would be the result? Why, so far, nothing would happen, but that the Whig party would have changed its name. That would be all. Instead of being the Whig party, it would be the Free-Soil party. We should be all there, exactly upon the same principles upon which we have always stood.'

"Now, contrast this full, explicit, comprehensive, and apparently ingenuous subscription and adhesion to all the doctrines and articles of the Buffalo platform, in 1848, with the 7th of March speech in 1850, and with all that has since followed it from the same source."

Yes, contrast it, and find, if you can, a single *principle* in the one, that is contradicted in the other. But Mr. Horace Mann is too thick-headed to understand, or too fanatical to acknowledge, (he may take which horn he pleases,) the difference between principles and measures,—that while these change, those remain. The truth is, Mr. Webster's career, "more forcibly than that of any other statesman of the time, illustrates the saying that, in applying principles to the changing affairs of life, the man who is true to his idea must often submit to the risk of being deemed inconsistent in his measures." Try Mr. Webster by the most rigid test, and see if you can detect, during the whole course of a long public life, a single deviation from *principle*, and if you cannot, then hold your tongues about apostasy, for very shame.

Apostasy, forsooth! The South knew better. They knew that Mr. Webster's hostility to the extension of slave territory was as uncompromising as ever, and it was on that account, and *that only*, that while they respected the man, they could not give him their vote in Convention, (not even in the way of compliment when it became certain he could not be nominated,) lest they should be charged with endorsing his doctrine on that point. I regret that it was so: I regret that his determination was so unalterable, for I believe most fully that the extension of slave territory will be for the benefit of the blacks as well as the whites, and that the best interests of the country demand it, as soon as it can be honorably brought about. But that Mr. Webster did not believe it, there can be no doubt, for if there is any one thing that is certain, it is that the *principles* of the "Buffalo Platform," were those of his whole public career.

And yet, in the face of all this, Mr. Horace Mann characterizes the doctrines of the 7th of March speech as "apostate doctrines," "cold, relentless, and blaspheming," and Mr. Whittier, in reference to that same speech, wrote the following:

ICHABOD.

So fallen! so lost! the light withdrawn
    Which once he wore!
The glory from his gray hairs gone
    For evermore!

Revile him not—the Tempter hath
    A snare for all;
And pitying tears, not scorn and wrath,
    Befit his fall!

Oh! dumb be passion's stormy rage,
    When he who might
Have lighted up and led his age,
    Falls back in night.

Scorn! would the angels laugh, to mark
    A bright soul driven
Fiend-goaded down the endless dark,
    From hope and heaven!

Let not the land, once proud of him,
    Insult him now,
Nor brand with deeper shame his dim,
    Dishonored brow.

But let its humbled sons, instead,
    From sea to Lake,
A long lament, as for the dead,
    In sadness make.

Of all we loved and honored, nought
    Save power remains—
A fallen angel's pride of thought,
    Still strong in chains.

All else is gone; from those great eyes
    The soul has fled;
When faith is lost, when honor dies,
    The man is dead!

Then, pay the reverence of old days
    To his dead fame;
Walk backward, with averted gaze,
    And hide the shame!

Shame, sayest thou?

"Blistered be thy tongue
For such a wish! He was not born to shame!
Upon his brow shame is ashamed to sit!
For 'tis a throne where honor might be crowned
Sole monarch of the universal earth."

But even had the above lines been as true as they are poetical, Mr. Whittier should have been the last person to give utterance to them, as my readers will probably admit, when they read the following, addressed by him some years ago to the Hon. Henry Clay, a slaveholder, and one, moreover, who stood side by side with Mr. Webster, on the "Compromise Measures:"—

Not fallen! No! as well the tall
And pillared Alleghany fall!
As well Ohio's giant tide!

Roll backward on its mighty track
As he, Columbia's hope and pride,
The slandered and the sorely tried,
In his triumphant course turn back.

He is not fallen! Seek to bind
The chainless and unbidden wind,
Oppose the torrent's headlong course
And turn aside the whirlwind's force,
But deem not that the mighty mind
Will cower before the blast of hate,
Or quail at dark and causeless ill,
For though all else be desolate
It stoops not from its high estate,
A Marius 'mid the ruins still.

He is not fallen! Every breeze
That wanders o'er Columbia's bosom,
From wild Penobscot's forest trees,
From ocean shore, from inland seas,
Or where the rich magnolia's blossom
Floats, snow-like, on the sultry wind,
Is booming onward to his ear,
A homage to his lofty mind,
A meed the fallen never find,
A praise which none but patriots hear.

Star of the West! A million eyes
Are turning gladly unto him,
The shrine of old idolatries
Before his waning light grows dim;
And men awake as from a dream
Of meteors dazzling to betray,
And bow before his purer beam,
The earnest of a better day.

All hail! the hour is hastening on,
When, vainly tried by slander's flame,
Columbia shall behold her son
Unharmed, without a laurel gone,
As from the flames of Babylon
The angel-guarded Triad came;

The slanderer shall be silent then,
His spell shall have the mind of men,
And higher glory wait upon
The Western Patriot's future fame.

Such were formerly Mr. Whittier's feelings towards a leading slave-holder. Yet he was then as much a Quaker as he is now; but he was not then an abolitionist, in any other sense than that in which Daniel Webster always was one; and, had his feelings at that time remained the same to 1850, he would have cut off his right hand sooner than have written the lines first above quoted.

Sed tempora mutantur;—

Twenty years have made a wonderful change in him and his associates. He and nine-tenths, ay, ninety-nine-hundredths, of those who act with him, were then (those of them, I mean, who were old enough to have an opinion,) as bitterly opposed to Garrison as the sturdiest conservative Whig, or Hunker Democrat, of them all, as Garrison, himself, could testify. But time does not alter truth, and Mr. Whittier must, therefore, excuse me, if, when he changes, I refuse to "veer and turn" with him.

Note 13.—Extension of Slave Territory.

I have already remarked in the preceding Note, that I most fully believe that the extension of slave territory will be for the benefit of the blacks as well as the whites, and that the best interests of the country demand it, as soon as it can be honorably brought about; and I am happy to believe that I can find plenty to agree with me "all over our land." Certainly, there has been a wonderful change in men's minds on this subject within the last ten years, and still more within the last fifty. A great deal of superfluous evidence has lately been brought forward by Free-Soil writers and speakers, to prove what nobody denies,—what, indeed, is perfectly notorious,—that at the time of the formation of the Federal Constitution nobody dreamed of the extension of slave territory, and very few, (hardly any, indeed, out of South Carolina and Georgia,) even of the extension of slavery, but that men generally were looking forward to its gradual and not very distant extinction. But then, it is equally true that nobody dreamed of the extension of territory at all, whether slave or free; and hence there is no provision for extension in the Constitution. And yet, since its adoption, the extent of our territory has been nearly tripled, and a considerable slice of the new portion, —more than one-fourth, and that the best for agricultural purposes,—is now slave territory. And still the cry is, More! and that not merely at the South, but even louder at the North, where it is fast becoming general. Witness the following from the New York Times, (Weekly,) of May 14, 1853:

"The selection of Mr. Buchanan for St. James', and Mr. Soulé for the Escurial, if significant at all, signifies that the United States has an inextinguishable appetite for Cuba; a fact of which no evidence is wanted. Has it not infested all our diplomacy; prevailed in all our Presidential messages; been inexhaustibly expressed in Congress and by the press? *The most conservative of us admit that the absorption of the island is only a question of time.* The selection is utterly devoid of other meaning."

And the following from the Boston Journal, of May 23, 1853:

"Whether the administration will be slow to take offence at the folly of our Mexican neighbors remains to be seen; but an important movement is undoubtedly in contemplation. Sooner or later the limits of our territory must and will be extended further South. Its course is as plainly marked out as the path of the sun in heaven; but it is only blind enthusiasts, hot-headed politicians, and reckless demagogues, that would precipitate matters before the time. Enlightened Mexicans, like General Arista, foresee it, and wish for such a result; but the true course for us to adopt is to leave Mexico to herself. Her tyranny and anarchial rule will alienate the northern provinces, which will shake off her yoke, successively following the example of Texas, and become independent States. The people of the United States will emigrate thither and settle among them, carrying civilization, the love of republican liberty, and the ability of self-government; and when in this way they become regenerated, and fit to be admitted, they will drop like ripened fruit into the lap of the Union, becoming really valuable acquisitions."

As to the Sandwich Islands, it seems to be generally conceded that we are to have them during the present administration; probably, within the present year.

And this we call "manifest destiny." I rather refer it to the leadings of Providence,—that

> "Divinity that shapes our ends,
> Rough-hew them how we will;"—

that leads us by a way we knew not, working out by our (often unconscious) agency his purposes of wisdom and love;

> "From seeming evil still educing good,"

and carrying the world, slowly but surely, forward, to its final redemption.

And what are to be the consequences of all this to the negro?

First and foremost, increased value to his labor, and consequent kinder treatment from his master:

Then, a more rapid elevation in the scale of being:

And finally, a speedier exodus to the land of his fathers.

I say to the land of his fathers; for that in that direction lies his final exodus, I have no doubt. I do not believe, with Mr. Secretary Walker, that it is to be through Texas into Mexico. On the contrary, I believe that his mission is to civilize and Christianize his native Africa, and that therefore Providence *frowns* upon every attempt of his to form a free and independent community in this Western Hemisphere. Cuba may, perhaps, become eventually the home of the Quadroon; for with his Anglo-Saxon energy, and with just enough of African blood in his veins to make him proof against tropical diseases, he would be admirably adapted, in conjunction with the Anglo-Saxon, to develope the inexhaustible resources of that magnificent island. But, for the full-blooded negro there can be no *home* this side the water: he must be again "ferried o'er the wave:" Africa *must* be redeemed, and he only can work out its redemption.

NOTE 14.—SOUTHERN EMANCIPATORS.

Mrs. Stowe speaks of a class of slaveholders who may be appropriately designated by this title, and that there is such a class, is undoubtedly true; but she seems to think them numerous, and in this she is mistaken; they are but few, and of those few, the greater part are in the border slave States, principally in Northern Kentucky. These last look across the river, and contrast the rapid growth of Ohio with the comparatively slow growth of their own Commonwealth, and then jump to the conclusion that slavery is at the bottom of it. Now, undoubtedly, slavery is *a* cause of it, but if it is the only cause, how happens it that Georgia is one of the most flourishing States of the Union, and that her resources are developing with such giant stride as to have gained for her the cognomen of the "Empire State of the South?" How happens it, too, if slave labor is the only kind of labor which exhausts the soil, that two-thirds of the improved land of the State of New York has become exhausted to such a degree that "fully to renovate it would cost at least an average of twelve dollars and a half per acre, or an aggregate of *one hundred millions of dollars?*" (See Appendix, R.)

The truth is, slave labor in a border State is necessarily unprofitable, from the fact that it is constantly coming increasingly into competition with free labor, and that, in such a state of things, *both* operate to disadvantage. Such is now the condition of things in Kentucky: she is purchasing her redemption, and she is paying the price of it as she goes along. I say her *redemption*, for a community whose laborers are free, is better off, *ceteris paribus*, than one whose laborers are slaves. Meanwhile, she has no right,—no moral right, I mean,—to turn her slaves loose on the community: she is bound to take care of them, or to *send them where they will be taken care of*, till they become fit for freedom.

This is a consideration which seems to be entirely lost sight of by Southern Emancipators. I commend it to Cassius M. Clay, and his coadjutors: they are too impatient by half; they had a great deal better take things easy, and wait for the slow but sure operation of natural causes to place them on the vantage ground of the Ohio freeman. Any attempt to hurry matters will only make bad worse.

NOTE 15.—YANKEE OVERSEERS.

Mrs. Stowe has no good opinion of this class of persons, for she tells us (vol. ii. p. 316,) that they are "proverbially, the hardest masters of slaves." This is, no doubt, true; but it does not follow that they are, therefore, "renegade sons" (vol. ii. p. 15,) of New England. On the contrary, it is because they are *genuine* Yankees, that they are so hard masters: they have been accustomed to see men do a day's work,—they have done it themselves,—and they cannot understand how the negro can do only a half or a third of one.

I recollect the first time I saw Quashy at work in the field, I was struck with the lazy, listless manner in which he raised his hoe. It reminded me of the working-beam of the engine on the steamboat that I had just landed from—fifteen strokes a minute; but there was this difference, that whereas the working-beam kept steadily at it, Quashy, on the contrary, would stop about every five strokes and lean upon his hoe, and look around, apparently congratulating himself on the amount of work he had accomplished.

Mrs. Stowe may well call Quashy "shiftless." One of my father's hired men, who was with him seven years, did more work in that time than an average negro would do in his whole life. Nay, I myself have done more work in a day,—and followed it up too,—than I ever saw a negro do; and yet I was considered remarkably lazy with the plough or the hoe: certainly, I had no great liking for it, for my vocation did not seem to me to lie that way. Perhaps a similar reason was operating on Quashy.

Note 16.—Characters of the Work.

I have remarked in the Introduction that the life of the work is in its characters. Certainly the author has a wonderful power of descriptive portrait-painting, and where she has an *original* to sit to her, she invariably succeeds. She can paint a New England old maid, or a Kentucky negro, to the life, for she is at home among them. Equally successful is she in sketching the Kentucky drover, for genuine specimens of these are to be seen occasionally on the Ohio side of the river. So, too, with the Quakers: her family picture shows that she has been among them; there are Phinehas Fletcher's, and plenty of them too, in every Quaker community, not only of those who have married into the society, but such as have been "always born and brought up" in it. And this must necessarily be so. Quakerism is so unnatural, so contrary to human nature, not only unregenerate, but regenerate, that you cannot screw men up to it; or if you do, you cannot keep them screwed:

"Naturam expelles furca, tamen usque recurret."

Mrs. Stowe understands this, and she makes Simeon Halliday himself more than half acknowledge it.

But to proceed with the characters. Senator Bird and his wife is a true sketch, real and life-like. So is Tom Loker: I myself have seen at least "a dozen of him"—veritable flesh and blood—engaged in quite a different calling, though, from that of negro-catcher.

In all these characters, and several others that might be mentioned, Mrs. Stowe is at home; but when she comes to the Southern gentleman or lady, she is evidently out of her element. Her idea of the former, we have in Mr. Shelby, "a well sketched *average* Kentucky gentleman," as her friend, the London Examiner, calls him: if he is, God help the Kentuckians, for they are sadly in need of help! But more of Mr. Shelby further on: let us turn to our author's idea of ladyship. This we have in Marie St. Clare! But certainly no lady, not to say, no Southern lady, ever sat for that portrait: not only is it a caricature,—*that* we might put up with,—but there is in it an essential and ingrained vulgarity. For proof of this, see both volumes *passim*, and particularly vol. ii. pp. 98 and 148. A lady might be cruel, if it were *simple* cruelty, and still, *possibly*, remain within the charmed circle of *ladyship;* but any one who could so far forget herself as to use the language, "You good-for-nothing *nigger!* Get along off with you!" and could deliberately and systematically set about breaking down and destroying all "delicacy and sense of shame" in one of her own sex, would find herself out of that circle irrecoverably; or rather, such language and such conduct would show that she was never in it.

Mrs. Stowe is more at home among the Kentucky negroes; but, even here, she cannot help exaggerating. Uncle Tom himself is an exaggeration, though not to such a degree as the London Times would have us suppose: to judge from its language, one would suppose that negro piety was an incredible, or, at any rate, a very questionable thing. The Times goes as far to the one extreme, as Mrs. Stowe to the other: the truth lies midway between them.

As to George Harris and Eliza, I am inclined to look upon them as true representations: at any rate, they are close approximations to them. But then they are few; not more than one in ten thousand: and of them all, George Harris and his wife a e, probably, the only ones that ever got off into Canada. Certainly, most of the fugitives there are of a very different stamp. Says Prof. Ansted in his first Letter to the London Times, "Nearly all those runaway slaves who escaped into Canada—and the number is not inconsiderable—are found to be idle, useless, and unimproving in every sense of the word. *Their idea of liberty is an escape from labour, and the indulgence of a mere animal existence with as little effort as possible.* They are bad servants and bad citizens, and rarely rise above the very lowest position in the social scale. *This is matter perfectly notorious*, and we must not be surprised if before long the people of Canada refuse to admit a population *which has no value*, and frequently becomes a drag on the resources of the country."

Now why did not Mrs. Stowe take negroes of this stamp

for her runaways? Because they would not answer her purpose. Wherever outrageous cruelties are to be enacted, such as would excite our indignation even if inflicted on a beast, there she introduces full-blooded negroes; but when our sympathies are to be enlisted in behalf of fugitives, she takes care to have them not negroes, nor even mulattoes, but quadroons,—men and women all but white, and who, therefore, according to the *fitness of things*, ought not to be in slavery at all.

Had it been a strapping negro wench, black as a coal and ugly as sin, that had called with her boy at Senator Bird's, she might have got off as she could: certainly the Senator never would have helped her off. This, Mrs. Stowe very well knew, and therefore she took care to have her fugitives all but white. True she has two black ones with them,—Jim and his aged mother; but they are only accessory. She tries indeed to make Jim out a hero, but with poor success. Speaking of one who had run similar ventures, she asks, (vol. ii. p. 298.), My good sir, is this man a hero or a criminal? *Not* a hero, Mrs. Stowe; no, not a hero: you yourself have settled that point. Uncle Tom is the hero. But had he run away, instead of staying to suffer martyrdom, would he have been a hero, you yourself being judge? You know he would not, and therefore you made him a martyr.

NOTE 17.—INCONSISTENCIES AND IMPROBABILITIES OF THE STORY.

These lie at the foundation of the work: the very first chapter is *full* of them. First we have Mr. Shelby, "an average Kentucky gentleman," entertaining at his own table a professional slave-trader, "a short, thick-set man, with coarse, commonplace features, and that swaggering air of pretension which marks a low man who is trying to elbow his way upward in the world." (See his description at large, in the second paragraph of the chapter.) Now I can assure Mrs. Stowe that no Southern gentleman would ever invite such a personage to his table; it is morally, I had almost said, physically, impossible: I should as soon expect to see the Duchess of Sutherland entertaining the public hangman at Stafford House, or Mrs. Stowe marrying her children to runaway negroes.

But even supposing Mr. Shelby could, by any possibility, have so far forgotten himself as to invite Haley to his table, the utmost stretch of his complaisance could have gone no farther than a cold and constrained civility. And yet we have him, here, setting a favorite little quadroon slave-boy to playing off "monkey-shines" for the amusement of his guest!

However, all this is nothing compared with the next improbability,—the sale of Uncle Tom; an improbability *so* improbable that the allegation of it as a fact is simply ludicrous. I challenge Mrs. Stowe to bring forward *a single instance* in which such a slave as Uncle Tom is here represented to have been, was *ever* sold by his master to a slave-dealer. Servants like Uncle Tom are known throughout the community, (see vol. i. p. 148.), and valued, too; or rather they are justly considered invaluable; and Mr. Shelby had only to let it be known that he was obliged to part with Tom, to have had a dozen of his neighbors in competition for the purchase, and at a higher price, too, than any prudent dealer would be willing to offer; for they would know what they were purchasing, and the dealer, whatever his own knowledge, would find it no easy matter to transfer that knowledge to his customer.

But what need of selling Uncle Tom at all? There were plenty of other negroes on the estate, if we may believe Aunt Chloe:—"Why, laws me, Missis! other folks hires out their niggers and makes money on 'em! Don't keep such a tribe eatin 'em out of house and home." (Vol. ii. p. 57.) Why not sell some of these?—Andy and Black Sam, for instance, who would have gone off with their hands in their pockets, whistling as they went, and congratulating themselves on the chance they had of rising in the world. But this would have spoiled the *story*.

Absurd as all this is, it is not the only absurdity: not only must Uncle Tom go, but little Harry must go with him;—little Harry the only child of Mrs. Shelby's favorite waiting maid. Mr. Shelby deliberately agrees to sell the child, though he knows it will spoil the value of the mother *as a servant*. But then Mr. Shelby is not like other men: other men take care of their own property; Mr. Shelby deliberately sets about ruining his. I say, ruining; for he must have known that it *would* ruin it: Eliza, we are told, had lost "two infant children, to whom she was passionately attached, and whom she mourned with a grief so intense as to call for gentle remonstrance from her mistress, who sought, with maternal anxiety, to direct her naturally passionate feelings within the bounds of reason and religion. After the birth of little Harry, however, she had gradually become tranquillized and settled; and every bleeding tie and throbbing nerve, once more entwined with that little life, seemed to become sound and healthful." (Vol. i. p. 30.)—Of course the loss of little Harry, in *such* a way,* would

* Those who are represented as separating mother and child, are represented as doing it ordinarily as a business transaction, a simple matter of dollars and cents: they are represented, moreover, as shrewd business men, and must therefore know the effect of the separation on the mother. Now, one of two things must be true: either the separation injures the mother *as property*, or it does not; in other words, either the mother easily gets over the separation, or she does

be tenfold worse than the death of the other two, and if she *was* as she is here described, it would manifestly have ruined her *as property;* and Mr. Shelby knowing this, (and he must have known it,) and still deliberately consummating the bargain, whether "an average Kentucky gentleman," or not, had not certainly an average share of brains.

Ridiculous as all this is, the reason given for it is still more ridiculous:—"I'm sorry you feel so about it, Emily,—indeed I am," said Mr. Shelby; "and I respect your feelings, too, though I don't pretend to share them to their full extent; but I tell you now, solemnly, it's of no use—I can't help myself. I didn't mean to tell you this, Emily; but, in plain words, there is no choice between selling these two or selling everything. Either they must go, or *all* must. Haley has come into possession of a mortgage, which, if I don't clear off with him directly, will take everything before it. I've raked, and scraped, and borrowed, and all but begged,—and the price of these two was needed to make up the balance, and I had to give them up. Haley fancied the child; he agreed to settle the matter that way, and no other. I was in his power,* and *had* to do it. If you feel so to have them sold, would it be any better to have *all* sold?" (vol. i. p. 57.)

not: if she does, then the alleged strength of her maternal affections is unfounded; if she does not, then the trader who makes the separation, is not a shrewd business man. Mrs. Stowe may take which horn of the dilemma she pleases.

* "Did his life, or that of any, or all his family, depend on his submission to this ruthless tyrant?

"Oh, no.

"What then? Had he the planter so completely in his power that, unless he submitted to his whim to have old Tom and little Henry, he could so ruin him at once as to reduce himself and family to beggary?

"Nothing of all this.

"What then?

A queer mortgage this, that can be "cleared off" only by the sale of one particular negro and one particular little quadroon boy; that no other negro, or negroes,—no, nor the hard cash itself, can cancel! A very queer mortgage, isn't it?

And this is gravely put forward as an adequate reason for the sale of Uncle Tom and little Harry, and we are expected to receive it as such! Archbishop Whately, wo are told, is among Mrs. Stowe's English friends: what will he say to such logic?

And all this lies at the *foundation* of the story: that being swept away, the superstructure falls, as a matter of course. However, to show that the inconsistencies and improbabilities of the story are not in the foundation alone, but that there are plenty of them in the superstructure, I will briefly notice two or three.

The first is on page one hundred twenty-fifth, volume second. We have seen that it took a violent improbability, or rather, *several* violent improbabilities, to get Tom off from Kentucky to New Orleans. We see here that it takes another and an equally violent one to transfer him from New Orleans to Red River. We are told that there was one thing that St. Clare did, soon after his return to New Orleans, "and that was to commence the legal steps necessary to Tom's emancipation, which was to be perfected as soon as he could get through the necessary formalities:" and again, (p. 151.), Miss Ophelia says to Marie St. Clare, "Augustine promised Tom his liberty, and began the legal

"Why, he held a promissory note against him. And *by the time that the planter could grow two crops, he might force the payment of it.* So much; no more, is the planter in the trader's power. Such is the slight foundation on which Mrs. Stowe has erected the main building of her showy and admired edifice." The Planter, or Thirteen years in the South, p. 35.

N*

forms necessary to it. I hope you will use your influence to have it perfected."

It would seem from this that the emancipation of a negro in Louisiana is a very difficult and intricate matter,—almost as much so as the formation of a new State Constitution in this second half of the nineteenth century. If so, why did n't St. Clare make Tom over to Miss Ophelia, as he did Topsy, (p. 131.)? that could have been done in a half-hour's time, and would have been tantamount to giving Tom his liberty. Oh! but that would have prevented Tom's martyrdom, and so would have spoiled the *story!*

But *is* the emancipation of a negro in Louisiana so difficult a matter, after all? If so, how happens it that there are seventeen thousand five hundred and thirty-seven free negroes in that State,—nearly two thousand more than in all the other "coast planting" States put together,—and that in the year ending June, 1st., 1850, there were one hundred and fifty-nine manumitted, being forty-one more than in all the other States south of Virginia and Kentucky, and more than one-ninth of all the manumissions in the United States during that year?

The truth is, this alleged difficulty is all "humbug": there is n't a State in the Union in which a solvent master cannot manumit his slave at any time, *provided* he sends him out of the State,—a restriction (in many of the more Southern States) designed to prevent the accumulation of a refuse population that might, and probably would become a charge to the community, either as paupers or as criminals. St. Clare had, therefore, only to give Tom his "walking papers," and he might have "made tracks" for Kentucky at once. And even when the master lay a dying, and his thoughts were running on "Tom! poor fellow!" (p. 142.), he had only to make a parole declaration, in the presence of the Doctor and Miss Ophelia, that he gave Tom his liberty, and all the laws of Louisiana could not have retained him in bondage. So much for the inconsistencies and improbabilities in the second stage of the story.

We come now to the third stage, and here we make the acquaintance of Simon Legree, first at the slave warehouse, then on the steamboat, and finally at his plantation on the Red River. In the warehouse scene there are no inconsistencies and improbabilities that call for particular observation, but the steamboat scene is full of them.

First we have Legree holding out his hand to a gentleman for examination:—" Just feel of my knuckles, now; look at my fist. Tell ye, sir, the flesh on 't has come jest like a stone, practising on niggers,—feel on it." (p. 172.) This gentleman, we are told, (p. 311.), was the author's brother, "then collecting clerk to a large mercantile house, in New Orleans." Speaking of Legree, he says, "He actually made me feel of his fist, which was like a blacksmith's hammer, or a nodule of iron, telling me that it was 'calloused with knocking down niggers.' When I left the plantation, I drew a long breath, and felt as if I had escaped from an ogre's den."

Now a coarse, brutal man might make such a boast in the presence of negroes, or of men of his own sort, but the supposition that he could make it *bona fide*, and in *sober earnest*, to a *gentleman*, is, really, too ridiculous for any but the greenest of greenhorns to swallow. Without presuming to call in question the truth of Mr. Beecher's statement, I think I find an easy and natural explanation of it in the following paragraph from the January number of the Southern Quarterly Review: — "The testimony of this brother is the only one which she cites, except in the general 'all over the land' style, which we have noticed; and we think any one who has spent six months of his life in a southern city will recognize the type of this her solitary authority. Who has not seen the green Yankee youth opening his eyes and mouth for every piece of stray intelligence; eager for horrors; gulping the wildest tales, and exaggerating even as he swallowed them? Why, this fellow is to be met with in every shipload of candidates for clerkships who come out like bees to suck our honey. * * * Seriously, is it not easy here to perceive that a raw, suspicious Yankee youth having "happened" (as he would say) in contact with a rough overseer, a species of the *genus homo* evidently quite new to him, has been half gulled by the talk of the fellow, who has plainly intended to quiz him, and has half gulled himself with his own fears while in the vicinity of this novel character, whom he, poor gentle specimen of Yankee humanity, has absolutely mistaken for an ogre, because his hand is hard." (p. 85.)

I was mentioning this explanation, a short time ago, to a young lawyer of my acquaintance in Baltimore. "Why," said he, "I myself have done pretty much the same thing. I recollect I was once on a visit to a cousin in Philadelphia, and one day we started off in the stage-coach for Doylestown, Bucks County, to call on some friends there. We were then boys, and up to almost anything in the way of a joke. Our only travelling companions were two ancient maidens, apparently some years on the shady side of thirty. We soon found they were abolitionists, ready to swallow anything *black*, however monstrous, and I determined at once to have some fun out of them. Accordingly, I set about relating to my companion all sorts of horrible cruelties inflicted on negroes, inventing the materials as I went along and making myself the *hero* of the greater part of them; my companion putting leading questions to me, every now and then, to *draw me out*. Such atrocities as I recounted! I presume the like of them were never heard of, or even dreamed of before. I told them all, however, with a grave face, as though they were commonplace, every-day occurrences, giving to my fair auditors the impression, all the while, that I thought such inflictions all right where negroes were the subjects of them. Thus I went on, pouring out horror after horror, with a fertility of invention that I had never before imagined myself possessed of, and which seems truly wonderful when I look back upon it. The ancient maidens listened, all the while, with open eyes and mouth, swallowing my inventions *easily*, and with throats apparently capacious enough to admit 'a few more of the same sort;' but, unluckily for our sport, the coach brought me and my companion to our journey's end, and I had to break off in the midst of a horror which, for that reason, has remained untold to this day."

Now all this was very naughty, no doubt, and the only apology we can make for it is in Black Sam's language, (vol. i. p. 113,) *mutatis mutandis:*—"It was ugly on me,—there's no disputin' that ar; and of course *good people* wouldn't encourage no such works. I'm sensible of dat ar; but a *wild fellow* like me's 'mazin' tempted to act ugly sometimes, when *ancient maidens and 'collecting clerks' will be so green.*"

So much for the "fist and knuckles." Now for another inconsistency and improbability: "'I don't go for savin' niggers. Use up, and buy more, 's my way;—makes you less trouble, and I'm quite sure it comes cheaper in the end;' and Simon sipped his glass.

"'And how long do they generally last?' said the stranger.

"'Well, donno; 'cordin' as their constitution is. Stout fellers last six or seven years; trashy ones gets worked up in two or three. I used to, when I fust begun, have considerable trouble fussin' with 'em, and trying to make 'em hold out,—doctorin' on 'em up when they's sick, and givin'

20

on 'em clothes and blankets, and what not, tryin' to keep 'em all sort o' decent and comfortable. Law, 't was n't no sort o' use; I lost money on 'em, and 'twas heaps o' trouble. Now, you see, I just put 'em straight through, sick or well. When one nigger's dead, I buy another; and I find it comes cheaper and easier, every way.'" (p. 173.) Now I challenge Mrs. Stowe to bring forward any authority, or shadow of an authority, for such a representation. She cannot find a single instance of the kind *since the abolition of the foreign slave-trade:* before that time, there may have been instances, for *then* it really was cheaper to "use up niggers," but now it is dearer, "every way;" and Mrs. Stowe herself admits that it is dearer, for she makes Cassy say to Legree, "I've saved you some thousands of dollars, at different times, by taking care of your hands;" so hard it is to be consistent in fiction that professes to be founded on fact, and whose whole aim and end is, to put the worst face possible upon things.

But enough of the inconsistencies and improbabilities of the story: to expose the whole of them would require a volume. Let these serve for a specimen.

NOTE 18.—IRRELIGIOUS TENDENCY OF THE WORK.

At the "breakfast" given to Mrs. Stowe, the morning after her arrival in Liverpool, Professor Stowe, in his *after*-breakfast speech, is thus reported:—"Speaking of the success of his gifted lady's book, he said—Incredible as it may seem to those who are without prejudice, it is nevertheless a fact, that this book was condemned by the leading religious newspaper in the United States as antichristian, and its author associated with infidels and disorganizers."

I have not seen the article referred to, but I find the following extract from it in "The Planter: or, Thirteen Years in the South:"—"We have read the book, and regard it as antichristian. We have marked numerous passages in which religion is spoken of in terms of contempt, and in *no* case is religion represented as making a master more humane; while Mrs. Stowe is careful to represent the indulgent and amiable masters as without religion. This taint pervades the work, just as it does the writings of all the modern school of philanthropy. It is certainly a non-religious, if not anti-evangelical school. Mrs. Stowe labors through all her book to render ministers odious and contemptible, by attributing to them sentiments unworthy of men or Christians." (p. 24.)

Now all this I fully concur with: I have myself "marked numerous passages," and I presume they are the same with those marked by the Editor of the Observer. They may be found on pages 58, 139, 181, 191, 262, 264, 265, and 266, of volume first, and on pages 10 and 127, of volume second. In each of these passages there is an open or covert sneer at the Church or the Clergy. As a set-off to all these, there is but one redeeming passage in the book: it is to be found on page 137 of volume second. How Mrs. Stowe could reconcile it with the passages above referred to, or, indeed, with the whole spirit of her Work, is past my comprehension.

I say, with the whole spirit of her work; for unless the Church of Christ has, from the beginning, utterly misapprehended the character of Christianity, that spirit is an antichristian spirit; it is the spirit of the so-called *moral reforms* of the present day; the atheistic spirit of the old French Revolution: its sympathies are not with Christ, but with "the false prophet." Even the temperance movement,—the most plausible of them all,—is a Mahommedan, and not a Christian movement: years ago, in one of the Congregational Churches in Lowell, Mass., (the third, I believe,) it substituted for wine, in the Lord's Supper, *molasses-and-water;* and recently, in the Unitarian Church in Bedford, (the place of my nativity,) reversing the miracle of our Lord, it has changed wine into water! Mrs. Stowe may not be *ready yet* to go to such a length, but her tendencies are in that direction: the spirit of her work is the spirit of the several "movements;" her sympathies are not with Christ, and with St. Paul, and St. Peter, and St. Jude, but with Theodore Parker and Horace Mann. Like them, she is "presumptuous," "self-willed," "not afraid to speak evil of dignities."

It is painful to have to speak thus of a woman, but she has left me no alternative. Who would have supposed that a woman *could* deliberately pen so shockingly irreverent a sentence as that at the end of the first paragraph on page fifteenth of volume second? And what could we expect from such an one but that she should be found, as she actually is found, arraying herself in open hostility to the laws of her country, and not merely encouraging passive non-obedience for conscience sake—*that* we might respect, however much we thought the conscience misguided—but actually inciting to active resistance to the execution of those laws, even to the extent, if need be, of taking human life?

Alas for my country, when such a work, from such a source, is read by such multitudes—thousands upon thousands,—I had almost said, millions upon millions! I solemnly believe that it has done more, considering its immense circulation, to debauch public sentiment and sap the foundations of social order, and lead men to infidelity and open atheism, than any other publication, with the single exception of the New York Tribune. The Independent, judging from the little I have seen of it, is as bad, but its circulation is comparatively limited. As to the Herald, even in its worst days, it was a good Christian, side by side with the Tribune, and *now* it is an angel of light in the comparison. By its ridicule of "Philosopher Greely" it has furnished the young men of New York, and of the country, with an antidote to the Tribune's bane, and I should look upon its discontinuance,—the Tribune still continuing to be issued,—as a public calamity.

NOTE 19.—KEY TO UNCLE TOM'S CABIN.

This the author evidently considers a "settler," and it is certainly *ponderous* enough to settle almost anything. Uncle Tom's Cabin is probably the first one of its kind that ever had a key, and therefore it seems to have been thought fitting that it should have a large one,—larger, strange to say, than the Cabin itself. It is evidently a permutation and combination key; it carries on the face of it the marks of more than one person having been engaged in the manufacture of it, and of there having been a shifting (not sifting) of materials from time to time. The author, having made a handsome speculation on the Cabin, has invested a part of the proceeds in a new venture, and a paying one, too, for there is no end to human gullibility:

> "Doubtless the pleasure is as great
> Of being cheated as to cheat,"

if not a little greater; and this innocent pleasure Mrs. Stowe has very benevolently ministered to, and on a magnificent scale. Having abundant resources at her command, she has spread a drag-net from the Rio *Grande* to Cape *Sable*, "which, when it was full," with much ado and great flourish of trumpets, she has succeeded in "drawing to land;" but instead of "gathering the good into vessels and casting the bad away," she has pretty nearly reversed the process, having saved only enough of the good to keep up a *show* of candor: and now, all the enemies of freedom in the Old World "sacrifice unto her net, and burn incense unto her drag." "Shall they therefore empty their net and not spare continually to slay the nations?" (Hab. i. 16, 17.). No! thank God! it is too late in the day. Had Mrs. Stowe written ten years earlier, there is no telling to what an indefinite period the oppression of the toiling millions of Europe might have been prolonged by her gross, ay, wholesale misrepresentations. But now, hundreds of thousands of Irishmen escaped from the grinding oppression of the English Commercial System, and Germans and other Europeans escaped from the hampering of outworn political and social institutions are enjoying in this land, where

> "The free spirit of mankind at length
> Casts its last fetters off,"

a blessing on their honest toil, such as they, in their wildest dreams, had never even imagined; and every transatlantic mail takes out hundreds and thousands of letters to their friends, with remittances, to bring them over. And they will come, spite of Uncle Tom's Cabin and the Key into the bargain.

But this Key! What is it for? To clench the *story*. "At different times," it seems, "doubt has been expressed whether the representations of 'Uncle Tom's Cabin' are a fair representation of slavery as it at present exists." The representations doubtful! Well, that is a good joke! One might almost imagine the author were quizzing us! Doubtful? Yes! doubtful, (as Coleridge would say,) in the same sense in which it is doubtful whether the moon is made of green cheese! When Mrs. Stowe has proved the one, she may consider the other proved also.

Nothing daunted, however, she undertakes the proof: and by what kind of evidence?

1. "Personal observation."

2. Formal testimony, written or oral.

3. Published documents, including newspaper paragraphs and advertisements.

Well, these are all legitimate means of proof, provided they are properly employed. But what does she mean by "personal observation?" If we turn to part 1. chap. 2., we shall find, at the end of the first paragraph, the following: "The author's first *personal observation* of this class of beings [the slave-traders] was somewhat as follows." She then goes on to relate how it was, and it turns out that her "personal observation" of "this class of beings" was merely a "personal observation" of a letter handed to her, or rather, "pushed towards her," by a "colored woman" with a "surly, unpromising face," and *purporting* to be written by one of "this class of beings," *and*, the answer of the aforesaid colored woman to the question, "What sort of a man is this?" "Dunno, ma'am; great Christian, I know,—member of the Methodist church, any how." And this the author calls "personal observation!" And it is'nt a slip of the pen, either. In chapter ii. p. 49., middle of the second column, she tells us, "An incident of this sort [referring to the narrative just before quoted by her, from Uncle Tom's Cabin, of the sale of a mother from her child because she fell asleep from exhaustion while nursing her master,] *came under the author's observation* in the following manner." The "observation turns out to be the *testimony* of a "liberated quadroon slave family," that the mother of a "little quadroon boy" living with them, had been so sold!

This is what the author understands by "personal observation," and I have called the reader's attention to it for two reasons: first, that he may not misunderstand her, and think that, when she speaks of "personal observation," she means what other persons mean by it; and second, that he may be able to judge what are the qualifications of one who can use language thus loosely, to comment on testimony, and interpret legal documents, and may not therefore be surprised, if he finds her, in the sequel, involved in the most ludicrous blunders.

So much for the "personal observation:" now for the testimony. This, the reader, after what has been said above, will not be at all surprised to find, is, much of it, the *ex parte* testimony of runaway slaves against their master or mistress, given without the sanction of an oath and without opportunity for cross-examination; all which, nevertheless, the author is so "verdant," (to use one of her own expressions,) as to expect us to take for gospel!

Her first witness of this kind is Lewis Clark, her second, Frederick Douglass, and her third, Josiah Henson; (see chap. iv. pp. 13, 19.). "Now all these incidents that have been given [in the pages here referred to,] are," she tells us, "*real** incidents of slavery, related by those who know slavery by the best of all tests—experience;" and she *naively* adds, a few sentences after: "It is supposed by many that the great outcry among those who are opposed to slavery comes from a morbid reading of unauthenticated accounts gotten up in Abolition papers, &c. This idea is a very mistaken one. The accounts which tell against the slave-system are derived from the continual living testimony of the poor slave himself; *often* from that of the *fugitives* from slavery who are *continually* passing through our Northern cities. As a specimen of some of the incidents thus developed, is given the following fact of recent occurrence," &c., &c.; (p. 19.).

Now I am not going to deny the truth of their statements, but I do say that the testimony of a runaway apprentice,—and they *do* run away, sometimes, witness the advertise-

* The *italics* are hers.

ments so common in the Northern newspapers, headed, "A basket of chips reward!" "One cent reward, and no charges paid!"—I say the testimony of a runaway apprentice against his master or mistress would be received *cum grano salis*, with a grain,—ay, with a good many grains of allowance, and I do not see why a colored skin should gain more credence for its possessor than a white one.

I said I was not going to *deny* the truth of the statements, but it may be well to give a specimen of them, that the reader may know what it is he is expected to gulp down. So, here goes! "Gape, sinner, and swallow!"*—"The slaves often say, when cut in the hand or foot, 'Plague on the old foot' or 'the old hand! It is master's,—let him take care of it. Nigger don't care if he never get well.'" (Testimony of Lewis Clark, last paragraph, p. 16.) St. Paul says that "No man ever yet hated his own flesh; but nourisheth and cherisheth it;" (Eph. v. 29,): but St. Paul didn't live in the nineteenth century. The same Apostle says in the preceding verse, "So ought men to love their wives as their own bodies;" but, if Lewis Clark and Mrs. Stowe are *both* to be believed, Quashy has *improved upon* the Apostle, for he loves his wife, ay, and his children, too, *better* than his own body: otherwise, he would say, when parted from them, "Plague on de ole woman! Plague on de little woolly-head! They are master's,—let him take care on 'em. Nigger don't care if he never see 'em again."

So much for testimony.

The third kind of evidence is published documents, &c., and these, as I have not the means of authenticating them, or testing the truth of their statements, I shall let pass for what they are worth.

And what *are* they worth? What is the whole evidence of the book, that from personal observation, that from testi-

* *Meg Merrilies.*

mony, and that from published documents—worth as a justification of the representations of Uncle Tom's Cabin? Just nothing at all. The alleged facts in the Key might, every one of them, be real facts, without exception, and without exaggeration, and Uncle Tom's Cabin still be an outrageous caricature: the fancy-sketch of *Horace*, half woman and half fish, with a covering of parti-colored feathers, is made up of constituent parts, each of which exists *in verum natura*, but the *combination* never has been seen, and, *I rather think*, never will be. Some men are lascivious, and some are wantonly cruel, but the two characters were never yet found united in the same person: there are "disjunctive conjunctions" in rhetorical composition, but not in the composition of human nature. Because there is "coarse-fine"* salt in Northern warehouses, it does not follow that there are coarse-fine ladies in Southern drawing-rooms; because "blackberries are always red when they are green," it does not follow that Quashy is always white when he is yellow or brown. To father all the cruelties to apprentices on one master, and all the cruelties to wives on one husband, and then hold these up as specimens of a class, and legitimate results of a system, would be to follow in Mrs. Stowe's footsteps, but it would be a poor excuse for the foul libel, in the estimation of all honorable men, to say that each of the alleged cruelties had been actually committed, somewhere, at some time, by some body, and that very many of them had, through the imperfection of the law, or the worse than imperfection of its administration, gone unpunished.

But enough of preliminaries: I come now to the work itself, and shall notice a few, and but a few, of its statements and comments; to notice them all would require a volume, and I can spare but a few pages. I shall follow, for the most part, the order of the "Key."

* So the Liverpool salt is called in New-England.

The first chapter of the work is introductory. The second is entitled, "Mr. Haley," and at the end of this chapter, (p. 8.) Mrs. Stowe says, "If there is an ill-used class of men in the world, it is certainly the slave-traders." "These men," she tells us, "are exceedingly sensitive with regard to what they consider the injustice of the world in excluding them from good society," &c.—Now when I shall see Mrs. Stowe receiving at her table and in her drawing-room public whippers (and we have these last in all our prisons,—the prison discipline could not be maintained without them,) or even horse-jockeys, I shall acknowledge that she is *sincere*, but not that she is right. She forgets that Providence makes use of vile instruments to do things necessary and proper to be done, but which are so repulsive in the doing that none but vile instruments will do them;—that, in this world of sin, moral scavengers are as necessary as physical ones: we may respect a constable, but not a public whipper; a drover, but not a horse-jockey. It might be difficult to assign a reason, *a priori*, why the profession of a horse-jockey should make a man repulsive to a person of refinement and a nice moral sense, but that it does, as really, (if not to the same extent,) as that of a negro-trader, is undeniable.

The third chapter presents "the fairest side of slave-life," and as "there is," in the author's view, "no kind of danger to the world in letting the very fairest side of slavery be seen," and she can therefore afford to be generous, she magnanimously devotes to it the very liberal allowance of *four pages and three-quarters*, out of two hundred and fifty-six!

The fourth chapter is devoted to "intelligent" negroes and colored persons, and contains not a few improbabilities, that speak for themselves: the advertisements at the end of the chapter, I shall notice further on, under the head of *outlaws*.

The fifth chapter treats of quadroon girls and Ohio justices. The following is characteristic :—

"Last spring, while the author was in New York, a Presbyterian clergyman, of Ohio, came to her and said, 'I understand they dispute that fact about the woman's crossing the river. Now, I know all about that, for I got the story from the very man that helped her up the bank. I know it is true, for she is now living in Canada."

Last spring, Mrs. Stowe *swam across the Atlantic.* I know it is true, *for* she is now travelling in England! I got the *story* from the man that *didn't* see her swim.

As to "Justice D——," if Professor Stowe and the magistrate on whom he called knew the said Justice to be such a rascal, why did not they bring him before the authorities. It was their duty to do it as good citizens.

"He 's the man that does all this kind of business, and he 'll deliver her up, and there 'll be an end to it."

Rachel Parker was "delivered up," but was *there* "an end to it?" On the contrary, she was delivered back again. And so it would have been with the girl in question: if, "by the laws of Ohio, she was entitled to her freedom, from the fact of her having been brought into the State, and left there, temporarily, by the consent of her mistress," the Courts in any of the slave States would have adjudged her free, for these cases are always decided according to the *lex loci.*

Professor Stowe, it seems, was the "Senator Bird" of the story; but instead of helping off a fugitive slave, as the Senator is represented as having done, he merely helped off a free woman, to save her from kidnappers; a praiseworthy deed in him, and one in which no Southerner would consent to be left behind.

The sixth chapter is devoted to "pious negroes." The following extract from the account of "the venerable Josiah

Henson," "now a clergyman in Canada," is commended to the consideration of those who oppose the "Fugitive Law," and try to obstruct its execution:—

"Henson forthwith not only became a Christian, but began to declare the news to those about him; and, being a man of great natural force of mind and strength of character, his earnest endeavors to enlighten his fellow-heathen were so successful, that he was gradually led to assume the station of a negro preacher; and though he could not read a word of the Bible or hymn-book, his labors in this line were much prospered. He became immediately a very valuable slave to his master, and was intrusted by the latter with the oversight of his whole estate, which he managed with great judgment and prudence. His master appears to have been a very ordinary man in every respect,—to have been entirely incapable of estimating him in any other light than as exceedingly valuable property, and to have had no other feeling excited by his extraordinary faithfulness than the desire to make the most of him. When his affairs became embarrassed, he formed the design of removing all his negroes into Kentucky, and intrusted the operation entirely to his overseer. Henson was to take them alone, without any other attendant, from Maryland to Kentucky, a distance of some thousands of miles, giving only his promise as a Christian that he would faithfully perform this undertaking. On the way thither they passed through a portion of Ohio, and there Henson was informed that he could now secure his own freedom and that of all his fellows, and he was strongly urged to do it. He was exceedingly tempted and tried, but his Christian principle was invulnerable. No inducements could lead him to feel that it was right for a Christian to violate a pledge solemnly given, and his influence over the whole band was so great that he took them all with him into Kentucky. Those casuists among us who lately seem to think and teach that it is right for us to violate the plain commands of God whenever some great national good can be secured by it, would do well to contemplate the inflexible principle of this poor slave, who, without being able to read a letter of the Bible, was yet enabled to perform this most sublime act of self-renunciation in obedience to its commands."

Now I do not wish to be understood as vouching for the truth of the above; on the contrary, certain portions of it seem to me to have a very apocryphal air, especially the second, third, fourth and fifth sentences: but the last two sentences are valuable as showing Mrs. Stowe's opinion of her friends, the "higher-law" men, and how, in her view, the conduct of "this poor slave" puts them to the blush. The advocates of the Fugitive Law could not desire a more complete justification than Mrs. Stowe has here volunteered for them.

The seventh chapter treats of the Northern prejudice against negroes, and in what the author says of the unchristian character of this prejudice, I go with her *to the fullest extent;* and I am happy to see that she admits—what indeed she could not help admitting—that there is no such prejudice at the South. But she tells us further that this prejudice at the North is a residuum of slavery, which, although it "has been abolished in the New England States," has "left behind it" this its "most baneful feature." And herein, I think she is mistaken: I am satisfied, from the testimony of those who lived under the old regime, and can remember the state of society at that time, that there was then no such prejudice. My grandfather had a slave, a faithful body-servant, and there was certainly no such prejudice against him: on the contrary, all the children were as much attached to "Black Peter," as are the children of Southern slave-owners, at the present day, to the slaves with whom they have grown up from childhood; and I believe it was so generally; and, indeed, if I were disposed to branch off into a philosophical speculation on the subject, I think I could find, in the nature of the relation that existed between them, some reasons why it should be so. If, then, slavery is to be abolished in the Southern States, and the negro remain on the soil, either the Southerner must be a good deal superior to his Northern brother in sympathy for whatever is human, or the same prejudice will develope itself there that has borne so hard upon the negro here. I hope I may never see the Southern negro reduced to such a condition.

Chapter eighth is headed, "Marie St. Clare," and contains a good deal of truth about certain *northern* ladies. What is here said about whipping, requires no other remark than has already been made on the subject.

Chapter ninth is entitled, "St. Clare," and opens as follows:—

"It is with pleasure that we turn from the dark picture just presented, to the character of the generous and noble-hearted St. Clare, wherein the fairest picture of our Southern brother is presented."

And what, in our author's view, is this "fairest picture?" That of a sneering sceptic, (vol. i. pp. 264–266,) who "had only that kind of benevolence which consists in lying on a sofa, and cursing the church and clergy for not being martyrs and confessors," (vol. ii. p. 137,) who, according to his own account of himself, (vol. ii. p. 24,) "instead of being actor and regenerator in society," was "a piece of drift-wood," "floating and eddying about," and his life, "a contemptible *non-sequitur*."

Now I do not find fault with Mrs. Stowe for drawing the picture of such an easy, good-for-nothing, "graceless dog," (vol. i. p. 264,) but I do protest, most emphatically, against her calling it "the fairest picture of our Southern brother." What! *They* the best men among the slaveholders who believe in their conscience that it is wrong to hold slaves, and yet continue to hold them? So, strange to say, Mrs. Stowe teaches: "Such men," she tells us, "are shocked to find their spiritual teachers less conscientious than themselves;" that is to say, those "spiritual teachers" (and, of course, those of their flock who think and act with them,) who believe in their consciences that it is right to hold slaves, and who act up to that belief, are, in Mrs. Stowe's opinion, less conscientious than the sneering and scoffing St. Clare's, who, believing that it is wrong to hold slaves, do, nevertheless, *deliberately and systematically*, violate their consciences by continuing to hold them! This is the meaning of Mrs. Stowe's language: I defy her, or anybody else, to make anything else out of it.—A *queer* conscientiousness, reader, this, of Mrs. Stowe's, isn't it?

"What a sorrowful thing it is that such men live an inglorious life, drawn along by the general current of society, when they ought to be its regenerators!" Its regenerators? No! Mrs. Stowe! The regenerators of society are made of sterner stuff: they are men of conscience, who, if you can convince them that they are in the wrong, will at once set about righting that wrong: men of nerve, however, who will not be led away, by their sympathy with particular instances of hardship, to save here and there an individual at the expense of ruin to the race, and thus turn a sporadic disease into an epidemic; men whose motto is, "Slow and sure;" who go as fast and as far as they can see their way clear, and no faster and no farther. Such men are the hope of humanity, and when and where *they* go, society must *perforce* go with them. There are plenty of such men at the South; they know what they are about, and they are not to be turned aside from it by false issues: "in quietness and in confidence" they are regenerating the negro and helping on his final redemption. They are "doing a great work," steadily, but noiselessly, as did the builders of the temple at Jerusalem. They are not of the Jehu's of society, who boast and bluster and brag: they have no confidence in such boasting and blustering and bragging; they know that it is at the expense of the interests of humanity, and these interests in their estimation outweigh everything earthly. God speed them in their work of love! God speed those Northern men, too, who are with them in heart and soul! They are of the noblest of the sons of the North. Strong in the might of truth, they can afford to be taunted and sneered at by such men as John Randolph and "Mr. Mitchell,"—men who, by their own confession, are deliberately and systematically violating their own consciences, and who, therefore, if they had a particle of modesty, would be ashamed to set themselves up as censors of the morals of others. May God give them "repentance and a better mind!"

There is one other thing requiring notice in the chapter before us, and that is the "kind of preaching" and the "scriptural expositions" that St. Clare says "don't edify him." Of this we have two specimens, one from the Rev. Mr. Clapp, and to this I must take two exceptions; the first, as a matter of taste, to the epithet "fascinating," which, as here employed, seems to me to belittle the subject, the second, as a matter of substance, to the word "every" in the fourth sentence: I would *not* say "to *every* slave in the United States" what Mr. Clapp says *he* would, but I *would* say it to the slaves as a body—to ninety-nine out of every hundred of them. With these two qualifications, I endorse every word of the extract, and if Mrs. Stowe objects to the sentiment of the first three sentences, (as it would seem that she does, from her calling the paragraph a "specimen of *ethics*,") she has yet to learn "which be the first principles of the oracles of God."

The other extract is from the Rev. Mr. Smylie, and if by the first paragraph he means to imply merely that it is *not* the "legitimate tendency of the gospel" to make man free, outwardly *and* inwardly if possible, *but*, *at any rate*, *outwardly*, which, I suppose is his meaning, then I go with him ; but if he means to imply (which I cannot for a moment believe) that it is not the "legitimate tendency of the gospel" to make man free with an inward, and thereby, *eventually*, with an outward freedom, then I want words to express my utter dissent from his doctrine ; for I hold most undoubtingly that it *is* the legitimate tendency—the very end and aim of Christianity to make man free inwardly, and that where a *race* has become *thus* free, it cannot longer be continued in slavery by a Christian people.* And when the colored *race* in this country shall become thus free, if I live to see the day, (which I do not anticipate, for I believe it is a long way off,) I will preach nothing *but* abolition to the Southern people, or rather, I shall have no need to preach it to them, for they will enter into it spontaneously, and by acclamation.

The tenth chapter is entitled "Legree," and the author discusses in it, amongst other things, the *possibility* of the character : I shall have something to say upon that before I get through, but at present I will take it for granted. Here follow a few extracts :—

"Legree is introduced not for the sake of vilifying masters as a class, but for the sake of bringing to the minds of honorable Southern men, who are masters, a very important feature in the system of slavery, upon which, perhaps, they

* The horror of "White Slavery in the Barbary States" is, that it subjects a people internally free, like St. Vincent de Paul, to a people internally slaves.

have never reflected. It is this: that *no Southern law requires any test of* CHARACTER *from the man to whom the absolute power of master is granted.*

* * * * *

"Now it is respectfully submitted to men of this high class, who are the law-makers, whether this awful power to bind and to loose, to open and to shut the kingdom of heaven, ought to be intrusted to every man in the community, without any other qualification than that of property to buy.

* * * * *

"Now, in all the theory of government as it is managed in our country, just in proportion to the extent of power is the strictness with which qualification for the proper exercise of it is demanded. The physician may not meddle with the body, to prescribe for its ailments, without a certificate that he is properly qualified. The judge may not decide on the laws which relate to property, without a long course of training, and most abundant preparation. It is only this office of MASTER, which contains the power to bind and to loose, and to open and shut the kingdom of heaven, and involves responsibility for the soul as well as the body, that is thrown out to every hand, and committed without inquiry to any man of any character.

* * * * *

"Are there such men as Legree? Let any one go into the low districts and dens of New York, let them go into some of the lanes and alleys of London, and will they not there see many Legrees? Nay, take the purest district of New England, and let people cast about in their memory and see if there have not been men there, hard, coarse, unfeeling, brutal, who, if they had possessed the absolute power of Legree, would have used it in the same way; and that there should be Legrees in the Southern States, is only saying that human nature is the same there that it is everywhere. The only difference is this,—that in free States Legree is chained and restrained by law; in the slave States, the law makes him an absolute, irresponsible despot."

A word, now, upon these extracts.

As to the first one, I can assure Mrs. Stowe that the "honorable Southern men, who are masters," are not the unreflecting persons she seems to think them, but that they have *thought* upon the subject of slavery more than she has, and understands its practical working better than she does, if she could only be persuaded to think so.

She tells us in this extract that *no test of* CHARACTER is required in order to be a master, and yet she admits, in the next extract, that the master must have sufficient property to buy the slave, which, *at the South*, is, *practically*, a very stringent test. "It is only this office of MASTER," she continues, "that is thrown out to every hand, and committed without inquiry to any man of any character," and yet she knows perfectly well that the office of *father* is "committed without inquiry" and without even the *property test*, "to any man of any character;" and she admits that there are Legrees among fathers at the North: "the only difference," she tells us, "is this,—that in free States Legree is chained and restrained by law; in the slave States, the law makes him an absolute irresponsible despot."

What! Legree chained in free States in any other sense than he is in the slave States! Many a poor wife could tell a different story, and so could many a poor child, the victim of domestic tyranny.

Oh, but the *law!* the law! Don't you know that Legree is chained by it, in free States, and that his wife or child is thereby *protected?* Indeed! "What a charming freshness of nature is suggested by this assertion! A thing could not have happened in a certain State because there is a law against it!" This is the way you dispose of a law that "chains Legree" in Louisiana! It is a poor rule, Mrs. Stowe, that won't work both ways.

The truth is, Legree is chained as really in the slave States as in the free, only his chain is a little longer,—a disadvantage that is more than made up for by the comparative rarity of the animal in these States and by the operation of self-interest which protects the slave from the bad master ten times as often, in proportion, as parental affection protects the child from the bad father. In proof of the comparative rarity of the animal at the South, I myself could name at least half a dozen in my native village in Massachusetts, (a village of less than a thousand inhabitants,) now living, or that have been living within the last twenty years, that never ought to have been parents, and if I were to take my cue from Mrs. Stowe, I should seek to procure the enactment of a law prohibiting men like them from becoming such, or else, I should seek to take away from *all* parents that power which at least one in twenty of them (a far greater proportion than among masters) use to so bad purpose; but in doing this, I should be acting very foolishly, for the restriction of the parent's power would work mischief, and only mischief to children *as a class*, however it might protect now and then an individual; and what is true in this respect of the power of the parent over the child is equally true of the power of the master over the slave, if Mrs. Stowe could only be brought to see it.

I have gone thus far in these remarks upon the hypothesis of the *possibility* of such a character as Legree; but, as the reader is aware, I have already denied that possibility. "But," says Mrs. Stowe, "the reader will have too much reason to know of the possibility of the existence of such men as Legree, when he comes to read the records of the trials and judicial decisions in Part II." I have read those records, and I find no instance of a Legree, or anything approaching to one. Instances of cruelty, I find,—ay, outrageous cruelty, though they are but few, notwithstanding she has *raked and scraped* "all over" the South. It is wonderful, the small number of the instances she has succeeded in finding.* Could any free State, at the North, or in Europe, stand the sweep of such a drag-net, and come out as free from scath?

No one doubts that there are instances of cruelty,—*horrible* cruelty,—at the South, as well as elsewhere. It was not the cruelty that I had in mind when I denied the possibility of such a character as Legree; I had in mind, amongst other things, the conversation on board the steamboat (vol. ii. pp. 172, 173.) and especially this portion of it:—

"I used to, when I fust begun, have considerable trouble fussin' with 'em, and trying to make 'em hold out,—doctorin' on 'em up when they's sick, and givin' on 'em clothes, and blankets, and what not, trying to keep 'em all sorts o' decent and comfortable. Law, 't want no sort o' use; I lost money on 'em, and 't was heaps o' trouble. Now, you see, I just put 'em straight through, sick or well. When one nigger's dead, I buy another; and I find it comes cheaper and easier, every way."

Now none but a madman ever uttered such superlative nonsense, and from the madman the law takes away the control of his slaves as well as his other property, and also, of his children.

Mrs. Stowe tries to justify her putting such language into the mouth of Legree, but she fails utterly. She quotes the Report of the Agricultural Society of Baton Rouge, La., for 1829, as stating that the annual waste of life on well-conducted sugar estates was *two and a half per cent.*, over

* And among them all, is there one like that from the London Guardian, of February 2., (Appendix K. 3, (7.),) and was there ever such a verdict returned in such a case at the South?

and above the natural increase. And she adds, "The late Hon. Josiah S. Johnson, member of Congress from Louisiana, addressed a letter to the Secretary of the United States' Treasury, in 1830, containing a similar estimate, *apparently made with great care, and going into minute details.* Many items in this estimate differ from the preceding; but the estimate of the annual *decrease* of the slaves on a plantation was the same,—TWO AND A HALF PER CENT.!"

This is, no doubt, a correct estimate,* but how does it tally with the hearsay testimony of Mr. Blackwell, and Dr. Demming, that the annual waste of life was 12½ to 14 *per cent.*,—in other words, that the master "could afford to sacrifice a set of hands once in seven or eight years," instead of once in forty? And how does this latter tally with the statement of Simon Legree, that the waste was from 15 to 50 per cent.? Mrs. Stowe must excuse me if I prefer the authentic official statement to the hearsay testimony; especially as I can demonstrate, *from her own data*, the truth of the one, and the falsehood of the other; that is to say, that the planter *can* afford to sacrifice a set of hands once in forty years, and that he *cannot* afford to sacrifice a set of hands once in seven years: the former, she will of course admit; the latter, I proceed to demonstrate.

Mrs. Stowe states, from Professor Ingraham, that the negroes work during the *season* from eighteen to twenty hours, the gang being divided, at night, "into two watches,

* Perhaps Mrs. Stowe will think it very awful to use up human life even at the rate of two and a half per cent.: if so, then she must think stone-cutting, glass-grinding, house-painting, and a good many other trades that might be mentioned, very awful ones, for they use up human life at a much more rapid rate. As to the sugar culture, more lives are lost in the transportation (by sea) than in the cultivation. Query: Did any Yankee abolitionist while eating his salt fish, ever reflect how many lives were lost by the cod-fishery, annually?

one taking the first and the other the last part of the night." Let us take the longest period,—twenty hours, and let us suppose a planter starting an estate with a gang "of seven hundred blacks," a number just sufficient to work the estate, working twenty hours a day during the *season*, and at the ordinary rate the rest of the year; let us further suppose the negroes to be fresh hands, just purchased from a Virginia trader, of the average age of twenty-five years, which is a *high* average, judging from Mrs. Stowe's advertisements and comments, (pp. 133—150,) and at the average cost of one thousand dollars, which is a *low* average in Louisiana, as they are now bringing nearly that in Virginia. If the planter were to purchase three hundred more negroes and work the estate with a gang of one thousand at the rate of fourteen hours a day during the *season*, and seven-tenths of the ordinary rate the rest of the year, he would accomplish the same amount of labor as with the seven hundred on the other supposition, and Mrs. Stowe herself must admit that they would not in that case be overworked nor their lives shortened. According to the Baton Rouge Agricultural Society Report, and the Hon. Mr. Johnson's letter, the estate could be worked with the seven hundred, working twenty hours a day during the *season*, and a *set* be worked up only once in forty years; and this would be more profitable than to work it with one thousand. According to Mr. Blackwell and Dr. Demming, the estate being worked with seven hundred, a *set* would be worked up in seven years; and this would be less profitable—*far* less profitable than to work it with one thousand, as I am now to show.

In the following demonstration, the several examples have been worked out to the nearest cent, and the results are here set down to the nearest dollar.

According to Mrs. Stowe, the expense of *keeping* a negro in Lousiana,—"two pairs of pantaloons and a pair of shoes a year, with enough food and shelter to keep him in working order," (vol. ii. p. 20,)—cannot be more than twenty dollars, at the outside, as thus: Two pairs of (thin) pantaloons and a pair of shoes, $5,00 ; a peck of corn a week, or thirteen bushels a year, at fifty cents a bushel, (Key, p. 45,) $6,50 ; rent of *shanties*, such as are described in the Key, (p. 44,) *per head*, $6,00 ; (a shanty containing ten, would thus rent for $60,00 ; high enough, in all conscience !) doctor's bill, $2,50 ;—in all, $20,00. We will put it, however, at double that amount, viz. $40,00, which is $3,60 more than it costs to "board, nurse, *clothe* and doctor" a pauper in the cold climate of Massachusetts, (see Appendix, F., LEOMINSTER,) and more than three times the sum ($12,00) which the American missionaries in Ceylon required, thirty years ago, for boarding, clothing and educating a Tamul youth; (see Missionary Herald, of that period, *passim.*) This item is to be charged against both systems,—the using up, and the saving. To this latter is to be charged another item,—that of life-insurance, as on this system the capital is not to be sunk at all. The charge for this, at the age of twenty-five, is $1,90 on the hundred; or, $19,00 per head. The debtor side of the account, then, will stand as follows :—

1. On the *saving* system :

Compound interest on capital—1,000 negroes, at $1,000 each—$1,000,000, at 6 per cent., for 7 years,		$507,630
Cost of keeping, at $40,00 each, per annum, for 7 years,		280,000
7 years' comp'd interest on 1st year's keeping,	$20,305	
6 " " 2d "	16,741	
5 " " 3d "	13,529	
4 " " 4th "	10,499	
3 " " 5th "	7,641	
2 " " 6th "	4,944	
1 " " 7th "	2,400	76,059
Life Insurance—7 years' premium, at $19,000,		133,000
Interest on ditto, computed as on the keeping,		36,128
Total,		$1,032,817

2. On the *using up* system:

Capital sunk—700 negroes, at $1,000, - - - - -	$700,000
Compound interest on it, for 7 years, - - -	355,341
Cost of keeping, at $40,00, - - - - - - -	196,000
Interest on ditto, computed as above, - - -	53,241
Total, - - - - - - - - -	$1,304,582
Deduct as above, - - - - - - -	1,032,817
Balance *against* the *using up* system, - - -	$271,765

Being a dead loss *annually*, on the average, of $38,824! For every dollar that we diminish the estimated cost of keeping, we *increase* the above loss by $381,49, and if we put the keeping, as we ought to, at $20,00, according to the estimate above from Mrs. Stowe's data, it will bring the annual dead loss up to $46,453. For every hundred dollars, on the contrary, that we diminish the estimated value of the negro, we *diminish* the annual dead loss by $5,408,-30. If, therefore, we take the highest estimate of the *keeping*, the negroes must not cost over $283,00 per head, to make it more profitable to *use up* seven hundred on an estate every seven years, than to work the estate *in perpetuity* with one thousand, and if we take the lowest estimate of the keeping, they must not cost over $141,00! When, therefore, Legree told the "collecting clerk to the large mercantile house," (if he ever did tell him,) that he worked his estate on a system by which he suffered a dead loss of $40,000 a year, he was plainly trying how much the raw youth could swallow! Certainly, no man, of woman born, ever told such a story in sober earnest; and if the "collecting clerk" *took* it in earnest, I, for one, shall not doubt his *vo*racity.

I commend this "NEW ARABIAN NIGHT'S ENTERTAINMENT" (Key, p. 257) of FIGURES VS. FANCY, to Mrs. Stowe's especial consideration, and hope she will go through the calculations for herself, or, (if, as I shrewdly suspect, her *forte* does n't lie that way, but rather in *figures* of RHETORIC,) get some one of "those legal gentlemen who have given her their assistance and support in the legal part of the discussion," (Preface to the Key,) to do it for her; and I should not wonder if the result should be, the conclusion on her part, "that these nomadic Arabs, the digits, are making a very unfair use, among us, of the family reputation gotten up during the palmy days of their innocence, when they were a breezy, contemplatively unsophisticated race of shepherds," and never thought of tripping up a *lady*, even though she *would* wrestle with them. Alas! the days of chivalry are over; and now, "every one must look out for his own toes, as the jackass said to the chickens:" if I "step on" *hers*, let her "*mention* it." (Vol. i. p. 239.) But perhaps, after all, Mrs. Stowe, finding herself a sharer in "the bewilderment of the few old-fashioned people" she refers to, and having a *shrewd suspicion*, if she "does not know with very great clearness," "what 'percentage'* and 'average' mean," may say that she meant Legree's language to be taken "in a Pickwickian sense:" "I should n't wonder."

We come now to the "peck of corn a week," which Mrs. Stowe tells us (Key, p. 45,) is the negro's "usual allowance." And how much would she *have* him have? Is not a peck

* Mrs. Stowe's (or her friend, "that most respectable female person, Mrs. Partington's") idea of "per-centage" seems to be about as luminous as that of the retailer out in Illinois, who "came," as Mrs. Stowe would say, "under my *personal observation*," some ten or twelve years ago: at any rate, if *he* did not, the *anecdote* did; and that, according to her, is all one. He was boasting that he made "three per cent." in his business, and on some one's expressing a doubt whether he understood clearly the meaning of the term, "Well," said he, "I don't know anything about your 'per cent.,' but I know this,—that every dollar I pay out, *brings in three:* that's what *I* call *three per cent.!*"

enough? Can she eat more herself? A peck of corn a week, is two pounds a day; and two pounds of corn will make three pounds of bread, as every cook knows. Now her friend Dr. Hitchcock will tell her that a pound to a pound-and-a-half, is an *ample* allowance, (see his "Dyspepsia Forestalled and Resisted,") and if he practises what he preaches, he has given a twenty years' proof of it. For my part, though those who know me say I am "death on corn-cakes," and I confess to their being "my particular wanity," and would rather be confined to them, than to any other *one* article of food, I am sure I would not eat three pounds a day; and if Mrs. Stowe can, then I will admit *her* voracity, as well as the "collecting clerk's," and shall begin to think it *runs in the family!*

But "the slaves down the Mississippi," says Mrs. Stowe, (Key, p. 46,) "are *half-starved!*" And the proof of it! Ay, the *proof* of it! Open your eyes *wide*, reader:—"The boats, when they stop at night, are constantly boarded by slaves, begging for something to eat." Verily, "Mr. Tobias Baudinot, St. Albans, Ohio, a member of the Methodist Church," (I trust it has some better timber,) "who for some years was a navigator" (by *traverse* sailing, no doubt) "on the Mississippi," must be a *rare bird.* Mothers! look out for him, when he comes into your houses, and don't let him hear your children "begging for bread," or he'll certainly go away and report that they are *half-starved!*

And you, ye sturdy farmers of the North, who are generally supposed to have *some* common sense, read the statement of "Mr. Asa A. Stone" (Query: Any relation to Miss Lucy?) "a theological student, who resided near Natchez, Miss., in 1834-5," that "on almost every plantation, the hands suffer more or less from hunger at some seasons of almost every year. There is always a *good deal of suffering* from hunger. On many plantations, and particularly in Louisiana, the slaves are in a condition of *almost utter famishment*, during a great portion of the year," and remembering that a slave costs ten times as much as a horse, or a yoke of oxen, and considering with yourself how you treat *your* horses and *your* oxen, and how you would almost as soon suffer, yourself, as see even those dumb animals suffer, then say what you think of a theological student who could gravely tell such a *story*, and say further, how you would like to hear such a one in the pulpit! For my part, I should expect him

"At times to vend a rousing whid,
And nail 't wi' Scripture!"

And these are Mrs. Stowe's *proofs!* She must excuse me, but I cannot accept them. To all her allegations of short fare, I have one all-sufficient answer to oppose,—the *fact*, namely, that the negroes *thrive* upon their "common doings," (even where they cannot get "chicken fixins,") and *prove* that "the sleep of a laboring man is sweet, whether he eat little or much, (Eccl. v. 12,) and that they "increase and multiply" ten per cent. faster than their white brethren. But I forget: Mrs. Stowe does n't like "percentage." This is singular, considering the lessons she has taken in it, with a certain publishing house in Boston during the past twelve months. However, "there is no disputing about tastes."

There is one other allegation under this head, that I had almost forgotten: "The negroes," Mrs. Stowe tells us, "have to grind their own corn." Well, that is better than to have no corn to grind. However, as she seems to think it such a hardship, if she will read, in the N. Y. Daily Times, of June 14, 1853, the twenty-fourth of a series of excellent "Letters on the Productions, Industry, and Resources of the Slave States," by one who, though not an anti-slavery propagandist, because he is a fair-minded man, has yet no liking for slavery, she will learn, what, if she had ever lived at the South, she would have known without, "that the negroes prefer to take their allowance of corn and 'crack' it for themselves, rather than to receive meal, because they think the mill-ground meal does not make as sweet bread." Quashy, I am thinking, won't thank Mrs. Stowe for wanting to take away the *sweetness* from his "peck of corn:" she had better *understand* him, before she undertakes to cater for him, or, in her ignorance, she may get him into "a peck of trouble."

In what I have said thus far on the food of the negro, I have taken Mrs. Stowe's representation of it. I must now add that large numbers of them—nearly, or quite, all, in Maryland, and probably full one half, in the South generally, have their regular weekly allowance of animal food,* and that there are very few who do not get it occasionally. But even where they do not, they are better off than the peasant in Ireland or in Hindostan, the former of whom would gladly exchange his potatoes, and the latter his rice,† for the

* "Oh, Missis, my husband,—he working now out on de farm,—*so* he hab 'lowance *four pounds bacon* and one peck of meal ebery week." Letter to Mrs. Stowe, "from a *friend*," (Key, p. 153.) According to "Uncle Tom at Home," (a work in *defence* of Uncle Tom's Cabin,) "In Alabama, the act of her Legislature provides *a proper ration of meat every day* for the slave, establishing a penalty if the master withholds it." (p. 100.)

† The *Maryland Journal and Baltimore Advertiser*, May 30, 1788, says, "A single peck of corn, or *the same measure of rice*, is the ordinary provision for a hard-working slave, to which a small quantity of meat is occasionally, though rarely, added." (Key, p. 45)

A tea-cupful of rice will make a pretty good-sized pudding, as a bachelor friend of mine in Virginia can testify. He once undertook to make one, and having tied the rice in a bag, in default of a pot, put it into a *tea-kettle*, where it swelled so much that he could not *get it out whole*. Moreover, in tying it up, he had not left room *enough* for it to swell in; accordingly, he had to *dig* it out, for it was nearly as hard as a rice snuff-box; I tried some of it, but my *molars and bi-cuspids* gave it negro's "peck of corn a week," and both of whom would gain by the bargain.

A word on the negro cabins. The description of them on page 44, is not by any means a fair description of them *now*, though it *may* have been ten or fifteen years ago; but ten or fifteen years ago, I could have shown Mrs. Stowe plenty of such in Illinois, and those not always of the lowest class of whites either, but of those who had seen better days.

As to the "Cachexia Africana," it is not a very *fatal* disease, judging from the increase of the negro population, and, though not by any means desirable, it is not so loathesome, by half, as a certain other disease, for some time past, epidemic at the North, in certain "localities,"—Worcester, for instance, and Syracuse,—I mean, the *Cacoethes Africana*, *anglice*, AFRICAN ITCH; a disease, of which, in my opinion, the *Old Scratch* is at the bottom.

In chapter eleventh, Mrs. Stowe informs us that "The custom of unceremoniously separating the infant from its mother, when the latter is about to be taken from a Northern to a Southern market, is a matter of every-day notoriety in the trade. It is not done occasionally and sometimes, but always, whenever there is occasion for it; and the mother's agonies are no more regarded than those of a cow when her calf is separated from her."

Will it be believed that the only shadow of evidence she has given, throughout the whole chapter, of this "custom" is, *negro testimony* to *four isolated instances!* Could she not bring up, with her *drag-net*, a single white witness to a "custom" of "every-day notoriety?" After such absolute failure to substantiate her assertion, what are we to think

up, as a bad job. Now if a tea-cupful will fill a tea-kettle, a peck would swell to a pretty good week's allowance: yet the negroes prefer the peck of corn, and "complain of being faint when fed on rice." (Key, p. 45.)

of the last two sentences of the following, the *italics* of which are her own?

"An American gentleman from Italy, complaining of the effect of 'Uncle Tom's Cabin' on the Italian mind, states that images of fathers dragged from their families to be sold into slavery, and of babes torn from the breasts of weeping mothers, are constantly presented before the minds of the people as scenes of every-day life in America. The author can only say, sorrowfully, that it is *only the truth* which is thus presented.

"These things *are*, EVERY DAY, part and parcel of one of *the most thriving trades that is carried on in America.*"

What, I repeat, are we to think of such language? Could it have been believed beforehand that one with an American heart in her bosom, could, even if the allegation were true, thus sully the fair fame of her country and publish its shame to the world? For my part, if I could hope to make my voice heard by her, I would say to her, in such case, in the noble language of Whittier already quoted—noble but for his false *application* of it,—

> "Then pay the reverence of old days
> To *its* dead fame:
> Walk backward, with averted gaze,
> And *hide* the shame!"

The path of filial irreverence, is a down-hill path: what wonder then, if we find her in a foreign land, on a public occasion, *sitting under a mutilated flag of her country!*

I have said that she has failed to substantiate her charge by argument: she seems to be sensible of this, herself, and accordingly when argument fails, she betakes herself to philosophizing. *Assuming* that the children are *customarily* separated from the mother when she is to be taken "to a Southern market," she gives a reason why it *must be*, viz: that "they detract from the value of the mother as a field-hand;" and yet she tells us, on the very next page, that it is a "pitiful lie" which says "that these unhappy mothers" "do not feel when the most sacred ties are thus severed." Now one of two things is certain: either the mother does not feel *much*, and therefore does soon get over it, or else, the separation does *not* add to her value "as a field-hand," and therefore the "trader" has no such motive to make it. If the cow, when separated from her calf, instead of getting over it in a few days, did not get over it at all, what should we think of the brains of the Northern farmer who should gravely argue for the separation *as a means of increasing the cow's value!* Do, Mrs. Stowe, forego your woman's privilege, and for *once*, give us an argument that shall be consistent with *itself*, if you can; and if you cannot, get some one of the "legal gentlemen," you speak of in the preface, to do it for you: it is altogether too hard upon your reviewer to give him *nothing* that he can't answer,—nothing, even, that does not answer itself. No wonder the London Athenæum (June 4, 1853) should say of Mr. William Goodell's "American Slave Code in Theory and Practice," "It is the best commentary on 'Uncle Tom' that we have yet seen—not excepting the 'Key' by Mrs. Stowe herself, because it is *more critical and logical.*" Verily Mr. Goodell must feel very much beholden to the Athenæum for thus damning his work with faint praise.*

* The Athenæum says, further, that it is "a startling contribution to the Anti-Slave cause." If, as I shrewdly suspect, Mr. Goodell is one of the "legal gentlemen" of the preface, it must be a "startling contribution," so far as the *comments* are concerned. I recollect a missionary subscription paper was carried round in my native village, some five-and-twenty years ago, and among the subscriptions obtained, was one of fifty cents, from "A friend to the *caws*." The

Mrs. Stowe affirms that it is a *custom* of the trade, also, to part husband and wife; and to *prove* this *custom* she brings forward two witnesses, (white ones, for a wonder,) who testify each to one *isolated instance!* That the thing is occasionally done, no one doubts; but that it should be done *customarily* I have shown (Note 5) to be contrary to known principles of human action.

Chapter Twelfth treats of "the degradation of the negro's *position*," and contains a letter from the Rev. Dr. Pennington, (formerly a slave in Maryland,) in which is the following:—

"O, Mrs. Stowe, slavery is an awful system! It takes man as God made him: it demolishes him, and then mis-creates him, or perhaps I should say mal-creates him!"

If Dr. Pennington means this of slavery as it exists in Africa, it is true: if he means it of slavery as it exists in America, it is false. American slavery takes the negro as slavery *in Africa* has made him, a brute in human shape,* (see Appendix, B.) and humanizes him, and Christianizes him, and elevates him to a *man*; and of this, Dr. Pennington is in his own person an illustrious example. He should be the last one to speak ill of American slavery: it has made him all he is, and all he hopes for. But for it, he would have been a degraded creature in the land of his ancestors, with Reason and Conscience, those glorious endowments of humanity, undeveloped, and nothing but the "human form divine" to say to the beholder, This is a man.—And there are hundreds of Dr. Pennington's, and hundreds of thousands, ay, millions, of *approximations* to

emendation was considered rather doubtful at the time; but I am inclined to think it would now come in very pat: certainly we have had plenty of contributions, within the last year or two, to the Anti-Slavery *Caws*; plenty of iterations and reiterations.

* Or if it has not made him so, it has found him so, and *left* him so.

him,—*made* so by their "position;" and when, *as a race*, they shall have attained his stature of humanity, American slavery is doomed: it will fall to pieces by its own weight; if it did not, the outraged sentiment of Christendom would rise *en masse* to exterminate it.

The thirteenth chapter is devoted to the Quakers. I have space to notice only two or three passages in it, which are particularly noteworthy as partially letting us into the author's idea of Christianity, and showing that the Key, as well as the original work, is anti-christian.

It seems that "a family, consisting of Samuel Hawkins, a freeman, his wife Emeline, and six children, who were afterwards *proved slaves*," were arrested and committed as such to Newcastle (Delaware) jail; and that, at the instance of John Garret, a Quaker, who supposed not only the father, but the mother and the "four youngest children," free, they were brought by *habeas corpus* before Chief Justice Booth, and by him set at liberty, *on the ground of defect in the commitment*. The rest of the account, I give in Garret's own words:

"The day was wet and cold; one of the children, three years old, was a cripple from white swelling, and could not walk a step; another, eleven months old, at the breast; and the parents being desirous of getting to Wilmington, five miles distant, I asked the judge if there would be any risk or impropriety in my hiring a conveyance for the mother and four young children to Wilmington. His reply, in the presence of the sheriff and my attorney, was there could not be any. I then requested the sheriff to procure a hack to take them over to Wilmington."

The whole family escaped. Garret was brought to trial, convicted and fined $5,400; $3,500 for hiring the "hack," and $1,900, as the value of the slaves. If this were the whole story, it would be a hard case. But let us hear Mrs. Stowe:

"After John Garret's trial was over, and this heavy judgment had been given against him, he calmly arose in the court-room, and requested leave to address a few words to the court and audience.

* * * * * * *

"After showing conclusively that he had no reason to suppose the family to be slaves, and that they had all been discharged by the judge, he nobly adds the following words: '*Had I believed every one of them to be slaves, I should have done the same thing!*'"

"Thus calmly and simply," says Mrs. Stowe, "did this Quaker *confess Christ before men.*" (!) And, speaking of the result of the trial: "Our European friends will infer from this that it costs something to *obey Christ* (!) in America, as well as in Europe."

Now for another instance of "obeying Christ,"—that of Richard Dillingham:

"Some unfortunate families among the colored people had dear friends who were slaves in Nashville, Tennessee. Richard was so interested in their story, that when he went into Tennessee he was actually taken up and caught in the very act of helping certain poor people to escape to their friends."

"For this," says Mrs. Stowe, "he was seized and thrown into prison. In the language of this world (!) he was imprisoned as a 'negro-stealer.'"

One more instance, in another part of the book, (p. 219,) *not* of a Quaker: "Torrey, meekly patient, died in a prison, saying, 'If I am a guilty man, I am a very guilty one, for I have helped four hundred slaves to freedom, who but for me would have died slaves;'" *and*, four lines below, Mrs. Stowe's comment upon this: "Jesus Christ has not wholly deserted us yet."

Now, in answer to all this, I have only to say, (and it is

all that *need* be said,) Picture to yourself, reader, if you *can* picture such a thing, St. Paul *running off* four hundred slaves, and at the same time preaching, "Servants, be obedient to them that are your masters according to the flesh!" (Eph. vi. 5.) "Let as many servants as are *under the yoke* count their own masters worthy of all honour, that the name of God and HIS DOCTRINE be not blasphemed," (1. Tim. vi. 1,) and then say, where is his character as an Apostle? Gone irretrievably, even abolitionists themselves being judges. Garrison and Theodore Parker would have no patience with such shuffling; they abhor the *doctrine* now; they would then abhor the *man;* for whatever their faults, hypocrisy is not one of them.

The fourteenth chapter is entitled, "The Spirit of St. Clare," and contains several "testimonials from Southern men" in favour of Uncle Tom's Cabin, in the shape of letters, some anonymous, and some authentic: the former, of course, require no notice, as, for aught we know, they may be, every one of them, from Northern abolitionists,—"ancient maidens" or "collecting clerks;" of the latter, all but one are from the class of "Southern Emancipators" (see Note 14.) in the border States, and that one, though "hailing" from Charleston at the time of writing, has since published a book entitled, "Uncle Tom at Home," (designed to *prop up* the Cabin,) on the title page of which he describes himself as "*late* of Charleston," at which I am not surprised, for I should suppose, after he had thus fouled his own nest, he would want to be out of it as soon as possible. The book is a literary curiosity, and I had marked some *sixty-seven* "elegant extracts," wherewith to enliven my own pages, as specimens of the author's noble independence of the King's English, and to show how much reliance was to be placed on the testimony of such a *muddle-head.* But I find I cannot afford the space for them; so I have concluded to spare "the *harmless* albatross." I advise all my readers, however, to get the book, and if they don't find it a rich treat, then they have no relish for *Nick-Bottomism.*

I have now gone through the whole of PART I., having, I believe, noticed every chapter. I might go on in the same way with the remaining "PARTS," but I have not the space for it: I must, therefore, confine myself to a few of the more prominent points.

PART II. is devoted to the slave-code, and here it is that the author is so beholden to the "legal gentlemen who have given her their assistance and support." (Preface to the Key.) Who these "legal gentlemen" are, I have a great curiosity to know, for they, or she, or all together, have certainly given some queer interpretations. However, out of respect for the gentlemen of the green bag, I am inclined to hold them innocent of the interpretations aforesaid, and to *mother* those interpretations upon *her.*

A story is told of a preacher who, while delivering a sermon made up of shreds and patches from the old divines, was very much annoyed by an old gentleman in the pew below repeating in a semi-audible tone, as passage after passage came out, the name of its author—"Barrow!"—"Tillotson!"—"Jeremy Taylor!" At last, provoked beyond all endurance, he called out, Turn that man out! "That's his own," said the man.

Now, though the portion of the work before us is evidently a hodge-podge, and jumbled together, too, in beautiful confusion, I think I can put my finger on passage after passage, and say, without fear of mistake, That's her own! and among these passages are certain odd misinterpretations, to two or three of which I must now call the reader's attention.

The first is on page 70. Mrs. Stowe cites the law of South Carolina as enacting that "slaves shall be deemed sold, (?) taken, reputed and adjudged in law, to be chattels personal in the hands of their owners and possessors, and their executors, administrators, and assigns, TO ALL INTENTS, CONSTRUCTIONS AND PURPOSES WHATSOEVER," and then adds, "Let the reader reflect on the extent of the meaning in this last clause;" evidently showing that she understands "chattels personal" to be here used in opposition to "persons," whereas, any lawyer, and *one* who is *no* lawyer, could have told her that it is used simply in opposition to "chattels *real;*" that in Maryland and Virginia, and, I believe, in most of the Southern States, slaves are, for ordinary purposes, chattels personal, but, for testamentary and administrative purposes, chattels real; whereas, in South Carolina, and, perhaps, some other States, they are chattels personal, for *all* purposes, and chattels real, for none. This is the simple meaning of the South Carolina law, in which Mrs. Stowe has found such a mare's nest.

Yet she will have it that, in Southern law, the negro is not a person, or, at any rate, that it is a mooted point, and accordingly she cites (p. 75,) the case of WITSELL VS. EARNEST AND PARKER, which the reader will find in the Appendix, (E. 3,) and on which she thus comments:

"IF *we consider the negro a person,* says the Judge; and, from his decision in the case, he evidently intimates that he has a strong leaning to this opinion, though it has been contested by so many eminent legal authorities that he puts forth his sentiment modestly, and in an hypothetical form."

Now to place in a strong light the *logic* of this comment, let me request the reader's attention, for a moment, to the following "Report of a Case not to be found in any of the Books."

Professor Stowe, we will suppose, having lately been in England, and seen how Englishmen flog their wives, and what good results follow from it, takes it into his head to introduce the custom here; but his wife not being as submissive as the English ladies, the case comes into court, and the evidence being all in, and the lawyers having made their speeches, the Judge charges the jury thus: "If we consider Mrs. Stowe merely as a woman, plainly she is not liable to chastisement at the hands of a private person; nor, if we consider her as a *wife*, can the Professor be justified, for the English law which allows a man to flog his wife is not in force here."

On this charge, taking my cue from Mrs. Stowe, I comment on this wise: "IF *we consider Mrs. Stowe as a wife*, says the Judge; and, in his charge, he evidently intimates that he has a strong leaning to this opinion, though he puts it forth in a hypothetical form." Now I submit it to the common sense of the reader, whether this logic is not as good as Mrs. Stowe's, and whether, according to her mode of reasoning, it would not prove, in the case supposed, that the Judge was at least in doubt whether she were a wife or not!

Now turn to page 111, and read the following: "The act regulating patrols, as quoted by the editor of Prince's [Georgia] Digest, empowers *every justice of the peace to disperse* ANY *assembly or meeting of slaves* which *may* disturb the peace, &c., of his majesty's subjects." Observe the emphasis on the word "may," (for the *italics*, &c., are hers,) and the comment implied in it. She seems not to have the remotest suspicion that the word means here, as often elsewhere, the same as "shall." Other languages have a subjunctive mood to express such meaning unmistakeably, but the English language is the language of common sense, and expects common sense in its interpreters.

The reader has now had a taste of Mrs. Stowe's quality

as a commentator. The interpretations put forth are such, that it is difficult to believe she could be in earnest in them. They remind me of a *passage* between Judge P. and Mr. Q., of the Baltimore bar. Mr. Q. was pleading a case in court, and had just laid down a very singlar proposition, when he was interrupted by Judge P.: "Is it possible, Mr. Q., that you can think that *that* is law?" "Oh, no, your honor! *I* didn't think it was, but I didn't know but the *Court* might!"

I now pass to consider Mrs. Stowe's positions and comments generally; or rather, to *touch* upon them, for I have not space to do more.

In chapter second, after some preliminary flourishes, she lays down the following proposition: "That the slave-code is designed *only for the security of the master, and not with regard to the welfare of the slave.*" If this proposition is not very good English, it isn't my fault: it was fitting that the rhetoric of the proposition should be in keeping with the logic of its proofs. Among these "proofs," not one of which *proves* the proposition, or even "begins" to prove it, is one which completely upsets it. I refer to the "opinion" of Judge Ruffin, (pp. 77, 78,) in which, after recognizing "the full dominion of the owner over the slave," except in "particular instances of cruelty and deliberate barbarity," *and* "when the exercise of it is forbidden by statute,"—pretty broad exceptions, (see Appendix, E., *passim*,) he adds, in the concluding paragraph:

"And this we do upon the ground that *this dominion is essential to the value of slaves as property, to the security of the master and the public tranquillity, greatly dependent upon their subordination;* and, in fine, as most effectually securing the general protection and comfort of the slaves themselves."

The *italics* are Mrs. Stowe's, and if the reader will carefully examine the last clause, he will be at no loss to perceive why she left *that* "in roman:" *she* thought it knocked her proposition in the head, but then, like the Baltimore lawyer, she didn't know what "the *court*" might think,—especially if she could draw off their attention to the first part of the paragraph! It won't do, Mrs. Stowe! The public are at least *as* sharp as the *Old* Baltimore Court.

As to the rest of Judge Ruffin's opinion, if there is anything in it inconsistent with the paragraph above, it is not my fault. I have as great respect for him as Mrs. Stowe; especially as he is a sound Churchman, as I gather from his having been chosen delegate from the diocese of North Carolina to the next General Convention. Possibly, Mrs. Stowe would not have been so laudatory of him, had she been aware that he "belonged to" a Church which "has never done anything *but* comply, either North or South." In justice to the Judge, I should state that this opinion was delivered more than twenty-three years ago, and was among the first, perhaps the very first, delivered by him on the bench of the Supreme Court.

Chapter Third is entitled, "SOUTHER VS. THE COMMONWEALTH." The N. Y. *Courier and Enquirer* had *correctly* stated the decision in this case to be, that "The killing of a slave by his master and owner, by wilful and excessive whipping, is murder *in the first degree: though it may not have been the purpose and intention of the master and owner to kill the slave.*" Mrs. Stowe *admits* this, but then because the *jury* in the court below, (*not* the *judge*,) decided the crime to be murder in the *second* degree, and sentenced the prisoner to the *penitentiary for five years*, and the prisoner could not, in Virginia, any more than in Massachusetts, or any other civilized State, be tried again, she thinks the law is at fault, or, as she elsewhere expresses it, (chap. xiii. p. 110,) that "the men are better than their laws." And yet, she would not have allowed him the benefit of a trial at all: "One would think," says she, "that * * * the community would have risen by an universal sentiment, to shake out the man, as Paul shook the viper from his hand. It seems, however, that they were quite self-possessed; that lawyers calmly sat, and examined, and cross-examined, * * * * and that an American jury found that the offence was murder *in the second degree.*"

Now what is this but the very spirit of *lynch law*—against which Mrs. Stowe is, elsewhere, (p. 186,) so virtuously indignant, when abolitionists are the victims! And this is from one of the softer sex! "Tell me of the lovely rule of woman!" (vol. ii. p. 91.)

She goes on:—"Any one who reads the indictment will certainly think that, if this be murder in the *second degree*, in Virginia, one might earnestly pray to be murdered in the first degree, to begin with."

And she adds, speaking of this very case, (p. 106.) "Such *extreme* cases of bodily abuse from the despotic power of slavery are comparatively rare. Perhaps they may be paralleled by cases brought to light in the criminal jurisprudence of other countries. They might, perhaps, have happened anywhere; at any rate, we will concede that they might. But where under the sun did *such* TRIALS, of such cases, ever take place, in any nation professing to be free and Christian?"

I will tell you, Mrs. Stowe: In the good old Commonwealth of Pennsylvania, which is, if I mistake not, "under the sun" (unless, indeed, you refer to the torrid zone,*) and which, I believe, professes to be "free and Christian."

I was in the city of Pittsburg, (now, the head-quarters of Pennsylvania Abolitionism,) in June, 1842, and being

* Even then, I won't say *it is n't*, judging from some specimens of hot weather I have met with in it.

detained there some days, and having nothing else to occupy me, I attended a murder trial that was then going on in one of the courts. I forget the names of the parties, but these, as well as the particulars of the case will be found in the newspapers of the day. The evidence was, that the prisoner, after beating and abusing his wife, so that the neighbours heard her cries and shrieks, *tied her in a chair* and set fire to the house and *burned her up* in it, and the jury brought in a verdict of murder *in the second degree!** What sort of laws must those be, under which such a verdict was possible? Very naughty, you will say. O no! It was n't a black man that was tortured to death; it was only a white woman! only a *wife!* that's all!

But why did not the neighbours interfere, as you think the people of Raleigh should have interfered in the case of Mima? Ah! Mrs. Stowe, it is very dangerous to come between husband and wife. If the "*supposed* case," two or three pages back, the "case not to be found in any of the books," were to become an *actual* one, I should be very loth indeed to interfere, on the score of safety to my own skin; for as Marks says, (vol. i. p. 282,) "It's the best I've got, and I don't know why I *should n't* save it."

But this verdict was in "repudiating" Pennsylvania. "Was ever such a trial held in England as that in Virginia, of SOUTHER VS. THE COMMONWEALTH?" (p. 106.) O yes, Mrs. Stowe, no longer ago than last February, as you will see, if you turn to the extract from the London Guardian, (Appendix, K. 3. (7.).) You will see by that, that while according to a Virginia jury, torturing and burning a black man to death is murder in the second degree, according to an English jury, torturing and burning a white *child* to death is only *manslaughter!* Verily, if the English jury

* Recollect that "Legree is chained in free States." Mrs. Stowe says so, (p. 40,) *and she knows!*

were in the right, Souther was n't so far out of the way in thinking that the verdict in his case ought to have been "manslaughter" too.

We come now to the subject of the *Outlawry* of negroes in North Carolina. The following is the law on the subject, as cited by Mrs. Stowe (Key, p. 83) from the Revised Statutes, chap. cxi. sec. 22:

"Whereas, MANY TIMES *slaves run away and lie out, hid and lurking in swamps, woods, and other obscure places*, killing cattle and hogs, and committing other injuries to the inhabitants of this State; in all such cases, upon intelligence of any slave or slaves lying out as aforesaid, any two justices of the peace for the county wherein such slave or slaves is or are supposed to lurk or do mischief, shall, and they are hereby empowered and required to issue proclamation against such slave or slaves (reciting his or their names, and the name or names of the owner or owners, if known,) thereby requiring him or them, and every of them, forthwith to surrender him or themselves; and also to empower and require the sheriff of the said county to take such power with him as he shall think fit and necessary for going in search and pursuit of, and effectually apprehending, such outlying slave or slaves; which proclamation shall be published at the door of the court-house, and at such other places as said justices shall direct. And if any slave or slaves against whom proclamation hath been thus issued stay out, and do not immediately return home, it shall be lawful for any person or persons whatsoever to kill and destroy such slave or slaves by *such ways and means as he shall think fit*, without accusation or impeachment of any crime for the same."

Now what sort of persons are these outlaws, and what is the reason that North Carolina alone has such a statute? Read the following from Number Thirteen of the Letters on the South, before referred to, and you will see:

"The Dismal Swamps are noted places of refuge for runaway negroes. They were formerly peopled in this way much more than at present; a systematic hunting of them with dogs and guns having been made by individuals who took it up as a business about ten years ago. Children were born, bred, lived and died here. The negro, my guide, told me he had seen skeletons, and had helped to bury bodies recently dead. There are people in the swamps now, he thought, that are the children of fugitives, and fugitives themselves *all their lives*. What a strange life it must be!

"There can be, though, but very few, if any, of these 'natives' left. They cannot obtain the means of supporting life without coming often either to the outskirts to steal from the plantations, or to the neighbourhood of the camps of the lumbermen. They live mainly upon the charity or the wages given them by the latter. The poorer white men owning small tracts of the swamps will sometimes employ them, and the negroes frequently. In the hands of either they are liable to be betrayed to the 'drivers,' as the negro hunters are called, or to their owners if they are known. The negro told me that they had huts in 'back places,' hidden by bushes, and difficult of access, and had apparently been himself quite intimate with them. He said when the shingle negroes employed them, they made them get up logs for them, and would give them enough to eat and some clothes, and perhaps two dollars a month in money. But some when they owed them money, would betray them instead of paying them.

"He said the 'drivers' sometimes shot them. When they saw a fugitive, if he tried to run away from them, they would call out to him, that if he did not stop they would shoot, and if he did not, then they would shoot, and sometimes kill him. 'But some of 'em would *rather* be shot than be took, Sir,' he added, simply. A farmer living near the swamp confirmed this account, and said he knew of three or four being shot in one day. I suppose when the drivers first commenced their business in a large way, they made a practice of killing those that would not surrender, without mercy, that they might strike terror into those that remained, and prevent others from continuing to join them. In this purpose they have been in a great degree successful. I judged that the drivers were looked upon with repugnance by the community in general."

Now I ask, as a Christian, which is best,—that these pests of society should be rooted out and their haunts broken up,—or that they should be suffered to go on preying upon the community, increasing in numbers, and sinking daily deeper and deeper in barbarism? Is it not better that one thousand should be exterminated, if need be, than that ten thousand should be added to them, and thus ruined for time and eternity? The truth is, these men are at war with society, and society has therefore an undoubted right to protect itself against them. If the sovereign State of North Carolina has the right to call out the military to subdue, and, if need be, exterminate them, as none will question who admit that the magistrate "beareth not the sword in vain," then it has the right to make use of any other equally effective and less burdensome way of accomplishing the object. If it were white men who were thus "lying out," no one would doubt this; but a black skin makes a wonderful difference.

A word, now, upon the advertisements offering rewards for the apprehension of runaways, DEAD or ALIVE, (p. 21.) The first of these advertisements is evidently of an *outlaw*, and the second, probably so. In every one of them, it is implied that the slave is to be killed *legally*, that is, ONLY when *resisting capture*, and in three of them it is expressly so stated. Moreover, in one of them no reward at all is offered for killing, and in another, only *one-third as much* as for taking alive. To the argument intended to be drawn from these advertisements, it is a sufficient answer, that under *none* of them could the pursuer kill the fugitive *unresisting*, without finding himself liable to the owner for the pecuniary value of the *chattel*, and to the State, for the murder of the MAN. So much for the advertisements at which Mrs. Stowe is so shocked.

Chapter Fifth is devoted to *Protective Statutes.* After stating the penalty for killing a slave "on a sudden heat or passion, or by undue correction," she goes on:

"The next protective statute to be noticed, is the following from the act of 1740, South Carolina.

'In case any person shall wilfully cut out the tongue, put out the eye, * * * or cruelly scald, burn, or deprive any slave of any limb, or member, or shall inflict any other cruel punishment, *other than* by whipping or beating with a horse-whip, cowskin, switch or small stick, or by putting irons on, or confining or imprisoning such slave, every such person shall, for every such offence, forfeit the sum of one hundred pounds, current money.'—*Stroud, p.* 40. 2 *Brevard's Digest,* 241.

"The language of this law, like many other of these protective enactments, is exceedingly suggestive; the first suggestion that occurs is, What sort of an institution, and what sort of a state of society is it, that called out a law worded like this?"

I will tell you, Mrs. Stowe. An "institution" and a "state of society" such as existed, *less than eighty years ago*, "all over our land;" such as your fathers, and mine, were *familiar* with; a state of society in which Massachusetts men, and Rhode Island men, and Connecticut men, could engage in the foreign slave-trade, and yet hold up their heads in the community, like other Christians; a state, however, happily, long since past away, never to return. The "protective statutes" of this stamp, and also those relating to food, amount of labour, &c., (p. 90,) date back, all of them, to a period when the foreign slave-trade was in full vigor, and the price of slaves was low, and masters, therefore, could *afford* to abuse them.

It will be observed that they prohibit the *use* of *improper* modes of punishment, not the *abuse* of *proper* ones,* the exceptions introduced by the words, "*other than*," in the act above quoted, being, *every one of them*, proper modes, and those that are prohibited, every one of them, improper. Mrs. Stowe calls this an "awful principle † of slave laws." (p. 81.) In answer, I have only to say that it is a principle recognized by God himself, by express enactment, (Ex. xxi. 20, 21, 26, 27,) and if she chooses to charge God with recognizing an "awful *principle*," on her be the responsibility: I would not have it on my soul, for worlds. The "malicious, cruel and excessive beating" of a slave is, indeed, "awful" wickedness, but there are a great many awfully wicked things that the law cannot punish without, on the whole, doing more harm than by leaving them unpunished, and this is one of them, or we may be sure God would never have given his people such an enactment.

Chapter Seventh is devoted to the case of Eliza Rowand, and Chapter Ninth to that of James Castleman. They *may* have been guilty, but according to Mrs. Stowe's own showing, there was no *evidence* against them, and a good deal for them.

In Chapter Eleventh, Mrs. Stowe draws a comparison between "the Roman *law* of slavery," and "the American,"

* Unless that abuse result in death, or, *in Louisiana*, (Civil. Code, Art. 173,) "expose him" (the slave) "to the *danger* of loss of life."

† Mrs. Stowe draws a false "corollary" (p. 81, at the bottom,) from this. Souther *could* have been indicted for the "burning" and for any other of the *modes* of punishment employed by him, not recognized in the above act, even if they had *not* resulted in death.

and after giving (p. 110,) the last item in Blair's description of Roman slavery, adds:

"To this alone, of all the atrocities of the slavery of old heathen Rome, do we fail to find a parallel in the slavery of the United States of America."

And yet, according to her own showing, the 1st, 3d, 5th, 8th, 9th, 10th, 12th and 13th "atrocities," (more than half the whole number,) of Roman slavery,—that is, slave-*law*, for it is that of which she is speaking, (see the title of the chapter,)—have no parallel in American.

Chapter Fourteenth compares the Hebrew with the American slave law. This chapter is *full* of blundering, or worse than blundering, comments, and ludicrous misinterpretations, —*so* ludicrous, on their very face, as not to need examination, even had I room for it. I will just remark, however, in passing, (what the reader, I fear, will hardly thank me for, as it seems to imply his own shallowness,) that the practices referred to in the first three items of Professor Stowe's "summary," (p. 116,) are every one of them expressly *prohibited* by Christianity, whereas slavery and *slave-holding Christians*, "faithful and beloved," are expressly *recognized* by it. As to the "cities of refuge," the provision would be a perfectly proper one now, if there were any necessity for it. A similar provision—the Truce of God—*did* exist in the middle ages, and did immense service to civilization. "The Israelites," says Professor Stowe, "were commanded to exterminate the Canaanites, men, women and children." Well! when God shall command *us* to "exterminate the Canaanites," I will take hold and do my part, and I trust the Professor will his.

One omission in this chapter is noteworthy, as showing the authors *prudence*: in the passage cited by me two or three paragraphs back, (Ex. xxi. 20, 21, 26, 27,) she cites the 26th and 27th verses, and *omits* the other two! See also an equally *significant* omission in Lev. xix. 20.

On pages 88 and 90, (chapters 5 and 6,) are provisions of law requiring the accused master, in certain cases, to *purge* himself by oath, or suffer punishment. On these provisions the author tries to be facetious: she speaks of the "virtuous solemnity and gravity" of one of the acts, and shows herself, thereby, "to be in the enjoyment of an amiable ignorance and unsophisticated innocence with regard to the workings of human society generally, which is, on the whole, rather refreshing." (p. 92.) She thinks a master who should *neglect* to allow his slave sufficient clothing, covering or food, would necessarily be bad enough to perjure himself for the sake of saving a "sum *not exceeding* twenty pounds current money!" And, speaking of the act on page 86, she asks, "What was this law made for? Can any one imagine?" Yes, Mrs. Stowe! *I* can imagine: and my imagination is n't half as fertile as yours, either. The law was evidently made for *this:* If possible, to secure the punishment of the offender here; or, failing that, to send him into eternity with the awful guilt of perjury on his soul, to receive a double punishment hereafter.

"Chapter Tenth: PRINCIPLES ESTABLISHED.

"From a review of all the legal cases which have hitherto been presented, and of the principles established in the judicial decisions upon them, the following facts must be apparent to the reader:

"*First*, That masters do, now and then, kill slaves by the torture."

True! "But," as Mrs. Stowe says, "the actual number of them, compared with the whole number of masters, we take pleasure in saying, is small. It is an injury to the cause of freedom to ground the argument against slavery upon the *frequency* with which such scenes as these occur. It misleads the popular mind as to the real issue of the subject." (p. 106.)

"*Second*, That the fact of so killing a slave is not of itself held presumption of murder, in slave jurisprudence."

False ! see the closing paragraph of Judge Field's opinion, (p. 80,) and the slave-code *passim*.

"*Third*, That the slave in the act of resistance to his master may always be killed."

True ! *Per Contra:* "If a slave, in defence of his life, and under circumstances strongly calculated to excite his passions of terror *and resentment*, kill his overseer or *master*, the homicide is, by such circumstances, mitigated to manslaughter." State vs. Will, (Key, p. 105.)

"From these things it will be seen to follow, that, if the facts of the death of Tom had been fully proved by two white witnesses, in open Court, Legree could not have been held by any *consistent* interpreter of slave-law to be a murderer; for Tom was in the act of resistance to the will of his master." (p. 105.)

True ! But under the statute enacted by God himself, (Ex. xxi. 20, 21,) it would have been the same : Legree could not have been punished. The law of the land, even when enacted by God himself, is not, and was not designed to be, omnipotent. "A system of government which would raise a barrier against every evil disposition in man, would be a clog about his feet." (Slavery in the S. States, By a Carolinian, p. 12.)

"In conclusion, as the accounts of these various trials contain so many shocking incidents and particulars, the author desires to enter a caution against certain mistaken uses which may be made of them, by well-intending persons. The crimes themselves, which form the foundation of the trials, are NOT to be considered and spoken of as specimens of the *common* working of the slave system." (Key, p. 106.)

I come now to PART III., on Public Opinion in the slave States, and this I shall dispatch in a single paragraph, for it needs no more. It is made up, in good part, of advertisements and comments, the *spirit* of which latter may be gathered from the first paragraph on the second column of page 140. The principal object of them, however, is to show the frequency of the separation of families; and yet each of these advertisements, separately, is consistent with their being no separations at all, and all of them together, with there being very few. Indeed, she seems to suspect as much; for, after having given a long string of them, (pp. 129—142,) she says, (p. 144,) "We have shown in the preceding chapters, the kind of advertisements which are usual in those States; but, as we wish to produce on the minds of our readers something of the impression which has been produced on our own mind by their *multiplicity* and *abundance*, we shall add a few more here;" and then goes on to give "a few more:" and of these "few *more*" six are *repetitions*, several of them word for word, and all of them, substantially, of advertisements already given!!! McLendon's, (p. 144,) being found also on page 139; Harker's, (p. 145,) on 142; McLean's second one (p. 145,) on 140; Bolton, Dickens & Co's, (p. 145,) on 138; Griffin and Pullum's, (p. 147,) on 139; and James's, (p. 147, col. 1, on 138: nay, she has even gone so far as to give John Mattingly's twice on the same column, (p. 146,) and with only one other between them! It may be said that these advertisements are often actually repeated in the same paper, on different pages, to draw attention to them, and that she was, in this way, misled by them; but this excuse will not serve her, for she was perfectly aware of this custom of repetition, as is shown by her comment on the first advertisement on page 140, and therefore her repetition of them shows, I will not say deliberate misrepresentation, but, certainly, unpardonable carelessness.

I come now to PART IV., and last, on the "Influence

of the American Church on Slavery." On this part of her work I could say a great deal, but I have already considerably exceeded my limits, and I must therefore be very brief.

"If," says Mrs. Stowe, "the argument of Charles Sumner be contemplated, it will be seen that the history of this Presbyterian Church and the history of our United States have strong points of singularity. In both, at the outset, the strong influence was anti-slavery, even among slaveholders. In both there was no difference of opinion as to the desirableness of abolishing slavery ultimately; both made a concession, the smallest which could possibly be imagined; both made the concession in all good faith, contemplating the speedy removal and extinction of the evil; and the history of both is alike. The little point of concession spread, and absorbed, and acquired, from year to year, till the United States and the Presbyterian Church stand *just where they do.* Worse has been the history of the Methodist Church. The history of the Baptist Church shows the same principle; and, as to the Episcopal Church, it has never done anything *but* comply, either North or South. It differs from all the rest in that it has never had any resisting element, except now and then a protestant, like William Jay, a worthy son of him who signed the Declaration of Independence."

I thank you, Mrs. Stowe, for this admission. It shows that the Church understands her mission,—the "plan" of her Divine Founder—too well, to mix herself up with the institutions of society and the affairs of State. She receives alike within her fold the Free-Soiler and the Pro-Slavery man, asking no questions of either: she would as soon think of asking her candidates for baptism or the communion, whether they were whigs or democrats. Enough for her that they are churchmen: as such she receives them; as such they submit themselves to her. On this point her members are all agreed: there is no difference of opinion amongst us in regard to it. In our conventions we never discuss Anti-Masonry, or Anti-Slavery, or any other *anti*,—Teetotalism or Fourierism, or any other *ism*: we ignore their very existence. Outside the Church, indeed, in our capacity of citizens and individuals, we have our opinion upon each and all of these, and we do not hesitate to express it, on all fitting occasions. But even here, we harmonize to a far greater extent than most other religious bodies. No sound churchman *could* go all lengths with the Free-Soil party. I am acquainted with one, and but one, who is a prominent member of that party,—the one you quote from on page 6, and that he does not go all lengths with them, you have his own declaration in his speech at the Hale dinner. There is a good deal in this book that he would not agree with, but there is a good deal more that you would not agree with, that he would. I have the best reason for saying that he utterly disapproves of the proceedings of Torrey and Chaplin, but you sympathize with those proceedings, and try to make your readers sympathize with them. Again: you object to the Church that it "has done nothing *but* comply." What you meam by this, viz., that it has never taken any action at all, upon the subject, pro or con, he and I agree in considering its glory.

I have mentioned two points in which you differ from him and me: I am happy to say that there are two other points in which we all three agree.

First, we agree in our estimate of the Smiths, the Southers and the Castlemans *et id omne genus*. You, however, think the law of the land should take hold of them for carrying a proper kind of punishment to excess, even though it do not result in death: I do not, and I very much doubt if he does.

Second, we agree in looking upon the slave as a man and a brother; a sharer in that humanity in which the Lord of Glory walked our earth; in which he suffered, was crucified, dead and buried, rose again, ascended into heaven, sitteth on the right hand of God the Father, and shall come to judge the quick and the dead. But even here, you cannot enter with us into the full meaning of all this, you cannot look on the slave in the same light that we do, unless you are far, very far, in advance of ninety-nine-hundredths of the New England Congregationalists. So much for the course of the Church on this subject.

The fourth and fifth chapters are full of paralogisms; I can only notice a single one. I refer to the parallel you draw at the end of the fifth chapter, which is, in truth, no parallel, but a parody. Did you really think, when writing the last paragraph, that the white man, at the South, had taken anything from the negro?—that he had not, on the contrary, given him all he has, and all he hopes for, for time, and for eternity? If you did, then I have nothing further to say: it would be a waste of breath to no purpose.

In Chapter Sixth is the following:

"There is an argument which has been much employed on this subject, and which is specious. It is this. That the apostles treated slavery as one of the lawful relations of life, like that of parent and child, husband and wife.

"The argument is thus stated: The apostles found all the relations of life much corrupted by various abuses.

"They did not attack the *relations*, but reformed the *abuses*, and thus restored the relations to a healthy state.

"The mistake here lies in assuming that slavery is the lawful relation. Slavery is the corruption of a lawful relation. The lawful relation is *servitude*, and slavery is the *corruption* of servitude.

"When the apostles came, all the relations of life in the

Roman empire were thoroughly permeated with the principle of slavery. The relation of child to parent was slavery. The relation of wife to husband was slavery. The relation of servant to master was slavery."

The sophistry of this argument is transparent, and the wonder is that you did not see through it yourself. If, as you say, "the lawful relation is *servitude*, and slavery is the *corruption*" of "that lawful relation," why did not our Lord require of all who would be his disciples that they should *manumit* their slaves and turn them into *hired servants*. This they could have done without coming into collision with the civil power, as I have already shown (p. 63), and as you yourself admit in the paragraph next following the one last above quoted, in which you tell us that "by Roman law," (and the whole civilized world was then under Roman law,) the son could be "formally liberated" only "by an act of manumission three times repeated, while the slave could be manumitted by performing the act only once;" and it would have been, moreover, nothing strange, for hired servants were not at all uncommon, as is shown by St. Luke xv. 17, and St. James v. 4. The fact, therefore, that while our Lord *did* prohibit even the formal relation of polygamy and concubinage, as being corruptions of the marriage relation (Matt. xix. 3—9, Luke xvi. 18, et al.) he did *not* prohibit the formal relation of slavery, shows clearly that he did not regard it as a "*corruption* of servitude."

"What is to be done?" This is the title of your last chapter. "What is to be done?" Nothing! Let the whole subject alone! Every time you touch it, you make things worse, not only for the slave but for the free colored man. They understand this, if you don't. Read the following resolutions, being the first and second of a series adopted by a "Convention of the Free Colored People of Maryland," composed of Delegates from the several counties, and which assembled in Baltimore, July 26, 1852, and continued in session for several days.

Resolved, That while we appreciate and acknowledge the sincerity of the motives and the activity of the zeal of those who, during an agitation of twenty years, have honestly struggled to place us on a footing of social and political equality with the white population of this country, yet we cannot conceal from ourselves the fact that no advance has been made towards a result to us so desirable; but that on the contrary, our condition as a class is less desirable than it was twenty years ago.

Resolved, That in the face of an immigration from Europe, which is greater each year than it was the year before, and during the prevalence of a feeling in regard to us, which the very agitation intended for good, has only served apparently to embitter, we cannot promise ourselves that the future will do that which the past has failed to accomplish.

Take their advice; the advice implied in these resolutions. This, of all subjects, should be let alone by empirics. No good can come of bungling:

Stat contra ratio, et secretam garrit in aurem,
Ne liceat facere id, quod quis vitiabit agendo.

Bend all your efforts another way. Give your time, your talents, and, let me add, your *money*, to help on the success of the Liberia experiment: it is the only atonement you can make to the black man for the wrongs you have done him. Engage your English friends in the work—and a great work it is—of regenerating the Jamaica negro; and let your and their efforts conspire together to build up a great African Empire. In this way you may do something for "this persecuted race," and every *real* well-wisher to the colored man will bid you God speed in the doing of it.

APPENDIX.

Appendix, A

The following are a few of the many specimens that might be given of Abolition Literature:

From the Boston Traveller, of June 1, 1850.

New-England Anti-Slavery Convention.

The meeting on Wednesday morning was fully attended. Calvin Fairbanks addressed those in attendance—mostly in the gallery—who were unwilling to listen patiently to the sentiments of the Convention. He said he was ready to go even further than S. S. Foster did yesterday, in relation to the sanction of slavery by the Old Testament. He believed that it did sanction oppression, and he was prepared to trample under foot all sentiments in it which were contrary to known natural truths. He said, perhaps this would be thought saying considerable for a Methodist minister (cheers and hisses).

From the Boston Commonwealth.

Rev. Dr. Fuller.—Wednesday's Journal says "it is gratifying to witness a Christian slaveholder welcomed to the hearts and pulpits of *his brethren* here." This "Christian slaveholder" is the Rev. Richard Fuller. He was welcomed to the hearts and pulpits of the churches in Rowe street and Charles street, as we have before mentioned. A million of this Christian slaveholder's sisters have no protection against the lusts of a million of his brothers. Husband, father, mother, brother, victim,—all equally powerless! With a knowledge of this, the churches in Rowe street and Charles street welcome a Rev. "Christian slaveholder,"—one of those who hold the keys of this vast brothel,—to their "hearts and pulpits."

From the New York Herald, (Weekly,) of May 14, 1853.

AMERICAN ANTI-SLAVERY SOCIETY:—FANATICISM RUN MAD.

The Chairman next introduced Mr. Wendell Phillips of Boston, who addressed the assembly as follows:—I can say, with the utmost sincerity, that so far as the Anti-Slavery Society is concerned, there is no necessity that I should address this audience, and I think it almost a waste of time that I should spread either facts or arguments before an intelligent American audience, in the twenty-second year of the Anti-slavery Society. The motto of our organ in this city is, "Without concealment—without compromise." I read with great satisfaction some of the speeches with which our faithful friend Mr. Hale was received in Boston; and yet it seems to me that the tone with which that meeting addressed the American public should be distinct from that which we should address it. They are full of hope —we are not. They can call this a glorious Union. May my tongue cleave to the roof of my mouth before I call it a glorious Union. (Applause and hisses.) Two adjectives distinguish them from us. With them the Union is glorious—with us it is accursed. With them the character of Washington is heroic; and with me I dare not thank God for giving him to us. (Great hisses.) Do you suppose that the brutal slaveholders could ever have sustained slavery in this country till the year 1853? Do you suppose that profligate priests could have dragged slavery behind the altar? No. She would have sunk a hissing and a shame were it not that she hid herself behind the great proportions of Washington's name. (Hisses.) It is because Americans dare not call things by their right name; it is because we like the great names of the present and the past; it is because that we spread a beautiful mist before the Union—that idol which we worship —that slavery still continues. It is to tear away the veil from the American eyes that the object of this society is. Our friends tell us that the Union must be preserved; it is a part of the soil—a part of the blood—not to be spoken of, much less abjured. I do not deny that it has some merits—but so had Nero. A rose bush was planted on his tomb some months after his death—planted by some Roman to whom his life was not an unmitigated tyranny. The pulpit, with only here and there an exception, if it speaks freely, speaks itself out of its pulpit. The press that lives on the popular voice and reflects it, what is it? Pro-slavery. Free speech is only to be bought here at the price of martyrdom. It is with pain I have asked the tenants of country pulpits to preach an anti-slavery sermon, knowing that if they obeyed me they obeyed me at the sacrifice of the bread of their children. You send your delegates to the June Anniversaries of London—they will be hissed there. Our religion is ever a butt. There is an American religion, distinct from Christianity. This is a glorious Union! We cannot reprint an English book without expurgating it. Your Bible Society dare not offer a Bible to one having a drop of black blood in his veins. 'Tis a glorious Union. Free speech! Men walk about, and dare not tell their names, and that's your glorious Union. The man who stands under the shadow of the Union is bound to think it a good establishment, but we wash our hands of it. The only platform we stand on is this: our religion is this, where there is neither male nor female, African or Anglo-Saxon, bond or free. (Applause.) The Fugitive Slave Law in some sense has succeeded, because it has crushed in some pulpits the rising sense of anti-slavery principles. It is no occasional, or temporary expedient; it is the foundation corner of this Union. When we picture the Italian we do so with his fine arts. The Greek is described with his severe and classic beauty; and England comes to us in the names of Hampden and Sydney; and when the European, either with his pencil or his pen, wishes to picture America, how does he do it?—with a slave on the one side and the slaveholder and scourge on the other. Over the world there is no other emblem for this glorious Union than the slave whip. Can you object to the picture? Which of the last seven Presidents can you admire? We have but one book that we have contributed to the literature of the world, and every respectable newspaper, and every conservative pulpit, declares it a libel. There is many a man who weeps over Uncle Tom and swears by the HERALD. (Laughter and cheers.) But you know, and I know, that the governing mind of this country is not in the pulpit nor in the editor's chair—it is in the counting house. We are a commercial people, and that by the nobility which the possession of wealth creates. The counting house is the real great representative of the sentiment of the country. If we cannot play on a flute, we can say, with Pericles, we know how to make a wilderness blossom with fertility. Do these merchant princes report progress on Uncle Tom? Why, they sell their principles at the same time that they sell their goods; or rather they sell their goods and throw their principles in to swell the bargain. (Applause.) We come up here on these anniversaries, not for argument, but merely for a word. We come amid this Babel of piety in the May week, and we write on your walls our old motto: "Immediate and complete emancipation of the slave." But what is slavery, and how is it supported? Some men think it is supported by the New Testament and the Bible. Nonsense. Dr. Spring will pray quietly enough the moment pro-slavery becomes a losing question. (Hisses and applause.) Find me a balance on the wrong side of the ledger, and I will show you that scores of doctors of divinity will find out that Onesimus was not a slave. (Laughter.) It is our duty to show that the Christianity which the Puritans left us is a Christianity which does not veil its crest before a hundred thousand slaveholders and two hundred millions of dollars. The Rev. Dr. Rogers, of our city, published a sermon, in which he told us it was our duty to obey the Fugitive Slave law, right or wrong, and that in the first centuries of Christianity they obeyed the laws. Thus then, you will find according to Dr. Rogers, that our Divine Master and eleven of his disciples died violent deaths for obeying the law. And this is the ecclesiastical learning of Dr. Rogers! Point me to the page of history on which such a fact stands as that of three millions of slaves kept in bondage by thirty thousand slaveholders. What keeps them in slavery? The Union does. I would turn the Southern bankrupts out from the shelter of the national roof. But we render it possible for the South to keep three millions of ignorant toiling slaves in the nineteenth century. Disunion would turn them out to pay their own debts; and I say that disunion is the slave's best hope, planting the cannon of self-interest on his side. Now, you may think that when we talk of the Union being a curse we are talking fanaticism. No, we are simply talking commercial truth. Could England have kept Ireland where she is were it not that her people were kept in ignorance by Catholicity? Slavery, intrenched in dollars and cents, must be attacked by the same weapons and tools. You may ridicule our ideas as mad now, but when the South has girdled the Gulf with slave States—when she has bought or bullied Cuba into the Union—when she thinks she can stand alone—then the proposition may come from the other side. You know that it is idle to speak with the slave interest—you know there is neither public opinion or principle enough in the Union to oppose the annexation of Mexico and Cuba. I met a gentleman the other day who asked me if there was no spirit in New England to oppose this, and I told him of Dr. Spring being afraid to pray, and of Dr. Dewey wanting to get rid of his mother. (Applause and hisses.) For once I have the audience with me—some of you are applauding me, and the rest hissing Dr. Dewey. (Laughter.) It is said that slavery will be gradually annihilated—that Kentucky will abolish slavery, and that other States will follow its example; and if this were so, you will have slavery dying for centuries. But it will still be spreading southward, and like the Dutchman's coat, what will be cut off the collar will be appended to the tail. (Laughter.) If we shall ever abolish slavery we owe it to the Hampdens and the Sydneys, the Cromwells, and the men of the Mayflower. Your system is to be gradual. Yes, and in the meantime your counting houses will be just as servile, the pulpits just as timid, and the newspapers just as pro-slavery. We live in a land where newspapers make Presidents. We live in a land where the HERALD makes the law. (Cheers and laughter.) Now I would fain make it possible for Daniel Webster to be an honest man. (Hisses.) God gives us great men, and we take and sacrifice them. I hate the Union because it does not let us bury any of our greatest men except in tears. (Hisses.) Our great men—I say it not reproachfully. I am an American—oh, no! thank God, I am a Massachusetts man. (Hisses.) An American in Europe is a walking apology. (Hisses.) It is easy to hiss it in the city of New York, but it is hard to meet it in the streets of Europe. It is nevertheless true that all over Europe an American has nothing to do but to explain and apologize. O'Connell didn't shake hands with an American until he told him what State he was from. This country makes it almost the business of our lives to explain. And that's your glorious Union—none of mine. I would not acknowledge glorious a country which rendered it almost impossible for great men to lead symmetrical lives. With us so flagrant are the evils of our great men's examples, that their epitaphs must be examples to those who come after them. And that's your Union. I would make the service of the State privately honorable. The service of the State now is private dishonor, private infamy. And yet how shall men stand before their wives and children, and practise at home the lessons they give from the forum. Call slavery something else—slavery, piracy, adultery—and we will recognize its deformity. I would therefore break up all these national arrangements. My problem is, that we want men as disinterested as the apostles to put down slavery. We cannot war against two thousand millions of dollars, and Gardner Spring in the pulpit. It was not Daniel Webster's fault that he acted as he did. God made him as good as any of us, but he sunk before temptation; and you sunk as low as he when you worshipped and idolized him. Every time I have alluded to Dr. Spring you have hissed me. The existence of such a monster is not my fault, nor that of the Anti-Slavery Association. It is the fault of your school and counting houses; I say, given a Wall street committee and Dr. Gardner Spring in the pulpit, and the problem is to make twenty millions of people equal in honesty to the Apostles. How soon can it be done? "These be thy gods, O Israel." (Laughter.) That is your religion. (Hisses.) Hiss it, certainly. There was a Greek, who was not a Phidias nor Praxiteles, and he painted something which he got a Greek slave by his side to declare a horse. And so you describe a contemptible timeserver as a Doctor of Divinity or a politician. (Laughter.) I would move as my resolution this:—

Resolved, That we re-affirm our old principle, "Immediate and unconditioned emancipation of the slave;" and we also reaffirm our conviction that there is no probability for that except by the dissolution of the Union and the re-constitution of the American church.

An old lady here advanced to the foot of the platform, and in a confidential tone assured Mr. Garrison that she had been listening to sermons and speeches on the subject of slavery, for the last ten years, but had never heard so fine a sermon as that just delivered by Mr. Phillips.

From the Boston Weekly Commonwealth, of Aug. 7, 1852.

ONE OF OUR MASTERS.

A MARYLAND FARMER.—The Easton (Md.) Star says that Col. Edward Lloyd, of that county, with his own servants—numbering near four hundred—some nine or ten farms—about six thousand acres of land, including timber land, raises annually between 30,000 and 40,000 bushels of wheat, and a much larger quantity of corn; besides various other valuable products. Besides these extensive operations in Talbot, he has a plantation carried on in the State of Mississippi, worth several hundred thousand dollars, and his annual income cannot fall short of $150,000. His residence is one of the most splendid in this country, and has been the homestead of the Lloyd family since their first settlement in Maryland.

Very grand and fine. And very convenient, and comfortable, and agreeable, no doubt, to Col. Edward Lloyd, "of that county." But where does it all come from? Wrung by the whip, the chain, the pistol, and the bowie-knife, out of the four hundred "servants," as the

Easton Star delicately phrases it, who cultivate the farms in Maryland, to say nothing of those who toil and sweat upon the plantation in Mississippi "worth several hundred thousand dollars." This nabob lives in a "splendid" residence, while his four hundred "servants" spend their days in the corn fields and their nights in wretched huts —unpaid for their labor, or paid only as horses are paid, that is, fed and sheltered well enough to keep them fit for work; uneducated, nay, strictly debarred from education, even from enough to enable them to read the Word of God; debarred also from all opportunities to better their condition; and not sure from one moment to another that their wives, or husbands, or children are their own, for they are liable to be sold at any time, on the least whim or caprice of Col. Edward Lloyd, or whenever that gentleman may wish for a little more pocket money. No feudal lord, no nobleman in any country, even the most absolute and most barbarous, holds his serfs in such complete subjection as this Maryland slave driver. Yet every one of them is a native born American, a citizen of this "free republic," and many of them may be and probably are greatly superior to their "owner" in all that constitutes human worth or excellence. Frederick Douglass, as able a man as Maryland has produced, a man of greater intellect and nobler character than any public man of that State at this day, was born and held a slave for twenty years on one of the plantations of this same Col. Edward Lloyd. No man can tell how many more black Douglasses there may be withering in ignorance and wretchedness on these plantations, that Col. Edward Lloyd may live in aristocratic pomp and luxury.

Freemen of New England and the North, working men, mechanics, laborers and farmers, look again at this account of this Maryland slave driver. You have a personal interest in it. We all have a personal interest in it. Col. Edward Lloyd is one of our masters. He is one of those who dictate the policy which is pursued at Washington—one of those who have extended their peculiar institution over our once free soil, so that they may hunt their fugitives upon it—one of those who declare that if we murmur or "agitate" about it, or send representatives to Congress to speak about it, they will dissolve the Union, and overthrow the Republic which our fathers founded by their valor, and built up by their wisdom.

However, it is a consolation to remember, amid our degradation, that if we are slaves, we have magnificent masters—that our owners are not "common white men," but gentlemen who live in splendid residences, and have incomes of one hundred and fifty thousand dollars. Let us be thankful at least for *that*.

APPENDIX, B.

CONDITION OF THE NEGRO IN AFRICA.

The following Extracts are taken from Fletcher's Studies on Slavery, pp. 138–155:

So far as we have means, it may be well to examine the negro in his native ranges.

About thirty years ago, we had a knowledge of an African slave, the property of Mr. Bookter, of St. Helena Parish, La. Sedgjo was apparently about sixty years of age—was esteemed to be unusually intelligent for an African. We propose to give the substance of his narrative, without regard to his language or manner. For a length of time we made it an object to draw out his knowledge and notions; and on the subject of the Deity, his idea was that the power which made him was *procreation;* and that, as far as regarded his existence, he needed not to care for any other god. This deity was to be worshipped by whatever act would represent him as *procreator.* It need not be remarked that this worship was the extreme of indecency; but the more the act of worship was wounding to the feelings or sense of delicacy, the more acceptable it was to the god. The displays of this worship could not well be described.

Sedgjo's account put us in mind of Maachah, the mother of Asa. In this worship, it was not uncommon to kill, roast, and eat young children, with the view to propitiate the god, and make its parents prolific. So also the first-born of a mother was sometimes killed and eaten, in thankfulness to the god for making them the instruments of its *procreation.* The king was the owner and master of the whole tribe. He might kill and do what else he pleased with them. The whole tribe was essentially his slaves. But he usually made use of them as a sort of soldiers. Those who were put to death at feasts and sacrifices were generally persons captured from other tribes. Persons captured were also slaves, might be killed and eaten on days of sacrifice, or sold and carried away to unknown countries. If one was killed in battle, and fell into the hands of those who slew him, they feasted on him at night. If they captured one alive who had done the tribe great injury, a day was set apart for all the tribe to revenge themselves, and feast on him. The feet and palms of the hands were the most delicious parts. When the king or master died, some of his favourite wives and other slaves were put to death, so that he yet should have their company and services. The king and the men of the tribe seldom cultivated the land; but the women and captured slaves are the cultivators. They never whip a slave, but strike him with a club; sometimes break his bones or kill him: if they kill him, they eat him.

Sedgjo belonged to the king's family; sometimes commanded as head man; consequently, had he not been sold, would have been killed and eaten. The idea of being killed and eaten was not very dreadful to him; he had rather be eaten by men than to have the flies eat him.

He once thought white men bought slaves to eat, as they did goats. When he first saw the white man, he was afraid of his red lips; he thought they were raw flesh and sore. It was more frightful to be eaten by red than by black lips.

On shipboard, many try to starve, or jump into the sea, to keep themselves from being eaten by the red-lips. Did they but know what was wanted of them, the most would be glad to come. He cannot tell how long he was on the way to the ships, nor did he know where he was going; thinks he was sold many times before he got there; never saw the white man till he was near the sea; all the latter part of his journey to the coast the people did not kill or eat their slaves, but sold them. Their clothing is a small cloth about the loins. The king and some others have a large cloth about the shoulders. Many are entirely naked all their lives. Sedgjo has no wish to go back; has better clothing here than the kings have there; if he does more work, he has more meat. If he is whipped here, he is struck with a club there. There, always afraid of being killed; jumped like a deer, if, out of the village, he saw or met a stranger; is very glad he came here; here he is afraid of nobody.

Such is the substance of what came from the negro's own lips. It was impossible to learn from him his distinct nation or tribe. Mr. Bookter thought him an Eboe, which was probably a mistake.

The following is from Lander, p. 58: "What makes us more desirous to leave this abominable place, is the fact (as we have been told) that a sacrifice of no less than *three hundred* human beings, of both sexes and all ages, is shortly to take place. We often hear the cries of many of these poor wretches; and the heart sickens with horror at the bare contemplation of such a scene as awaits us, should we remain here much longer."

And page 74: "We have longed to discover a solitary virtue lingering among the natives of this place, (Badagry,) but as yet our search has been ineffectual."

And page 77: "We have met with nothing but selfishness and rapacity, from the chief to the meanest of his people. The religion of Badagry is Mohammedanism, and the worst species of paganism; that which sanctions and enjoins the sacrifice of human beings, and other abominable practices, and the worship of imaginary demons and fiends."

Page 110: "It is the custom here, when a governor dies, for two of his favourite wives to quit the world on the same day, in order that he may have a little pleasant, social company in a future state."

Page 111: "The reason of our not meeting with a better reception at Loatoo, when we slept there, was the want of a chief to that town the last having followed the old governor to the eternal shades, for he was his slave. Widows are burned in India, just as they are poisoned or *clubbed* here; but in the former country, I believe no male victims are destroyed on such occasions."

"At Paoya, (page 124,) several chiefs in the road have asked us the reason why the Portuguese do not purchase as many slaves as formerly; and make very sad complaints of the stagnation in this branch of traffic."

Page 158: "At Leograda, a man thinks as little of taking a wife as cutting an ear of corn. Affection is altogether out of the question."

Page 160: "At Eitcho, it will scarcely be believed, that not less than one hundred and sixty governors of towns and villages between this place and the seacoast, all belonging to Yariba, have died from natural causes, or have been slain in war, since I was last here; and that of the inhabited places through which we have passed, not more than a half-dozen chiefs are alive at this moment, who received and entertained me on my return to Badagry, three years ago."

Page 176: "They seem to have no social tenderness; very few of those amiable private virtues which would win our affection, and none of those public qualities that claim respect or command admiration. Their love of country is not strong enough in their bosoms to incite them to defend it against the irregular incursions of a despicable foe. * * * Regardless of the past as reckless of the future; the present alone influences their actions. In this respect, they approach nearer to the brute creation than perhaps any other people on the face of the globe."

Page 181: "In so large a place as this, where two-thirds of the population are slaves." " " "

Page 192: "The cause of it was soon explained by his informing us that he would be doomed to die with two companions, (slaves,) as soon as their governor's dissolution should take place."

Page 227: "In the forenoon we passed near a spot where our guides informed us a party of Falatahs, a short time ago, murdered twenty of their slaves, because they had not food sufficient," &c.

Page 232: "At Coobly, he would rather have given us a boy (slave) instead of the horse."

Page 232: "Monday, June 14th.—The governor's old wife returned from Boossa this morning, whither she had gone in quest of three female slaves who had fled from her about a fortnight since. She has brought her fugitives back with her, and they are now confined in irons."

Page 272: "Both these days the men have been entering the city; and they have brought with them only between forty and fifty slaves."

Page 278: "The chief benefits resulting to Bello from the success of the rebels, were a half-yearly tribute, which the magia agreed to pay him in slaves."

Page 282: "At Yaooris.—And many thousands of his men, fearing no law, and having no ostensible employment, are scattered over the face of the whole country. They commit all sorts of crimes; they plunder, they burn, they destroy, and even murder, and are not accountable to any earthly tribunal for their actions."

Page 312: "At Boossa.—The manners of the Africans, too, are hostile to the interest and advancement of woman, and she is very rarely placed on an equality with her husband."

Page 228: "A man is at liberty to return his wife to her parents at any time, and without adducing any reason."

Page 345: "The Sheikh of Bornou has recently issued a proclamation, that no slaves from the interior countries are to be sent for sale farther west than Wowow,—so that none will be sent in future from thence to the seaside. The greatest and most profitable market for slaves is said to be at Timbuctoo, whither their owners at present transport them to sell to the Arabs, who take them over the deserts of Sahara and Libya to sell in the Barbary States. An Arab has informed us that many of his countrymen trade as far as Turkey, in Europe, with their slaves, where they dispose of them for two hundred and fifty dollars each. * * * Perhaps it would be speaking within compass to say that four-fifths of the whole population of this country, (the Eboe,) likewise every other hereabouts, are slaves."

Vol. ii. page 208: "It may appear strange that I should dwell so long on this subject, for it seems quite natural that every one, even the most thoughtless barbarian, would feel at least some slight emotion on beng exiled from his native land and enslaved; but so far is this from being the case, that Africans, generally speaking, betray the most perfect indifference on losing their liberty and being deprived of their relatives; while love of country is seemingly as great a stranger to their breasts as social tenderness and domestic affection. We have seen many thousands of slaves; some of them more intelligent than others; but the poor little fat woman whom I have mentioned,—the associate of beasts, and wallowing in filth,—whose countenance would seem to indicate only listlessness, stupidity, and perhaps idiotism, without the smallest symptom of intelligence—she alone has shown anything like regret on gazing on her native land for the last time."

Page 218: "It has been told us by many that the Eboe people are confirmed Anthropophagi; and this opinion is more prevalent among the tribes bordering on that kingdom than with the nations of more remote districts."

We shall close our extracts from Lander's work, by the following, showing that the Africans made slaves of the two Landers themselves.

Page 225: "The king then said, with a serious countenance, that there was no necessity for further discussion respecting the white men, (the two brothers Lander,) his mind was already made up on the subject; and, for the first time, he briefly explained himself, to this effect: That circumstances having thrown us in the way of his subjects, by the laws and usages of the country he was not only entitled to our own persons, but had equal rights to those of our attendants. That he should take no further advantage of his good fortune than by exchanging us for as much English goods as would amount in value to twenty slaves."

The following we transcribe from Stedman's Narrative, vol. ii. page 267: "I should not forget to mention that the Gingo negroes are supposed to be Anthropophagi, or cannibals, like the Caribbee Indians, instigated by habitual and implacable revenge. Among the rebels of this tribe, after the taking of Boucore, some pots were found on the fire, with human flesh, which one of the officers had the curiosity to taste; and declared that it was not inferior to some kinds of beef or pork. I have since been informed, by a Mr. Vaugils, an American, who, having travelled a great number of miles inland in Africa, at last came to a place where human arms, legs, and thighs hung upon wooden shambles, and were exposed to sale like butcher's meat. And Captain John Keen, formerly of the Dolphin, but late of the Vianbana schooner, in the Sierra Leone Company's service, positively assured me that, a few years since, when he was on the coast of Africa, in the brig Fame, from Bristol, Mr. Samuel Briggs, owner, trading for wool, ivory, and gold-dust, a Captain Dunningen, with the whole crew belonging to the Nassau schooner, were cut in pieces, salted, and eaten by the negroes of Great Drewin."

But this is nothing to what is related, on good authority, respecting the Giagas, a race of cannibals who are said to have overrun a great part of Africa. These monsters, it is said, are descended from the Agows and Galia, who dwell in the southern extremity of Abyssinia, near the sources of the Nile. Impelled by necessity or the love of plunder, they left their original settlements, and extended their ravages through the heart of Africa, till they were stopped by the Western Ocean. They seized on the kingdom of Benguela, laying to the south of Angola; and in this situation they were found by the Romish missionaries, and by our countryman, Andrew Battel, whose adventures may be found in Purchas's Pilgrim. Both he, and the Capuchin Cavozzi, who resided long among them, and converted several of them to Christianity, gave such an account of their manners as is enough to chill the blood with horror. We shall spare our readers the horrid detail, only observing that human flesh is one of their delicacies, and that they devour it, not from a spirit of revenge, or from any want of other food, but as the most agreeable dainty. Some of their commanders, when they went on an expedition, carried numbers of young women along with them, some of whom were slain almost every day, to gratify this unnatural appetite." See Modern Universal History, vol. xvi. p. 321; also Anzito; also Edin. Encyc. vol. ii. p. 185.

In continuation of this subject, permit us to take a view of these tribes, at a time just before the slave-trade commenced among them with Christian nations. The Portuguese were first to attempt to colonize portions of Africa, with the double view of extending commerce and of spreading the Christian faith. They commenced a settlement of that kind in the regions of Congo, as early as 1578; shortly after which, the Angolas, an adjoining nation, being at war with each other, one party applied to Congo and the Portuguese for aid, which was lent them. Soon a battle took place, in which 120,000 of the Angolas and Giagas were slain. See Lopez's Hist. of Congo.

About the same time, we find in *Dappus de l' Afrique*, the following data:

"The natives of Angola are tall and strong; but, like the rest of the Ethiopians, they are so very lazy and indolent, that, although their soil is admirably adapted to the raising of cattle and the production of grain, they allow both to be destroyed by the wild beasts with which the country abounds. The advantages which they enjoy from climate and soil are thus neglected. * * * We are told that the people in some of the idolatrous provinces still feed on human flesh, and prefer it to all other; so that a dead slave gives a higher price in market than a living one. The cannibals are, in all probability, descended from the barbarous race of the Giagas, by whom the greater part of the eastern and south-eastern provinces were peopled. One most inhuman custom still prevails in this part of the kingdom, and that is, the sacrificing of a number of human victims at the burial of their dead, in testimony of the respect in which their memory is held. The number of these unhappy victims is therefore always in proportion to the rank and wealth of the deceased; and their bodies are afterwards piled up in a heap upon their tombs. * * * This prince (Angola Chilvagni) became a great warrior, enlarged the Angolic dominions, and died much regretted; and was succeeded by his son, Dambi Angola. Unlike his father, he is described as a monster of cruelty, and, happily for his subjects, his reign was of short duration. Nevertheless, he was buried with great magnificence; and, according to the barbarous custom of the country, a mound was erected over his grave, filled with the bones of human victims, who had been sacrificed to his manes."

"He was succeeded by Ngola Chilvagni, a warlike and cruel prince, who carried his victorious arms within a few leagues of Loando. * * * Intoxicated with success, he fancied himself a god, and claimed divine honours. * * * Ngingha was elected his successor, a prince of so cruel a disposition that all his subjects wished his death; which, happily for them, soon arrived. Nevertheless, he was buried with the usual pomp, with the usual number of sacrifices. His son and successor, Bandi Angola, discovered a disposition still more cruel than his father's. * * * To counteract these and other idolatrous rites, and to soften that barbarity of manners which so generally prevailed, the Portuguese, when they established themselves in the country, (1578,) were at great pains to introduce the invaluable blessings of Christianity. * * * So that from the year 1580 to 1590, we are informed, no less a number than 20,000 were converted, and publicly professed Christianity." * * *

"Her remains were no sooner deposited beside her sisters, in the church which she had built, than Mona Zingha declared his abhorrence to Christianity, and revived the horrid Giagan rites. Five women, of the first rank, were by his orders buried in the queen's grave, and upwards of forty persons of distinction were next sacrificed. * * * He wrote the viceroy at Loando, that he had abjured the Christian religion, which he said he had formerly embraced merely out of respect * * * to his queen, and that he now returned to the ancient sect of the Giagas. That there might remain no doubt of his sincerity in that declaration, he followed it with the sacrifice of a great number of victims, in honour of their bloody and idolatrous rites, with the destruction of all Christian churches and chapels, and with the persecution of the Christians in all parts of his kingdom."

And we may here remark, that even the nations of the coast could never be persuaded to abolish human sacrifice, nor to the introduction of Christianity, to any extent, until after the introduction of the slave-trade with Christian nations. See also Osborn's Collection of Travels, vol. ii. p. 537; Mod. Universal Hist. vol. 43; and Edin. Encyc. vol. ii. pp. 107, 109, 110, 113.

Over two hundred years ago, and during the reign of Charles I. of England, Sir Thomas Herbert, (not Lord Edward Herbert, who wrote a deistical book, entitled "Truth,") a gentleman of most elevated connection, and a scholar devoted to science and general literature, with a mind adorned by poetry, and influenced by the strongest impulses of human sympathy; and one, of whom Lord Fairfax said,

"He travelled, not with lucre sotted,
But went for knowledge—and he got it!"

This author, in his Tour in Africa, writes thus: "The inhabitants here along the Golden coast of Guinea, and Benin, bounded with Tombotu, (Timbuctoo,) Gualata, and Mellis, and watered by the great river Niger, but, especially in the Mediterranean (inland) parts, know no God, nor are at all willing to be instructed by nature—'Scire nihil jucundissimum.' Howbeit the Divel, who will not want his ceremonie, has infused prodigious idolatry into their hearts, enough to relish his pallet, and aggrandize their tortures, when he gets power to fry their souls, as the raging sun has scorched their cole-black carcasses. * * * Those countries are full of black-skinned wretches, rich in earth, as abounding with the best minerals and with elephants, but miserable in Demonomy. * * * Let one character serve for all. For colour they resemble chimney-sweepers; unlike them in this, they are of no profession, except rapine and villany make one; for here, *Demonis omnia plena.* * * * But in Loango and the Anziqui the people are little other than divels incarnate; not satisfied with nature's treasures, as gold, precious stones, flesh in variety, and the like; the destruction of men and women neighbouring them, whose dead carcasses they devour with a vulture relish and appetite; whom if they miss, they serve their friends such scurvy sauce, butchering them, and thinking they excuse all in a compliment that they know no better way to express love than in making two bodies in one, by an inseparable union; yea, some, as some report, proffering themselves to the shambles, accordingly are disjointed, and set to sale upon the stalls. * * * The natives of Africa being propagated from Cham, both in their visages and natures, seem to inherit his malediction. * * * They are very brutes. A dog was of that value here that twenty salvages (slaves) have been exchanged for one of them; but of late years the exchange here made for negroes, to transport in the Cariba isles and continent of America, is become a considerable trade."

It will be remembered how great have been the exertions of the British Government to abolish totally the slave-trade in Africa. A great number of slave ships were captured, and the negroes found on board sent to Sierra Leone. Strong hopes were entertained that "*poor, suffering Africa*" was about to be civilized.

We quote from the Hibernian Auxiliary Missionary Report, Christian Observer, 1820, pages 888 and 889:

"The slave-trade, which, like the (fabled) upas, blasts all that is wholesome in its vicinity, has, in one important instance, been here overruled for good. It has been made the means of assembling on one spot, and that on a Christian soil, individuals from almost every nation of the western coast of Africa. It has been made the means of introducing to civilization and religion many hundreds from the interior of that vast continent, who had never seen the face of a white man, nor heard the name of Jesus. And it will be made the means, under God, of sending to the nations beyond the Niger and the Zaire, native missionaries who will preach the Redeemer in the utmost parts of the country, and enable their countrymen to hear in their own tongue the wonderful works of God. European avarice and native profligacy leave no part of Africa unexplored for victims; and these slaves, rescued by our cruisers, and landed on the shores of our colony, are received by our missionaries, and placed in their schools."

The sympathies of the world were excited on this subject, and every civilized heart cried *amen*, in union with the impulsive feelings of this Hibernian Report.

But let us remember to inquire a little into the facts, and examine whether these hopes were well or ill founded. We quote from vol. xix. of the Christian Observer, page 890:

"Mr. Johnson was appointed to the care of Regent's Town, in the month of June, 1816. On looking narrowly into the actual condition of the people intrusted to his care, he felt great discouragement. Natives of twenty-two different nations were there collected together. A considerable number of them had been but recently liberated from the holds of slave-vessels. They were greatly prejudiced against one another, and in a state of continual hostility, with no common medium of intercourse but a little broken English. When clothing was given to them, they would sell it, or throw it away: it was difficult to induce them to put it on; and it was not found practicable to introduce it among them, until led to it by the example of Mr. Johnson's servant-girl. None of them, on their first arrival, seemed to live in a state of marriage; some of them were soon afterwards married by the late Mr. Butscher; but all the blessings of the marriage state and of female purity appeared to be quite unknown. * * * Superstition, in various forms, tyrannized over their minds; many devil's houses sprang up, and all placed their security in wearing gregrees. Scarcely any desire of improvement was discernable. * * * Some, who wished to cultivate the soil, were deterred from doing so by the fear of being plundered of the produce. Some would live in the woods, apart from society; and others subsisted by thieving and plunder: they would steal poultry and pigs from any who possessed them, and would eat them raw; and not a few of them, particularly of the Eboe nation, the most savage of them all, would prefer any kind of refuse meat to the rations which they received from Government."

Doubtless Mr. Johnson and his successors have done all that good men could do, even under the protection of the British Government; but have they, in the least, affected the slave-trade of Africa, otherwise than to divert its direction, or have they diminished it to any observable extent? True, its course has been changed, and its enormities thereby increased tenfold. Instead of its subjects being brought under the regenerating influences of Christianity, they are sacrificed at the shrine of friends at home, or sent among pagans or Mohammedans! Let the Christian philosopher think of these things.

While we recollect the proclamation of the Emperor of Bourno, let us look at the slave-trade as now carried on with the Barbary States, the Arab tribes, and Egypt and Asia, as well as Turkey in Europe. We quote from "Burckhart's Travels in Nubia," as reported in the Christian Observer, vol. xix. p. 459:

"The author had a most favourable opportunity of collecting intelligence and making observations on this subject, (slavery,) as connected with the northeastern parts of Africa by travelling with companies of slaves and slave-merchants through the deserts of Nubia. * * * The chief mart in the Nubian mountains, for the Egyptian and the Arabian slave-trade, is Shendy. * * * To this emporium, slaves are brought from various parts of the interior, and particularly from the idolatrous * * * tribes in the vicinity of Darfour, Bozgho, and Dar Saley."

Our traveller calculated the number sold annually in the market of Shendy at five thousand. "Far the larger part of these slaves are under the age of fifteen."

See page 460: "Few slaves are imported into Egypt without changing masters several times. * * * A slave, for example, purchased at Fertit, is transferred at least six times before he arrives at Cairo. These rapid changes, as might be expected, are productive of great hardship to the unfortunate individuals, especially in the toilsome journey across the deserts. Burckhart saw on sale at Shendy, many children of four or five years old, *without their parents.* * * * Burckhart has entered into the details of cruelties of another kind, practised on the slaves to raise their pecuniary value. The particulars are not suitable for a work of miscellaneous perusal. * * * The great mart, however, for the supply of European and Asiatic Turkey with the kind of slaves required as guardians for the harem, Mr. Burckhart informs us, is not at Shendy, but at a village near Siout, in Upper Egypt, *inhabited chiefly by Christians.*" (Abyssinians, we suppose.)

The mode of marching slaves is described as follows: "On the journey, they are tied to a long pole, one end of which is tied to a camel's saddle, and the other, which is forked, is passed on each side of the slave's neck, and tied behind with a strong cord, so as to prevent him drawing out his head: in addition to this, his right hand is also fastened to the pole, at a short distance from the head, thus leaving only his legs and left arm at liberty. In this manner he marches the whole day behind the camel: at night he is taken from the pole and put in irons. While on the route to Souakim, I saw several slaves carried along in this way. Their owners were afraid of their escaping, or of becoming themselves the objects of their vengeance; and in this manner they would continue to be confined until sold to a master, who, intending to keep them, would endeavour to attach them to his person. In general, the traders seem greatly to dread the effects of sudden resentment in their slaves; and if a grown-up boy is to be whipped, his master first puts him in irons."

Page 333: "Females with children on their backs follow the caravans on foot; and if a camel breaks down, the owner generally loads his slaves with the packages; and if a boy in the evening can only obtain a little butter with his *dhourra* bread, and some grease every two or three days to smear his body and hair, he is contented, and never complains of fatigue. Another cause which induces the merchants to treat the slaves well (?) is their anxiety to dissipate the horror which the negroes all entertain of Egypt and the white people. It is a common opinion in the black slave countries that the Ouleder Rif, or children of Rif, as the Egyptians are there called, devour the slaves, who are transported thither for that purppose: of course, the traders do everything in their power to destroy this belief; but, notwithstanding all their endeavours, it is never eradicated from the mind of the slaves."

Page 462: "The manners of the people of Souakim are the same as those I have already described in the interior, and I have reason to believe that they are common to the whole of eastern Africa, including Abyssinia, where the character of the inhabitants, as drawn by Bruce, seems little different from that of these Nubians. I regret that I am compelled to represent all the nations of Africa, which I have yet seen, in so bad a light."

We next quote from the Family Magazine, 1836, page 439, as follows: "Many of the Dayaks have a rough, scaly scurf on their skin, like the Jacong of the Malay Peninsula. * * * The female slaves of this race, which are found among the Malays, have no appearance of it. * * * With regard to their funeral ceremonies, the corpse * * * remains in the house till the son, the father, or the next of blood, can procure or purchase a slave, who is beheaded at the time the corpse is burned, in order that he may become the *slave* of the deceased in the next world. * * * Nobody can be permitted to marry till he can present a human head of some other tribe to his proposed bride. * * * The head-hunter proceeds in the most cautious manner to the vicinity of the villages of another tribe, and lies in ambush till he can surprise some heedless, unsuspecting wretch, who is instantly decapitated. * * * When the hunter returns, the whole village is filled with joy, and old and young, men and women, hurry out to meet him, and conduct him, with the sound of brazen cymbals, dancing, in long lines, to the house of the female he admires, whose family likewise come out to greet him with dances, and provide him with a seat, and give him meat and drink. He holds the bloody head still in his hand, and puts part of the food into his mouth, after which the females of the family receive the head from him, which they hang up to the ceiling over the door. If a man's wife die, he is not permitted to make proposals of marriage to another, till he has procured another head of a different tribe. The heads they procure in this manner, they preserve with great care, and sometimes consult in divination. The religious opinions connected with this practice are by no means correctly understood: some assert they believe that every person whom a man kills in this world becomes his *slave* in the next. * * * The practice of stealing heads causes frequent wars among the tribes of the Idean. Many persons never can obtain a head; in which case they are generally despised by the warriors and the women. To such a height is it carried, however, that a person who has obtained eleven heads has been seen, and at the same time he pointed out his son, who, a young lad, had procured three."

James Edward Alexander, H. L. S., during the years 1836 and 1837, made an excursion from the Cape of Good Hope into the interior of South Africa and the countries of the Namaquas, Boschmans, and Hill Damaras, under the auspices of Her Majesty's Government, and the Royal Geographical Society, which has been published in two volumes; from which we extract, vol. i. page 126: "I was anxious to ascertain the extent of knowledge among the tribe (Damaras) with which I now dwelt; to learn what they knew of themselves, and of men and things in general; but I must say that they positively know nothing beyond tracing game and breaking in jack-oxen. They did not know one year from another; they only knew that at certain times the trees and flowers bloom, and then rain was expected. As to their own age, they knew no more what it was than idiots. Some even had no names. Of numbers, of course, they were nearly or quite ignorant; few could count above five; and he was a clever fellow who could count his ten fingers. Above all, they had not the least idea of God or of a future state. They were, literally, like the beasts which perish."

Page 163, 164, and 165: "At Chubeeches the people were very poor. * * * Standing in need of a shepherd, I observed here two or three fine little Damara boys, as black as ebony. * * * I said to the old woman to whom Saul belonged, 'You have two boys, and they are starving; you have nothing to give them.' 'This is true,' she replied. 'Will you part with Saul?' said I; 'I want a shepherd, and the boy wants to go with me.' 'You will find him too cunning,' returned the old dame. 'I want a clever fellow,' said I. 'Very well,' she replied; 'give me four cotton handkerchiefs, and he is yours.' 'Suppose,' said I, 'you take two handkerchiefs and two strings of glass beads?' 'Yes! that will do;' and so the bargain was closed; and thus a good specimen of Damara flesh and blood was bought for the value of about four shillings. * * * I told him to go and bring his skins; on which he informed me that he had none, saving what he stood in—and that was his own sable hide, with the addition of the usual strap of leather around his waist, from which hung a piece of jackal's skin in front. Constant exposure to the vicissitudes of the weather, without clothes, hardens the skin of the body like that of the face; and still it is difficult to sleep at nights without proper covering. In cold weather, the poor creatures of Namaqua Land, who may have no karosses, sit cowering over a fire all night, and merely doze with their heads on their knees."

Vol. ii. page 23: "Can any state of society be considered more low and brutal than that in which promiscuous intercourse is viewed with the most perfect indifference; where it is not only practised, but spoken of without any shame or compunction? Some *rave* about the glorious liberty of the savage state, and about the innocence of the children of nature, and say that it is chiefly by the white men that they become corrupt. The Boshmans of Ababres had never seen white men before; they were far removed from the influence of the Europeans."

Vol. i. page 102. "Notwithstanding that some people maintain that there is no nation on earth without religion in some form, however faintly it may be traced in their minds, yet, after much diligent inquiry, I could not discover the slightest feeling of devotion towards a higher and invisible power among the Hill Damaras."

In Mohammedan countries, the most unfavourable portions of the slave's existence, as such, is while in the hands of the geeleb, or slave-merchant, and until he is sold to one who designs to keep him permanently. In the first instance, if negroes, they suffer much in the journey from the place of purchase to that of sale. For instance, it has been known, in the journey from Sennaar and Darfour to the slave-mart at Cairo, or even the intermediate one at Siout, the loss in a slave caravan, of men, women, camels, and horses, amounted to not less than 4000. The circumstances of the mart itself scarcely appear in a more favourable aspect than those of the journey,—whether we regard the miserable beings, as in the market at Cairo, crowded together in enclosures like the sheep-pens in Smithfield market, amid the abominable stench and uncleanness which result from their confinement; whether, as at another great mart at Muscat, we perceive the dealer walking to and fro, with a stick in his hand, between two lots of ill-clothed boys and girls, whom he is offering for sale, proclaiming aloud, as he passes, the price fixed on each; or else leading his string of slaves through the narrow and dirty streets, and calling out their price as he exhibits them in this ambulatory auction. * * * The slaves, variously exhibited, usually appear quite indifferent to the process, or only show an anxiety to be sold, from knowing that as slaves, finally purchased, their condition will be much ameliorated. * * * How little slavery is dreaded is also shown by the fact that even *Mohammedan parents or relatives* are, in cases of emergency, ready enough to offer their children for sale. During the famine which a few years since drove the people of Mosul to Bengal, one could not pass the streets without being annoyed by the solicitations of parents to purchase their boys and girls for the merest trifle; and even in Koordistan, where no constraining motive appeared to exist, we have been sounded as to our willingness to purchase young members of the family. Europeans in the East are scarcely considered amenable to any general rules, but Christians generally are not allowed to possess any other than negro slaves." *London Penny Mag.* 1834, pp. 243, 244; also, *Sketches of Persia*, and *Johnson's Journey from India.*

Appendix, C.

From Havana.

The Cherokee—The Slave Trade—General News.

Correspondence of the New York Daily Times,

Havana, Wednesday, Dec. 15, 1852.

* * * * * * *

The mysterious working of the law is still retaining Capt. Grey and his son under bonds, preventing their return to the United States. There should be in all this month two barks cleared from the United States, bound for the coast of Africa,—one from Baltimore and one from New York, or an Eastern port. There are two fitting out in the harbor of Havana, as I was informed by a friend interested in the black "fleece" of this Spanish "Colchis," schooners of light draught, to get into good concealment up the rivers, and clipper built; at the east end of the island there are two brigs now ready for sea, and one or two to be ready very shortly on the south side—so the work for redemption from barbarism goes bravely on. The lighter vessels, if it should prove expedient for security, are used between the coast and the islands on the coast of Brazil, and they frequently pack into a space where twenty or thirty men would be uncomfortable, from one hundred and fifty to two hundred and fifty negroes—and often they leave the coast with so many on board, that they have scarcely space for provisions and water; and make sail for the Island of Cuba, where they arrive with the numbers vastly diminished by the discount of death, owing to the close and uncomfortable quarters to which they are confined for the long voyage. Can this systematic and regular return of notorious slavers, and their clearance from the ports of Cuba, be accomplished without the knowledge and consent of the authorities? It is impossible; and this charity that covers a multitude of sins, I am compelled to place to the credit of those who could restrain the traffic, if they would exercise the power they possess. In the reign of Alcoy, we had a remarkable instance, which shows the power, even after pocketed compensation, of control over the introduction, when there are found those bold enough to make denunciation in given cases. A cargo had been introduced not far from Havana, within the reach of the railroad, before breakfast, and regularly paid for. But an officer in the infected district was to be removed to make place for a parasite favorite, and before going out of office, he seized some two hundred of the negroes, and they were brought within the reach of the "British and Spanish mixed Court of Justice," and thus secured their eventual freedom, unless they should happen to die, by report and well authenticated documentary evidence, before the expiration of seven years service, the term for covering the expenses incidental to their liberation from life bondage, and protection of the two Governments. The actuating motive was revenge upon the Captain General, who had received the bonus—but his object was very far from being accomplished. The parties called upon Alcoy, with great delicacy, to refund the four or six ounces he had received, but it was one of those cases where correction was impossible—they knew nothing of any such transaction at the palace! The money was not delivered; but under *the usage*, the negroes were sold to the best bidders for the service of seven years, and a good part of the price paid, fell again into the all-absorbing purse of the Captain-General, which he kept well bound with the clasps of charity.

From the Baltimore Sun, of Dec. 8, 1852.

INCREASE OF THE SLAVE TRADE IN CUBA.—All accounts represent a large increase of the slave trade in Cuba, at which, it is alleged, the Spanish officials wink. A letter from Havana gives a list of nine vessels, which have landed at different ports of Cuba, during the present year, 4,170 slaves from Africa. The letter referred to adds:

"This is but the beginning. There is a tacit understanding for the extension of this scheme until ten thousand more have been brought hither, on each of which is paid to officials, for winking at it, three ounces, or fifty-one dollars, making in the aggregate $510,000."

From the same paper, of Jan. 10, 1853.

THE AFRICAN SLAVE TRADE.—Letters from the coast of Africa state that the British government are about to withdraw their naval forces from the coast, and, of course, by such an act, abandon its efforts in that quarter for the suppression of the slave trade.

From the same paper, of Feb. 7, 1853.

A CONFLICT BETWEEN THE BRITISH AND SPANISH AUTHORITIES ABOUT A SLAVER.—A slaver, in possession of an English prize crew, was lately taken possession of by a number of Spanish soldiers, at Havana. The English captain (Hamilton) prepared for immediate recapture, and manned his boats for that purpose, but the English consul interfered, and advised waiting instructions from home. Thus the matter remains, while it is said, the soldiers are busy in effacing the evidence which would condemn her as a slaver. It is believed the Queen-mother is the owner of the brig, and hence this bold measure of the Captain-General. Meanwhile, much ill-feeling is manifested by the officials towards the English residents.

From the New York Weekly Times, of April, 30, 1853.

SLAVE TRADE: ITS ABOLITION.

Clarkson, Wilberforce and Pitt advocated the abolition of the slave-trade, upon the supposition that the abolition of slavery would follow as the necessary result. It was the prevalent error of that time. The idea prevailed in the Convention which framed the Constitution of the United States. It was imagined that the existing negro stock must naturally disappear beneath the rigor of labor and hard treatment. It was taken for granted that the cessation of the former supply would burden the actual slaves with additional toils and sufferings, in order to make up the requisite return, per annum, of the mill or plantation. Mortality was therefore set down as a crescent quantity; while marriages and births, as always where the conditions of life are unfavorable, were assumed to be steadily decreasing. There would be nothing to repair the exhaustion; and the period between the termination of the slave-trade and the termination of slavery was regarded as a question of time. It might be half a century; possibly more; probably less. It never seems to have been thought of, that the legitimate effect of the slave-trade suppression might be beneficial to the institution of Slavery, and calculated to prolong it indefinitely.

But such is the evidence of facts. We have only to draw a comparison between Cuba and the Southern States of this Union, to ascertain it. Cuba may be regarded as representing the condition of things where the slave population is still kept up by importations. The slave-trade between Cuba and Africa has been very slightly affected by the several conventions for its extinction. It has only been rendered more hazardous. The negroes have been males; because males are better able to bear the terrors of the transit, prolonged and heightened as they were by the necessity of avoiding the English cruisers; and because the planters have preferred them, as field hands, to women, who were found, in other respects, expensive and troublesome. The prospect of the importations ceasing was too indefinite to excite apprehensions of the stock perishing from this short-sighted policy. It was only in 1834, when the remonstrances, threats and redoubled vigilance of England gave the alarm, that the demand for females became active, and the dealers were induced to proportion their shipments more wisely. But there has been no sensible falling off in the number and bulk of the cargoes. The slave population, according to the census of the island, taken in 1819, amounted to 195,145. The return made no separate returns for the two sexes. The census of 1841 did so, however, showing the number of males to be 281,250; of females, 155,245; in all, 436,495. Now there is every reason to believe that previous to 1834, the proportion of male to female slaves was as ten to one. It was notorious that whole plantations, employing two or three hundred hands, had not one woman on them. The partiality to the males was general. There is no doubt that the gain of 241,350, which is noted between 1819 and 1841, is entirely the fruit of the African trade. Nor is this all. With such disparity between the sexes, the increase could not begin to replace the annual mortality. Signor Tenaza, an intelligent Cuban, who has just published a tract on the subject at Paris, estimates the actual importations into the Island at 431,925 in the twenty-one years ending in 1841, or about *twenty thousand per annum*. This is probably the fact; and although we have no official returns of the population, or the extent of the traffic since that date, we know that, although the influx has diminished very considerably, it has not done so sufficiently to render the breeding of negroes a profitable business. It is still cheaper to buy men, than to buy women and rear children. And because the external supply still continues, the exaction of excessive labor and the infliction of the cruelties, which so harrowed up the souls of Wilberforce and his followers, continue; only increasing as the price of negroes diminishes. The Island planter applies the "sweating" system to his serfs, because there is no difficulty in replacing the wear and tear, from the cargoes of such men as Captain Capo, whom our letters described the other day. The natural effect of this inhuman system is plainly visible. England protests against it. One measure has been taken to obviate a portion of the mischief, and the rest will presently yield to the influences now brought to bear upon the Court of Madrid. Slavery will be presently abolished in Cuba; and it will be abolished a century before the advantages of free labor are understood at the South, and the institution dispensed with.

For in spite of "Uncle Tom," the treatment of the southern slave is not grossly inhuman. It is always fair to apply the principles of natural increase to such questions; and the application to American slavery shows a very large yearly increase, which could not possibly have place, were labor excessive, fare meagre, and general treatment unindulgent. All the evidence, including that of our own correspondent in Virginia, goes to prove that the planting interest is impoverished because the labor exacted from the slave is so trifling and so totally inadequate to the cost of living. This moderation results from the cessation of the foreign slave traffic. The slave is valuable in proportion to his price. If he have cost the expense of rearing his value is great, and he is treated accordingly. When free trade in negroes was the rule, they cost little and were abused terribly. Since prohibition was decreed they have cost extensively and are treated considerately. And while the institution retains this mild type, and domestic slave-trade alone exists, transferring the chattel from the less to the more profitable field of labor, but nowhere encouraging barbarity of treatment, the indignation requisite to enforce abolition, will scarcely reach the proper pitch of intensity. If ever slavery at the South attain the degree of mischief, direct or indirect, which it has elsewhere occasioned, the public opinion of mankind will act upon it as in Cuba: where slavery is, after all, attacked less for its own demerits than for the encouragement it affords the man-stealer. The peculiar influences we have referred to, make the continuance of slave labor on the island, contingent upon the continuance of the slave traffic; and the slave traffic can only be suppressed by the abandonment of the island by the Spanish Government.

From the London Guardian, of Jan. 26. 1853.

In this state of things, when the Government of Madrid must be well aware that the United States is only waiting for the favorable opportunity, what is its conduct? It allows its officials in Cuba to involve themselves in petty squabbles with the officers of American merchant steamers touching at the island, and it does its best to get up a quarrel with its best ally, Great Britain, by its unblushing prosecution of the slave-trade. In defiance of the most solemn engagements, and of assurances repeated *usque ad nauseam,* to our ambassador at Madrid, slavers are daily leaving Cuba with the manifest connivance of the authorities, and cargoes of slaves are regularly landed, and a duty paid to the Government as if on ordinary merchandise. Already the United States journals are chuckling over the prospect of a quarrel between Spain and Great Britain, which they seem to consider would greatly facilitate their own ulterior designs on the Island. The Spaniards have generally contrived to render it impossible for their best friends to help them, and so it may perhaps be again. And, dangerous as the proximity of the Americans in Cuba to our own West Indian colonies might appear to ourselves, there is little doubt that the interests of humanity in general would gain by the substitution of the Anglo-Saxon for the Spanish race in that magnificent island.

As a pendant to this, take the following, which tells its own story, and needs no comment:—

Proclamation.—Whereas, Messrs. Hyde, Hodge & Co. of London, contractors with Her Britannic Majesty's government, to furnish laborers from the African coast for the West Indies, have sent some of their ships to the coast of the republic, offering an advance of ten dollars for every person who may be induced to emigrate; and whereas, the extinction of the slave trade has left large numbers of predial and other laborers in the possession of the chiefs and principal men of the country, while the offer of ten dollars each is nearly equivalent to the amount formerly paid for slaves, during the prevalence of the slave trade, and which operated mainly in producing and sustaining the wars, by which the country was distracted; and whereas, certain refractory chiefs are reported to have engaged with the agents of said Company to furnish a number of laborers, and are further known to have in concealment, near Grand Cape Mount, a number of the unhappy victims of their predatory excursions; and whereas, complaint has been made to the government that persons are held to be sent off without their voluntary consent, or the consent of their natural guardians; therefore, to prevent the abuses and evils which might otherwise result from the enterprise:

Be it known by this proclamation, to all whom it may concern, that the law regulating passports must be strictly observed—that vessels carrying or intending to carry away emigrants must come to this port with their emigrants on board, to obtain passports, in order that an opportunity may be presented to the government to ascertain whether the emigration be free or constrained. Every violation of the law regulating passports will be visited with the utmost penalty of the law in that case made and provided,

Done at Monrovia, this twenty-sixth day of February, in the year of our Lord one thousand eight hundred and fifty-three, and of the republic the fifth. J. J. ROBERTS.

(L. S.) By the President, H. TEAGE,
Secretary of State.

Appendix, D.

Negro Communicants.

The Editor of the New York Observer, in an article introductory to Miss M'Intosh's letter, speaking of the descendants of the Highlanders and Germans, who were the first settlers of Georgia, says:—

"They inherit the religious principles of their fathers. They have the Bible and love to read it. They go to that blessed book, and not to Northern men or Englishmen, to Northern ladies or English ladies, to learn their duties to their slaves. They do not find in any part of that book the doctrine of the immediate abolitionists. They find there that the slave is a man and a brother; that God made him; that God loves him; that Christ died for him; and that God will not bless, and Christ will not love, the master who does not love his slave, or the slave who does not love and obey his master. With this simple teaching, and withdrawing themselves, as the Apostle directs, from those who teach otherwise, they have been laboring quietly and unostentatiously, amidst all the discouragements caused by the curse of slavery on one side, and the agitations of abolitionists on the other, to establish schools and churches, and to fit the negro for the enjoyment of all the happiness of which he is capable here and hereafter; and with such success, that they and their co-laborers count, as one of the fruits of their toil, more than 300,000 negro members of evangelical churches—a greater number, as has been frequently stated, than the aggregate number in all the churches under Protestant missionaries in all the countries of the heathen world."

APPENDIX, E.

EXTRACTS FROM THE STATUTES AND DECISIONS OF SOME OF THE SLAVE STATES.

1. Slaves are persons and not *mere* chattels. *Devereaux's N. C. Reports*, 4. 340. STATE VS. EDMOND, A SLAVE.—This was a trial for concealing a slave on board a vessel with intent to convey her out of the State and enable her to escape. On this charge the prisoner was convicted, but various exceptions being taken to the ruling of the Court below, it came up for a hearing before the Superior Court, where it was contended, amongst other things, that the prisoner, being a slave, was but a chattel, a thing, and not to be considered a "person" within the meaning of the Act of Assembly. Decided by the Court that, "The prisoner, although a slave, is a 'person' *in the natural acceptation of that term.*" "A slave is a person capable of committing crime, and subject to punishment." "I think the prisoner is a person, within the words and meaning of the Act of Assembly." (See also the passages in *italics* below in the next citation.)

2. Power of the Master over his slave:—Does not extend to life or limb.

THE STATE OF MISSISSIPPI VS. JONES. *June T.* 1820. *Walker's Rep.* 83. *Per Cur. Clarke, J.* "The question in this case, arising in arrest of judgment, transferred on doubts from Adams superior court, is, whether, in this State, murder can be committed on a slave. Because individuals may have been deprived of many of their rights by society, it does not follow, that they have been deprived of all their rights. *In some respects*, slaves may be considered as chattels, *but in others, they are regarded as men.* The law views them as capable of committing crimes. This can only be upon the principle, that they are men and rational beings. The Roman law has been much relied on by the counsel of the defendant. That law was confined to the Roman Empire, giving the power of life and death over captives in war, as slaves, but it no more extended here, than the similar power given to parents over the lives of their children. Much stress has also been laid by the defendant's counsel, on the case cited from Taylor's Reports, decided in North Carolina; yet, in that case, two judges against one were of opinion, that killing a slave was murder. Judge Hall, who delivered the dissenting opinion in the above case, based his conclusions, as we conceive, upon erroneous principles, by considering the laws of Rome applicable here. His inference, also, that a person cannot be condemned capitally, because he may be liable in a civil action, is not sustained by reason or authority, but appears to us to be in direct opposition to both. At a very early period in Virginia, the power of life over slaves was given by statute; but Tucker observes, that as soon as these statutes were repealed, it was at once considered by their courts, that the killing of a slave might be murder. Commonwealth vs. Dolly Chapman; indictment for maliciously stabbing a slave under a statute. It has been determined in Virginia *that slaves are persons.* In the Constitution of the United States, slaves are *expressly designated as "persons."* In this State the legislature have considered slaves as reasonable and accountable beings, and it would be a stigma upon the character of the State, and a reproach to the administration of justice, if the life of a slave could be taken with impunity, or if he could be murdered in cold blood, without subjecting the offender to the highest penalty known to the criminal jurisprudence of the country. *Has the slave no rights, because he is deprived of his freedom?* He is still a human being, and possesses all those rights of which he is not deprived by the positive provisions of the law; but in vain shall we look for any law passed by the enlightened and philanthropic legislature of this State, giving *even to the master*, much less to a stranger, power over the life of a slave. Such a statute would be worthy the age of Draco or Caligula, and would be condemned by the unanimous voice of the people of this State, where cruelty to slaves, much less [more?] the taking away of life meets with universal reprobation. By the provisions of our law, a slave may commit murder, and be punished with death, why then is it not murder to kill a slave? *Can a mere chattel commit murder, and be subject to punishment?*

Villeins, in England, were more degraded than our slaves. It is true, that formerly the murder of a villein was not punished with death, but neither was the murder of a freeman then so punished. The only difference between the freeman and the slave was in the magnitude of the fine. In England, killing a villein was as much murder as killing a lord. Yet villeins were then the most abject slaves, and could be bought and sold as chattels; but because slaves can be bought and sold, it does not follow that they can be deprived of life. The right of the master exists, not by force of the law of nature or nations, but by virtue only of the positive law of the state; and although that gives to the master the right to command the services of the slave, requiring the master to feed and clothe the slave from infancy till death, yet it gives the master no right to take the life of the slave; and if the offence be not murder, it is not a crime, and subjects the offender to no punishment. The taking away the life of a reasonable creature, under the king's peace, with malice aforethought, express or implied, is murder at common law. Is not a slave a reasonable creature?—is he not a human being? And the meaning of this phrase, *reasonable creature*, is a human being. For the killing a lunatic, an idiot, or even a child unborn, is murder, as much as the killing a philosopher; and has not the slave as much reason as a lunatic, an idiot, or an unborn child? All are in the king's peace, except alien enemies *flagrante bello*. A distinction once existed in England, between the killing a Dane and a Saxon; but even in Coke's time, the killing any rational being was murder. Jews were then regarded in a light more odious than the most abject slave; yet to kill them was murder. So to kill one attainted, or an outlawed felon, or even an alien enemy, except in battle, might be murder. The term, "king's peace," means the place where the crime is committed, the actual venue, and not a particular class of human beings.

At one period of the Roman history, a history written in the blood of vanquished nations, slaves were regarded as captives, whose lives had been spared in battle, and the savage conqueror might take away the life of the captive, and therefore he might take away the life of the slave. But the civil law of Rome extirpated this barbarous privilege, and rendered the killing a slave a capital offence. When the northern barbarians overran Southern Europe, they had no laws but those of conquerors and conquered, victors and captives; yet, even by this savage people, no distinction was recognized between the killing, in cold blood, a slave or a freeman. And shall this court, in the nineteenth century, establish a principle too sanguinary for the code even of the Goths and Vandals, and extend to the whole community, the right to murder slaves with impunity?

The motion to arrest the judgment must be overruled."

State vs. Reed, June T. 1823. 2 Hawk's N. C. Reports, 454. "This was an indictment for the murder of a slave, which concluded at *common law*. The prisoner was found guilty, and moved in arrest, because of the insufficiency of the indictment. The motion was overruled, and sentence passed, from which the prisoner appealed.

Henderson, J. This record presents the question, Is the killing of a slave, at this day, a statute or common law offence? And if a common law offence, what punishment is affixed to the act charged in this record? Homicide is the killing any reasonable creature. Murder is the killing any reasonable creature, within the protection of the law, with malice prepense, that is, with a design, and without excuse. That a slave is a reasonable creature, or more properly, a human being, is not, I suppose, denied. But it is said, that being property, he is not within the protection of the law, and, therefore, the law requires not the manner of his death; that the owner alone is interested, and the state no more concerned, independently of the acts of the legislature on that subject, than in the death of a horse. This is an argument, the force of which I cannot feel, and leads to consequences abhorrent to my nature: yet if it be the law of the land, it must be so pronounced. I disclaim all rules or laws in investigating this question, but the common law of England, as brought to this country by our forefathers, when they emigrated hither, and as adopted by them, and as modified by various declarations of the legislature since, so as to justify the foregoing definition. If, therefore, a slave is a reasonable creature, within the protection of the law, the killing a slave with malice prepense, is murder by the common law. With the services and labors of the slave, the law has nothing to do; they are the master's, by the law; the government and control of them belong exclusively to him. Nor will the law interfere upon the ground that the State's rights, and not the master's, have been violated.

In establishing slavery, then, the law vested in the master the absolute and uncontrolled right to the services of the slave, and the means of enforcing these services, follow as necessary consequences; nor will the law weigh with the most scrupulous nicety his acts in relation thereto;* but the life of a slave being noways necessary to be placed in the power of the owner for the full enjoyment of his services, the law takes care of that, and with me it has no weight, to show that by the laws of Ancient Rome or Modern Turkey, an absolute power is given to the master over the life of his slave. I answer, *these are not the laws of our country*, nor the model from which they were taken; it is abhorrent to the hearts of all those who have felt the influence of the mild precepts of Christianity; and if it is said, that no law is produced to show that such is the state of slavery in our land, I call on them to show the law by which the *life* of a slave is placed at the disposal of his master. In addition, I must say, that if it is not murder, it is no offence, not even a bare trespass. Nor do I think that anything should be drawn from the various acts of the legislature on the subject. Legislative exposition is good while the system of law thus expounded is in force; but when the whole system is abandoned, as is done by the act of 1817, exposition should be laid aside. But if the legislative exposition is to have weight, the last should be received, and the act last mentioned speaks the language of declaration, and not that of enactment. But it is not admitted that the acts prior to the act of 1817, are by any means a clear legislative declaration, that it was no offence to kill a slave anterior to any statutory provision. The first enactment that we have on the subject, is a simple declaration, that if any person shall maliciously kill a slave, he shall suffer imprisonment. From this we are not absolutely to conclude, that the legislature thought that before that time it was no offence; it is quite possible that juries had not applied the principles of the common law in their purity to the offence; for we see the spirit of the times by the legislative act; but that spirit is happily no more. I would mention as an additional argument, that if the contrary exposition of the law is correct, then the life of a slave is at the mercy

* The same is true in other and very different relations in life. Parents and schoolmasters may correct a child: "but the correction must be moderate, and in a proper manner, and for the good of the child: but if the parent or master have not acted in great violation of justice and propriety, their conduct *will not be weighed in golden scales.*" Bouvier, Institutes of American Law, vol. 3. p. 497, and marginal references.

of any one, even a vagabond; and I would ask, What law is it that punishes, at this day, the most wanton and cruel dismemberment of a slave, by severing a limb from his body, if life should be spared? There is no statute on the subject; it is the common law cut down, it is true, by statute or custom, so as to tolerate slavery, yielding to the owner the services of the slave, and any right incident thereto, as necessary for its full enjoyment, *but protecting the life and limbs of the human being;* and in these particulars, it does not admit that he is without the protection of the law. I think, therefore, that judgment of death should be pronounced against the prisoner."

The statute of Georgia, of Dec. 2, 1799, requires, (Sec. 2, marginal title,) "the same mode of prosecution and measure of punishment for killing a slave as a white person."

The statute of South Carolina, of 1740, P. L. 173, enacts that "if any person shall on sudden heat of passion, or by undue correction, kill *his own slave*, or the slave of any other person, he shall forfeit the sum of three hundred pounds current money.

STATE VS. CHEATWOOD.—Fall T. 1834. 2 Hill's S. C. Rep. 459. *Harper, J.*, held that the object of the act of 1821, relative to the murder of slaves, was, to make the murder of a slave, of the same grade and character as the murder of a white man or free man at common law, and is to be made out by the same kind of proof."

3. Not even when fleeing from his master.

WITSELL VS. EARNEST & PARKER.—Jan. T. 1818. 1 Nott & M'Cord's S. C. Rep. 182. *Per. Cur. Colcock, J.* "By the statute of 1740, any white man may apprehend, and moderately correct any slave who may be found out of the plantation at which he is employed; and if the slave assaults the white person, he may be killed; *but a slave who is merely flying away cannot be killed.* Nor can the defendants be justified by the common law, if we consider the negro as a person; for they were not clothed with the authority of the law to apprehend him as a felon, and without such authority he could not be killed."

4. Nor to inflicting cruel punishment.

MARKHAM VS. CLOSE.—Sept. T. 1831. 2 Louisiana Rep. 581. Held by the court, Porter, J., that the infliction of cruel punishment on the slave, by his master, is a criminal offence, and must be punished by a criminal prosecution, and not before a civil tribunal.

Laws of Georgia. Cobb's Digest, Athens, Ga. 1851. p. 971. Act of May 10, 1770. Preamble. "*Whereas*, from the increasing number of slaves in this province, it is necessary as well to make proper regulations for the future ordering and governing such slaves, and to ascertain and prescribe the punishment of crimes by them committed, as to settle and *limit* by positive laws, the extent of the power of the owners of such slaves over them, so that they may be kept in due subjection and obedience, and owners or persons having the care and management of such slaves, *may be restrained from excessive and unnecessary rigor or wanton cruelty* over them: *Therefore, be it enacted,*" &c.

Laws of Maryland, 1715. Chap. 44. Sec. 21. "*And be it further enacted by the authority aforesaid,* That if any master or mistress of any servant whatsoever, or overseer by order or consent of any such master or mistress, shall deny, and not provide sufficient meat, drink, lodging and clothing, or shall unreasonably burthen them beyond their strength with labour, or debar them of their necessary rest and sleep, or excessively beat and abuse them, or shall give them above ten lashes for any one offence, the same being sufficiently proved before the justices of the county courts, the said justices have hereby full power and authority for the first and second offence, to levy such fine upon such offender as to them shall seem meet, not exceeding one thousand pounds of tobacco, to the use of his majesty, his heirs and successors, for the support of government, and for the third offence, *to set such servant so wronged at liberty, and free from servitude*."

Laws of Kentucky. Morehead & Brown's Digest. Frankfort, 1834. Act of Jan 28, 1830, Sec. 4. "*Be it further enacted*, That if any owner of a slave shall treat such slave cruelly and inhumanly, so as in the opinion of the jury to endanger the life or limb of such slave, or shall not supply his slave with sufficient food and raiment, it shall and may be lawful for any person acquainted with the fact or facts, to state and set forth in a petition to the circuit court, the facts or any of them aforesaid of which the defendant hath been guilty, and pray that such slave or slaves *may be taken from the possession of the owner* and sold for the benefit of such owner, agreeably to the seventh article of the constitution."

Sec. 5, Makes it obligatory on the court to inquire into the truth of the allegations, and if they are found to be sustained, to grant the petition.

Civil Code of Louisiana. Article 192. "In like manner, no owner shall be compelled to sell his slave, but in one of two cases, to wit: the first, when * * *; the second, when the master shall be convicted of cruel treatment of his slave, and the judge shall deem proper to pronounce, besides the penalty established for such cases, that the slave shall be sold at public auction, in order to place him out of the reach of the power which his master has abused."

5. The Lord's day, a day of rest to the slave.

Laws of Maryland. 1723. Chap. 16, sec. 10, *enacts*, "That no one having children, servants or slaves, shall command, or wittingly, or willingly suffer any of them to do any manner of work or labor on the Lord's day, (works of necessity and charity always excepted,) on penalty of two hundred pounds of tobacco."

Laws of Georgia. Cobb's Digest, p. 971. Act of May 10, 1770, sec. 41. "If any person shall on the Lord's day, commonly called Sunday, employ any slave in any work or labor, (work of absolute necessity, and the necessary occasions of the family only excepted,) every person so offending shall forfeit and pay the sum of ten shillings for every slave he, she, or they shall so cause to work or labor."

6. Provision for the old and infirm.

Laws of Georgia. Act of Dec. 24, 1832. "An act to establish an Infirmary for the relief and protection of aged and afflicted negroes, in the State of Georgia," sec. 5, provides for receiving slaves, on payment by their masters of a sum to be determined by the Directors, the payment to go to the support of the Institution.

The Act of Dec. 12, 1815, makes it the duty of the Inferior Courts of the several Counties to relieve old or infirm slaves, neglected by their masters, and empowers the said Courts to sue for, and recover from the owner the amount expended.

There is a similar provision in Maryland, and, I presume, in the other slave States.

7. Husband and wife.

Laws of Maryland. 1832, chap. 317, sec. 8. "*And be it enacted*, That in all cases where the wife or the husband, or the male or female united in wedlock with any slave held and owned in this State by any citizen thereof shall be a slave owned and possessed by an inhabitant of any adjoining State, district or territory, it shall and may be lawful for the owner aforesaid of such wife or husband, or person united in wedlock, to purchase, import, and bring into this State, from such adjoining State, district or territory, the said wife, husband or person; *Provided*, the solemnization of the marriage ceremony between such slaves, according to the form of some one of the churches or religious communities of this State, and by a minister of such church or religious community, be proved by the affidavit in writing of the person so purchasing such slave, or by the affidavit of some other creditable white person, and left to be recorded," &c.

8. Mother and child.

Laws of Louisiana. Act of Jan. 31, 1829, sec. 16. *Be it further enacted*, That if any person or persons shall sell the mother of any slave child or children, under the age of ten years, separate from said child or children, or shall, the mother living, sell any slave child or children, of ten years of age, or under, separate from said mother, [he] shall incur the penalty of the sixth section of this act;" that is, (see sec. 6,) "suffer a fine *not less than one thousand dollars*, nor more than two thousand dollars, and an imprisonment of *not less than six months*, nor more than one year, and shall moreover *forfeit the slave or slaves*."

In the Code of Alabama, p. 392, Title 5, chap. 4, secs. 2056 and 2057, is a similar provision, when the sale is under legal process.

So too in the Decisions of the Courts:

Fitzhugh et Ux. vs. Foot et al. April T. 1801. 3 Call's Va. Rep. 13.

Held by the court, that an equal division of slaves, in number and value, is not always possible, and sometimes improper, when it cannot be exactly done without separating infant children from their mothers, which humanity forbids, *and will not be countenanced in a court of equity;* so that a compensation for excess must, in such cases, be made and received in money.

9. Amalgamation.

Laws of Maryland. 1715, chap. 44, sec. 27. "Any white man that shall beget any negro woman with child," "*shall become a servant* for and during the term of seven years."

1728. Chap. 4. Preamble. "Whereas by the act of Assembly relating to servants and slaves, there is no provision made * * * for the punishment of free negro women, having bastard children by white men; *and forasmuch as such copulations are as unnatural and inordinate as between white women and negro men*," &c.

10. Testimony.

STATE vs. SIMS. Dec. T. 1830. 2 Bailey's S. C. Rep. 29. The defendant being convicted of being accessory to a murder by a number of slaves, who had been tried, convicted, and executed, he moved for a new trial, on the ground "that the declarations of the said slaves, as to their agency in the murder, and the mode in which they perpetrated it, were received in evidence; and the declaration of each slave was received, not only as to his own guilt, but as to the acts of others."

The Court, Johnson, J., overruled the motion for a new trial, and decided that the confession of a slave of his own guilt, as principal, is admissible in evidence on the trial of a free white man as accessory before the fact.

South Carolina. Cooper and McCord's Statutes at large, vol. 7: Charleston, 1840. Act of May 10, 1740, sec. 39. "And *whereas*, by reason of the extent and distance of plantations in this Province, the inhabitants are far removed from each other, and many cruelties may be committed on slaves, because no white person may be present to give evidence of the same, unless some method be provided for the better discovery of such offences; and as slaves are under the government, so they ought to be under the protection of masters and managers of plantations; *Be it therefore enacted* by the authority aforesaid, That if any slave shall suffer in life, limb, or member, or shall be maimed, *beaten or abused*, contrary to the directions and true intent and meaning of this Act, when no white person shall be present, or being present, shall neglect or refuse to give evidence, or be examined upon oath, concerning the same, in every such case, the owner or other person who shall have the care and government of such slave, and in whose possession or power such slave shall be, shall be deemed taken, reputed and adjudged to be guilty of such offence, and shall be proceeded against accordingly, without further proof, unless such owner or other person as aforesaid, can make the contrary appear by good and sufficient evidence, *or shall, by his own oath, clear and exculpate himself;* which oath, every court where such offence shall be tried, is hereby empowered to administer, and to acquit the offender accordingly, if clear proof of the offence be not made by two witnesses at least; any law, usage or custom to the contrary notwithstanding."

Disqualification as a witness does not extend to remote admixtures of negro blood.

STATE vs. DAVIS AND HANNA. Dec. T. 1831, 2 Bailey's S. C. Rep. 558. "Harper, J., in delivering the opinion of the court, observed, * * * 'It is certainly true, as laid down by the presiding judge, that 'every admixture of African blood with the European, or white, is not to be referred to the degraded class.' It would be dangerous and cruel to subject to this disqualification a person bearing all the features of a white, on account of some remote admixture of negro blood; nor has the term mulatto, or person of color, I believe, been popularly attributed to such person. The shades are infinite, and it is difficult to fix a limit. I do not know that we can lay down any other rule than to give what appears to be the popular meaning of the word: to wit, that where there is a distinct and visible admixture of negro blood, the person is to be denominated a mulatto, or person of color. It is a question for the jury. In determining it, they may have the evidence of inspection as to color, and the peculiar negro features; the evidence of reputation, as to parentage; and such evidence as was offered in the present case, of the person having been received in society, and exercised the privilege of a white man."

In Lousiana and North Carolina, a presumption of slavery arises from a black complexion, but none from that of a mulatto:—*vide* State vs. Cecil, 2 Martin's La. Rep. 208; Pilie vs. Lalande et al. 19 Martin's La. Rep. 648; Gobu vs. Gobu, 1 Taylor's N. C. Rep. 164; Scott vs. Williams, 1 Devereaux's N. C. Rep. 376; and others.

Prescription is never pleadable against a claim of freedom.

Delphine vs. Deveze, June T. 1824, 14 Martin's La. Rep. 650. Per. Cur. Porter, J. "The plaintiff urges, she is descended from one Marie Catherine, a negro woman now deceased, who was the slave of a certain Marie Durse, and that the said Marie emancipated, and set free, Catherine and her children, Florence, Luce, and Catherine, the mother of the petitioner. She complains that the defendant illegally holds her in slavery, and prays that she may be decreed free, and recover damages for the injury she has sustained by being held in servitude. The defendant pleaded the general issue, and prescription. We shall, before entering on the merits, dispose of the exception, which forms the second ground for defence in the defendant's answer. We do so by referring to the third Partida, title twenty-nine, law twenty-four, in which we find it provided, that if a man be free, no matter how long he may be held by another, as a slave, his state or condition cannot be thereby changed, nor can he be reduced to slavery, in any manner whatever, on account of the time he may have been held in servitude. The plaintiff is entitled to her freedom."

Oatfield vs. Waring. May T. 1817, 14 Johnson's N. Y. Rep. 188. Per Cur. Spencer. J. * * * "All presumptions in favor of personal liberty ought to be made."

Metayer vs. Metayer. Jan. T. 1819, 6 Martin's La. Rep. 16. Held by the court a slave who enjoyed her freedom in Hispaniola during the late revolution, may reckon that time in establishing her right to freedom by prescription.

In suits for freedom, hearsay evidence is admissible to prove pedigree:—*vide* Jenkins vs. Tom et al. 1 Wash. Va. Rep. and Vaughan vs. Phebe, 1 Martin and Yerger's Tenn. Rep. 1.

Mahoney vs. Ashton. Oct. T. 1797, 4 Harris and M'Henry's Md. Rep. "On a trial for freedom, the deposition of Henry Davis was read, in which he stated, that he had heard his uncle, David Davis, (who is deceased,) say, that it was the report of the neighbourhood that if she, Joice, (meaning the ancestor of the petitioner,) had had justice done her, she ought to have been free; and this he heard sundry times from his uncle when talking the matter over. The counsel for the defendant objected to reading the evidence to the jury.

The court, Chase, Ch. J., overruled the objection, and determined it should be given to the jury."

11. The Fugitive Slave Law.

No. 31. *An Act to amend and supplementary to the Act entitled "An Act respecting fugitives from justice and persons escaping from the service of their masters," approved February* 12, 1793. Commissioners of the Circuit Court of the United States, now, or hereafter to be, appointed under any act of Congress, and thereby authorized to exercise powers given in section 33 of the act of September 24, 1789, are authorized and required to perform the duties required by this act. The Superior Courts of the organized Territories may appoint commissioners, who shall have the same powers as commissioners of the said Circuit Courts, and the number of commissioners shall be from time to time enlarged, with a view to afford reasonable facilities to reclaim fugitives from labor, and promptly to discharge the duties imposed by this act. They shall have concurrent jurisdiction with the judges of the said courts in term time and vacation, and shall grant certificates to claimants, upon satisfactory proof, with authority to take and remove such fugitives, under the restrictions herein contained, to the State or Territory from which such persons may have escaped or fled, and shall receive in full for services a fee of $10, if a certificate is granted, or of $5 where the proof does not allow the granting of a certificate, in either case to be paid by the claimant. And the better to enable the said commissioners to execute their duties faithfully and efficiently, they are hereby empowered, within their counties respectively, to appoint, in writing, any suitable persons, from time to time, to execute all such processes as may be issued by them in the lawful performance of their respective duties, with authority to such commissioners, or the persons to be appointed by them, to execute process as aforesaid, to summon and call to their aid the bystanders or *posse comitatus* of the proper county, when necessary, and the persons thus appointed shall each receive from the claimant $5 for each person arrested and taken before a commissioner, with other reasonable fees for additional necessary services. All good citizens are hereby commanded to aid and assist in the prompt and efficient execution of this law, whenever their services may be required, as aforesaid, for that purpose, and said warrants shall run and be executed by said officers anywhere in the State within which they are issued. If any marshal or deputy marshal shall refuse to receive any process, when tendered, or to use all proper means diligently to execute the same, he shall, on conviction thereof, be fined in the sum of $1000, to the use of such claimant, on the motion of such claimant, by the Circuit or District Court for the district of such marshal, and after arrest of such fugitive by such marshal or his deputy, or whilst at any time in his custody under the provisions of this act, should such fugitive escape, whether with or without the assent of such marshal or his deputy, the marshal shall be liable on his official bond to be prosecuted for the benefit of such claimant, for the full value of the service or labor of said fugitive in the State, Territory, or District whence he escaped. The marshal, deputies, clerks, &c., shall be paid for their services like fees as for similar services in like cases, to be paid wholly by the claimant, if the services are rendered exclusively in the arrest, &c., of a fugitive.

§ 6. When a person held to service or labor in any State or Territory of the United States has heretofore or shall hereafter escape into another State or Territory of the United States, the person or persons to whom such service or labor may be due, or his, her, or their agent or attorney, duly authorized, by power of attorney, in writing, acknowledged and certified under the seal of some legal officer or court of the State or Territory in which the same may be executed, may pursue and reclaim such fugitive person, either by procuring a warrant from some one of the courts, judges, or commissioners aforesaid, of the proper circuit, district, or county, for the apprehension of such fugitive from service or labor, or by seizing and arresting such fugitive, where the same can be done without process, and by taking, or causing such person to be taken, forthwith before such court, judge, or commissioner, whose duty it shall be to hear and determine the case of such claimant in a summary manner; and upon satisfactory proof being made, by deposition or affidavit, in writing, to be taken and certified by such court, judge, or commissioner, or by other satisfactory testimony, duly taken and certified by some court, magistrate, justice of the peace, or other legal officer authorized to administer an oath and take depositions under the laws of the State or Territory from which such person owing service or labor may have escaped, with a certificate of such magistrate or other authority, with the seal of the proper court or officer thereto attached, which seal shall be sufficient to establish the competency of the proof, and with proof, also by affidavit, of the identity of the person whose service or labor is claimed to be due, that the person so arrested does in fact owe service or labor to the person or persons claiming him or her, in the State or Territory from which such fugitive may have escaped, and that said person escaped, to make out and deliver to such claimant, his or her agent or attorney, a certificate setting forth the substantial facts as to the service or labor due from such fugitive to the claimant, and of his or her escape from the State or Territory in which such service or labor was due, to the State or Territory in which he or she was arrested, with authority to such claimant, or his or her agent or attorney, to use such reasonable force and restraint as may be necessary, under the circumstances of the case, to take and remove such fugitive person back to the State or Territory whence he or she may have escaped. In no trial or hearing under this act shall the testimony of such alleged fugitive be admitted in evidence; and the certificates shall be conclusive of the right of the person or persons in whose favor granted to remove such fugitive to the State or Territory from which he escaped, and shall prevent all molestation of such person or persons by any process issued by any court, judge, magistrate, or other person whomsoever.

§ 7. Any person who shall knowingly and willingly obstruct, hinder, or prevent such claimant, his agent or attorney, or any person or persons lawfully assisting him, her, or them, from arresting such fugitive from service or labor, either with or without process as aforesaid; or shall rescue, or attempt to rescue, such fugitive from service or labor from the custody of such claimant, his or her agent or attorney, or other person or persons lawfully assisting, when so arrested, pursuant to the authority herein given, or shall aid, abet, or assist such person so owing service or labor, directly or indirectly, to escape from such claimant, his agent or attorney, or other person or persons legally authorized as aforesaid; or shall harbor or conceal such fugitive, so as to prevent the discovery and arrest of such person, after notice or knowledge of the fact that such person was a fugitive from service or labor, shall, for either of said offences, be subject to a fine not exceeding $1000, and imprisonment not exceeding six months, by indictment and conviction before the District Court of the United States for the district in which such offence may have been committed, or before the proper court of criminal jurisdiction, if committed within any one of the organized Territories of the United States; and shall moreover forfeit and pay, by way of civil damages, to the party injured by such illegal conduct, the sum of $1000 for each fugitive so lost, to be recovered by action of debt, in any of the District or Territorial Courts within whose jurisdiction the said offence may have been committed.

§ 9. Upon affidavit made by the claimant of such fugitive, his agent or attorney, after such certificate has been issued, that he has reason to apprehend that such fugitive will be rescued by force before he can be taken beyond the limits of the State in which the arrest is made, it shall be the duty of the officer making the arrest to retain such fugitive in his custody, and to remove him to the State whence he fled, and there to deliver him to said claimant, his agent or attorney. And to this end, the officer is hereby authorized and required to employ so many persons as he may deem necessary to overcome such force, and to retain them in his service so long as circumstances may require. The said officer and his assistants, while so employed, to receive the same compensation, and to be allowed the same expenses, as are now allowed by law for the transportation of criminals, to be paid out of the treasury of the United States.

§ 10. When any person held to service or labor in any State or Territory, or in the District of Columbia, shall escape therefrom, the party to whom such service or labor shall be due, his, her, or their agent or attorney, may apply to any court of record therein, or judge thereof in vacation, and make satisfactory proof to such court, or judge in vacation, of the escape aforesaid, and that the person escaping owed service or labor to such party. Whereupon the court shall cause a record to be made of the matters so proved, and also a general description of the person so escaping, with such convenient certainty as may be; and a transcript of such record, authenticated by the attestation of the clerk and of the seal of the said court, being produced in any other State, territory, or District in which the person so escaping may be found, and being exhibited to any judge, commissioner, or other officer authorized by the law of the United States to cause persons escaping from service or labor to be delivered up, shall be held and taken to be full and conclusive evidence of the fact of escape, and that the service or labor of the person escaping is due to the party in such record mentioned. And upon the production by the said party of other and further evidence, if necessary, either oral or by affidavit, in addition to what is contained in the said record of the identity of the person escaping, he or she shall be delivered up to the claimant. And the said court, commissioner, judge, or other person authorized by this act to grant certificates to claimants of fugitives, shall, upon the production of the record and other evidences aforesaid, grant to such claimant a certificate of his right to take any such person identified, and proved to be owing service or labor as aforesaid, which certificate shall authorize such claimant to seize or arrest and transport such person to the State or territory from which he escaped: *Provided,* That nothing herein contained shall be construed as requiring the production of a transcript of such record as evidence as aforesaid. But in its absence the claim shall be heard and determined upon other satisfactory proofs competent in law. September 18, 1850.

APPENDIX F.

PAUPER SYSTEM OF MASSACHUSETTS.

The following extracts are taken from the "Report of the Commissioners appointed by an order of the House of Representatives, Feb. 29, 1832, on the subject of the Pauper System of the Commonwealth of Massachusetts.—Boston; Dutton & Wentworth, State Printers, 1833." The Commissioners, Hon. William B. Calhoun, Hon. Henry Shaw, Joseph Caldwell, Esq., George A. Tufts, Esq., and Rev. Joseph Tuckerman, under authority from the House of Representatives, appointed one of their number agent to visit various towns in the State and collect statistics, and these statistics are appended to the report, and published by order of the House.

The towns whose statistics are given are classified under two heads,—those that have Alms-houses and land for the support of the poor, and those that have not; of the former class are 43, and of the latter, 26.

In the quotations that follow, I have *italicised* certain passages, to call particular attention to them, as showing that, twenty years ago, certain practices, which are commonly spoken of as peculiar to the slave States, such, for instance, as selling men and women at auction, and separating husbands and wives, were not unknown in the "model Commonwealth," and therefore, *a fortiori*, it may be presumed, in the other free States. I give them here, not to bring reproach upon my native State, than which the sun does not shine upon a worthier, or a happier, but to show that every social system has its evils,—evils that are much more easily perceived than got rid off,—and that it does not become the pot to call the kettle *black*. Here follow the quotations:—

"BOSTON. The House of Industry contains fifty-five lodging rooms in the main house for the poor, and thirty-two in two out-houses. * * * *Husbands and wives are not allowed to live in the same room.*"

"LYNN. The Alms-house was built in 1819. * * * *It does not admit of a classification of the poor* [that is, *of a separation of the sexes*]; *and great evils result from this defect in the institution.*"

"ANDOVER. The Alms-house * * * has eleven lodging rooms for the poor. *Considerable evils result from the impracticability of separating and classifying its inmates.*"

☞ This town is the place of Mrs. Stowe's present residence, Mr. S. being Professor Stuart's successor in the Theological Seminary. It is to be hoped, therefore, that, for the honour of her sex, she will look into this matter, and see whether the above "impracticability" has been got over, or whether the town is still too *poor* to take care of the morals of its paupers.

"HAVERHILL. *Great difficulties are experienced from the impracticability of classifying the inmates.*"

"MALDEN. *The house does not admit of a classification of the inmates; and there is cause for the apprehension of evil from this circumstance.*"

"LEXINGTON. There are eight lodging rooms for the inmates, and from one to three sleep in a room. *Great care is required for security against immoralities.*"

"WESTFORD. There are six lodging rooms for the poor, and from two to six sleep in a room. *Immoralities have resulted from the impracticability of classifying the inmates.*"

"ROXBURY. The males live in one wing, and the females in the other. *Husbands and wives are not allowed to live together*, and the sexes are kept quite apart from each other. This circumstance has brought the house into disfavor with some who would otherwise have taken up their abode in it."

The *naiveté* with which this last remark is made, is very amusing.

"WORCESTER. There is a small *out-building* which contains two lodging rooms *for the blacks.*"

This town, it should be recollected, is the Head-Quarters of Massachusetts Abolitionism.

"SPRINGFIELD. It has nine lodging rooms for the poor, and from four to eight sleep in a room. No classification can be made of the inmates. *Immoralities have resulted from this circumstance, but not recently.*"

The above are from the first class, or those which have Alms-houses, and they are only a *specimen*, as may be seen by turning to the Report. The following are from the second class:—

"STOUGHTON. The poor of this town are annually *sold at auction to the lowest bidder.* * * * Within twelve years past, the expense of supporting the poor who were *sold* has varied from *sixty-two cents* to one dollar a week for each of them."

"LEOMINSTER. The present contractor has this class of the poor [the permanent poor,] for *seventy cents* per week." For this sum they are "boarded, nursed, clothed, and attended by a physician, if necessary." "Small children are boarded out in families till they are *eight years old, at which average age they are bound out.* The cost for these is *forty cents* per week. * * * Only one man of the permanent poor is capable of half a day's work."

"*Seventy cents* per week," each, for "boarding, nursing, and clothing," through the rigors of a Northern winter, *seventeen* human beings, (see Table II., appended to the Report,) and only one of the seventeen able to do anything towards earning his living, and he only "half a day's work." A magnificent sum truly! Why, "a peck of corn a week" would swallow up one-third of it, and the other two-thirds wouldn't clothe a negro in the mild climate of Maryland and Virginia, to say nothing of nursing and the Doctor's bill. And yet this is by no means an unfair specimen; indeed, it is considerably above the average price, as shown by Tables II. and III.

"BRIMFIELD. Of the poor *taken by the lowest bidder*, the average cost per week for adults is *seventy-five cents*. For children, *thirty-five cents*. The children in charge of the overseers are *bound out* between the ages of *eight* and twelve years, till they are sixteen years old."

"MONSON. Of the poor *taken by the lowest bidder*, the average cost for adults has been *sixty cents* per week. For children, *thirty cents* per week. The practice in regard to children is, *to bind them out as soon as possible.*"

After this, we are prepared for the second sentence in the following extract:—

"WEST SPRINGFIELD. Previous to the last six years, the poor *were separated into lots, and bid off at auction* to those who would take them for the lowest sum. *They were then, however, neither well fed nor well clothed*, and a change was found necessary in the manner of disposing of them."

"SANDISFIELD. Poor children are bound out *as soon as they are capable of any service.*"

"EGREMONT. The poor of this town are *put up at auction* to the lowest bidder."

APPENDIX, G.

1. EMANCIPATION IN THE BRITISH WEST INDIES.

The following extracts are from a work entitled, "Jamaica in 1850: or, The Effects of Sixteen Years of Freedom on a Slave Colony. By John Bigelow. *Magnas inter opes inops.*—Horace. New York and London: George P. Putnam. 1851." Mr. Bigelow was, at the time he published this, and, I believe, is still, a Free-Soiler, and one of the Editors of the New York Evening Post; he will not, therefore, be suspected of exaggerating.

"Before the ship had fairly stopped, we were surrounded with boats filled with negroes, some dressed decently, and some indecently, and some not at all." (p. 7.)

"We had four colored oarsmen under command of Commodore Brooks, himself a very black man, with very white linen, whose broad pennant of red, with a white ball, swung at the masthead, to indicate that he was senior officer of the port. * * * * He was about two hours in getting us over to Kingston, a distance of about five miles." (pp. 8, 9.)

"My largest trunk, which was handled by the coachman in New York without difficulty, engaged the devoted exertions of four negroes, in the effort to draw it from the boat, which they effected by instalments, after turning it over, as they did every article of luggage, several times, and trying it in various ways, and from opposite sides, as if to see if they could not in some way get the advantage of it. They were two hours in transporting our luggage from the boats to our lodgings, not half a mile distant." (p. 11.)

"They (the hotels) are all kept and served by colored people. * * * They have no idea of doing anything within any specified period. * * * If breakfast was ordered at 8 o'clock, it was sure not to be ready till 10. If dinner was ordered at 3, we congratulated ourselves if we got it by 5." (p. 12.)

"Rents are exceeding low, less than half a fair interest on the cost of the building alone—while the vacant lots cannot be said to have any market value, there being no sales." (p. 14.)

"Though Kingston is the principal port of the Island, it has but little of the air of a commercial city. One looks and listens in vain for the noise of carts and the bustle of busy men; no one seems in a hurry; but few are doing anything, while the mass of the population are lounging about in idleness and rags." (p. 15.)

"At the Surry Assize, there were two *colored* lawyers and nine *colored* jurors. All the officers of the Court, except the clerk, were *colored.*" (p. 23.)

"Seven-tenths of the Police force on the Island, also, were *colored.* Of the forty-eight or fifty members of the Legislative Assembly, ten or a dozen were *colored.* The public printers, Jordan and Osborn, who were also publishers of the Kingston Journal, were *colored.* One or two of the regiments, and nine-tenths of the Penitentiary officers, were *black.* The Island is eventually to be given up to them." (pp. 24, 25.) In the above paragraphs, the terms "colored" and "black" are to be carefully distinguished.

"While the *entente cordiale* between the whites and the colored population is apparently strengthening daily, a very different state of feeling exists between the negroes or Africans, and the browns. The latter shun all connection by marriage with the former, and can experience no more unpardonable insult, than to be classified with them in any way. They generally prefer that their daughters should live with a white person upon any terms, than to be married to a negro. Few will need to be told that where such is the condition of public sentiment in a class, the standard of female virtue among them cannot be very high. It is, perhaps, a trifle higher than among the slaves." (p. 26.)

Intermarriages between the whites and "browns" are constantly occurring. (p. 20.)

The population of the Island is about 400,000. Of these about 16,000 are whites, 68,529, colored, and 293,128, black, (p. 40.)

"It is difficult to exaggerate, and yet more difficult to define, the poverty and industrial prostration of Jamaica. The natural wealth and spontaneous productiveness of the Island are so great that no one can starve, and yet it seems as if the faculty of accumulation were suspended. All the productive power of the soil is running to waste; the finest land in the world may be had at any price, and almost for the asking; labour receives no compensation, and the product of labour does not seem to know the way to market. Families accustomed to wealth and every luxury, have witnessed the decline of their incomes, until now, with undiminished estates, they find themselves wrestling with poverty for the commonest necessaries of life. There are no public amusements here of any kind, for amusements are purchased with the surplus wealth of a people, and here there is no surplus. * * * * But the Island abounds with more palpable, if not more significant evidences of prostration than these.

"Since the year 1833, when the British Slavery Emancipation act was passed, the real estate of the Island has been rapidly depreciating in value, and its productiveness has been steadily diminishing to its present comparatively ruinous standard. Whatever diversity of views may exist respecting the influence which the abolition of slavery may have had in producing this state of things, there is no doubt, I believe, entertained by any, that the passage of the Emancipation Act of 1833, was followed by the disasters I have referred to, as promptly as it could have been if it had been their cause. * *

"Since 1832, out of the 653 sugar estates then in cultivation, more than 150 have been abandoned and the works broken up. This has thrown out of cultivation over 200,000 acres of rich land, which in 1832, gave employment to about 30,000 laborers, and yielded over 15,000 hogsheads of sugar, and over 6,000 puncheons of rum.

"During the same period, over 500 coffee plantations have been abandoned, and their works broken up. This has thrown out of cultivation over 200,000 acres more of land which in 1832, required the labor of over 30,000 men." (pp. 53, 54, 55.)

The depreciation of real estate between 1833, (the year of Emancipation) and 1850, may be judged of by the following instances, which are but a few of those given by the author, and which, he says, "may be *relied on.*"

The "Spring Valley" estate, containing 1,244 acres, together with "machinery, works, &c." depreciated from £18,000 sterling to £1000. The "Tremoles" estate, of 1,450 acres, from £68,000 to £8,400, and, in 1850, would not probably have sold for half that sum. The "Golden Valley" estate, of 1200 acres, with machinery, &c., to £620. "Caen Wood," from £18,000 to £1500. "Fair Prospect," (which at one time produced 500 hogsheads of sugar,) from £40,000 to £4,000. "Ginger Hall," (which, prior to 1833, brought in an annual income of £1200,) to £1400. "Bunker Hill," (which, at one time, was mortgaged for £30,000,) to £2,500. (pp. 56, 57.)

In the other West India Colonies, there has been a similar falling off in exports, and a similar depreciation in real estate.

In Demerara and Essequibo, there were in 1838, 258 estates in profitable cultivation. Of these, 71 have been abandoned, and 111, sold under execution. (p. 58.)

In Berbice, up to 1849, 3 cotton, 30 coffee, and 9 sugar estates had been abandoned *in one county alone*, and were, at that time, "relapsing into a wilderness." (p. 60.)

In British Guiana, in 1850, there were 27 estates under sequestration,—25 of them, sugar estates,—and the real estate valuation had fallen from £20,000,000 sterling to £660,000! (p. 61.)

"Jamaica embraces about 4,000,000 acres of land, of which there are not, probably, any ten lying adjacent to each other, which are not susceptible of the highest cultivation, while not more than 500,000 acres have ever been reclaimed, or even appropriated." (p. 64.)

"The richness of the soil may be inferred from a usage which has existed since long previous to the abolition of slavery, of setting apart to the negroes one day in seven for the cultivation of their own little grounds from which they gathered nearly their entire support. On Saturdays they are never expected to work for any one but themselves. They devote that day to tilling their grounds and marketing their produce. This one day's labor in each week is all they require to keep up to the highest power of production, from three to five, and sometimes ten acres of provision grounds." (p. 65.)

"Very little of the soil has been manured, or requires to be, and such a thing as an exhausted estate is hardly known." (p. 64.)

The productions of the Island are rum, molasses, sugar, coffee, pimento, ginger, copper and coal. (pp. 65—69.)

"Such are some of the natural resources of this dilapidated and poverty-stricken country. Capable as it is of producing almost every thing, and actually producing nothing which might not become a staple with a proper application of capital and skill, its inhabitants are miserably poor, and daily sinking deeper and deeper into the utter helplessness of abject want.

Magnas inter opes inops.

Shipping has deserted her ports; her magnificent plantations of sugar and coffee are running to weeds; her private dwellings are falling to decay; the comforts and luxuries which belong to industrial prosperity have been cut off one by one, from her inhabitants; and the day, I think, is at hand when there will be none left to represent the wealth, intelligence and hospitality for which the Jamaica planter was once so distinguished." (p. 70.)

The *Planters'* reasons for this are the following:—

1. Price of free labour.

2. The small compensation they received for their slaves. The Commissioners appraised the slave-property of all the British West Indies at £43,104,889 8s. 6d., and the government finally allowed the owners only £16,638,937 8s. 1¾d., or less than 50 per cent.

3. Reduction of the sugar duties in 1846, to the amount of some £5,000,000, annually. (pp. 71, 72.)

The *Author's* reasons, on the contrary, are these:—

1. Degradation of labour:—

"I could not perceive that sixteen years of freedom had advanced the dignity of labour, or of the labouring classes one particle. That fell legacy which slavery always leaves behind it, I found here, neither wasted nor reduced. The operative occupies a decidedly lower social position in Jamaica now, than he does in South Carolina." (p. 77.)

2. Absenteeism. $3000 a year to Agents, &c.

3. Encumbered Estates. Mortgages paid off, in part, by the money received from Government. (p. 89.)

"But the question arises, why have not the properties been sold by the necessitous, and purchased upon terms that would admit of careful and remunerating cultivation; in other words, why have not the laws of supply and demand dispossessed the absentee landlords, converted the mortgagees into resident proprietors, and thus restored the equilibrium between labor and capital?

"This is the Jamaica problem. Without presuming to be able to give it a scientific solution with the means at present within my reach, I think I can indicate the direction in which such a solution is to be found, by those who may choose to go in quest of it." (pp. 103, 104.)

He then goes on to mention what he considers some of the principal obstacles to the return of prosperity, and which therefore require to be got rid of. Among these, are the employment of agents at a high salary; the expense of having sugar-works on each estate; and finally the size of the estates themselves:—"140, taken at random, averaged over 1200 acres each." (p. 105.) He then adds:—

"Hence it happens that when a proprietor sells a property, whether from necessity or choice, he insists upon selling the whole of it, and the purchaser generally insists upon buying the whole. The residents of the Island are, for the most part, too poor to buy, and hence non-residents have usually been the purchasers, when any sales were made." (p. 107.) In this way, he tells us, Absenteeism has been perpetuated. And yet in another place, he says,

"I was greatly surprised to find that the number of these colored proprietors is already considerably over one hundred thousand, and constantly increasing." And again:—

"When one reflects that only sixteen years ago, there was scarcely a colored landholder upon the Island, and that now there are a hundred thousand, &c. * * * * Their properties average from three to five acres." (p. 116.)

After stating (p. 159) that the vacancies in the population created by emigration and death are not filled up by the births in the white families, because their children are sent abroad for education and have no inducement to return, he goes on:

"Of course, the loss of every white man is a loss of capital to a greater or less extent; it strengthens the influences already operating to depress the price of property, increases facilities for the colored people to appropriate it, and is hastening that partition of the soil which I have supposed necessary to a realization of its highest protective power. It is also hastening a result which I have reason to believe the home government anticipate and are prepared for—the gradual occupation of the whole island by the blacks. They see and know that the two races cannot prosper together, if both are free; that the superior intelligence and advantages of the whites will prevent the blacks from acquiring that independence and self-reliance which are the sinews of enterprise and the basis of national prosperity; and as the blacks are so much the more numerous, and enjoy so great an advantage in their natural adaptedness to the climate of the tropics, it has been wisely determined to surrender the Island to them, as soon as it can be done consistently with the vested rights of the white population." (p. 160.)

Nothing is more probable, in respect to the political fate of the

Island, twenty years hence, than that it will be one of the United States of America." (p. 161.)

2. Hayti.

The following Official Correspondence is from the Washington Union, of Dec. 21, 1852.

Hayti.

Mr. Walsh to Mr. Webster.

Port au Prince, February 5, 1851.

Sir: I embarked at Norfolk on the 25th of last month, the Saranac having been detained there until that date, and arrived here on the afternoon of the 2d instant, after a pleasant but not very rapid passage, of nearly eight days. The vessel, though an admirable one in many respects, does not seem to be remarkable for speed. From the commodore and officers I received every courtesy, and immediately on our arrival, Mr. Usher, the consular agent of the United States, came on board and tendered me the hospitalities of his house, which I was glad to accept, *the warm welcome of an inn being a luxury not to be had in this place.*

* * * * * *

Faustin the First is stout and short, and very black, with an unpleasant expression, and a carriage that does not grace a throne. He is ignorant in the extreme, but has begun to learn to read and write, and is said to exhibit commendable diligence in his studies. Energy and decision are his most important traits, and no soft feelings are likely to interfere with their full display when occasion calls them forth, as it frequently does. There has been considerable demand for them of late, in consequence of a formidable conspiracy which was discovered a short time since, the object of which was to restore the republic.

* * * * * * * *

I have the honour to be, with great respect,
your obedient servant,
ROB'T. M. WALSH.

Hon. Daniel Webster, Secretary of State.

Mr. Walsh to Mr. Webster.

Port au Prince, April 8, 1851.

Sir: In my last I announced the opening of the Chambers, and enclosed a copy of the Emperor's speech. The ceremony was performed with all possible parade, as you will perceive by the journal which I have the honour to transmit. His Majesty and suite were robed for the occasion in costumes just arrived from France, making such a display as I never seen rivalled, except at "Franconi's," in Paris; and certainly none but theatrical magnificoes would venture to exhibit such glittering and variegated splendor in any other metropolis, however imperial. The toilet of Soulouque himself was quite wonderful, especially the chapeau, with its numerous feathers tipped with different hues.

* * * * * * * *

You will see by the journal the correspondence which has taken place between the Minister of Foreign Affairs and the Chambers, in regard to a request made by my colleagues and myself to be present at the discussion of the Dominican question. It seems to have embarrassed the legislators, and at last they determined to sit with closed doors, so that we can obtain no satisfactory intelligence of their proceedings.

With great respect, your obedient servant,

ROBERT M. WALSH.

Hon. DANIEL WEBSTER, Secretary of State.

Mr. Walsh to Mr. Webster.

PORT AU PRINCE, April 10, 1851.

SIR: I am informed that the Chambers have appointed a joint committee to make a report upon the Dominican question, and that the Emperor has added to it six generals, in order that the army may be represented in the business. The town is now full of military personages, all the principal officers of the empire having been summoned here, to the number of nearly five hundred generals, and twice as many colonels, for the double purpose of ascertaining their views concerning the war, and of giving them the decorations, just arrived from France, of the order of St. Faustin—an order instituted by the Emperor in honor of himself and the saint whom he has selected as his patron. I say selected, because his real name is Quassie, and not Faustin; but there being no saint of the former appellation in the calendar, he exchanged it for an epithet of more civilized and Christian sound. The order is a strict imitation of similar institutions in other monarchies, with all the different gradations of knighthood, and ribands and crosses; and these are bestowed upon the "princes, dukes, counts, barons, and chevaliers of the empire," in recompense for their "zeal, patriotism, merit and talents," as military worthies. That the civilians also who "merit distinctions for the services which they have rendered, and continue to render, to the country," might be duly rewarded, another order, the "Legion of Honor," was established, which already, in consequence of the quantity of meritorious and distinguished Haytiens, rejoices in nearly as many members as its French namesake, originated by Napoleon.

A Haytien without a decoration is a very rare as well as very unhappy individual, at least among the inhabitants of the towns. In the country, a banana is generally regarded with more interest and admiration than even the Grand Cross of St. Faustin. Two other orders, it is said, are soon to be instituted in honor of the empress and the princess, and their patron saints St. Anne and St. Olive, for which the insignia are now in course of preparation by Parisian artists. Ladies of eminence are to be the amiable recipients of them when they arrive; and it is said that they will be almost as multitudinous as those appertaining to the confraternities of cavaliers.

I trust, sir, you will pardon me if I sometimes wander from the serious tone appropriate to a despatch; but it is difficult to preserve one's gravity with so absurd a caricature of civilization before one's eyes, as is here exhibited in every shape.

Nothing saves these people from being infinitely ridiculous, but the circumstance of their being often supremely disgusting by their fearful atrocities. The change from a ludicrous farce to a bloody tragedy is here as frequent as it is terrible; and the smiles which the former irresistibly provoke can only be repressed by the sickening sensations occasioned by the latter.

It is a conviction which has been forced upon me by what I have learned here, that negroes only cease to be children when they degenerate into savages. As long as they happen to be in a genial mood, it is the rattle and the straw by which they are tickled and pleased; and when their passions are once aroused, the most potent weapons of subjugation can alone prevent the most horrible evils. A residence here, however brief, must cause the most determined philanthropist to entertain serious doubts of the possibility of their ever attaining the full stature of intellectual and civilized manhood, unless some miraculous interposition is vouchsafed in their behalf. In proportion as the recollections and traditions of the old colonial civilization are fading away, and the imitative propensity, which is so strong a characteristic of the African, is losing its opportunities of exercise, the black inhabitants of Hayti are reverting to the primitive state from which they were elevated by contact with the whites—a race whose innate superiority would seem to be abundantly proved by the mere fact that it is approaching the goal of mental progress, while the other has scarcely made a step in advance of the position in which it was originally placed. It is among the mulattoes alone, as a general rule, that intelligence and education are to be found; but they are neither sufficiently numerous, nor virtuous, nor enlightened to do more than diminish the rapidity of the nation's descent, and every day accelerates the inevitable catastrophe by lessening their influence and strength.

The contrast between the picture which is now presented by this country, and that which it exhibited when under the dominion of the French, affords a melancholy confirmation of what I have said. It was then, indeed, an "exulting and abounding" land—a land literally flowing with milk and honey; now it might be affirmed without extravagance, that where it is not an arid and desolate waste, it is flooded with the waters of bitterness, or covered with noisome and poisonous weeds. "When I arrived here," to quote the words of an intelligent foreigner who has been in Hayti since the epoch of its independence, "there was abundance of everything; now there is a want of everything." The cultivation of sugar, which was once the main fountain of wealth, is now entirely abandoned, except for the production of an intoxicating drink; and that of coffee has so much decreased, that it would not in the least be a matter of surprise if, ere long, the supply of that indispensable article for Haytien commerce were to be insufficient for the ordinary consumption of the inhabitants themselves.

The government, in spite of its constitutional forms, is a despotism of the most ignorant, corrupt, and vicious description, with a military establishment so enormous that, while it absorbs the largest portion of the revenue for its support, it dries up the very sources of national prosperity, by depriving the fields of their necessary laborers to fill the town with pestilent hordes of depraved and irreclaimable idlers. The treasury is bankrupt, and every species of profligate and ruinous expedient is resorted to for the purpose of obtaining the means of gratifying an insane passion for frivolous expenditure. A great portion of the public revenue is wasted upon the personal vanities of the Emperor, and his ridiculous efforts to surround himself with a splendor which he fancies to be pre-eminently imperial. It is a fact that the same legislature which voted him several hundreds of thousands of francs for some absurd costume, refused an appropriation of twenty-five thousand francs for public schools. The population, for the most part, is immersed in Cimerian darkness that can never be pierced by the few and feeble rays which emanate from the higher portions of the social system, whilst there is a constant fermentation of jealousies and antipathies between the great majority and the only class at all capable of guiding the destinies of the land, which threatens at every moment to shatter the political vessel in which they are so perilously working. As to the refining and elevating influences of civilized life —the influences of religion, of literature, of science, of art—they do not exert the least practical sway, even if they can be said to exist at all. The priests of the altar set the worst examples of every kind of vice, and are universally mere adventurers, disowned by the church, who alone can come here in consequence of the assumption by the Emperor of ecclesiastical authority, which militates with that of the Roman pontiff. The press is shackled to such a degree as to prevent the least freedom of opinion, and people are afraid to give utterance, even in confidential conversation, to aught that may be tortured into the slightest criticism upon the action of the government.

In short, the combination of evil and destructive elements is such, that the ultimate regeneration of the Haytiens seems to me to be the wildest of Utopian dreams. Dismal as this picture may appear, its coloring is not exaggerated. It is as faithful a representation as I can sketch of the general aspect of this miserable country—a country where God has done everything to make his creature happy, and where the creature is doing everything to mar the work of God.

Of the individual in whose hands the whole power of the nation is lodged, I have already, in my previous despatches, endeavored to convey some idea; and it may be easily inferred, that his character offers little guarantee of prosperity or tranquillity from day to day. Even if he were animated by the purest intentions, he is utterly incapable of grappling with the difficulties with which he is surrounded, and ameliorating the condition of his subjects. It is not believed that he can sustain himself for any length of time; and when he is overthrown, the beginning of the end may be anticipated. Universal confusion will probably ensue, with all its possible horrors. It is the dread of such a consequence of his fall which is perhaps the strongest support of his throne. Beneath its ruins, in the apprehension of the most intelligent, not only the empire but the nationality of Hayti may be irretrievably buried—a result, however, which, deplorable as it may be to individual interests and feelings, will not eventually be a source of regret to enlightened philanthropy in its largest sense.

When a nation has proved itself utterly unfit to perform its duty for its own benefit and that of mankind, its destruction can scarcely be considered a cause of grief, and its epitaph will have no claim to be written with a pen dipped in tears.

With great respect, your obedient servant,

ROBERT M. WALSH.

Hon. DANIEL WEBSTER, Secretary of State.

APPENDIX, H.

FLOGGING AS A MEANS OF DISCIPLINF.

The following extracts are from "Two years before the Mast, by Richard H. Dana, Jr." I wish I had space for all relating to the subject; as I have not, I am obliged to content myself with only a part.

"'Now for you,' said the captain, making up to John and taking his irons off. As soon as he was loose, he ran forward to the forecastle. 'Bring that man aft,' shouted the captain. The second mate, who had been a shipmate of John's, stood still in the waist, and the mate walked slowly forward; but our third officer, anxious to show his zeal, sprang forward over the windlass, and laid hold of John; but he soon threw him from him. At this moment I would have given worlds for the power to help the poor fellow; but it was all in vain. The captain stood on the quarter-deck, bareheaded, his eyes flashing with rage, and his face as red as blood, swinging the rope, and calling out to his officers, 'Drag him aft!—Lay hold of him! I'll *sweeten* him!' &c., &c. The mate now went forward and told John quietly to go aft; and he seeing resistance in vain, threw the blackguard third mate from him; said he would go aft of himself; that they should not drag him; and went up to the gangway and held out his hands; but as soon as the captain began to make him fast, the indignity was too much, and he began to resist; but the mate and Russell holding him, he was soon seized up. When he was made fast, he turned to the captain, who stood turning up his sleeves and getting ready for the blow, and asked him what he was to be flogged for. 'Have I ever refused my duty, sir? Have you ever known me to hang back, or to be insolent, or not to know my work?'

"'No,' said the captain, 'it is not that that I flog you for; I flog you for your interference—for asking questions.'

"'Can't a man ask a question here without being flogged?'

"'No,' shouted the captain; 'nobody shall open his mouth aboard this vessel, but myself;' and began laying the blows upon his back, swinging half round between each blow, to give it full effect. As he went on, his passion increased, and he danced about the deck, calling out as he swung the rope,—'If you want to know what I flog you for, I'll tell you. It's because I like to do it! It suits me! That's what I do it for!'

"The man writhed under the pain, until he could endure it no longer, when he called out, with an exclamation more common among foreigners than with us—'Oh, Jesus Christ! Oh, Jesus Christ!'

"'Don't call on Jesus Christ,' shouted the captain; '*he can't help you. Call on Captain T———.* He's the man! He can help you! Jesus Christ can't help you now!'

"At these words, which I never shall forget, my blood ran cold. I could look on no longer. Disgusted, sick, and horror-struck, I turned away and leaned over the rail, and looked down into the water. A few rapid thoughts of my own situation, and of the prospect of future revenge, crossed my mind; but the falling of the blows and the cries of the man called me back at once. At length they ceased, and turning round, I found that the mate, at a signal from the captain, had cut him down. Almost doubled up with pain, the man walked slowly forward, and went down into the forecastle. Every one else stood still at his post, while the captain, swelling with rage and with the importance of his achievement, walked the quarter-deck, and at each turn, as he came forward, calling out to us,—'You see your condition! You see where I've got you all, and you know what to expect!' 'You've been mistaken in me—you didn't know what I was! Now you know what I am! I'll make you toe the mark, every soul of you, or I'll flog you all, fore and aft, from the boy, up!' You've got a driver over you! Yes, a *slave-driver—a negro driver*! I'll see who'll tell me he isn't a negro slave!' With this and the like matter, equally calculated to quiet us, and to allay any apprehensions of future trouble, he entertained us for about ten minutes, when he went below. Soon after, John came aft, with his bare back covered with stripes and wales in every direction, and dreadfully swollen, and asked the steward to ask the captain to let him have some salve, or balsam, to put upon it. 'No,' said the captain, who heard him from below; 'tell him to put his shirt on; that's the best thing for him; and pull me ashore in the boat. Nobody is going to lay-up on board this vessel.' He then called to Mr. Russell to take those two men and two others in the boat, and pull him ashore. I went for one. The two men could hardly bend their backs, and the captain called to them to 'give way,' 'give way!' but finding they did their best, he let them alone." (pp. 126—129.)

"In the treatment of those under his authority, the captain is amenable to the common law, like any other person. He is liable at common law for murder, assault and battery, and other offences; and in addition to this, there is a special statute of the United States which makes a captain or other officer liable to imprisonment for a term not exceeding five years, and to a fine not exceediug a thousand dollars, for inflicting any cruel punishment upon, withholding food from, or in any other way maltreating a seaman. This is the state of the law on the subject; while the relation in which the parties stand, and the peculiar necessities, excuses, and provocations arising from that relation, are merely circumstances to be considered in each case. As to the restraints upon the master's exercise of power, the laws themselves seem, on the whole, to be sufficient. I do not see that we are in need, at present, of more legislation on the subject. The difficulty lies rather in the administration of the laws; and this is certainly a matter that deserves great consideration, and one of no little embarrassment.

"In the first place, the courts have said that public policy requires the power of the master and officers should be sustained. Many lives and a great amount of property are constantly in their hands, for which they are strictly responsible. To preserve these, and to deal justly by the captain, and not lay upon him a really fearful responsibility, and then tie up his hands, it is essential that discipline should be supported. In the second place, there is always great allowance to be made for false swearing and exaggeration by seamen, and for combinations among them against their officers; and it is to be remembered that the latter have often no one to testify on their side. These are weighty and true statements, and should not be lost sight of by the friends of seamen." (pp. 462, 463.)

"I could not do justice to this subject without noticing one part of the discipline of a ship, which has been very much discussed of late, and has brought out strong expressions of indignation from many,—I mean the infliction of corporal punishment. Those who have followed me in my narrative will remember that I was witness to an act of great cruelty inflicted upon my own shipmates; and indeed I can sincerely say that the simple mention of the word flogging, brings up in me feelings which I can hardly control. Yet, when the proposition is made to abolish it entirely and at once; to prohibit the captain from ever, under any circumstances, inflicting corporal punishment; I am obliged to pause, and, I must say, to doubt exceedingly the expediency of making any positive enactment which shall have that effect. If the design of those who are writing on this subject is merely to draw public attention to it, and to discourage the practice of flogging, and bring it into disrepute, it is well; and, indeed, whatever may be the end they have in view, the mere agitation of the question will have that effect, and, so far, must do good. Yet I should not wish to take the command of a ship to-morrow, running my chance of a crew, as most masters must, and know, and have my crew know, that I could not, under any circumstances, inflict even moderate chastisement. I should trust that I might never have to resort to it, and, indeed, I scarcely know what risk I would not run, and to what inconvenience I would not subject myself, rather than do so. Yet not to have the power of holding it up *in terrorem*, and indeed of protecting myself, and all under my charge, by it, if some extreme case should arise, would be a situation I should not wish to be placed in myself, or to take the responsibility of placing another in.

"Indeed, the difficulties into which masters and officers are liable to be thrown, are not sufficiently considered by many whose sympathies are easily excited by stories, frequent enough, and true enough of outrageous abuse of this power. It is to be remembered that more than three-fourths of the seamen in our merchant vessels are foreigners. They are from all parts of the world. A great many from the north of Europe, beside Frenchmen, Spaniards, Portuguese, Italians, men from all parts of the Mediterranean, together with Lascars, Negroes, and perhaps worst of all, the off-casts of British men-of-war, and men from our own country who have gone to sea because they could not be permitted to live on land.

"As things now are, many masters are obliged to sail without knowing anything of their crews, until they get out at sea. There may be pirates or mutineers among them; and one bad man will often infect all the rest; and it is almost certain that some of them will be ignorant foreigners, hardly understanding a word of our language, accustomed all their lives to no influence but force, and perhaps nearly as familiar with the use of the knife as with that of the marline-spike. No prudent master, however peaceably inclined, would go to sea without his pistols and handcuffs. Even with such a crew as I have supposed, kindness and moderation would be the best policy, and the duty of every conscientious man; and the administering of corporal punishment might be dangerous, and of doubtful use. But the question is not, what a captain ought generally to do, but whether it shall be put out of the power of every captain, under any circumstances, to make use of even moderate chastisement. As the law now stands, a parent may correct moderately his child, and the master his apprentice; and the case of the shipmaster has been placed upon the same principle. The statutes, and the common law, as expounded in the decisions of courts, and in the books of commentators, are express and unanimous to this point, that the captain may inflict moderate corporal chastisement, for a reasonable cause. If the punishment is excessive, or the cause not sufficient to justify it, he is answerable; and the jury are to determine, by their verdict in each case, whether, under all the circumstances, the punishment was moderate, and for a justifiable cause.

"This seems to me to be as good a position as the whole subject can be left in. I mean to say, that no positive enactment, going beyond this, is needed, or would be a benefit either to masters or men, in the present state of things. This again would seem to be a case which should be left to the gradual working of its own cure. As seamen improve, punishment will become less necessary; and as the character of officers is raised, they will be less ready to inflict it; and, still more, the infliction of it upon intelligent and respectable men, will be an enormity which will not be tolerated by public opinion, and by juries, who are the pulse of the body politic. No one can have a greater abhorrence of the infliction of such punishment than I have, and a stronger conviction that severity is bad policy with a crew; yet I would ask every reasonable man whether he had not better trust to the practice becoming unnecessary and disreputable; to the measure of moderate chastisement and a justifiable cause being better understood, and thus, the act becoming dangerous, and in the course of time to be regarded as an unheard-of barbarity—than to take the responsibility of prohibiting it, at once, in all cases, and in whatever degree, by positive enactment?" (pp. 468—471.)

APPENDIX I.

INFIDEL TESTIMONY.

From the Boston Post, of June 4th, 1853.

Extract from a memorial to the convention assembled to revise the constitution of Massachusetts, asking "that the constitution be so amended, that the doctrines of no religion shall be established or recommended therein, and that no religious or ecclesiastical interference with the laws of the State, its official institutions, or its public schools, shall be hereafter possible in the Commonwealth :"—

"A large and rapidly increasing class of citizens are by the constitutional rulings of the courts of law in this Commonwealth, denied the protection of the State, declared incompetent to give evidence in any case whatever, or to hold any office, and positively proscribed as unsafe members of society, because they cannot believe in the infallibility of certain religious doctrines.

"Against such deprivation of political character and civil rights, because of theological opinions, we most respectfully, but most firmly, protest.

"We hold that the right to doubt underlies the right to believe; that a man has the same right to be an infidel or an atheist, that he has to be a Christian; that the State, having to take cognizance of men's acts and not of their opinions, has no authority whatever to make any religious faith a test of citizenship; that it has nothing to do with the belief or the unbelief of any individual, nor with any publication of sentiments; but that it is held, by the first principles of republicanism, to conserve the entire freedom of all its people, to know citizens, not sects, and to guarantee to all men an absolute equality before the law.

"Your memorialists submit, that the ostracism of infidels by the government is not only theoretically false and despotic, but that it is, at every point, an injustice to society, and utterly incapable of effecting the minutest good. If it be thought a cure to scepticism, we beg leave to suggest that no surer method of increasing infidelity could be adopted, inasmuch as proscription invariably creates sympathy for the proscribed, and weakens confidence in the religion which needs persecution to sustain it. Besides, it is the strictly conscientious man who is made to suffer the application of the law. An individual may say that he believes in the Christian religion, and his evidence is received in court, though truth be a stranger to his lips. But a man who does not thus believe, and is honorable enough to avow his sincere convictions, is met by the State with the preposterous charge of moral imbecility, and the law excludes his testimony, reckless of any wrong which follows. And this brand of legal incompetency affects the infidel in every department of business, and condemns his trustworthiness, however unblemished may be his integrity. Every contract to which he is a party must be written or proven by others, else it is worthless to him; and his accounts, except they be kept by a Christian clerk, are invalid and uncollectable.

"And it is not alone the infidel who is interested in this matter, but the safety of society also requires that credibility should be determined by character and not by belief. An opportunity is now given for defeating the ends of justice, of which advantage is often taken to shield the guilty from conviction and punishment. Instances are constantly occurring in your criminal courts, where the only persons who can give evidence in a case avoid appearing against their friends or accomplices, by designedly stating, before witnesses, that they do not believe in a God or in a future state. When called upon to testify, the defence objects to their evidence, on the ground of atheism; the disqualifying statement is proved to have been made, the witness has leave to withdraw, and the guilty party escapes. Moreover, it is to the direct personal interest of the Christian, that his infidel neighbor should be possessed of the same civil ability as himself, inasmuch as when a transaction occurs, as any day it may, the just settlement of which is of importance to the Christian, and the essential evidence of which is the acquaintance of an infidel friend with the facts, if his testimony be excluded, the rights and interests of the Christian may be sacrificed beyond hope of relief. A Christian may be foully wronged, within the knowledge of an infidel, or he may be murdered in the presence of twenty infidels, all honorable and respected men, and yet the wronger and assassin cannot be brought to justice, and need fear no law.

"A recent judicial decision in this Commonwealth presents the injustice of excluding the testimony of infidels in the strongest light. It having been shown, as it is known to you, that a murdered man had been a sceptic upon certain points of ordinary belief, the murderer, by the ruling of the court, walked out an innocent man and worthy citizen—the court deciding, in effect, that to kill an infidel is not a crime known to Massachusetts law!

"The relation of the infidel to the State is now identical to that of a chattel. His humanity is disowned; his political existence denied. His rights are violated with impunity; he is outraged in person and possessions, and the law recognizes no offence, unless, indeed, some Christian may happen to know the facts. With only this reservation, no matter how great an indignity is inflicted upon heretics, no matter how unjust the act, or how atrocious the wrong, they have no protection, and no redress.

"Your memorialists believe it to be a fundamental maxim of common law, that when the State withdraws its protection from the individual, *then the obligations of the individual to support the State become annulled, his responsibility to the laws of the State extinguished,* and he is thrown back upon his reserved right of self-protection by whatever means he may. Such of your memorialists as are now put in this relation to the law, wishing no longer to hold such position, and having no desire to be forced upon their last alternative in any instance, because despoiled by the State of their civil or their social rights, knock respectfully at the door of the convention for the recognition of their citizenship, and the relief of their political disabilities. And here we beg leave particularly to represent that we seek no favor, nor ask any privilege, but that we claim at your hands, as our plain, absolute and unqualified RIGHT, that constitutional protection against injustice, and that constitutional *equality before the law*, to which, as citizens of this Commonwealth, we are entitled, wholly irrespective and independent of whatever religious or anti-religious theories be entertained."

APPENDIX K.

CONDITION OF THE "LABOURING CLASSES" IN ENGLAND, AND OTHER NON-SLAVEHOLDING COUNTRIES.

1. English labouring classes:—General statements.

From the London Guardian of Jan. 19, 1853.

"UNITED STATES.—The *New York Courier and Enquirer* publishes a rejoinder from the American ladies to the Stafford-house remonstrance against slavery in America. It is entitled an 'Affectionate and Christian Address of many Thousands of the Women of the United States of America to their Sisters, the Women of England.' They will not dwell upon the 'flagitious and bloody modes' by which England extends her territories in Southern Africa, Southern Asia, and the Southern Seas; the iniquitous Chinese war, or Irish misrule; but speak 'of the ignorant and poverty-stricken, and the degraded population of your own land; and we shall do it with faithfulness, yet with kindness.' 'Sisters, your land is filled with slaves—slaves to ignorance, slaves to penury, and slaves to vice.' England has no system of public instruction worthy of the name. In New York alone, more is spent in education than the annual Parliament grant for the same purpose in England. In New York one-third of the population are at public schools, in England only one-eleventh:—

"'You, whom we are addressing, live in all parts of England, but everywhere, in the metropolis, in the manufacturing towns, and in the country, you see about you the most pitiable destitution and degradation. In London there are, we understand, more than 1,000,000 of immortal beings who are never seen in the house of God, and practically think the thoughts and live the lives of absolute heathens. The condition of a large portion of the labouring population of that vast city may be judged from the fact that of its 20,000 journeymen tailors, 14,000 can barely earn a miserable subsistence by working fourteen hours a day, Sunday included; and that it contains 33,000 needlewomen, who earn on an average only 4½d. a day, by working fourteen hours. There are 50,000 people in London who obtain their living in the streets, and Henry Mayhew, an authority whom you will not venture to question, says of them, 'When the religious, moral, and intellectual degradation of the majority of these 50,000 people is impressed upon us, it becomes positively appalling to contemplate the vast amount of vice, ignorance, and want existing in the very heart of our land.' There are 30,000 costermongers; of these he says 'only one-tenth—at the outside one-tenth—of the couples living together and carrying on their costermongering trade are married;' that 'not three in a hundred of them had ever been in the interior of a church or any place of worship, or knew what was meant by Christianity, and only one in ten of them is able to read.' In your manufacturing towns the case is no better. In Glasgow there are 60,000 women engaged in factories or needlework, whose average earnings do not exceed 7s. or

8s. a week. Dr. Patterson, whom you know and respect as one of the most eminent divines in that city, stated, in a public speech not long since, that in three wynds, constituting but a portion of his parish, there were, in a population of 3,232, only 83 church sittings, or little more than an average of 2½ to 100, and that in the whole locality there were only 117 Bibles. 'Certain it is,' he exclaims, 'that nothing short of a levy *en masse* of whatever there is of living Christianity in the city, in all the branches of the Church of Christ, will suffice to make head against the augmenting ignorance and ungodliness and infidelity with which we have to deal. If we do not destroy the evil, it will destroy us.' Out of 10,461 burials in that city in 1850, no less than 2,381, or nearly a fourth, were at the public expense. Glasgow, in these particulars, is but a specimen of your manufacturing towns generally. So, too, of your country population. A very large number of your agricultural population live in filthy and crowded cottages, where the sexes are in close and perilous contact night and day, where decency is difficult and comfort impossible; the effect of which is to break down the barriers of morality, to obliterate all the sweet and saving attractions of a home, to weaken and desecrate all domestic ties, and to brutalise the manners and debase every natural feeling. The cottage accommodation of your villages is little or no better; and the low tone of morality which this, in conjunction with other unfavourable influences, has caused, may be inferred from the following sad statement made last May in the *North British Review*:—'There are few things more remarkable in the sight of observant residents in many country villages than the small number of marriages solemnised in the course of the year. Among these few things, we are afraid, must be mentioned the number of illegitimate children that are born into the world. In some villages, indeed, these events are of such frequent occurrence as to excite neither surprise nor indignation. . . . . . There is something in this kind of insensibility which is very chilling and disheartening. This obtuseness of the moral senses, this deadness to shame, makes one almost despair over it. When the standard of public opinion is so low, there is little hope of practical improvement.'

"'But, sisters, we have said enough; and we now appeal to you very seriously to reflect, and to ask counsel of God how far such a state of things is in accordance with his Holy Word, the inalienable rights of immortal souls, and the pure and merciful spirit of the Christian religion. . . . . .

"'Now, sisters, we do not shut our eyes to the difficulties that might beset the sudden elevation of your degraded population to the rights and the dignity of manhood. But, nevertheless, we cannot be silent on those systems of your society which, in direct contravention of God's own law, deny in effect to the poor labourer the sanctity of marriage, with all its joys, rights, and obligations; nor can we be silent on that awful policy which, either by law, or by the absence of law precludes any race of men, or any portion of the human family, from that education which alone can enable them to understand the truths of the Gospel and the ordinances of Christianity. We appeal to you as sisters, as wives, and as mothers, to raise your voices to your fellow-citizens, and your prayers to God, for the removal of England's shame from the Christian world.' "

2. Physical Condition.

From the London Guardian of Jan. 19, 1853.

(1.) THE POOR AND THE POLICE.

"The report of Capt. Hay, one of the Commissioners of the Metropolitan Police, on the operation of the Common Lodging-house Act, just made to the Secretary of State of the Home Department, has laid bare a state of things in reference to the habitations and mode of living of the very poor which might, perhaps, have been suspected, but could hardly be thoroughly realized by any of us until the wretched details were thus published by authority. Have any of us ever asked ourselves what becomes at night of those destitute creatures who prowl about the thoroughfares of London and our other great towns, who rise in the morning without the certainty of a meal during the day,—who exist partly by petty pilfering, and whom not even the efficiency of the modern system of police has hitherto appeared perceptibly to affect. If we wish to see how a portion of our fellow-beings are lodged, this official report will tell us. In a small eight-roomed house in a fœtid alley, built up close at the back, so that the circulation of even the smallest current of air is rendered impossible, are to be found seventy or eighty persons huddled together, several families in a single small room, each occupying its respective corner. These places are never white-washed, not even cleansed, and are utterly destitute of the most ordinary appliances of decency. Not to dwell on these disgusting details any longer, let us pass on to another feature of the report. We are told that great good has already been effected,—that the inspecting police-sergeants walk several hundred miles every week in the performance of their duties, and that by their exertions, aided by the co-operation of the magistracy, numbers of these dens have been cleaned out and white-washed, and the owners compelled to obey the law by limiting the numbers of their lodgers. So far as it goes this is well enough. It must be an unspeakable blessing to the better part of a neighbourhood to get these hotbeds of filth, and its accompanying typhus and small pox, put in some sort of order; but how came such a state of things ever to arise at all, and may we not be quenching the evil in one part to reappear with increased malignity in another?

"We ask—and we should like the attention of those to whom the administration of the Common Lodging-house Act is intrusted, to turn their attention to the point—how much of the evil is of comparatively recent date, and whether it is not in great measure clearly attributable to the careless indifference of Parliament and the public? At the time when New Oxford-street was being opened, and Victoria-street in Westminster projected—vast improvements undoubtedly to the surrounding property—it was asked by ourselves, in common with some of our contemporaries, whether any one had considered for an instant the inevitable fate of the people thus turned into the streets.

That portion of St. Giles' traversed by New Oxford-street, and the Almonry, now extinguished by Victoria-street, were, no doubt, two of the vilest haunts in our great metropolis. But for all that, they were then inhabited by several thousands of human beings, who were remorselessly turned out without a thought being given to their future fate. Lodge somewhere they of necessity must, and where were they to go, except to places already occupied by those in a like condition with themselves? It was pointed out at the time, that, as a consequence of providing no substitute for the dwellings pulled down in the course of the alterations, other haunts of wretchedness would henceforth be doubly crowded, and that, while the shopkeepers of Oxford-street, and the dwellers near the Houses of Parliament, might with reason congratulate themselves on the removal from their neighbourhood of a mass of dirt and crime, the evil would infallibly show itself in an aggravated form in some other quarters. And so it has come to pass; thenceforth common lodging-houses have become the most valuable description of property. The floor of a room is let out at so much a foot—it might almost be said at so much an inch; and where, some years ago, forty or fifty people might be found in one small dwelling, seventy or eighty are now congregated.

"And now that the evil is laid bare, are any steps being taken to remedy it? None, or next to none, it would seem. A course of fining and imprisoning may indeed compel the lodging-housekeepers of a particular quarter to clean out their houses, and admit no more than a certain number at a time, but what has been done to house the people displaced? Take the case of a house in which, prior to the visits of the inspecting sergeant of police, eighty wretches were piled, and suppose that, thanks to magisterial severity and an active police supervision, the number is henceforth reduced to thirty, what has become of the remaining fifty? The question is not difficult to answer. Lodge they must somewhere. It appears by the reports that, according to the calculations of the police, about half the houses only, subject to the operation of the act, have hitherto been visited. We may feel quite sure that those who have been displaced from their old quarters in the inspected half, have been driven to find shelter in that portion which the visits of the police have not yet reached. It may be fully expected that if the authorities continue these reports periodically, the evil, though apparently narrowed in area, will increase in intensity. In a class of houses where eighty people may now be stowed, it must not surprise us if we read of a hundred or so on some future occasion. But even let it be supposed, for the sake of argument, that every common lodging-house has been visited and set in order, and its inmates reduced to the legal number, and that a strong staff of police takes care that the law is not again infringed. It is said that the houses already inspected amount to one-half of the total number of those in existence in London, and that they form the habitation of fifty thousand persons. So that it may be assumed there are in London one hundred thousand persons or so who live in this way. It is quite clear that the least the police can do is to clear out at least one-half of the number from each house, and even then they would be probably too crowded. Nevertheless, suppose one half are allowed to remain, and then where are the other half to go to? What is to become of the fifty thousand men, women, and children turned out to sleep in the streets? Have our legislators ever given this view of the question a single thought? The fact is, we are all of us apt to be careless and indifferent except to what immediately affects us; and it is only when the matter is forced on our notice, that we try to realize the condition of those in a different sphere. It is not merely in London that this blind sanitary zeal has manifested itself. Some years ago it was found that there were numbers of people in Liverpool living in damp, close, unwholesome cellars; the Corporation determined to make a clean sweep, a private Act of Parliament was obtained without difficulty, and the cellars were cleared, but their occupants had no where to go to. Legislation had not done anything for their accommodation, and frightful scenes of misery were the result of this indiscriminating reform.

"The remedy, indeed, is simple enough. To turn people out of their dwellings without providing places for them to go to, is manifestly beginning at the wrong end. Sanitary reform is an excellent thing, but what right have the rich to throw its weight exclusively on the poor? The rich man gets compensation when turned out of his dwelling, not so the poor vagrant. So far as street improvements are concerned, nothing can be simpler than the course which should invariably be adopted. Dwellings for the poor as well as for the rich should in every case be erected on a portion of the ground cleared for the improvements, in numbers sufficient to accommodate properly the poorer population displaced. It is no particular inconvenience to the rich man who keeps his carriage, or even to him who can afford his threepence for an omnibus, if he is obliged to live a little further from his place of business; but a large portion of the poor are of necessity obliged to live in the centre of the metropolis, and some accommodation ought to be provided for them. Nor have the richer inhabitants of the neighbourhood any reason to fear, if, when a rookery is cleared out, proper accommodation be provided in its stead, the upgrowth of a new St. Giles's or a new Almonry. The dwellings for the humbler classes erected in St. Pancras—not a particularly healthy situation—have proved that it is possible, and not very difficult, to keep the mortality of poor families in London below that of the average mortality of England. It is quite possible to make London a healthy place for all of us; and although, unfortunately, moral improvement does not necessarily keep pace with physical comforts, one thing is certain, that if any set of human beings be lodged and treated materially as beasts, or worse than beasts, their moral and intellectual natures will soon undergo an analogous degradation."

From the London Morning Herald of March 30, 1853.

(2) "CONDITION OF THE POOR IN LONDON.

"Not very far from the spot where we write, within no very great distance of the residences of many of our aristocracy, lies one of those dark and gloomy 'courts' which all over London are thronged by the poor. It is not, we believe, worse than hundreds of others, but it has been explored, and to the humanity of those who have visited its dismal chambers, we are indebted for a description of the dwellings, and the daily life of myriads of our swarming population.

"The 'court' of which we write, Charlotte-buildings, off Gray's-inn-lane, contains 15 houses, and these 15 houses give, each containing eight rooms, shelter, upon the very lowest calculation, to a population of very nearly 1000 persons!! The description of one of these houses is the description of all. Will our readers bear with us while we take them through its apartments, as they are described by an eye-witness. We begin with the two rooms upon the ground floor:

"In the front room 'there are no bedsteads, chairs, or tables; a few ragged clothes are drying before a little fire in the grate; above the mantel are a looking-glass about three inches high, and some torn prints of the crucifixion, &c.; in the cupboards, without doors, are pieces of broken crockery; a kind of bed in one corner, with children asleep; the floor rotten in many parts, the walls and ceiling sadly cracked. The rent is 2s. 3d. per week, which is called for every Monday, and must be paid on Wednesday.'

"We are not told who are the inmates of this chamber, but the room immediately behind it 'presents a sad scene of distress—*the man, his wife, and some children, earn a living by chopping fire-wood;* the man had been ill, and not able to rise for two days; he was lying on a quantity of wood-shavings, and was covered with an old black and ragged blanket; his skin did not appear as if it had been washed for weeks; he was very ill, and evidently in a state of fever; his wife was almost equally dirty. '*We have no wood to chop,*' was the expression of their ultimate distress. This room was much dilapidated, and they had suffered greatly during the late severe weather, owing to the broken condition of the windows. The rent was 1s. 9d. per week; the window overlooks a back yard, the condition of which was shocking.'

"These, it will be remembered, are not the haunts of the outcasts of society, who live by plunder. This wretched back room is the hiding-place of a miserable couple who, with their children, attempt to earn their bread by an humble, an ill-requited, but an honest industry. The expression of their worst distress is, 'We have no wood to chop.'

"'The first floor,' continues the writer, 'both back and front, was crowded with inhabitants. The people acknowledged that fifteen persons slept in the two little rooms last night; the walls were cracked and dirty, and the ceiling constantly falls upon the floor while the inmates are taking their food. One woman said that a part of the cracked hearthstone from above had fallen amongst the children. The rent of the front room is 2s. 3d.; back, 1s. 9d. Continuing our way up stairs, we found the state of the staircase of the rooms worse and worse. *In the front room two pair, when our eyes had become accustomed to the Rembrandtish gloom, we found fifteen persons!! Some had been selling onions, &c., in the streets,* some begging, *one or two were seemingly bricklayer's laborers,* and others had been working at the carrion heaps in the neighborhood.'

"The others presented the same dismal picture, with the addition of holes in the roof, through which the winds, and rains, and snows, made their way upon the inmates of this wretched tenement. For these attics the rent was the same as for the lower apartments—an anomaly accounted for by the fact that 'the landlord *removes to the upper rooms those who may be a shilling or so in arrear of rent.*' The annual sum extorted from these miserable beings for the hire of this one house amounts to upwards of £40!!—a rent infinitely greater, in proportion, than is paid for the noblest palaces of the West-End.

"It is difficult to realize the appalling truth, that in one small court of this great metropolis, one thousand human beings are at this moment thus existing. Multiply this number by that of the similar receptacles of human misery that surround us, and we may venture *to set against all the degradation of human nature that prevails over ten thousand square miles of the most savage district upon earth, the utter abasement of our fellow-creatures, which is, at the very hour when we write, contained within the limits of the metropolis of great and Christian England.*

"Let men prate as they will about our progress, we do not believe that scenes like these existed in the olden time. Discomfort there may have been—distress, and hard and pinching times, but we do not believe that any generation but our own has ever witnessed so hideous a congregation of squalid, abject, and hopeless destitution as is to be found in these loathsome receptacles to which our busy civilization drives its cast off and rejected victims to rot."

From the London Times, of March 30, 1853.

(3) "THE WHITE SLAVES OF ENGLAND.

"What is slavery? 'A slave,' says Dr. Noah Webster, in his dictionary published at New York, 'is a person wholly subject to the will of another; one who has no will of his own, but whose person and services are wholly under the control of another.' The learned lexicographer—and surely at New York men should be acquainted with the rights of the subject—proceeds to inform us that, in the early ages of the world, prisoners of war were considered and treated as slaves. 'The slaves of modern times,' he adds, 'are generally purchased like horses or oxen.' Our own Dr. Johnson defines a slave as being one 'mancipated to a master—not a freeman—a dependant—one who has lost the power of resistance.' Mr. Charles Richardson, on the other hand, considers a slave as a person 'who is reduced to captivity—to servitude—to bondage; who is bound or compelled to serve, labor, or toil for another.'

"There is always some little trouble about a definition, and probably it requires the cobbling and filing of more than one generation to produce anything like a perfect one. There are, however, certain conditions of life which any lexicographer would endeavor to include in his drag net, if he were attempting to give a definition of slavery. We are all agreed about the Uncle Toms and colored population of the Southern States of the American Union. They are slaves—not only in name, but in fact—kindly treated, we believe, in the majority of instances—but still essentially slaves. When we endeavor to go a little further we find ourselves considerably embarrassed. A man is the slave of his own bad passions,—of his lust after gain or power. But this will scarcely do, for, by enlarging the definition too much, the essence and reality of the thing to be defined is altogether lost.

"It may perhaps be better to begin at the other end, and ascend from particulars to generals. Granting that the negro gangs who are worked on the cotton grounds of the Southern States of North America, or in the sugar plantations of Brazil, are slaves, in what way should we speak of persons who are circumstanced in the manner we are about to relate? Let us consider them as inhabitants of a distant region—say of New Orleans—no matter about the color of their skins, and then ask ourselves what should be our opinion of a nation in which such things are tolerated. They are of a sex and age the least qualified to struggle with the hardships of their lot—young women, for the most part, between 16 and 30 years of age. As we would not deal in exaggerations, we would premise that we take them at their busy season, just as writers upon American slavery are careful to select the season of cotton-picking and sugar-crushing as illustrations of their theories. The young female slaves, then, of whom we speak, are worked in gangs in ill ventilated rooms, or rooms that are not ventilated at all, for it is found by experience that, if air be admitted, it brings with it 'blacks' of another kind, which damage the work upon which the seamstresses are employed. Their occupation is to sew from morning till night, and night till morning—stitch, stitch, without pause—without speech—without a smile—without a sigh. In the gray of the morning they must be at work, say at six o'clock, having a quarter of an hour allowed for breaking their fast. The food served out to them is scanty and miserable enough, but still, in all probability, more than their fevered system can digest.

"We do not, however, wish to make out a case of starvation; the suffering is of another kind—equally dreadful of endurance. From six o'clock, then, till eleven, it is stitch, stitch. At eleven, a small piece of dry bread is served to each seamstress, but still she must stitch on. At one o'clock, twenty minutes are allowed for dinner—a slice of meat and a potatoe, with a glass of toast and water to each workwoman. Then again to work—stitch, stitch—until five o'clock, when fifteen minutes are again allowed for tea. The needles are then set in motion once more—stitch, stitch—until nine o'clock, when fifteen minutes are allowed for supper—a piece of dry bread and cheese, and a glass of beer. From nine o'clock at night until one, two, and three o'clock in the morning, stitch, stitch; the only break in this long period being a minute or two—just time enough to swallow a cup of strong tea, which is supplied lest the young people should 'feel sleepy.' At three o'clock, A. M., to bed; at six o'clock, A. M., out of it again to resume the duties of the following day. There must be a good deal of monotony in the occupation.

"But when we have said that for certain months of the year these unfortunate young persons are worked in the manner we describe, we have not said all. Even during the few hours allotted to sleep—should we not rather say to a feverish cessation from toil?—their miseries continue. They are cooped up in sleeping-pens, ten in a room which would perhaps be sufficient for the accommodation of two persons. The alternation is from the treadmill—and what a treadmill!—to the Black Hole of Calcutta. Not a word of remonstrance is allowed, or is possible. The seamstresses may leave the mill, no doubt; but what awaits them on the other side of the door?—starvation, if they be honest—if not, in all probability, prostitution and its consequences. They would scarcely escape from slavery that way. Surely this is a very terrible state of things, and one which claims the anxious consideration of the ladies of England, who have pronounced themselves so loudly against the horrors of negro slavery in the United States. Had this system of oppression against persons of their own sex been really exercised in New Orleans, it would have elicited from them many expressions of sympathy for the sufferers, and of abhorrence for the cruel taskmasters who could so cruelly overwork wretched creatures so unfitted to the toil.

"It is idle to use any further mystification in the matter. The scenes of misery we have described exist at our own doors, and in the most fashionable quarters of luxurious London. It is in the dressmaking and millinery establishments of the 'West End,' that the system is steadily pursued. The continuous labor is bestowed upon the gay garments in which the 'ladies of England' love to adorn themselves. It is to satisfy their whims and caprices, that their wretched sisters undergo these days and nights of suffering and toil. It is but right that we should confess the fault does not lie so much at the door of the customers as with the principals of these establishments. The milliners and dressmakers of the metropolis will not employ hands enough to do the work. They increase their profits from the blood and life of the wretched creatures in their employ. Certainly the prices charged for articles of dress at any of the great West End establishments are sufficiently high—as most English heads of families know to their cost—to enable the proprietors to retain a competent staff of workpeople, and at the same time to secure a very handsome profit to themselves.

"Wherein, then, lies the remedy? Will the case of these poor seamstresses be bettered if the ladies of England abstain partially, or in great measure, from giving their usual orders to their usual houses? In that case, it may be said, some of the seamstresses will be dismissed to starvation, and the remainder will be overworked as before. We freely confess we do not see our way through the difficulty; for we hold the most improbable event in our social arrangements to be the fact, that a lady of fashion will employ a second-rate instead of a first-rate house for the purchase of her annual finery. The leading milliners and dressmakers of London have hold of English society at both ends. They hold the ladies by their vanity and their love of fine clothes, and the seamstresses by what appears to be their interest and by their love of life. Now, love of fine clothes and love of life are two very strong motive-springs of human action.

"A correspondent who has addressed us upon this subject, suggests that the ladies of England—the censurers of American slavery, with the Duchess of Sutherland at their head—should refuse to give their patronage to any houses in which the twelve-hour system was not strictly adhered to. We confess we see difficulties in the way, but not greater than 'woman's wit' might overcome, if fairly brought to bear upon the question. The customers, the principals, the seamstresses, are all women. They are more competent to deal with each other than men could by any possibility be. If the Sutherland-house committee would fairly set the example, and carry out their design with sufficient vigilance, we doubt not they could execute the task. They did not shrink from the wholesale difficulty of emancipating the 3,000,000 or 4,000,000 negroes of the United States,—why hesitate at grappling with the London mantuamakers, who are dependent for their existence upon the good will and patronage of their customers? No doubt their intelligence will find a way out of difficulties which puzzle the masculine brain.

"We should be glad indeed to see any effective movement afoot, which would compel the milliners of the metropolis to employ a sufficient number of hands, and consequently to work only for a limited number of hours. God knows, twelve hours of labor and confinement are quite sufficient for any young woman to go through in the course of a day. For ourselves, we can but point to other climates where toil meets with its appropriate reward, and urge these unfortunates to leave their native shores as soon as passage money can be scraped together. Those who go will find a better England at the other side of the globe, and those who remain will find the market in a more wholesome condition. Almost every week we have to record a strike for increase of wages among certain classes of male laborers—it is time that the turn of the overworked women had come."

From Hood's "Lay of the Laborer:"—

(4.) "'What matters?' said a grey-headed man, in fustian, in answer to a warning nudge and whisper from his neighbor. 'If walls has ears, they are welcome to what they can ketch—ay, and the stranger to boot—if so be he don't know all about us already—for it's all in print. What we yarn, and what we spend—what we eat, and what we drink—what we wear, and the cost on it from top to toe—where we sleep, and how many on us lie in a bed—our consarns are as common as waste land.'

"'And as many geese and donkeys turned on to them, I do think!' cried a young fellow in velveteens—'to hear how folk cackle and bray about our states. And then the queer remedies as is prescribed, like, for a starving man! A Bible, says one—a reading made easy, says another—a temperance medal, says another—or maybe a hagricultural prize. But what is he to eat, I ax? Why, says one, a Corkassian Jew—says another, a cricket-ball—says another, a may-pole—and says another, the Wenus bound for Horsetrailye.'

"'As if idle hands and empty pockets,' said the grey-headed man, 'did not make signs, of themselves, for work and wages—and a hungry belly for bread and cheese.'

"'That's true, any how,' said one of the water-drinkers. 'I only wish that a doctor would come at this minute, and listen with his *telescope* on my stomach, and he would hear it a-talking as plain as our magpie, and saying, I wants wittles.'

"There was a general peal of mirth at this speech, but brief, and ending abruptly, as laughter does, when extorted by the odd treatment of a serious subject—a flash followed by deeper gloom. The conversation then assumed a graver tone; each man in turn recounting the trials, privations, and visitations, of himself, his wife, and children, or his neighbor's—not mentioned with fierceness, intermingling oaths and threats, not with bitterness—some few allusions excepted to harsh overseers or miserly masters—but as soldiers or sailors describe the hardships and sufferings they have had to encounter in their rough vocation, and evidently endured in their own persons with a manly fortitude. If the speaker's voice faltered, or his eyes moistened, it was only when he painted the sharp bones showing through the skin, the skin through the rags, of the wife of his bosom; or how the traditional wolf, no longer to be kept from the door, had rushed in and fastened on his young ones. What a revelation it was! Fathers, with more children than shillings per week—mothers travailing literally in the straw—infants starving before the parents' eyes, with cold, and famishing for food! Human creatures, male and female, old and young, not gnawed and torn by single woes, but worried at once by winter, disease and want, as by that triple-headed dog, whelped in the realm of torments!

"My ears tingled, and my cheeks flushed with self-reproach, remembering my fretful impatience under my own inflictions, no light ones either, till compared with the heavy complications of anguish, moral and physical, experienced by those poor men. My heart swelled with indignation, my soul sickened with disgust, to recall the sobs, sighs, tears, and hysterics—the lamentations and imprecations bestowed by pampered selfishness on a sick bird or beast, a sore finger, a swelled toe, a lost rubber, a missing luxury, an ill-made garment, a culinary failure!—to think of the cold looks and harsh words cast by the same eyes and lips, eloquent in self-indulgence, on nakedness, starvation, and poverty. Wealth, with his own million of money, pointing to the new half-farthings as fitting money to the million—gluttony, gorged with dainties, washed down by iced champagne, complacently commending his humble brethren to the brook of Elisha and the salads of Nebuchadnezzar; and fashion, in furs and velvet, comfortably beholding her squalid sisters shivering in robes de zephyr, woven by winter itself, with the warp of a north, and the woof of an east wind!

"'The job up at Bosely is finished,' said one of the middle-aged men. 'I have enjoyed but three days' work in the last fortnight, and God above knows where I shall get another, even at a shilling a day. And nine mouths to feed, big and little—and nine backs to clothe—with the winter a-setting in—and the rent behind-hand—and never a bed to lie on, and my good woman, poor soul, ready to ——;' a choking sound and a hasty gulp of water smothered the rest of the sentence. 'There must be something done for us—there MUST,' he added, with an emphatic clap of his broad, brown, barky hand, that made the glasses jingle and the idle pipes clatter on the board. And every voice in the room echoed 'there must,' my own involuntarily swelling the chorus.

"'Ay, there must, and that full soon,' said the gray-headed man in fustian, with an upward appealing look, as if through the smoky clouds of the ceiling to God himself for confirmation of the necessity. 'But come, lads, time's up, so let's have our chant, and then squander.'

"The company immediately stood up; and one of the elders with a deep bass voice, and to a slow, sad air, began a rude song, the composition, probably, of some provincial poet of his own class, the rest of the party joining occasionally in a verse that served for the burden.

'A spade! a rake! a hoe!
A pickaxe, or a bill!
A hook to reap, or a scythe to mow,
A flail, or what you will—
And here's a ready hand
To ply the needful tool,
And skilled enough by lessons rough
In labor's rugged school.

'To hedge, or dig the ditch,
To lop or fell the tree,
To lay the swarth on the sultry field,
Or plough the stubborn lea,
The harvest stack to bind,
The wheaten rick to thatch;
And never fear in my pouch to find
The tinder or the match.

'To a flaming barn or farm
My fancies never roam;
The fire I yearn to kindle and burn
Is on the hearth of home;
Where children huddle and crouch
Through dark long winter days,
Where starving children huddle and crouch
To see the cheerful rays,
A-glowing on the haggard cheek,
And not in the haggard's blaze!

'To Him who sends a drought
To parch the fields forlorn,
The rain to flood the meadows with mud,
The blight to blast the corn—
To Him I leave to guide
The bolt in its crooked path,
To strike the miser's rick, and show
The skies blood-red with wrath.

'A spade! a rake! a hoe!
A pickaxe, or a bill!
A hook to reap, or a scythe to mow,
A flail, or what ye will—

The corn to thrash, or the hedge to plash,
The market team to drive,
Or mend the fence by the cover side,
And leave the game alive.

'Ay, only give me work,
And then you need not fear
That I shall snare his worship's hare,
Or kill his grace's deer—
Break into his lordship's house,
To steal the plate so rich,
Or leave the yeoman that had a purse
To welter in the ditch.

'Wherever nature needs,
Wherever labor calls,
No job I'll shirk of the hardest work,
To shun the workhouse walls;
Where savage laws begrudge
The pauper babe its breath,
And doom a wife to a widow's life
Before her partner's death.

'My only claim is this,
With labor stiff and stark,
By lawful turn my living to earn,
Between the light and dark—
My daily bread and nightly bed,
My bacon and drop of beer—
But all from the hand that holds the land,
And none from the overseer!

'No parish money or loaf,
No pauper badges for me,
A son of the soil, by right of toil,
Entitled to my fee.
No alms I ask, give me my task;
Here are the arm, the leg,
The strength, the sinews of a man,
To work, and not to beg.

'Still one of Adam's heirs,
Though doomed by chance of birth
To dress so mean, and eat the lean
Instead of the fat of the earth;
To make such humble meals
As honest labor can,
A bone and a crust, with a grace to God,
And little thanks to man!

'A spade! a rake! a hoe!
A pickaxe, or a bill!
A hook to reap, or a scythe to mow,
A flail, or what ye will—

Whatever the tool to ply,
Here is a willing drudge,
With muscle and limb—and wo to him
Who does their pay begrudge.

'Who every weekly score
Docks labor's little mite,
Bestows on the poor at the temple-door,
But robbed them over-night.
The very shilling he hoped to save,
As health and morals fail,
Shall visit me in the New Bastile,
The spital or the gaol!'

"As the last ominous word ceased ringing, the candle-wick suddenly dropped into the neck of the stone bottle, and all was darkness and silence.

* * * * * * * *

"The vision is dispelled—the fiction is gone—but a fact and a figure remain.

"Some time since, a strong inward impulse moved me to paint the destitution of an overtasked class of females, who work, work, work, for wages almost nominal. But deplorable as is their condition, in the low deep, there is, it seems, a lower still—below that gloomy gulf a darker region of human misery—beneath that purgatory a hell—resounding with more doleful wailings and a sharper outcry—the voice of famishing wretches, pleading vainly for work! work! work!—imploring as a blessing, what was laid upon man as a curse—the labor that wrings sweat from the brow, and bread from the soil!

"As a matter of conscience, that wail touches me not. As my works testify, I am of the working class myself, and in my humble sphere furnish employment for many hands, including paper-makers, draughtsmen, engravers, compositors, pressmen, binders, folders, and stitchers—and critics—all receiving a fair day's wages for a fair day's work. My gains consequently are limited—not nearly so enormous as have been realized upon shirts, slops, shawls, &c.—curiously illustrating how a man or woman might be 'clothed with curses as with a garment.' My fortune may be expressed without a long row of those ciphers—those 0's at once significant of hundreds of thousands of pounds, and as many ejaculations of pain and sorrow from dependent slaves. My wealth might all be hoarded, if I were miserly, in a gallipot or a tin snuff-box. My guineas, placed edge to edge, instead of extending from the Minories to Golden Square, would barely reach from home to Bread Street. My riches would hardly allow me a roll in them, even if turned into the new copper mites. But then, thank God! no reproach clings to my coin. No tears or blood clog the meshes, no hair, plucked in desperation, is knitted with the silk of my lean purse. No consumptive seamstress can point at me her bony forefinger, and say, 'For thee, *sewing in forma pauperis*, I am become this living skeleton!' or hold up to me her fatal needle, as one through the eye of which the scriptural camel must pass ere I may hope to enter heaven. No withered work-woman, shaking at me her dripping suicidal locks, can cry, in a piercing voice, 'For thee, and for six poor pence, I embroidered eighty flowers on this veil'—literally a veil of tears. No famishing laborer, his joints racked with toil, holds out to me in the palm of his broad, hard hand, seven miserable shillings, and mutters, 'For these, and a parish loaf, for six long days, from dawn till dusk, through hot and cold, through wet and dry, I tilled thy land!' My short sleeps are peaceful; my dreams untroubled. No ghastly phantoms with reproachful faces, and silence more terrible than speech, haunt my quiet pillow. No victims of slow murder, ushered by the avenging fiends, beset my couch, and make awful appointments with me to meet at the Divine bar on the day of judgment. No deformed human creatures—men, women, and children, smirched black as negroes, transfigured suddenly, as demons of the pit, clutch at my heels to drag me down, down, down, an unfathomable shaft, into a gaping Tartarus. And if sometimes in waking visions I see throngs of little faces, with features preternaturally sharp, and wrinkled brows, and dull, seared orbs—grouped with pitying clusters of the young-eyed cherubim—not for me, thank Heaven! did those crippled children become prematurely old; and precociously evaporate, like so much steam power, the 'dew of their youth.'

"For me, then, that doleful cry from the starving unemployed, has no extrinsic horror; no peculiar pang, beyond that sympathetic one, which must affect the species in general."

In proof (if proof is needed,) of what is said above, "Fathers, with more children than shillings per week," read the following from the London Guardian of Feb. 9th, 1853, and recollect that a shilling, sterling, is less than twenty-five cents, and that out of this pittance there are "nine mouths to feed, big and little—and nine backs to clothe"—and fuel to purchase, and rent to pay, besides,—and then say, is it to be wondered at, that the men "declined to split the difference?"

(5.) "The effects of emigration are being shown in a general demand for higher wages; the carpenters and joiners of the city of Bristol have publicly addressed a circular to their employers generally, in which they solicit an advance of 6d. per day on their present rate of wages. The shipwrights of Davenport have memorialised the Government for an increase; but the most determined demand has been made by the laborers of South Wiltshire. At Barford, Codford, and Fovant, they have struck for an advance of two shillings,—that is, from seven shillings to nine; and a settlement on Friday evening. The farmers resist; the peasants go for nine shillings or nothing. On Monday, nearly two hundred laborers marched from farm to farm stating their case, and behaving with propriety and good sense. The Reverend Mr. Waldegrave, Vicar of Barford, was called in to mediate; and he proposed to split the difference, urging the men to accept a uniform rate of eight shillings a-week. The men declined."

3. Moral Condition.

From the Boston Journal, of March 8, 1853.

"[Foreign Correspondence of the Journal.]

(1.) "LETTERS FROM ENGLAND.

"*Manchester and its Working Population—Their Amusements.*

'MANCHESTER, Feb. 17. 1853.

'Amid the excitement and bustle of this stirring place, one has little time to collect his thoughts; and it is only at a late hour of the night, the present time 12 o'clock—when all is still, that I can put a thought of, or a remark upon, what one sees, on paper. In going through the immense warehouses full of the products of skill and industry, we are struck with the magnitude of Britain's trade; we are lost in estimating its extent and endless variety; we are dazzled with the glare of wealth lying in heaps throughout them; we are amazed at the recital of the fortunes of self-made men, in some cases outstripping even the fortunes of Whittington and his feline friend. But then, going from these to view the immense machinery which produced all this, our amazement increases. Leaving this and viewing the human machines which work the former, or at least a great many of them, our amazement continues to increase, and in looking at these overwrought, hard-working, degraded-looking specimens of humanity, we ask the question—are these the ones who produce this wealth; are they the possesors of immortal souls like their employers, and do these employers know it? Where are they, and whither are they going? I, of course, speak now of the lower class of operatives here, *and not all of them*—but still a very large proportion. I know of nothing which England should first look to of more importance to her own interest, and to the interests of humanity, than this question—the condition of the working classes. Wages here are so low that the *comforts of a home* can be enjoyed by them in but few instances, and the desire for amusement of some kind, which is the ruling passion, drives them into the support, with their little earnings, of a kind of it which is most pernicious and demoralizing. The great fault is, the want of early education, both of the head and heart. The uneducated man, having nothing in himself on which he can depend for the gratification of his desire for amusement, seeks it in a way which is most congenial to his own feelings. An entertainment of a superior character he has no sympathy with. There is too much of the animal about him to relish the intellectual, and therefore, if we wish to elevate those classes, education must be the foundation—an education of the heart as well as the head—and then we may hope to raise a structure in which the fair proportions of true manhood may be developed. Mechanics' Institutions have been got up, and they have done much good, but they do not reach the classes I refer to. They are for the men who have had some education; they are like Greek or Hebrew to the lowest classes in English society. Ragged Schools are one of the means now resorted to, and the working of these have been, so far, successful. But the effort is not general enough, and until it be so we will [shall] not have a better state of things.

'These remarks are suggested by visits which, in company with a friend, I made to the places of amusement, which are the nightly resorts of thousands in this city. I went to four, for the purpose of seeing for myself. In the first place, we paid fourpence admission, which included a glass of ale or porter. The performances consisted of dances of the most obscene kind—and partly by children of only twelve or thirteen years of age—songs, &c., &c. The audience here was composed principally of young clerks of the lower grade and their female companions; little family parties, father, mother, and a few young shoots of the parent tree; the old lady now and then refreshing herself in the "dreadful 'ot place" with a drop of gin and some crackers which she generously assists her dear Joe and the little Joes to. A suspicious looking gentleman, wearing garments of a seedy black, but withal rather well informed and apparently anxious to impart his information to "green uns" like myself, who appeared to have the "cut of a fresh hand." Then there are the operatives of a better class, with their wives, and then again poor pale-looking creatures, wearing out their existence in the cellars of damp warehouses, with bleached cheeks and sunken eyes, and sharp-pointed, red noses, chuckling to themselves—laugh they cannot; they have forgotten how to do it; they used to laugh when they were children, but that was a long time ago, and there have been many changes since.

'But we go into another place; it is not so large, but the admission is the same. The performance is going on; it must be a good piece; roars of laughter are heard, but it is only at low jokes, and vulgar buffoonery, and burlesque imitations of an old Yorkshireman to act the part of a negro. Here the audience are of a lower grade, and in the *dress* circle the gentlemen are habited in moleskin jackets and greasy caps, the ladies in corresponding attire, and the whole appearance of them as human beings is sickening; a dull, heavy stare, or a sly, cunning, low look, or a heavy-breathing, wide-mouthed non-expressiveness, or a determined headstrong, heartless scowl, seemed to be settled on them all, and it was in vain that I looked for some whom I could look upon as something that might shed lustre upon the name of man. There they were, mostly very young persons—the children probably of those who were like the family in the former place—whose only comforts were found in the gin-bottle, whose happiness was only away from home, at such places, instead of *at home*, where only true pleasures can be found. This way of spending the evening is the fruit of the parents' example, and this fruit ripens until it is nipped by the gallows or the hulks.

'The other places are shades worse even; and in all, the inducements to attend are held out in this way: prices are low, say two pence, four pence and six pence, with a glass of ale or gin included. To show you the trade of these places, my friend informed me that only the week before, the lowest and poorest of them was taken by a man who paid £700 for the good will of the business, besides a large yearly rent, and it was thought quite a bargain. A visit to one of these places, among other things, to me at least, taught one lesson more powerfully than ever I heard the pulpit teach it—the duty of accepting Christianity and living in it—were it even for no higher object than that of its being the only means of preventing us from being the companions of the frequenters of such places in another world. This is certainly a low motive, and one which should not induce any man to embrace it, but still, when for ten minutes we could hardly bear the horror of such a place with such a company, how can we think of bearing with the companionship of such throughout an eternity, where no ray of hope can enter, and where the vilest wretches will be the leading powers. Oh! Britain, thou art a noble land, and the inhabitants of all lands must respect thee for what thou hast been; but, remove these leprous spots in your social system, or a disease may creep in, which will destroy your greatness far more effectually than any foreign invasion; which will sink you lower in the scale of nations than ever you have been high in this scale. I will return to this subject in future letters.

'Very truly yours, J. B.'"

From the Boston Courier, as copied by the National Ægis, of April 13th, 1853.

(2) "UNCLE TOM AND UNCLE JOHN.

"A month or two since, in commenting on what was done by those 'silly women,' the Duchess of Sutherland and her associates, we took occasion to advise them to 'look at home.' Our abolitionist friends waxed very wroth at this, and intimated that things were well enough in England, though Englishmen *did* now and then sell their wives at auction, with halters round their necks, nothing being done and very little said against it by their neighbours. John Bull, however—shall we say it—begins to think it high time to follow our advice. The London Morning Chronicle of March 12th has a leading article commencing as follows:

"'The bill for the protection of women and children, introduced by Mr. Fitzroy on Thursday night, is conceived in the right spirit. It will go far to redeem what is, we fear, a national disgrace. Whether we are in any degree indebted for it to the somewhat vivacious and personal reply which the 'Women of America' sent to a recent address from their British sisters, it is superfluous to inquire. Anyhow, the stern realities of our Police Courts equal, if they do not surpass, the fictitious horrors of Mrs. Beecher Stowe. *It is high time that we begin to look at home.* Whether the crime of trampling upon a wife, beating her with a poker, kicking and lacerating her person, are peculiar to England or to our own times, we know not. It is always difficult to register the origin or progress of crime—all we can do is to detect and suppress it. We suspect that even when 'England was merry England,' there was always a good deal of coarse brutality about the boasted British character; and savage domestic tyranny, at least in the lower ranks of society, is, we fear, no new phenomenon in our annals. Still it can hardly be doubted that cruel outrages upon women, chiefly perpetrated by their husbands and paramours, are largely increasing.'

"This, we think, is sufficient to show that the milk-and-water sentimentality of Stafford House is held at a cheap rate by sensible people in England, and that the ridiculous aspect of the pseudo-philanthropy, which melts into tears over romance, while it shuts its eyes and hardens its heart to the misery that lies weltering at its own door, is beginning to strike every thinking and feeling individual in that country. Some of the 'stern realities' above referred to are recapitulated in the course of what follows in the Chronicle. They form a catalogue of horrid brutalities too painful to quote. We will give a few of the London editor's comments.

"'Here then—including Mr. Fitzroy's list—are more than twenty instances, occurring within two months, in London alone, of the most foul and savage attacks committed mostly by men, on women and defenceless children. The old chivalry of common life, which held it base to lift a hand against a woman, seems to be extinct; and things have come to such a pass that a poor man's wife only claims from the law of England that measure of protection which is freely awarded to a dog or an ox.

"'It may be difficult to assign a special cause for this frightful degradation of the national character—for such we fear it is. We fully believe that this mass of misery, domestic hatred, cowardly assaults and murder, may in numberless instances be traced back to the miserable lodgings of the London poor, and to the moral disadvantages arising from the absence of those checks which society imposes. A London artisan, early and late at his work, is uninfluenced by social opinion—he has no neighbours—and thus, in the midst of a crowded population, he may relapse into a state akin to that of the solitary and the savage.'

"Stafford House, it is reasonable to think, should keep quiet for a while, at least on the subject of Uncle Tom. After the well-fed Duchess has lachrymated her prettiest over the pages of Mrs. Stowe, let her make a real step, with literal shoes and stockings, into one of these stern realities—'the miserable lodgings of the London poor'—and remember that London is *her* home, and not *ours*. When that is set to right, let the Duchess and her tender-hearted associates re-commence their denunciations of American slavery; but not till then."

Sometime since, I cut from an English newspaper an article headed, "History and Politics. Centralization and Local Self-Government." The name and date of the paper I did not preserve, and have forgotten, but it could, perhaps, be ascertained by the following description:—The columns are a quarter of an inch narrower than those of the London Guardian. On the reverse of the side containing the above-mentioned article, is the following:—"Law Intelligence. Admiralty Court. Wednesday. The Neptune. Salvage."—And under this, the following:—"Court of Bankruptcy. Wednesday. Before William Lionel Felix Tollemache.—Lord Hunting—r's [part of the last syllable is cut off,] Bankruptcy." In the paragraph that follows, the bankrupt is described as the eldest son of the Earl of Dysart. At the foot of the next column, is a paragraph on the "Railways Abandonment Bill."—I give the above as a clue to the name and date of the paper.—In the column last mentioned, is the following:—

(3.) A Very Young Pickpocket.

"*Thomas Connor*, not quite 7 years old, and whose head was scarcely level with the front of the dock, was convicted of picking the pocket of a lady named Linthwaite, of a purse containing a sovereign and six shillings. The father of the boy was in Court, and in answer to questions put by the learned Judge and several Magistrates upon the Bench, stated that he was a straw bonnet presser, at which business he earned a guinea per week. He had done what he could for the prisoner, but he unfortunately paid no attention to anything but thieving, and he was sorry to say that he had had another son, who was a trifle older than the prisoner, convicted in that Court. His children were unable either to read or write. The learned Judge said it was deplorable to see the extent to which the present system was carried. He meant the system by which such heartless and depraved creatures, as the father of this prisoner evidently was, sought to remove the responsibility of their children from themselves to the State, through the instrumentality of a trial and conviction. He had got rid of one child by those means, and he was with another no doubt hoping for a like result. The learned Judge then commented with severity upon the conduct of the father in not bringing up his children in honest habits, and said he sincerely regretted that he could not send him to the House of Correction for six months instead of the poor little creature then standing at the bar. Such a father was a disgrace to humanity, and he (the learned Judge) could only repeat what he had often said before, that the only effectual remedy for the evil would be a power vested in a criminal court to compel such parents to maintain their children whilst in prison. (To the father.) 'I suppose your other son was convicted of pocket-picking.' The father (sullenly)—'Well I suppose he was.' The Judge—'And they brought their plunder to you, didn't they?' The Father—'No; they always had it themselves.' The Judge—'I don't believe you, but I do believe that you gave them the first lessons in the art.' The prisoner was sentenced to six months' hard labor, the learned Judge intimating that that six months would be devoted to the moral and religious instruction of the prisoner in the excellent school of Westminster Bridewell."

Further down in the same column, is the following:—

(4) "SURREY SESSIONS.

"Picking Pockets at the Brighton Railway Terminus.

"Wednesday.—*James Helcock*, 13, was indicted for stealing, at St. Saviour's, Southwark, a silk pocket handkerchief, from the person of Henry Hasted. Prosecutor deposed that on the evening of the 13th inst. he came up by train from Brighton, and after he had left the platform, and was looking out for an omnibus, he felt some person at his pocket, and on turning round he perceived the prisoner behind him, with two other lads. He directly missed his handkerchief, and seized hold of the prisoner, when his companions commenced kicking prosecutor's legs, and prisoner endeavored to get away. A constable then came up and took the prisoner into custody with the handkerchief in his possession. A constable of the M division stated, that the prisoner was connected with a gang of young thieves who were a complete terror to the inhabitants of the borough. They infested the railway station, and it was a great difficulty to detect them, as they managed their business so systematically. Verdict, *Guilty*; sentence, three months, *and to be once whipped.*"

The following is from Henry Mayhew's London Labor and the London Poor, part 20, page 422, Harper's Reprint; (the *italics* are the authors:—

(5.) "*The chimney-sweepers generally are regardless of the marriage ceremony*, and when they do live with a woman it is in a state of concubinage. These women are always among the lowest of the street-girls—such as lucifer-match and orange-girls, some of the very poorest of the coster girls brought up among the sweepers. They are treated badly by them, and often enough left without any remorse. The women are equally as careless in these matters as the men, and exchange one paramour for another with the same levity, so that there is a promiscuous intercourse continually going on among them. I am informed that among the worst class of sweepers living with women, not one in 50 is married. To these couples very few children are born; but I am not able to state the proportion as compared with other classes."

(6.) The following is from a Review, in the London Guardian, of Feb. 9th, 1853, of a work entitled, "The Vicissitudes of Commerce:—

"Before leaving this book, we cannot but express our regret that so good a person as the writer appears to be, should seem by his language to concur in the term 'unfortunate,' as applied so often by the parties themselves to a sin *no less unhappily prevalent among our country population than it is in the manufacturing districts.* Let us show as much kindness as we please in hopes of a better mind; but let us avoid calling that a misfortune which is so undeniably a sin against the God of *purity.*"

(7.) *From the Baltimore Sun, of Nov. 17th,* 1852.

"INFANTICIDE is reported in the London papers to have increased fearfully among the factory operatives and agricultural laborers of England, caused, it is said, by their abject poverty and dire necessities. Burial clubs, which are mutual assistance institutions, formed among these poor persons for good objects, only increase the extent of the crime; as many are driven by want to murder their infants in order to obtain from these societies the few pounds of funeral money they give. In Leeds there are, as nearly as can be estimated, about *three hundred infants murdered yearly*, to avoid the consequences of their living, and the Coroner states that the murderers are never detected."

From the London Guardian, of Jan. 26th, 1853.

"Two shocking cases of child murder are reported this week. In the one case, at Agar town, the infant was found in a garden crushed to a mummy, it is supposed by placing it between two boards, and pressing it with heavy weights. No clue has been obtained to the inhuman author of the deed. The other case is that of Eliza Pallinger, a girl only 15, residing in the midst of a den of wretchedness, at No. 3, Claren-place, Camberwell, who has been committed for the murder of her new-born infant. On hearing of which, and having its paternity disputed by another man, the reputed father James Brown, aged 40, committed suicide by cutting his throat."

From the London Guardian, of Feb. 2d, 1853.

"The jury have returned a verdict of manslaughter against Mary Ann Oldham, the nurse at the Grenwich Union, who caused the death of a child *by compelling it to hold a hot burning coal.*"

4. Ireland.

(1.) *From the N. Y. Express, as copied by the Baltimore Sun, of Nov.* 16, 1852.

"A SAD PICTURE OF IRELAND.

"Ireland is rapidly undergoing a revolution, in many parts, such as does not attract much attention, but such, nevertheless, as is a great revolution. In an English paper before us, we see it stated that the county of Mayo is in a transition from the cottier state of society, in which the land was thickly peopled, and held by tenants in very small holdings, at very high rents, to the *grazing* system, in which it is occupied merely by a very few herds and care-takers, and held either by the landlord himself or by one or two great capitalist's tenants. The change is from being stocked with men, women, and children, to being stocked with sheep and cattle. A writer in the London Times, drawing the picture of the change, says:—

"'The whole population of a district many miles in extent are simply turned out into the roads to go where they please, and live or die as they can. Of course there are among them many old people hardly able to get along, many sick persons, many little children, many women in an advanced state of pregnancy—out they all go together. There seems to be in the ejecting landlords a very happy state of indifference to the question, what becomes of these people? But I confess my weakness. I have not yet attained this indifference. I inquired anxiously where the people were gone, who, a few months ago, inhabited one of these districts, lately thickly peopled, and now a sheep walk. I was told by a gentleman, and agent, who stoutly defended, upon the plea of necessity, the proceedings in question, that some of them, who had some little property, were gone to America; that many were in the Union workhouse; that some were in the lower parts of the great towns of England, Scotland and Ireland, but that, in his opinion, the greater part of them were dead.'

"A few years ago men, women and children were the most profitable stock which a landlord in this country could encourage upon his property; they lived upon the worst and least quantity of food, and paid rents which (considering the quality of the land and the total absence of any expenditure on the part of the landlord, either in fencing, draining, or the erection of tenements) would in any country be considered exorbitant. When, however, the potatoe failed, the human animal ceased to be a profitable rent paying stock; and as the Poor Laws had been imposed nearly at the same time it became an expensive one. Here we have in one word the *rationale* of the change.

"The most noble Lord Marquis of Sligo seems to be the great *operator* in this changing the habitations of men to the haunts of cattle. This writer in the Times, whence we quote, says:—

"'Near Westport, for several miles, the most noble the Lord Marquis of Sligo is at this moment clearing away the whole population. A few are already removed; in other cases their furniture is standing outside the cottage door, and the whole family are evidently on the point of plunging homeless, into the world. Meanwhile, a new and well built wall is rising between the road and the land, which is still the home of many lately happy families. It is sad to see that this very wall, not yet completed, (for there are breaches in many places, through which the tenants have to remove their all,) is built of the materials of demolished homes. The observant eye will see stones still stained with soot, which once formed the chimney of many a cottage.

"'Beyond Westport the wall is complete, and the people are gone. The most noble Marquis, I conceive, will see and hear no more of them, in this world at least. The remains of the cottages are here quite enclosed within the encircling wall. The district was cleared a few months ago.

"'As the traveller goes on he enters the territory of Sir Roger Palmer, and then that of the Right Hon. the Earl of Lucan. Here things are more advanced. A great part of the land is already in large grass fields, fed by sheep; fine crops of turnips are in others, and in some you may see the young grass among the fresh stubble. All will very soon bear the appearance of a district which man has never peopled.

"'I cannot exactly state the extent of the district operated upon. It begins three or four miles from Westport, and extends (though not without some considerable intervals of land belonging to other proprietors,) almost to the town of Ballinrobe, a distance of perhaps 25 miles. On both sides of the road it stretches as far as the eye can reach. I was informed and believe, (although I cannot state it of my own knowledge,) that the Earl of Lucan alone has lately laid down on grass about 20,000 acres of densely inhabited land.'

"What a mournful picture! What a frightful spectacle it must be! But it is from the country,—where this misery, if not this oppression exists,—that we hear the loudest reproaches of our African slavery, and where such books as Uncle Tom's Cabin find the largest encouragement."

(2.) *From the Baltimore Sun, of Sept. 14th*, 1852.

"The English Commissioners on Emigration report that the total emigration from Ireland in 1851 was 257,372, and that this year it will be considerably increased. Another remarkable fact is, that this emigration is self-sustained; in other words, it pays its own expenses, at least so far as the United States and Canada are concerned. The Commissioners state that last year there was either remitted from America, or expended for prepaid passages to America, by Irish settlers there, no less than £990,000 to enable their friends and relatives to follow them to their adopted homes. The number of emigrants from Ireland to the United States and Canada in 1851 was 238,016; the whole cost of which, as steerage passengers, would be £892,931 4s. 6d., or nearly £100,000 less than the sum absolutely remitted or paid, and which was retained, no doubt, for the use of relatives remaining in Ireland. This is a very suggestive subject. Ireland diminished 1,659,330 in her population between 1841 and 1851, and the result of fair calculation is, that there was a further decrease of 192,215 last year. Taking the United Kingdom as a whole, the annual increase of births over deaths will do little more than balance the annual emigration. Ireland will decrease this year 215,183; Great Britain will increase 227,368. For the first time upon record, without famine or plague, the population of the United Kingdom has become stationary."

From the Philadelphia North American and U. S. Gazette, of April 22d, 1853.

"Irish Emigration.

"Every foreign mail brings us some fresh evidence of the unusual degree of attention excited both in England and Ireland by the immense emigration from the last named country to the United States. We have frequently alluded to the subject, by way of chronicling the unabated progress of what the British writers call the great exodus; yet every successive arrival presents the same facts again in a new light. Nothing appears to stem this mighty torrent. The cessation of the potatoe rot, the diminution of pauperism, the improvement of crops and prospects, the great demand for laborers, with wages rising high, are of no effect. The events of late years seem to have destroyed that love of home and devotion to the isle of his nativity for which the 'exile of Erin' was once celebrated. His longings are now for the land of promise in the far-off world of the West, to which his friends, neighbors and relatives, who preceded him on the path, ever beckon. The attractions of the Australian gold fields fail to turn him aside from his purpose. There is but one bourne for him, and that is America. The Dublin Daily Express, of the 5th inst., says that almost all who possess the means of leaving the country are about doing so. All the vessels offering for passengers are filled up without delay. The Wexford Guardian says that the exodus in that locality has 'assumed a steady, increasing current, and emigration is the frequent topic of conversation in most parts of the country.' But the following extract from the Limerick Chronicle, of the 5th inst., presents the most striking picture :—

"'From the railway stations from Limerick to Clonmel, from Limerick and Galway to Dublin, and elsewhere throughout the country, the people are flying in crowds to the ports of Waterford and Liverpool, to take shipping for the New World; whilst in Limerick we believe we are correct in stating that the ships already announced for sailing are filled, and other ships are eagerly looked for by applicants every day. The rural districts and the smaller towns are the destination of remittances to an almost incredible amount from America; and those remittances are sent to enable those to bear their voyage expenses to whom they are directed. We have been informed by a respectable clergyman, within the last few days, that such is the scarcity of men in his extensive parishes, that he is obliged to send to a neighboring town for laborers to till his fields. Another clergyman informs us that he is daily receiving remittances from persons in America to pay passages for their relatives in his parish. It is apprehended in the neighborhood of the slate quarries, that the enterprising proprietor will be compelled to curtail the works, or to abandon them to some extent, such is the rage for emigration among the laborers he has been employing for some years. Altogether the exodus is alarming.'"

From the Boston Transcript, of April 20th, 1853.

"EXODUS FROM IRELAND.

"The emigration from Ireland, both to the United States and Australia, continues without abatement, and as a consequence, wages are advancing. A Cork paper gives the following illustration of what promotes this great efflux of the Irish population :—

"'A poor woman residing in the North of this city, whose husband emigrated to the United States about two years since, received yesterday a check for £10 to convey herself and child to New York. Her husband had on three previous occasions sent her £3 to assist her in supporting herself until he could send, as he promised her, sufficient to pay her passage out. This man was here one of the most wretched laborers. He must have done well when such a man could be in a position to forward £19 within one year and a half—a sum which, if he had remained at home, he never could have put together during his life.'"

5. The British West-Indies.

From the National Ægis, of April 6th, 1853.

"The condition of the Coolies in the British West India Island of Trinidad, is most deplorable, and certainly merits at least a share of the gushing sympathies of the Duchess of Sutherland and her coterie. A Martinique planter who visited the island, writes a letter, which we subjoin and commend to the consideration of the friends of Uncle Tom :—

"'My soul has been deeply afflicted by all that I have seen. How many human beings lost! So far as I can judge, in spite of their wasting away, all are young, perishing under the weight of disease. Most of them are dropsical, *for want of nourishment*. Groups of children, the most interesting I have ever seen, scions of a race doomed to misfortune, were remarkable for their small limbs, wrinkled and reduced to the size of spindles—and not a rag to cover them! And to think that all this misery, all this destruction of humanity, all this waste of the stock of a ruined colony, might have been avoided, but has not been! Great God! it is painful beyond expression, to think of such a neglect of duty and humanity on the part of the colonial authorities, as well of the metropolis as of the colony.

* * * * * * * *

"'I can prove a neglect to a great extent murderous; the victims are Indian Coolies of Trinidad, (in less than one year, as is shown by official documents, *two thousand* corpses of these unfortunate creatures have furnished food to the crows of the island,) and a similar system is pursued, not only without punishment, but without even forming the subject of an official inquest. Strange and deplorable contradiction! and yet the nation which gives us this example, boasts of extending the ægis of its protection over all its subjects, without distinction! It is this nation, also, that complacently takes to itself the credit of extending justice equally over all classes, over the lordly peer and the humblest subject without fear, favor, or affection!'"

See also Appendix, C., near the end.

Of the laboring classes of the European Continent, I have not sufficiently authentic information; so I pass them over, and come at once to our own country.

6. The "Northern States."

(1.) *From the N. Y. Journal of Commerce, as copied by the National Ægis, of April 13th*, 1853.

"The Rag Pickers and Bone Gatherers in New York.

"The deeper one descends in the gradations of social position in this city, the more apparent does it become that 'one-half of the world don't know how the other half live.' The bone and rag-gatherers,—answering to the 'Chiffonieres' of Paris,—are almost exclusively Germans, and are mostly congregated on the eastern side of the city, and from their clannish disposition, peculiarity of language and habits, form communities or 'colonies' as distinct as though no others surrounded them. Withdrawn from intercourse with their fellow men, they only emerge with their hooks and pokers, to add to their filthy accumulations. Under the escort of Capt. Squires, of the 11th police district, we were favored with a glimpse of 'real life,' among these degraded creatures.

"For dwellings, they generally select such as are constructed for the accommodation of numerous families under a single roof. These are put up very slightly, at a comparatively small expense, and the revenues accruing to the owners, from rents, form a large per centage on the capital invested. One structure on Third street, owned by a late State Senator, is calculated to yield a monthly income of $168, equal to $2,016 per annum. It is separated in the rear by a court from another building of the same description, yielding nearly the same amount of revenue. Each floor forms twelve apartments, filled by as many families, each of which pays $3 50, $4 50, or $5 per month, according to location. There is no pecuniary motive of putting up buildings of any other description in this locality. Though they are often filthy in the extreme, new buildings of a better quality would be filled by the same occupants with the same habits.

"There are many other houses of the same character, similarly occupied. On Sheriff street, is a large rear building containing about fifty families. The habitations of the rag-pickers may generally be recognized by the long rows of rags swinging from lines, to dry, and looking some like the brown wetted leaves in a tobacco shed.

"About daylight the colonies are in motion, and the able bodied, equipped with baskets and pokers, sally forth, each emulous to anticipate the rest in reaching the field of gain. Sometimes the city is partitioned off into districts, and it is as much a trespass to everstep the boundaries assigned, as for a fire engine to run out of its district. A few more favored than the rest, have carts with which to collect the refuse and offal of kitchen and butcher shops; and the wife and a dog, well harnessed, exert themselves in concert in urging it forward. At the close of the day, when the circuit has been completed, the baskets, bags and carts are emptied, and a pile formed of their contents. The latter are then carefully sorted, and generally afford, aside from the rags and bones, both food and fuel. The rags are sold to shops adjacent, for two cents a pound for cotton and linen, and something less for woollen, suitable for carpets. The bones are sold for thirty cents a bushel, after having been well scraped and boiled, to secure the nutritious portions for food. The bones from the gutter, after being washed, suffice to provide for necessities for the family proper, including the canine dependencies. The food and fuel thus secured, are the emoluments thus received over and above the income from bones and rags, and are incidental to the main purpose. The process rendered necessary by the transaction of business so various, all conducted in the apartment used as kitchen, bed-room, sitting and store room—imparts a peculiar odor to the atmosphere, discernable at some distance. It can easily be imagined that the melancholy mode of living thus described, with unsuitable food, and contracted and ill ventilated apartments, are not promotive of health. The cholera, accordingly, in past years, made a fearful havoc among these people.

"Notwithstanding the extreme degradation of the German rag pickers, they appear happy, and exhibit no signs of discontent. With many, the Western States is the promised land, and every effort is made to accumulate sufficient funds to enable them to emigrate. A colony of three hundred persons is mentioned, which occupied a single basement last year, living promiscuously together, with a common bone heap, to which all contributed, and from which was derived a portion of their sustenance. Though seeming to be in utter destitution, they all started for the West last spring to settle on farms.

"Snow storms are among the worse calamities that can befal the rag picker, as his means of livelihood are placed beyond his reach. In such emergencies, the girls turn out *en masse*, to sweep the street-crossings, asking each passenger for 'a penny,' and three or four shillings per day are often thus realized. A mild winter like the present is a blessing they can easily appreciate.

"The youth, both males and females, are marked by an unnatural precocity, resulting partly from the early age at which they are compelled to assist in gaining a livelihood, and partly from their addictedness to vice. Though young in years, many of them are adepts in vice. Destitution gives temptation an unwonted power, and they early learn to yield to it.

"It is gratifying to know that some benevolent and philanthropic individuals are interesting themselves in behalf of this wretched and long neglected population. A mission established by the Mercer Street Presbyterian Church has been for some time in operation, in Avenue D., and other plans are on foot, having in view the intellectual and moral benefit of these people, and others like them. Among other things, a Sabbath School for boys has been established, at which from 130 to 200 boys have been in attendance. Judge Mason superintends it personally, and there is much in the enterprise of an encouraging nature.

"Capt. Squires is one of the few police officers who have interested themselves in movements of this kind, though their peculiar duties eminently qualify them in many respects to co-operate in missionary efforts. It is now contemplated to establish a kind of workhouse, in which boys may be kept from idleness, and healthful instruction and discipline administered."

(2.) *From the Evangelical Catholic, as copied by the N. Y. Churchman, of Oct. 25th,* 1851.

"REPORT OF THE SHIRT-SEWER'S CO-OPERATIVE UNION.

"When an association commences to carry out and put into practice any measure of reform, it seems prudent and necessary to lay the subject before the public for their approval and sympathy, lest the designs and intentions of its protectors might be impugned, or its objects be deemed speculative—designed to benefit the few at the expense of the many, and thus alienate the sympathy of those who, when they should have a correct understanding of the purposes of the proposed reform, would more fully appreciate the motives, and aid in carrying forward the designs of the Association. In justice, then, to the Union, we have convened this meeting for the purpose of laying before the public a simple statement of the circumstances which induced us to form this Union, and to ask your friendly aid and co-operation. Forced by direct necessity, through want of employment and starvation wages, when we had work to do, some few of our present numbers combined together in the month of April last, and organized into an Association styled the Shirt Sewer's Co-operative Union. Our aims and objects were, to work together for mutual benefit, to share the profits accruing from our industry, according to our industry and willingness to do, instead of being, as formerly, compelled to give the *lion's share* of our labour to an employer. Briefly, it was an *experiment*, and it has succeeded. We have demonstrated the fact to our cast-down and suffering sisters, that full double the wages can be earned by less hours of toil, under our new plan of combination, than under the old arrangement. When our numbers were limited, and the work light, we were unable to pay our way; but as our members increased with the demand for labour, our profits increased, leaving us at present a net profit of 10 per cent. over the prices paid to the members. A statement of the prices of work given by employers, and that paid by the Association, will serve to show the advantage we have already gained by *combination.*

"Prices of shirts made for large shirt manufactories range from 5 to 50 cents; while our lowest prices are 25 cents for cheap shirts, and 75 cents for the best made article. Our prices range thus for the same article, only that ours are well made, which cannot be said of *sale shirts:*

Cheap Shirts, shop made,	8 to 10	cents.
Best Shirts, shop made,,	31 to 50	"
Cheap Shirts, Association made,	25 to 38	"
Best Shirts, Association made,	75	"
Collars, shop made,	1, 2, and 3	"
Collars, Association made,	8 to 10	"

"From these prices we are even now enabled to save 10 per cent., still to be divided or to be laid out in stock for the mutual advantage of all. Aside from these advantages, the members are not overtasked as much as under the old system, and we are sure of our being promptly paid, which very often was not the case in shop work. We therefore feel warranted in urging upon the public the necessity and expediency of enlarging our sphere of usefulness, by increasing our facilities for employing all who prefer working for themselves, and those dependent upon them, to toiling for the pittance wages grudgingly given by employers. Our Association at present employs 40 females, among whom are 15 widows—but not steadily, as, until the issue of the *appeal for aid*, (some three weeks since,) we had not full employment. That appeal, we are grateful and happy to say, has rallied around us many kind friends who have aided us very materially in procuring work, and now stimulate us further to lay our cause before the whole public. The time for such a movement seems to be *now*. There is a general feeling of sympathy and a lively interest for the 6,000 defenceless and deeply wronged shirt-makers of our city. Nobly are they striving to earn, in honesty and decent poverty, the bread that poorly feeds, and the humble raiment that but poorly covers, their wasted forms. They are patient sufferers, toiling unceasingly, ever hopeful of a brighter future. Very many are widows, descended by reverses to poverty; more of them are orphans,

'Too early thrown
On the cold world, unloved, alone.'

"Others are compelled to aid in the support of families and widowed mothers, and all have a pressing claim on society. Too long has this been lightly treated or totally disregarded. Occasionally, as the benevolent pass through our hospitals, their warmest sympathies are aroused for those who, worn down with toil, weary of life, diseased by sedentary habits, have come there to die. Not unoften the *prison-door* and the *mad-house* close upon them, and oftener the *house of shame* affords an asylum, denied to them by honest toil and a life of virtue. These are the every-day histories of the seamstress. Few of them enjoy the wholesome comforts of life, and more suffer for even the common necessaries. This should not be, or need not, when society begins to understand the duty of elevating the condition of her weak and defenceless sisters. The initiatory step in this reform is the associating together of the most depressed branches of industry for mutual aid and protection. One such organization, established by your aid and patronage, would be instrumental in accomplishing vast good to other depressed branches of trade, by a successful example. The advantages to accrue from a change in the uncertain tenure under which the needlewomen now hold their right to exist, (not to say live,) are apparent to every reflecting mind. All society would feel and benefit by the change, by placing in a position of comparative security and independence a large class of operatives, whose defenceless condition is now made to enure to the profit and aggrandizement of those who profit by their ill-paid labour. The change would lessen the numbers who at times are compelled to ask charity. It would rob the *living charnel houses of vice*, in which our city so abounds, of numberless victims. It would give a stimulus to industry, by placing thousands in positions to *need* and *consume* articles which their straitened circumstances now deprive them of. We will not enlarge further on the manifold advantages of so associating together, believing the fact apparent to all. We are anxious to try the experiment. Upon our failure or success depends the future comfort or misery of thousands in our city, who are even now 'sewing at once, with a double stitch, a shroud as well as a shirt.'

"The condition of the shirt-sewers of our city is lamentable, and calls for your kindest and warmest sympathies. It is estimated that their numbers at present exceed six thousand. Many of these are young and friendless orphans, early left to struggle with poverty, and solely dependent upon the precarious pittance of wages doled out by employers. Others are widows, depending upon the needle for the support of helpless children, and with the pittance of some $2 or $2 50 per week, trying to feed, clothe, and pay the rent of a family. We need not tell you this cannot be done. They bear in silence sufferings and trials that would chill the sternest hearts to recount. The defenceless girl often wrestles with poverty, hunger, temptation, until dire necessity forces sad and fearful alternatives upon her. Is this Christian? Is it human?

Oh, men, with sisters dear;
  Oh, men, with mothers and wives:
It is not linen you're wearing out,
  It's human creatures' lives.'

"But we will not murmur: we are ready to make any personal sacrifices to sustain and build up our Association. To this end we appeal to a generous public.

"We need your assistance now. We need a store in which to dispose of our stock when made, and the patronage of those who have employment to give. We need to be placed on a permanent basis, where daily necessities and wants will not circumscribe our usefulness and dampen our energies. Kind friends! Will you aid and assist us?"

(3.) *From the Worcester (Mass.) Weekly Transcript, of Dec.* 18, 1852.

"TERRIBLE EXPOSURE AND SUFFERING.—The Ogdensburg Sentinel states that a Mrs. McCurdy was found in the woods near that place, last week, in the last stages of exhaustion, produced by exposure and starvation. It seems that on Wednesday, *the day before Thanksgiving*, she had visited that village for the purpose of obtaining work for her needle, and, *failing in this*, had started on foot for Morristown. She was much exhausted and faint, and was compelled to sit down by the roadside a number of times to rest—and observing the passers-by stare at her, as she thought, as if they supposed her intoxicated, she retired into the woods to escape observation, and sitting upon the ground, between two trees, she fell asleep. When she awoke, she found she could not use her hands and feet. In this state she laid *till the ninth day*, exposed to the snow, and frost, and rain, unable to attract the attention of those who were passing near her, and till she was accidentally discovered. When found, the circulation had nearly ceased, and she could have survived but a short time."

From the Baltimore Sun, of Jan. 20, 1853.

"MAN FROZEN TO DEATH.—A man named Daniel Griffiths, a blacksmith by trade, *who has, for some time past, been wandering from place to place in search of work*, was found in some bushes by the roadside, near Brooklyn, on Monday morning, frozen to death."

7. International Interference.

This may seem inappropriate to the heading of the present Appendix, (Appendix, K.,) but there is so much respecting the laboring classes, interwoven with the following extracts, that I have thought best to give them here.

"*From the London Times, Dec.* 1.

"THE QUESTION OF AMERICAN SLAVERY—ADDRESS OF THE ENGLISH LADIES.

In one point there is a very general agreement among the nations of the earth. They all believe that they understand their own difficulties better than their neighbors do for them. We have had, and still have, many social problems, which events, and the spontaneous changes of society, rather than legislation, are solving in one way or another. But whether it be the condition of the Irish peasantry, or the Irish Church Establishment, or English pauperism, or factory labor, or the excess of our female population, we have never attached much importance to the opinions of French or German writers on these subjects. Indeed, if their remarks upon our social questions are ever read in this country, it is rather in the hope of coming upon some ridiculous misapprehension, or some queer intrusion of foreign peculiarities, than for any valuable suggestion we are likely to meet with. When we find this national jealousy so strong in ourselves, it is reasonable to expect something of the kind in our neighbors, and proper to make allowance for it. They all have their troubles, more or less ancient and inherited—more or less mixed up with their social and political institutions, so intimately at any rate as to defy the rude hand of the abstract reformer, and still more the unfriendly criticism of the foreign censor. Negro slavery, as it exists in the United States, is just such a deep and apparently incurable sore, and such are the feelings with which it is regarded in the Union. We, the great British nation, having our own Slave Colonies some six or seven thousand miles off, and having also more money and better credit than any other nation in the world, indulged our benevolence and our pride in abolishing slavery, and adding £20,000,000 to the figure of our national debt, with very little regard to the results either to the planter or to the slave. At the present moment, indeed, if there is one thing in the world that the British public do not like to talk about, or even to think about, it is the condition of the race for whom this great effort was made. We are not the less proud, however, of our achievement and its cost, and think that, having done so much ourselves, we may fairly impose the like sacrifice on our neighbors. But the precept, 'Go, and do thou likewise,' seldom comes with much force when the spokesman is urging his own example; and, as it happens in this case, the example does not apply quite so closely as it might do. In the United States the evil is constitutional and incorporate. It is political and domestic. It is gigantic and household. It is a question that affects families, institutions, States, and the whole Union. It affects slaves and freemen, both of every possible shade. Confessedly, and on the showing of the lady whose work has so spellbound every heart and every mind in this country, there are two great negro difficulties to be dealt with in the United States—the difficulty of the colored slave and that of the colored freeman; and, of the two, the latter is the worse. But, when England interferes in this matter, what is to be the exact manner and particular object of the interference? Are we to tell the Americans to love those whom they loathe, and associate with those against whom they feel an actual repulsion? If we do, we are dealing hard measure; if we do not, we are not touching the greater of the two difficulties to be dealt with.

"Of course, we are disposed to regard with every possible indulgence the proceedings of the select little convention of ladies that met the other day at Stafford-house. Never did anything more defy criticism; and it would really be breaking a butterfly on the wheel to remark on the affair as we should on the rough tustle of opinion in the House of Commons, or the tempestuous rhetoric of Exeter-hall. We may be permitted, however, to doubt whether women of the calibre that assembled the other day at Syracuse (United States,) will be able to appreciate the satin paper and rosewater of our female aristocracy; much more, whether the Haleys and Legrées, or even the Shelbys and the St. Clares of the Union, will take much heed of so softly-whispered a warning. The Americans are not very kindly-disposed to our aristocracy. They may rejoin, 'Are you so ready to drop all distinctions of classes? Do you consent, at the bidding of any monitor, to associate with all who are your equals in education and merit? Are there no castes, no *quasi* negroes, creoles, mulattoes, or quadroons, in the gradations of British society? The Court Circular, and the published catalogues of guests at your banquets and receptions, tell another story.' We will not anticipate the American rejoinders on the mere question of slavery itself, its physical distresses, and moral degradations. These must have occurred to the aristocratic, and not less philanthropic, circle at Stafford-house, who know too well the fragile materials of their own social system, not to fear the damaging reply they are bringing on themselves. Had we wished to say more, others have said it for us. Three letters in our columns this day show the delicate nature of the ground on which these ladies are trespassing, and how much exception may be taken both to the advisers and the advice. It is too late to ask them to reconsider their movement—for the movement is made, and, the address once before the world, we only hope it may receive a respectable number of lady signatures. Really and honestly, our chief motive in these remarks is to entreat the indulgence of the American public to a proceeding calculated to wound their *amour propre*, to rouse that jealousy which all nations feel towards one another—most of all, those nations which are most alike, and possibly even to augment the difficulties of the slavery question.

"Our fair readers, who are invited to enter on a crusade of a somewhat international character, will excuse one little warning, which we venture to make on the suggestion of 'Academicus,' in our columns to-day. We, of this free and happy country, are just the most extensive employers (indirectly, but not less really,) of slave labor in the world. Negro slaves, working under the lash in the mid-day sun, and 'keeping their toe well up to the mark,' as Mr. Legree would say, produce the material of our cravats, our stockings, and the simple and comprehensive garment in which we take our repose. They supply the muslins and prints, and nearly all the other fabrics of the female costume, from the dress of the Sovereign to that of the poorest needlewoman. Slaves produce our coffee, and the sugar that sweetens it. By day and by night, sitting down and rising up, we are still encouraging slavery by consuming its produce. The prime agent who moves the wheels of Southern slavery, we are told, is the Northern capitalist, who has his mortgage on the slave estate, or holds the bill of sale, and who secures himself, when necessary, by an order to his agent to sell off everything on the estate, slaves and all, for what they will fetch at the hammer. This man, Mrs. Stowe tells us, is really a guilty partner in the transaction, if not the most guilty,—the most guilty because he supplies the strongest stimulus of the system, and compels the most violent measures. But if the Northern capitalist pulls the strings of the Southern planter, who pulls the strings of the Northern capitalist? Most assuredly the merchants and brokers at New York are mainly dependent on the British market. *We* use the slave cotton. We supply the *slave* capital. *Our* money buys the negro,—*our* money buys his work. It is an indissoluble union of interests and operations, of which the white slave of this country is at one end, and the black slave of America at the other end of the chain. This should teach us a little more modesty, than if we were simply preaching to the people of Timbuctoo, to burn their idols and desist from human sacrifices. Perhaps it may suggest, also, that as a beginning, we had better not insist on *abolition*, or even talk about it—which is all, indeed, that the ladies of England are invited to do—but rather suggest *regeneration*. There are many who think that, with proper regulations, and particularly with a system for the self-enfranchisement of slaves, we might have brought about the entire emancipation of the British West Indies, with much less injury to the property of the planter and to the character of the negro than have resulted from the Abolition Act. Perhaps the warning will not be lost on the Americans, who may see the necessity of putting things in train for the ultimate abolition of slavery, and thereby save the sudden shock which the Abolitionists may one day bring on all the institutions of the Union, and the whole fabric of American society."

"*From Eliza Cook's Journal.*

"WILL IT BE BELIEVED?

"Will it be believed, a hundred years hence, that in 1842 the Government of Great Britain paid about £16,000,000 sterling per annum to keep up men-of-war and their appurtenances, and less than one-hundredth part the sum towards educating the children of the people throughout the nation?

"Will it be believed, that in England, a land of Bibles, and the most civilized and religious country in the world, one-half of the laboring people could neither read those Bibles nor write their own names?

"Will it believed, that the philanthropy of England exerted its ingenuity in the erection of palace-jails, and the perfecting of a system of education for criminals, but left the education and proper up-bringing of the children of honest poor men to charity and chance?

"Will it be believed, that though the charity-schools of England, and the endowed colleges of the nation, possessed an annual income of from four to five millions sterling, this revenue was devoted mainly to the education of the children of the rich, and furnishing rich sinecure offices for gentlemen; while the children of the poor, for whom these charities were bequeathed by pious men, were left chiefly to the education of the streets and the back lanes?

"Will it be believed, that the average pay of a policeman who looks after criminals was, in 1852, one-third more than the average pay of the schoolmaster appointed to educate immortal minds?

"Will it be believed, that the 14,000 armed police employed in Ireland received annual salaries of about thirty pounds a year, and that the 5,359 teachers of youth under the Irish National Board of

Education, received an average salary of only fourteen pounds a year?

"Will it be believed, that the British Judges got each from £4,000 to £5,000 a year for trying felons, and the British Astronomer Royal was paid with a fifth part of the sum—or no more than the salary of the deliverer of votes at the House of Commons?

"Will it be believed, that while we paid without objection several millions a year for arresting, trying and condemning criminals, we could not agree to provide one-half of the funds so to educate men as to prevent their becoming criminals?

"Will it be believed, that all the large towns of Great Britain paid more for the conviction and confinement of juvenile criminals, than they contributed for the education of children so as to prevent their becoming criminals?

"Will it be believed, that Great Britain excelled all other nations in working up raw materials—such as iron, cotton, flax and wool—into wondrously beautiful fabrics, but left the raw material of humanity in the most neglected state;—that she devoted infinite pains and skill to the perfection of machines of all kinds, but left Man, of all other machines, the least improved?

"Will it be believed, that it could be said in the House of Peers, of London—the seat and centre of modern civilization—that there were in that city '100,000 children who had received no education whatever; and that, with one or two exceptions, England was the least educated country in Europe?'

"And, will it be believed, that another noble lord, now a peer, could also have said in the House of Commons, without contradiction, 'I know that out of the pale of the church, beyond the limits of the 'denominations,' there is a vast, destitute, neglected mass, festering in our streets and alleys; with every sight and sound of contamination choking the accesses to every sense,—without any idea of duty to earth or heaven,—upon whom no word of instruction ever falls, upon whom no breath of love ever settles,—unclaimed by Lambeth, unknown to Geneva, unconverted by Rome;'—*and that, about such a time, the ladies and gentlemen of England were peering across the wide ocean for objects on which to bestow their tender philanthropy?*

"No, no! These things will *not* be believed some fifty years hence!"

From the Washington Union, of Dec. 21st, 1852.

"The Duchess of Sutherland, and her amiable and aristocratic sisters, the Viscountess Melbourne, Lady John Russell, Mrs. Macauley, &c., do not seem to be very extensively seconded in their abolition movement at Stafford House. The infection of 'Uncle Tom' has not been universally inhaled even in England—as witness an able and fair article we this day publish from the London Times. The Thunderer, we notice, also accords ready echo to some of the 'women of England,' whose co-operation in the anti-slavery crusade, in and against the United States, has been so earnestly invoked by the aristocratic circles of the British metropolis. Here are some generous examples:

'*To the Editor of the Times:*

'SIR: May I beg you to state that, although I feel deep interest in the abolition of slavery, (and who does not?) I did not authorize my name to be used in relation to the meeting at the Stafford House?

'So long as American women can justly taunt the women of England with the neglect, ill-usage, and starvation payment of the lady teachers employed in their families, there is little hope of their listening to our protests on the subject of slavery.

'Let us reform our school-rooms, and we may expect them to reform the cabins of their slaves.

'Had not illness prevented my attendance at the meeting, I should have stated this as my opinion.

'I am, Sir, your obedient servant,

'JANET KAY SHUTTLEWORTH.

'38 Gloucester Square, Nov. 30.'

"Another correspondent publishes what she predicts will be the retort of the women of America. We quote:

'Oh, bear your benign sympathies, gentlewomen of England, to your own male and female sufferers! Try what the blessed influence of unstained womanhood may yet effect on the unheeded victims of enslaving circumstances, such as it may be the main salvation of ourselves not to have encountered. Apply yourselves to this, and you shall not find reason to complain that we do not bear you company in mitigating whatever horrors of a like kind we can discover here. Believe that we are not so ignorant of womanly pity, so untrue to our sex, so forgetful of our common humanity, as to acquiesce in any system of cruelty and torture, whatever may be the exceptional instances of such from which romance writers may draw those conclusions which are naturally so startling to you.

'Once more—we will not believe that you are not merely 'sighing for wretchedness,' and 'shunning the wretched,' when we see you making a true effort to harmonize, by means of your magnificent resources, those dreadful face-to-face opposites of which we spoke. We will believe that your 'feelings' are not 'all too delicate for use;' we will believe that your sympathies with the remote miseries of which your orators tell you are more than mere sentiment, when we see you doing something, making some strenuous surrender of personal ease and comfort, to remove from your doors the greatest spectacle of virtual slavery which (as far as we can learn,) the whole world contains.

'Resign some larger portion of your splendors, your pleasures, your vacant hours, your influence, to the unreclaimed mass that is weltering behind your palaces, crying aloud, in bitter despair, *Usque quo Domine!* and convicting you, we say not, of conscious hypocrisy, but of that which subjects you, in the eyes of some, to the suspicion of unreality and partisanship.

'Believe me, Sir, nothing would induce me to ask to trespass thus on your columns, but that I am so well assured how unpractical, how hopeless of result, is this well-intended scheme of the circle of gentlewomen mentioned in the Times. I trust I have spoken of them with all the respectful deference which their sex and their high position demand, and that, however feeble my words, the thought which I desire to suggest may not be utterly disregarded.

'I remain, Sir, your faithful servant, 'R. G. D.'"

From the Baltimore Sun, of Jan. 25th, 1853.

"AMERICAN AND ENGLISH LADIES AND SLAVERY.

"We find in the London Daily News the entire resolutions adopted by the American ladies at Milan, in response to the ladies of England, on the subject of slavery. They are communicated to that paper by Mr. Hume, the veteran reformer, to whom they were sent by the American ladies, and who introduces them with some most judicious remarks. He says:

'The resolutions agreed to at Milan, by the American ladies of Anglo-Saxon origin, are well worthy of the attention of the Duchess of Sutherland, and of all those, her noble coadjutors, whose sympathies have been enlisted and excited by reports of the sufferings of the slaves in the United States of America.

'We should indeed be happy if misery and suffering could be removed from this and other lands; but we are assured, on the best authority, that there will always be poor and suffering mortals, and that legislation can never entirely prevent poverty and wretchedness. But, as Christians and considerate persons, we ought to look at home —to what is passing hourly before our eyes, or within the sound of our carriage-wheels—and, we may add, in almost every parish in our beloved country, and consider whether our legislation is just and equal.'"

(2.) *From the National Ægis, of April 6th,* 1853.

"We cannot help asking, as we peruse from time to time the accounts which reach us of the wrongs, abuses, and sufferings that tarnish the fame of all nations, and of our common humanity, whether any one of the leading nations of the earth can, with very great propriety, criminate and recriminate upon another. England may truly say to the United States, 'You have, in some of the States, legalized slavery;' and the United States can with equal truth reply, 'You gave it to us, and forced it upon us, against our wishes.' England may say to us, 'Your Southern slaves are at the mercy of their masters, with only such limitations as the interests and laws of slaveholders may suggest;' and the United States may with even greater truth reply, 'Our slaves are in a better condition, morally, socially, and physically, this day, than millions of your subjects, who are nominally free.' And so the work of mutual crimination might go on, in a progression that should end only in the far off, and perhaps seldom heard-of, oppressions and abuses in the most distant corner of the British empire. And as the United States have nothing to fear, and nothing to lose, in any international comparisons with Great Britain, so they can with honor declare, that this present and prevailing crimination and recrimination, is not of their seeking. It began in England. Aristocrats, purse-proud and overbearing, alike towards their tenants at home and their kindred abroad, have taken upon themselves to depreciate the American government, because of a system of slavery which our government cannot touch, and which our people cannot, but by annihilation to themselves, at once or at present abolish. It is, indeed, slavery; but it is not surcharged with all the horrors with which Mrs. Beecher Stowe has colored her romantic and profitable work. It is slavery, beyond a doubt; but, slavery as it is, it pales, in shades of cruelty, before the abolition of the West India bondage. Let American slavery and British West India emancipation, with their respective treatment and consequences, be placed in the scales together, and be weighed by the impartial judgment of the world, and we have no fears that in that comparison any MENE and TEKEL shall be pronounced upon us, that will not first and in more indignant tones be awarded to the vaunting philanthropists of England.

Appendix L.

Mrs. Stowe in England.

From the Boston Traveller, of April 30.

"The English papers, by the Canada, furnish us with a variety of details—more or less curious and interesting—of the manner in which our English brethren received and honored and rewarded Mrs. Stowe, the author of 'Uncle Tom's Cabin.' The Liverpool Journal speaks of her as the wife of Prof. Stowe of 'Brunswick College, Andover,' and thus describes her landing at Liverpool on Sunday, April 9th:—

"'Mrs. Stowe, closely veiled, and leaning upon the arm of the professor, was conducted to a cab, which drove off to the residence of Mr. John Cropper, Dingle Bank. A very large number of persons had collected to witness Mrs. Stowe's landing; and, as the vehicle drove away, several hearty cheers were given, to which she bowed her acknowledgments. Mr. John Cropper has been for some time much indisposed; but his brother, Mr. Edward Cropper, held a party on Monday morning, at his residence, to meet Mrs. Stowe at breakfast. The Rev. Dr. M'Neile and family, accompanied by the Rev. Mr. Burgess of Chelsea, arrived at nine o'clock; and the breakfast room was soon filled with guests anxious to pay their respects to the illustrious authoress. Mrs. Stowe received the warm congratulations of the company with unaffected simplicity, and seemed utterly unconscious of having done anything to merit such attention. At the request of the respected host, the Rev. Dr. M'Neile expressed to Mrs. Stowe, in neat terms, and with deep religious feeling, their hearty congratulations. After breakfast, Mr. Edward Cropper rose, and begged to add the name of Professor Stowe to the congratulatory address which had been so beautifully made by Dr. M'Neile. Professor Stowe then said a few words. Speaking of the success of his gifted lady's book, he said—Incredible as it may seem to those who are without prejudice, it is nevertheless a fact that this book was condemned by the leading religious newspapers in the United States as anti-Christian, and its author associated with infidels and disorganizers. And had it not been for the decided expression of the mind of English Christians, and of Christendom itself on this point, there is reason to fear that the pro-slavery power of the United States would have succeeded in putting the book under foot.'

"On Tuesday following, Mrs. Stowe and her husband were received by the Negro's Friend Society. On Wednesday she was presented with a purse containing about 600 dollars, which had been collected in Liverpool, chiefly in pence, by a committee of ladies. Mr Adam Hodgson addressed her in handing her the purse, and Prof. Stowe replied in her behalf as follows:—

"'It is impossible for me to express the feelings of my heart at the kind and generous manner in which I have been received upon English shores. Just when I had begun to realize that a whole wide ocean lay between me and all that is dearest to me, I found most unexpectedly a home and friends waiting to receive me here. I have had not an hour in which to know the heart of a stranger. I have been made to feel at home since the first moment of landing, and every where I have seen only the faces of friends.' Professor Stowe, in the course of his own speech which followed, said:—'We never could believe that slavery in our land would be a perpetual curse; but we felt and felt deeply, that there must be a terrible struggle before we could be delivered from it, and that there must be suffering and martyrdom in this cause, as in every other great cause; for eighteen years of immediate contact with the horrible thing, eighteen years of struggling and of suffering against it had shown to us its strength. And, under God, we rely very much on the Christian public of Great Britain; for every expression of feeling from the wise and good of this land, with whatever petulance it may be met by some, goes to the heart of the American people (hear, hear). You must not judge of the American people by the expressions which have come across the Atlantic in reference to the subject. Nine-tenths of the American people—nine-tenths of all the inhabitants of the land, at least—are in heart and feeling with you and with us on this great subject—(hear, hear);—but there is a tremendous pressure brought to bear upon all who are in favor of emancipation there. The whole political power, the whole money power, almost the whole ecclesiastical power, is wielded in defence of slavery, protecting it from all aggression; and it is as much as a man's reputation is worth to utter a syllable boldly and openly on the other side. They say there are social evils in England. Undoubtedly there are; but the difference between the social evils of England and this great evil of slavery in the United States is just here. In England, the power of the government and the power of Christian sympathy are all exerted to remove those evils. This is the difference. England repents and reforms. America refuses to repent and reform.'"

From the Boston Commonwealth, of May 7.

Extract from a speech of Professor Stowe; where delivered, the Commonwealth does not say:—

"Is it true that all this affectionate interest is merited? [Great applause.] I cannot help feeling in regard to that book, 'I don't specks anybody ever made that book, I 'specks it growed.' [Laughter.] Under the pressure of a horrid Fugitive Slave law, the book sprung out of the soil ready made. * * *

"I believe that the passage of the Fugitive Slave Law is the last desperate effort, and the dying struggle of the system. [Cheers.] But there are real difficulties connected with the slave question in those States in which slavery exists. All the social habits of the people are connected with the system, and they don't know what to do without slaves where they are so numerous, and where they have always been accustomed to them. There is another great difficulty connected with this question—that is, that the slaveholding States are, as political bodies, internally independent. The slaveholders possess all political power, and no movement can be made for the amelioration of the slave excepting by the slaveholders themselves. It is not the same as in this country, where your Parliament could hold a rod over the slave-owners. There it is the slaveholders themselves who hold the rod, and they are accustomed to use it. There are only two ways, therefore, in which a change can be looked for. Either the slaveholder himself must be persuaded to adopt a system for the abolition of the evil, or the evil will be brought to an end by a bloody revolution.

"The slaveholders have consciences, and these will be awakened in time by truth and Christian love. In coming along here from Liverpool, I have observed your wealth and comfort, and your abounding resources; but I have also observed that a great deal of it results from the products of slave labor. In this country is the great market for American cotton, and it is cotton which sustains American slavery. I do not say you can do without it. It is cotton which makes the system profitable, and cotton makes the price of a man £300 in the markets of the United States. It is my conviction that nine-tenths of the people of the United States feel in their hearts, on the subject of slavery, just as you do. [Cheers.] But there is such a tremendous power brought to bear against this feeling, that those who are comfortable and wish to live in an easy way don't want to meddle with the subject at all. * * *

"Referring to the Fugitive Slave Law, he stated that it had been and would be altogether inoperative; for out of the thousands of fugitive slaves in the States, not twenty-five of them had been carried back under the influence of that law. The Rev. Doctor concluded amid enthusiastic applause by stating that there was soundness in the American mind, which in due course would be unmistakably developed."

From the New York Times, of May 28.

"Mrs. H. B. Stowe at Stafford House.

"'On Saturday,' says the London Times, of the 9th inst., 'a number of ladies and gentlemen assembled at Stafford House, to welcome Mrs. H. B. Stowe to this country, and to give expression personally to the respect and admiration which are felt for that lady.

"The Duke of Sutherland having introduced Mrs. Stowe to the assembly, the following short address was read and presented to her by the Earl of Shaftesbury:—

"'Madam.—I am deputed by the Duchess of Sutherland, and the ladies of the two Committees appointed to conduct 'The Address from the Women of England to the Women of America, on the subject of Slavery,' to express the high gratification they feel in your presence among them this day. The address, which has received considerably more than half a million of the signatures of the women of Great Britain and Ireland, they have already transmitted to the United States, consigning it to the care of those whom you have nominated as fit and zealous persons to undertake the charge in your absence. The earnest desire of these committees, and, indeed, we may say of the whole kingdom, is to cultivate the most friendly and affectionate relations between the two countries, and we cannot but believe that we are fostering such a feeling when we avow our deep admiration of an American lady who, blessed by the possession of vast genius and intellectual power, enjoys the still higher blessing that she devotes them to the glory of God, and the temporal and eternal interests of the human race.'

"'Rev. Mr. Beecher (Mrs. Stowe's brother,) after a few prefatory remarks of acknowledgment and thanks, read the following letter from Hon. Cassius M. Clay, describing the progress of emancipation in Kentucky, and the service *Uncle Tom* had rendered the cause.

"After partaking of refreshments, the ladies who were present, congregated in one of the splendid saloons apart, and Mrs. Stowe, seated between the Duchesses of Sutherland and Argyll, entered freely into conversation with her numerous visitors.

"In the course of her observations, she stated that the ladies of England were not at all aware of the real state of feeling of the ladies of America on the subject of slavery; it must not be judged of by the answer sent to the address, nor by the statements in the American newspapers. The ladies of England seem not to be at all aware of the deep feeling of sympathy with which *Uncle Tom's Cabin* was received in America long before it was known in England. The press in America had invariably spoken highly of *Uncle Tom's Cabin.* The first word that ever appeared in print against *Uncle Tom's Cabin* was the article in the Times, which was reprinted and re-echoed in the American papers, and widely circulated in the form of a tract. The bitterness and anger manifested against the ladies' address showed how much its force had enraged the advocates of slavery. Ladies in England were happily ignorant of slavery; yet that address had shown sympathy, and sympathy was very sweet. There was no bitter feeling between the ladies of the two countries, but the ladies of America cannot, because of their husband's personal and political feelings, stand forth and say what they feel on the subject. Some had said that *Uncle Tom's Cabin* was now forgotten; but it should be mentioned that 60,000 copies of the *Key to Uncle Tom's Cabin* were sold in three days. The practical question was what can be done to forward this great work? She looked first to God, but man also could do something. Sympathy must continue to be expressed. British subjects in Canada must be educated. The use of free grown cotton must be encouraged, and there were other ways in which this great work may be aided by the people of England, remembering, that after all, the issue is in the hands of Him that ordereth all things.

"The company began to disperse soon after 5 o'clock, every one appearing to be thoroughly gratified with the interesting proceedings of the day.

"Mrs. Stowe and her friends were among the last to leave, and were accompanied to the entrance hall by the Duchess of Sutherland, who there took leave of her guests."

From the (Boston) Puritan Recorder, of June 9, 1853.

"LETTER FROM LONDON.

"We have been obligingly permitted to give our readers the following letter from an American clergyman, travelling abroad, to a relative in this city:—

'LONDON, May 16, 1853.

'Dear H.—I have spent three Sabbaths in this city, and have heard some of the great preachers of London; but I cannot say that I have heard any great preaching.

* * * * * * * *

'Rev. James Sherman, is the successor of Rowland Hill, at Surrey Chapel, and preaches to a congregation of 2500. There was nothing very striking about his discourse, excepting his allusion to slavery. Speaking of the importance of family religion,—"And here," he said, "lies one of the greatest evils of slavery. It denies to the children all instruction in the word of God. There, in that country over the waters, there are three millions of slaves; one million of whom are children—prohibited by law from reading the Bible and receiving religious instruction. God have mercy upon those Christian churches, and those Christian pastors, who uphold and advocate a system so prolific in curses to themselves." This he said with the greatest possible emphasis, and in a tone by no means the mildest. Upon further acquaintance, I found that Mr. Sherman represents the radical party here, the "Exeter Hall Abolitionists," as they are called. He is entertaining the Rev. Charles Beecher at his house. The moment we entered his study, before asking us to be seated, he opened upon us a heavy broadside, with a sweeping denunciation of the American ministry at large. The one great impression of Mrs. Stowe's book seems to be, that were it not for the support of the clergy of America, slavery would long since have disappeared.

'The great demonstration has at length come off,—at the Anniversary of the British and Foreign Anti-Slavery Society, on Monday evening. The clerk at the Secretary's office, who furnished us with tickets to the platform, told us, that never, since the days of Clarkson and Wilberforce, had there been such a rush for tickets. Even on Sunday, when the office was closed, the doors were besieged with applicants. Thousands had been sent empty away. On arriving at the appointed hour, I found the passage ways blocked up with outsiders, and the great Hall packed to the ceiling. The Earl of Shaftesbury took the chair, and made a flaming speech. When Mrs. Stowe entered the private gallery, the whole audience rose to their feet and received her with shouts of applause, and a general waving of hats and handkerchiefs, and when Mrs. Stowe rose in acknowledgment, supported by the Duchess of Sutherland, they gave three immense hurras. The same scene was repeated when she took leave, before the close of the meeting. Of course, it was to be expected, that many harsh things, many false things, many absurd things, would be said on such an occasion; but I confess, I was taken by surprise. The most extreme cases of cruelty were cited as the general rule, and the grossest misrepresentations were made of the free colored race at the North. When it was stated that President Pierce had announced his intention of enforcing the Fugitive Slave Law, hisses and cries of 'shame! shame!' rose from every part of the house.

'The indignation of these people seems to be directed more against America, than against slavery. *The Times* of the next morning, commented very severely on 'the frantic impotence' of Exeter Hall. Professor Stowe made the only sensible speech on this occasion, and one which seemed to confound the Stoweites themselves. He commenced by saying that there were only three ways to get rid of slavery. First,—by an appeal to arms, a bloody revolution. This none of the true friends of the Prince of Peace would desire to see. Secondly,—by an appeal to the conscience, convincing the slaveholder that he was wrong. This could not be done by denunciation and assault. It must be moderate and gradual. Thirdly,—by an appeal to the pocket, making the cotton business unprofitable. This the English had in their own hands. Americans never could support slavery;—the English supported four-fifths of the whole business. Cotton growers never could flourish without cotton consumers. It was very easy to talk about the right and the wrong, and to charge the slaveholder with the sin; 'but are you willing to sacrifice one penny of your own profits for the sake of doing away with this cursed business? It is a common maxim, that 'the receiver is as bad as the thief.'"

From the London Morning Chronicle.

"We can by no means commend the precedent which Professor Stowe has set to English husbands by bringing his wife to be exhibited on platforms as an object of public flattery. Long may it be before an English authoress is induced to prefer so dangerous and equivocal a gratification to the approbation of her readers, the love of her friends, and the applause of her own heart. *Long, very long, may it be before an Englishwoman is persuaded to parade in foreign lands the spectacle of her own merits, and her country's shame.* We are aware that the customs and opinions of American society on these points are very different from ours, and that an ovation of this kind would not be a novelty in that country. But it is a novelty in ours, and we must say, most emphatically, that we wish it may remain so."

Appendix, M.

Statistics of Slavery.

From Chambers' Journal, as copied into Littell's Living Age, No. 470, *page* 490.

* * * * * * * *

"The report of the *Prison Discipline Association* for 1845 throws some light on the morals, as well as the longevity, of negroes in the north. After giving the bills of mortality for the black and white population in the city and penitentiary of Philadelphia, the report says: 'Out of 1000 of each colour residing in the city, 196 blacks die for every 100 whites; and for every 1000 of each colour in the penitentiary, the astonishing number of 316 blacks to every 100 whites. Returns from the Philadelphia County Prison, for the last ten years, show that out of 101 deaths in that establishment, 54 died of consumption. Of these, 40 were coloured, and 14 white.'

"In 1845, Mathew L. Bevan, president of the Eastern Penitentiary of Pennsylvania, says: 'The increase of deaths comes from blacks. This increase of mortality is found in the fact, that those coloured inmates from the county of Philadelphia are so constitutionally diseased, as under any and all circumstances to be short-lived, from their character and habits. They die of constitutional and chronic disorders, which are general among their order, owing to the privations they undergo, and the want of proper attention in infancy, and their peculiar mode of living.' Mr. Bevan concludes: 'Indulging in the use of ardent spirits, subjected to a prejudice, which bids defiance to any successful attempt to improve their physical or moral condition, from youth to manhood, sowing the seeds of disease in their constitutions, and at last becoming inmates of prisons.'

"The southern planters, of course, point to these facts with exultation, and contrast their own treatment of the blacks with great advantage. It would indeed appear from several papers in these volumes (De Bow), and it is not an unlikely thing to occur as an epochal phenomenon, that a scientific spirit is gaining ground among the slave-owners, which extends not merely to improved cotton culture, but also to improved negro management. Some of the contributions of this character are both interesting and amusing. The suggestions about 'improved dwellings,' 'sanitary regulations,' and 'water supply,' not to mention provisions of a more spiritual character, would do credit to Lord Shaftesbury, or Prince Albert himself. Evidently, these planters consider themselves no mean philanthropists.

"One 'very sensible and practical writer' gives a description of his plantation, which would tempt any man to become a slave for the pleasure of living on it. His 'quarter,' has been selected on scientific principles, 'well protected by the shade of forest trees, sufficiently thinned out to admit a free circulation of air, so situated as to be free from the impurities of stagnant water;' and on this he has erected 'comfortable houses, made of hewn post oak, covered with cypress, 16 by 18, with close plank floors and good chimneys, and elevated two feet from the ground. The ground under and around the houses is swept every month, and the houses, both inside and out, white-washed twice a year.' Then there are 'good cisterns, providing an ample supply of pure water,' and 'ample clothing' for their beds, with a henhouse for each, so that he may have 'his chickens and eggs for his evening and morning meals to suit himself,' besides gardens for every family, in which 'they raise such vegetables and fruits as they take a fancy to.' The beauty of this description would be lost, were it regarded as drawn for European readers. It was written for a local magazine as a *bona fide* essay on the scientific management of negroes. This gentleman's treatment of his negroes is as precise as if he were conducting an hospital or superintending a nursery. 'Their dinners are cooked for them, and carried to the field, always with vegetables, according to the season. There are two hours set apart at mid-day for resting, eating, and sleeping, *if they desire it* [always consulting their wishes], and they retire to one of the weather-sheds or the grove to pass this time, not being permitted to remain in the hot sun while at rest.' A species of Harmony Hall has been erected for the children, 'where all are taken at daylight, and placed under the charge of a careful and experienced woman.' Moreover, continues our philanthropic planter, 'I have a large and comfortable hospital provided for my negroes when they are sick; to this is attached a nurse's room; and when a negro complains of being too unwell to work, he is at once sent to the hospital.'

"Nor are either lighter or weightier matters overlooked. Besides passing a 'liquor law' for his plantation, which secures sobriety, 'I must not omit to mention,' he says, 'that I have a good fiddler, and keep him well supplied with catgut; and I make it his duty to play for the negroes every Saturday night until twelve o'clock. They are exceedingly punctual in their attendance at the ball, while Charley's fiddle is always accompanied with Herod on the triangle, and Sam to 'pat!''

"Better still: 'I also employ a good preacher, who regularly preaches to them on the Sabbath-day, and it is made the duty of every one to come up clean and decent to the place of worship. As Father Garritt regularly calls on Brother Abram to close the exercises, he gives out and sings his hymn with much unction, and always cocks his eye at Charley the fiddler, as much as to say 'Old fellow, you had your time last night; now it is mine.'

"Neither the preaching nor the prayers have much effect on their morality, for the writer admits that they are very licentious. He attempted to improve them 'for many years by preaching virtue and decency, encouraging marriages, and by punishing with some severity, departures from marital obligations; but it was all in vain.'"

* * * * * * * *

Appendix, N.

From the Fifth Satire of Persius.

I had intended to give a long extract in English, but have room only for the following lines of the Original:

"Not Prætoris erat stultis dare tenuia rerum
Officia, atque usum rapidae permittere vitae.
Sambucam citius calōni aptaveris alto.
Stat contra ratio, et secretam garrit in aurem,
Ne liceat facere id, quod quis vitiabit agendo.
Publica lex hominum naturaque continet hoc fas,
Ut teneat vetitos inscitia debilis actus."
Sat. 5, l. 93—99.

Appendix P.

From the Boston Traveller, as copied into Littell's Living Age, No. 459, *page* 437.

Theodore Parker.

* * * * * * * *

"We refer now to two 'Sermons,' as he calls them—one delivered on the 14th November, 1852, when he was about to leave the Melodeon, and the other on the 21st, when he began his meetings in the new Music Hall—both of which have been published together in a pamphlet since this year (1853) came in, by Crosby, Nichols & Co. In these 'sermons,' he lets us somewhat more into his past history and future purposes, than the public had before been permitted to see; but still, it is quite plain, that the revelation is not complete.

"He tells us, that he came to Boston eight years ago, with great reluctance and misgiving, but with an 'idea' that he wished to teach and inculcate. Precisely what that idea *then* was, he does not here explain; but what his idea in preaching *now* is, he tells us pretty clearly. Probably it has been but one idea from the beginning.

"First, then, he tells us, under the two heads of his 'Ideas' of God and Man, and subsequently under two more heads, of the relations of God to Man, and of Man to God, what are his own notions of religion, and leaves no doubt that he is an unbeliever in Christianity as a divinely revealed religion. In short, he leaves no doubt that he is an infidel, of the class called Deists.

"But, secondly, lest there should be any mistake in the matter, he tells us what he does *not* believe. He says (pp. 14–15):—

"'I do not believe there ever was a miracle, or ever will be; everywhere I find law—the constant mode of operation of the infinite God. I do not believe in the miraculous inspiration of the Old Testament or the New Testament. I do not believe that the Old Testament was God's first word, nor the New Testament his last. The Scriptures are no finality to me. Inspiration is a perpetual fact. Prophets and Apostles did not monopolize the Father. He inspires men to-day as much as heretofore.

* * * * * * * *

"'I do not believe the miraculous origin of the Hebrew Church, or the Buddhist Church, or the Christian Church; nor the miraculous character of Jesus. I take not the Bible for my master, nor yet the Church; nor even Jesus of Nazareth for my master. I feel not at all bound to believe what the Church says is true, nor what any writer in the Old or New Testament declares true; and I am ready to believe that Jesus taught as I think, eternal torment, the existence of a devil, and that he himself should ere long come back in the clouds of heaven. I do not accept these things on his authority.

* * * * * * * *

"'He is my best historic ideal of human greatness; not without errors, not without the stain of his times, and I presume, of course, not without sins; for men without sins exist in the dreams of girls, not in real fact; you never saw such a one, nor I, and we never shall.'

"Of course, there can hereafter be no misapprehension about Theodore Parker's claims to be called a Christian minister; so that, if we *now* venture to say that he is not one, we shall, as we presume, no longer be told that we are uncharitable and calumnious; for to be a minister of Jesus Christ, and yet to ridicule Jesus Christ as a man who had the folly to teach 'that he should *ere long* come back in the clouds of heaven,' is an absurdity too strong for any reasonable person to accept. It is, however, worth notice that, on the title-page of these very 'sermons,' Mr. Parker is announced as the minister of the Twenty-Eighth Congregational Society in Boston, precisely as if he stood on the same footing with Dr. Blagden, or Dr. Adams, or any other of the Christian Congregational ministers of the city.

"So far, then, Theodore Parker has openly come out. He ridicules the idea of Christianity as a religion of miraculous authority, and he ridicules Jesus Christ, whom the Scriptures represent to be 'without sin,' as a character that can only 'exist in the dreams of girls;—not in real fact.' How much farther he will go in the same direction we cannot tell. Probably he cannot tell himself.

"But he gives us a glimpse of future possibilities. He says, p. 12, 'It may be possible that a man comes to the conviction of atheism, but yet has been faithful to himself.' We may, therefore, according to his own showing, have Theodore Parker preaching atheism among us, out of *faithfulness to himself*. At any rate, no man will say, that it is more unlikely he will do this fifteen years hence, than it was ten or fifteen years ago—(when as a Christian critic he attacked Dr. Palfrey so fiercely, or when as a Christian minister he received the degree of Master of Arts at our neighboring University,)—that he would, in 1852–3, be uttering in Boston such ribald attacks on Christianity as are contained in these two discourses.

"There is, however, another side of his public character and teachings, that it is important should be understood by the community in which he lives;—we mean, the *morals* he inculcates. Of this, from time to time, we have had intimations in a number of printed attacks on the judges of our courts, on our magistrates, on our clergy—in short, on anybody that did not hold opinions agreeable to Theodore Parker himself;—announcing his judgments, sometimes with brutal coarseness, though oftener in a tone that shows he is, after all, rather holding political caucuses on Sunday mornings, than anything else, and that his hearers so understand him by answering his appeals to their passions with clapping of hands and other signs of caucus-like applause. But, on one occasion, he went beyond the character even of a common political demagogue. We refer to his teaching that, in certain cases—which cases are to be judged of by each man for himself—perjury is the duty of a juryman. Mr. B. R. Curtis—now a Judge of the Supreme Court of the United States, and as much honored by the country as any man sitting on that bench—exposed this indecent outrage on public morals in a speech delivered at a very crowded meeting in Faneuil Hall, above two years ago. He said, with a plainness and sternness of rebuke, worthy the acknowledged elevation and integrity of his character:—

" 'Murder and perjury have been erected into virtues, and, in this city, preached from the sacred desk. I must not be suspected of exaggeration in the least degree. I read, therefore, the following passages from a sermon preached and published in this city—

" 'Let me suppose a case which may happen here, and before long. A woman flies from South Carolina to Massachusetts to escape from bondage. Mr. Greatheart aids her in her escape, harbors and conceals her, and is brought to trial for it. The punishment is a fine of one thousand dollars and imprisonment for six months. I am drawn to serve as a juror, and pass upon this offence. I may refuse to serve, and be punished for that, leaving men with no scruples to take my place; or I may take the juror's oath to give a verdict according to the law and the testimony. The law is plain, let us suppose, and the testimony conclusive. Greatheart himself confesses that he did the deed alleged, saving one ready to perish. The judge charges that if the jurors are satisfied of that fact, then they must return that he is guilty. This is a nice matter. Here are two questions. The one put to me in my official capacity as juror, is this—'Did Greatheart aid the woman?' The other put to me in my natural character as man, is this—'Will you help to punish Greatheart with fine and imprisonment for helping a woman to obtain her inalienable rights?' If I have extinguished my manhood by my juror's oath, then I shall do my official business and find Greatheart guilty, and I shall seem to be a true man; but if I value my manhood, I shall answer after my natural duty to love a man, and not hate him—to do him justice, not injustice—to allow him the natural rights he has not alienated, and shall say 'not guilty.' Then will men call me forsworn and a liar; but I think human nature will justify the verdict. * * *

" 'The man who attacks me to reduce me to slavery, in that moment of attack alienates his right to life, and if I were the fugitive, and could escape in no other way, I would kill him with as little compunction as I would drive a musquito from my face.'—*A Sermon of Conscience, by Rev. Theodore Parker.*

"'I should like to ask the Rev. Preacher, (continues Judge Curtis,) when he goes into court, and holds up his hand, and calls on his Maker to attest the sincerity of his vow to render a true verdict according to the law and the evidence, whether he does *that* as a man, or in some other capacity? And I should also like to ask him, in what capacity he would expect to receive the punishment which would await him here and hereafter, if he were to do what he recommends to others?'

"This was said by Judge Curtis, on the 26th of November, 1850. On the 18th of June next following, a juryman in Boston undertook to put in practice the precise doctrine here set forth, and was ignominiously struck from the panel of jurors for it, as soon as he was detected, by the Judge of the District Court of the United States. How many other persons—either to gratify their own passions, or the passions of their party—have acted on the same atrocious doctrine, *without* detection, Theodore Parker will know, when he meets them at the bar of God's judgment."

* * * * * * * *

Appendix, Q.

Legare on Slavery.

The Charleston Courier publishes the following eloquent remarks of Legare on the subject of Slavery in the United States. They are suggestive:—

"This is a great practical question, and needs to be treated by statesmen, and not by sophisters and fanatics.

"It is not *res integra,* and it is not necessary to discuss the justice or injustice, the fitness or unfitness of the institution in the abstract.

"The true question is, what is to be the destiny of this quarter of the world: what *race* is to inhabit and possess it? Shall it be given up (as to a great part of its surface) to barbarism—its inevitable fate under the dominion of the black race—or shall it continue to be possessed by the most improving, enterprising, active and energetic breed of men that have ever founded empires and peopled waste places—by that English race, whose conquests more extensive, whose power more gigantic, and whose Government more perfect than that of Rome, designate it as the fitting instrument, in the hands of Providence, for the great work of building up a world—that English race, of which the original stock has made itself the wonder of mankind—a people entirely peculiar in combining whatever is most dazzling in opulence and power, with well regulated liberty, and mild and equal administration of law—the most magnificent manifestations of the might and the grandeur of civilized life, that the world, in any age of it, has ever beheld. Look at Hayti, and contrast it with New-Holland!

"Does any man, who looks into the political character and effects of the cotton plant, doubt for a moment that slavery in the South has been and is a great instrument of civilization? Would the miracles, which the cotton trade has wrought, and is working, for the amelioration of the condition of mankind in Europe, have ever existed, had the negro of the South been emancipated in the revolution? Would this country have been what it is?

"The truth is, that civilization is more advanced by physical causes than by moral ones. I mean, supposing in both cases social order to be well established, and law administered. The steam engine is doing more for it than the *pulpit* itself. So of cotton. It is raising the standard of comfort, without which, men are doomed forever to be but half savage.

"The Roman conquests were attended with dreadful evils—millions of lives, it is said, were sacrificed by Cæsar in his Gallic wars, and so of all the rest. Does any one now doubt that, on the whole, the sword of Rome was a means of improvement to the whole race? that especially the spreading of Christianity was hastened and facilitated by it? Would any philanthropist, who did not assume that name to make it odious, wish the history of the Roman Empire blotted out?

"So of Greek art. Without doubt it had never existed—never, at least, in such an extraordinary perfection, without the institution of slavery. Suppose it were ascertained that, by establishing an English colony at the spot where Carthage once stood, at the end of some centuries, our race and institutions would spread over the whole of that continent, hitherto held to be doomed to everlasting silence and desolation; though the great result spoken of could only be accomplished by exterminating, as the red men of this continent have been, or reducing to bondage, under the white man, the negro, who is now the slave of his brother negro and brother savage—would it be considered inconsistent with humanity to have, yea, and to co-operate in producing a change so full of splendid improvement, so favorable to the dignity of human nature, and even to the beauty and glory of God's creation?

"Look at the state of South America, and compare it with the northern part of the continent.

"Therefore, I have always thought that the slave trade, inhuman, infernal as it was, had not been without its compensations; (certainly not enough to justify any one in taking part in continuing it, for so much evident and now known evil ought not to be done that good might come of it;) but that considered as a great evil, it was much more so to this continent than to Africa.

"In short, slavery is an evil, except under peculiar circumstances—generally speaking, certainly—and everything shows it *here;* but not such an evil as calls for violent, and still less destructive measures to arrest it."

Appendix, R.

Worn-out Lands.

"In the State of New York there are some twelve million acres of improved land, which includes all meadows and enclosed pastures. This area employs about five hundred thousand laborers, being an average of twenty-four acres to the hand. At this ratio, the number of acres of improved land in the United States is one hundred and twenty millions. But New York is an old and more densely populated State than an average in the Union; and probably twenty-five acres per head is a juster estimate for the whole country. At this rate, the aggregate is one hundred and twenty-five millions. Of these improved lands, it is confidently believed that at least four-fifths are now suffering deterioration in a greater or less degree.

* * * * * * * *

"Eight million acres [in the State of New York] are in the hands of three hundred thousand persons, who still adhere to the colonial practice of extracting from the virgin soil all it will yield, so long as it will pay expenses to crop it, and then leave it in a thin, poor pasture for a term of years. Some of these impoverished farms, which, seventy-five years ago produced from twenty to thirty bushels of wheat, on an average, per acre, now yield only from five to eight bushels. In an exceedingly interesting work entitled 'American Husbandry,' published in London in 1775, and written by an American, the following remarks may be found on page 98, vol. 1:—'Wheat, in many parts of the province, (New York,) yields a larger produce than is common in England. Upon good lands about Albany, where the climate is the coldest in the country, they sow two bushels and better upon an acre, and reap from *twenty* to *forty;* the latter quantity, however, is not often had, but from twenty to *thirty are common;* and with such bad husbandry as would not yield the like in England, and much less in Scotland. This is owing to the *richness* and *freshness* of the land.'

"According to the State census of 1845, Albany county now produces only seven and a half bushels of wheat per acre, although its farmers are on tide water and near the capital of the State, with a good home market, and possess every facility for procuring the most valuable fertilizers. Dutchess county, also on the Hudson river, produces an average of only five bushels per acre; Columbia, six bushels; Renssellaer, eight; West Chester, seven; which is higher than the average of soils that once gave a return larger than the wheat lands of England, even with 'bad husbandry.'

"Fully to renovate the eight million acres of partially exhausted lands in the State of New York, will cost at least an average of twelve dollars and a half per acre, or an aggregate of one hundred millions of dollars. It is not an easy task to replace all the bone-earth, potash, sulphur, magnesia, and organized nitrogen in mould consumed in a field which has been unwisely cultivated fifty or seventy-five years. Phosphorus is not an abundant mineral anywhere, and his *sub-soil* is about the only resource of the husbandman after his surface-soil has lost most of its phosphates. The three hundred thousand persons that cultivate these eight million acres of impoverished soils annually produce less by twenty-five dollars each than they would if the land had not been injured.

"The aggregate of this loss to the State and the world is seven million five hundred thousand dollars per annum, or more than seven per cent. interest on what it would cost to renovate the deteriorated soils. There is no possible escape from this oppressive tax on labor of seven million five hundred thousand dollars, but to improve the land, or run off and leave it."—*Patent Office Report*, 1849.

THE END.

CATALOGUE
OF
VALUABLE BOOKS,
PUBLISHED BY
LIPPINCOTT, GRAMBO & CO.,
(SUCCESSORS TO GRIGG, ELLIOT & CO.)

NO. 14 NORTH FOURTH STREET, PHILADELPHIA;

CONSISTING OF A LARGE ASSORTMENT OF

Bibles, Prayer-Books, Commentaries, Standard Poets,
MEDICAL, THEOLOGICAL AND MISCELLANEOUS WORKS, ETC.,

PARTICULARLY SUITABLE FOR

PUBLIC AND PRIVATE LIBRARIES.

FOR SALE BY BOOKSELLERS AND COUNTRY MERCHANTS GENERALLY THROUGHOUT THE UNITED STATES.

THE BEST & MOST COMPLETE FAMILY COMMENTARY.

The Comprehensive Commentary on the Holy Bible;

CONTAINING

THE TEXT ACCORDING TO THE AUTHORIZED VERSION,

SCOTT'S MARGINAL REFERENCES; MATTHEW HENRY'S COMMENTARY, CONDENSED, BUT RETAINING EVERY USEFUL THOUGHT; THE PRACTICAL OBSERVATIONS OF REV. THOMAS SCOTT, D. D.;

WITH EXTENSIVE

EXPLANATORY, CRITICAL AND PHILOLOGICAL NOTES,

Selected from Scott, Doddridge, Gill, Adam Clarke, Patrick, Poole, Lowth, Burder, Harmer, Calmet, Rosenmueller, Bloomfield, Stuart, Bush, Dwight, and many other writers on the Scriptures.

The whole designed to be a digest and combination of the advantages of the best Bible Commentaries, and embracing nearly all that is valuable in

HENRY, SCOTT, AND DODDRIDGE.

Conveniently arranged for family and private reading, and, at the same time, particularly adapted to the wants of Sabbath-School Teachers and Bible Classes; with numerous useful tables, and a neatly engraved Family Record.

Edited by Rev. WILLIAM JENKS, D. D.,

PASTOR OF GREEN STREET CHURCH, BOSTON.

Embellished with five portraits, and other elegant engravings, from steel plates; with several maps and many wood-cuts, illustrative of Scripture Manners, Customs, Antiquities, &c. In 6 vols. super-royal 8vo.

Including Supplement, bound in cloth, sheep, calf, &c., varying in

Price from $10 to $15.

The whole forming the most valuable as well as the cheapest Commentary published in the world.

A

NOTICES AND RECOMMENDATIONS
OF THE
COMPREHENSIVE COMMENTARY.

The Publishers select the following from the testimonials they have received as to the value of the work:

We, the subscribers, having examined the *Comprehensive Commentary*, issued from the press of Messrs. L., G. & Co., and highly approving its character, would cheerfully and confidently recommend it as containing more matter and more advantages than any other with which we are acquainted; and considering the expense incurred, and the excellent manner of its mechanical execution, we believe it to be one of the *cheapest* works ever issued from the press. We hope the publishers will be sustained by a liberal patronage, in their expensive and useful undertaking. We should be pleased to learn that every family in the United States had procured a copy.

B. B. WISNER, D. D., Secretary of Am. Board of Com. for For. Missions.
WM. COGSWELL, D. D., " " Education Society.
JOHN CODMAN, D. D., Pastor of Congregational Church, Dorchester.
Rev. HUBBARD WINSLOW, " " Bowdoin street, Dorchester.
Rev. SEWALL HARDING, Pastor of T. C. Church, Waltham.
Rev. J. H. FAIRCHILD, Pastor of Congregational Church, South Boston.
GARDINER SPRING, D. D., Pastor of Presbyterian Church, New York city.
CYRUS MASON, D. D., " " " " "
THOS. M'AULEY, D. D., " " " " "
JOHN WOODBRIDGE, D. D., " " " " "
THOS. DEWITT, D. D., " Dutch Ref. " " "
E. W. BALDWIN, D. D., " " " " "
Rev. J. M. M'KREBS, " Presbyterian " " "
Rev. ERSKINE MASON, " " " " "
Rev. J. S. SPENCER, " " " Brooklyn.
EZRA STILES ELY, D. D., Stated Clerk of Gen. Assem. of Presbyterian Church
JOHN M'DOWELL, D. D., Permanent " " " "
JOHN BRECKENRIDGE, Corresponding Secretary of Assembly's Board of Education.
SAMUEL B. WYLIE, D. D., Pastor of the Reformed Presbyterian Church.
N. LORD, D. D., President of Dartmouth College.
JOSHUA BATES, D. D., President of Middlebury College.
H. HUMPHREY, D. D., " Amherst College.
E. D. GRIFFIN, D. D., " Williamstown College.
J. WHEELER, D. D., " University of Vermont, at Burlington.
J. M. MATTHEWS, D. D., " New York City University.
GEORGE E. PIERCE, D. D., " Western Reserve College, Ohio.
Rev. Dr. BROWN, " Jefferson College, Penn.
LEONARD WOODS, D. D., Professor of Theology, Andover Seminary.
THOS. H. SKINNER, D. D., " Sac. Rhet. " "
Rev. RALPH EMERSON, " Eccl. Hist. " "
Rev. JOEL PARKER, Pastor of Presbyterian Church, New Orleans.
JOEL HAWES, D. D., " Congregational Church, Hartford, Conn.
N. S. S. BEAMAN, D. D., " Presbyterian Church, Troy, N. Y.
MARK TUCKER, D. D., " " " " "
Rev. E. N. KIRK, " " " Albany, N. Y.
Rev. E. B. EDWARDS, Editor of Quarterly Observer.
Rev. STEPHEN MASON, Pastor First Congregational Church, Nantucket.
Rev. ORIN FOWLER, " " " " Fall River.
GEORGE W. BETHUNE, D. D., Pastor of the First Reformed Dutch Church, Philada.
Rev. LYMAN BEECHER, D. D., Cincinnati, Ohio.
Rev. C. D. MALLORY, Pastor Baptist Church, Augusta, Ga.
Rev. S. M. NOEL, " " " Frankfort, Ky.

From the Professors at Princeton Theological Seminary.

The Comprehensive Commentary contains the whole of Henry's Exposition in a condensed form, Scott's Practical Observations and Marginal References, and a large number of very valuable philological and critical notes, selected from various authors. The work appears to be executed with judgment, fidelity, and care; and will furnish a rich treasure of scriptural knowledge to the Biblical student, and to the teachers of Sabbath-Schools and Bible Classes.

A. ALEXANDER, D. D.
SAMUEL MILLER, D. D.
CHARLES HODGE, D. D

The Companion to the Bible.

In one super-royal volume.

DESIGNED TO ACCOMPANY

THE FAMILY BIBLE,

OR HENRY'S, SCOTT'S, CLARKE'S, GILL'S, OR OTHER COMMENTARIES:

CONTAINING

1. A new, full, and complete Concordance;

Illustrated with monumental, traditional, and oriental engravings, founded on Butterworth's, with Cruden's definitions; forming, it is believed, on many accounts, a more valuable work than either Butterworth, Cruden, or any other similar book in the language.

The value of a Concordance is now generally understood; and those who have used one, consider it indispensable in connection with the Bible.

2. A Guide to the Reading and Study of the Bible;

being Carpenter's valuable Biblical Companion, lately published in London, containing a complete history of the Bible, and forming a most excellent introduction to its study. It embraces the evidences of Christianity, Jewish antiquities, manners, customs, arts, natural history, &c., of the Bible, with notes and engravings added.

3. Complete Biographies of Henry, by Williams; Scott, by his son; Doddridge, by Orton;

with sketches of the lives and characters, and notices of the works, of the writers on the Scriptures who are quoted in the Commentary, living and dead, American and foreign.

This part of the volume not only affords a large quantity of interesting and useful reading for pious families, but will also be a source of gratification to all those who are in the habit of consulting the Commentary; every one naturally feeling a desire to know some particulars of the lives and characters of those whose opinions he seeks. Appended to this part, will be a

BIBLIOTHECA BIBLICA,

or list of the best works on the Bible, of all kinds, arranged under their appropriate heads.

4. A complete Index of the Matter contained in the Bible Text.

5. A Symbolical Dictionary.

A very comprehensive and valuable Dictionary of Scripture Symbols, (occupying about *fifty-six* closely printed pages,) by Thomas Wemyss, (author of "Biblical Gleanings," &c.) Comprising Daubuz, Lancaster, Hutcheson, &c.

6. The Work contains several other Articles,

Indexes, Tables, &c. &c., and is,

7. Illustrated by a large Plan of Jerusalem,

identifying, as far as tradition, &c., go, the original sites, drawn on the spot by F. Catherwood, of London, architect. Also, two steel engravings of portraits of seven foreign and eight American theological writers, and numerous wood engravings.

The whole forms a desirable and necessary fund of instruction for the use not only of clergymen and Sabbath-school teachers, but also for families. When the great amount of matter it must contain is considered, it will be deemed exceedingly cheap.

"I have examined 'The Companion to the Bible,' and have been surprised to find so much information introduced into a volume of so moderate a size. It contains a library of sacred knowledge and criticism. It will be useful to ministers who own large libraries, and cannot fail to be an invaluable help to every reader of the Bible." HENRY MORRIS,
Pastor of Congregational Church, Vermont.

The above work can be had in several styles of binding. Price varying from $1 75 to $5 00.

LIPPINCOTT'S EDITION OF

BAGSTER'S COMPREHENSIVE BIBLE.

In order to develope the peculiar nature of the Comprehensive Bible, it will only be necessary to embrace its more prominent features.

1st. The SACRED TEXT is that of the Authorized Version, and is printed from the edition corrected and improved by Dr. Blaney, which, from its accuracy, is considered the standard edition.

2d. The VARIOUS READINGS are faithfully printed from the edition of Dr. Blaney, inclusive of the translation of the proper names, without the addition or diminution of one.

3d. In the CHRONOLOGY, great care has been taken to fix the date of the particular transactions, which has seldom been done with any degree of exactness in any former edition of the Bible.

4th. The NOTES are exclusively philological and explanatory, and are not tinctured with sentiments of any sect or party. They are selected from the most eminent Biblical critics and commentators.

It is hoped that this edition of the Holy Bible will be found to contain the essence of Biblical research and criticism, that lies dispersed through an immense number of volumes.

Such is the nature and design of this edition of the Sacred Volume, which, from the various objects it embraces, the freedom of its pages from all sectarian peculiarities, and the beauty, plainness, and correctness of the typography, that it cannot fail of proving acceptable and useful to Christians of every denomination.

In addition to the usual references to parallel passages, which are quite full and numerous, the student has all the marginal readings, together with a rich selection of *Philological, Critical, Historical, Geographical,* and other valuable notes and remarks, which explain and illustrate the sacred text. Besides the general introduction, containing valuable essays on the genuineness, authenticity, and inspiration of the Holy Scriptures, and other topics of interest, there are introductory and concluding remarks to each book—a table of the contents of the Bible, by which the different portions are so arranged as to read in an historical order.

Arranged at the top of each page is the period in which the prominent events of sacred history took place. The calculations are made for the year of the world before and after Christ, Julian Period, the year of the Olympiad, the year of the building of Rome, and other notations of time. At the close is inserted a Chronological Index of the Bible, according to the computation of Archbishop Ussher. Also, a full and valuable index of the *subjects* contained in the Old and New Testaments, with a careful analysis and arrangement of texts under their appropriate subjects.

Mr. Greenfield, the editor of this work, and for some time previous to his death the superintendent of the editorial department of the British and Foreign Bible Society, was a most extraordinary man. In editing the Comprehensive Bible, his varied and extensive learning was called into successful exercise, and appears in happy combination with sincere piety and a sound judgment. The Editor of the Christian Observer, alluding to this work, in an obituary notice of its author, speaks of it as a work of "prodigious labour and research, at once exhibiting his varied talents and profound erudition."

LIPPINCOTT'S EDITION OF

THE OXFORD QUARTO BIBLE.

The Publishers have spared neither care nor expense in their edition of the Bible; it is printed on the finest white vellum paper, with large and beautiful type, and bound in the most substantial and splendid manner, in the following styles: Velvet, with richly gilt ornaments; Turkey super extra, with gilt clasps; and in numerous others, to suit the taste of the most fastidious.

OPINIONS OF THE PRESS.

"In our opinion, the Christian public generally will feel under great obligations to the publishers of this work for the beautiful taste, arrangement, and delicate neatness with which they have got it out. The intrinsic merit of the Bible recommends itself; it needs no tinsel ornament to adorn its sacred pages. In this edition every superfluous ornament has been avoided, and we have presented us a perfectly chaste specimen of the Bible, without note or comment. It appears to be just what is needed in every family—'the *unsophisticated* word of God.'

"The size is quarto, printed with beautiful type, on white, sized vellum paper, of the finest texture and most beautiful surface. The publishers seem to have been solicitous to make a perfectly unique book, and they have accomplished the object very successfully. We trust that a liberal community will afford them ample remuneration for all the expense and outlay they have necessarily incurred in its publication. It is a standard Bible.

"The publishers are Messrs. Lippincott, Grambo & Co., No. 14 North Fourth street, Philadelphia." — *Baptist Record.*

"A beautiful quarto edition of the Bible, by L., G. & Co. Nothing can exceed the type in clearness and beauty; the paper is of the finest texture, and the whole execution is exceedingly neat No illustrations or ornamental type are used. Those who prefer a Bible executed in perfect simplicity, yet elegance of style, without adornment, will probably never find one more to their taste." — *M. Magazine.*

LIPPINCOTT'S EDITIONS OF

THE HOLY BIBLE.

SIX DIFFERENT SIZES,

Printed in the best manner, with beautiful type, on the finest sized paper, and bound in the most splendid and substantial styles. Warranted to be correct, and equal to the best English editions, at much less price. To be had with or without plates; the publishers having supplied themselves with over fifty steel engravings, by the first artists.

Baxter's Comprehensive Bible,

Royal quarto, containing the various readings and marginal notes; disquisitions on the genuineness, authenticity, and inspiration of the Holy Scriptures; introductory and concluding remarks to each book; philological and explanatory notes; table of contents, arranged in historical order; a chronological index, and various other matter; forming a suitable book for the study of clergymen, Sabbath-school teachers, and students.

In neat plain binding, from $4 00 to $5 00. — In Turkey morocco, extra, gilt edges, from $8 00 to $12 00. — In do., with splendid plates, $10 00 to $15 00. — In do., bevelled side, gilt clasps and illuminations, $15 00 to $25 00.

The Oxford Quarto Bible,

Without note or comment, universally admitted to be the most beautiful Bible extant.

In neat plain binding, from $4 00 to $5 00. — In Turkey morocco, extra, gilt edges, $8 00 to $12 00. — In do., with steel engravings, $10 00 to $15 00. — In do., clasps, &c., with plates and illuminations, $15 00 to $25 00. — In rich velvet, with gilt ornaments, $25 00 to $50 00.

Crown Octavo Bible,

Printed with large clear type, making a most convenient hand Bible for family use.

In neat plain binding, from 75 cents to $1 50. — In English Turkey morocco, gilt edges, $1 00 to $2 00. — In do., imitation, &c., $1 50 to $3 00. — In do., clasps, &c., $2 50 to $5 00. — In rich velvet, with gilt ornaments, $5 00 to $10 00.

The Sunday-School Teacher's Polyglot Bible, with Maps, &c.,

In neat plain binding, from 60 cents to $1 00. — In imitation gilt edge, $1 00 to $1 50. — In Turkey, super extra, $1 75 to $2 25. — In do. do., with clasps, $2 50 to $3 75. — In velvet, rich gilt ornaments, $3 50 to $8 00.

The Oxford 18mo., or Pew Bible,

In neat plain binding, from 50 cents to $1 00. — In imitation gilt edge, $1 00 to $1 50. — In Turkey super extra, $1 75 to $2 25. — In do. do., with clasps, $2 50 to $3 75. — In velvet, rich gilt ornaments, $3 50 to $8 00.

Agate 32mo. Bible,

Printed with larger type than any other small or pocket edition extant.

In neat plain binding, from 50 cents to $1 00. — In tucks, or pocket-book style, 75 cents to $1 00. — In roan, imitation gilt edge, $1 00 to $1 50. — In Turkey, super extra, $1 00 to $2 00. — In do. do gilt clasps, $2 50 to $3 50. — In velvet, with rich gilt ornaments, $3 00 to $7 00.

32mo. Diamond Pocket Bible;

The neatest, smallest, and cheapest edition of the Bible published

In neat plain binding, from 30 to 50 cents. — In tucks, or pocket-book style, 60 cents to $1 00. — In roan, imitation gilt edge, 75 cents to $1 25. — In Turkey, super extra, $1 00 to $1 50. — In do. do gilt clasps, $1 50 to $2 00. — In velvet, with richly gilt ornaments, $2 50 to $6 00.

CONSTANTLY ON HAND,

A large assortment of BIBLES, bound in the most splendid and costly styles, with gold and silver ornaments, suitable for presentation; ranging in price from $10 00 to $100 00.

A liberal discount made to Booksellers and Agents by the Publishers.

ENCYCLOPÆDIA OF RELIGIOUS KNOWLEDGE;

OR, DICTIONARY OF THE BIBLE, THEOLOGY, RELIGIOUS BIOGRAPHY, ALL RELIGIONS, ECCLESIASTICAL HISTORY, AND MISSIONS.

Designed as a complete Book of Reference on all Religious Subjects, and Companion to the Bible; forming a cheap and compact Library of Religious Knowledge. Edited by Rev. J. Newton Brown. Illustrated by wood-cuts, maps, and engravings on copper and steel. In one volume, royal 8vo. Price, $4 00.

The Clergy of America:

CONSISTING OF

ANECDOTES ILLUSTRATIVE OF THE CHARACTER OF MINISTERS OF RELIGION IN THE UNITED STATES,

BY JOSEPH BELCHER, D. D.,

Editor of "The Complete Works of Andrew Fuller," "Robert Hall," &c.

"This very interesting and instructive collection of pleasing and solemn remembrances of many pious men, illustrates the character of the day in which they lived, and defines the men more clearly than very elaborate essays." — *Baltimore American.*

"We regard the collection as highly interesting, and judiciously made." — *Presbyterian.*

JOSEPHUS'S (FLAVIUS) WORKS,

FAMILY EDITION.

BY THE LATE WILLIAM WHISTON, A. M.

FROM THE LAST LONDON EDITION, COMPLETE.

One olume, beautifully illustrated with Steel Plates, and the only readable edition published in this country.

As a matter of course, every family in our country has a copy of the Holy Bible; and as the presumption is that the greater portion often consult its pages, we take the liberty of saying to all those that do, that the perusal of the writings of Josephus will be found very interesting and instructive.

All those who wish to possess a beautiful and correct copy of this valuable work, would do well to purchase this edition. It is for sale at all the principal bookstores in the United States, and by country merchants generally in the Southern and Western States.

Also, the above work in two volumes.

BURDER'S VILLAGE SERMONS;

Or, 101 Plain and Short Discourses on the Principal Doctrines of the Gospel.

INTENDED FOR THE USE OF FAMILIES, SUNDAY-SCHOOLS, OR COMPANIES ASSEMBLED FOR RELIGIOUS INSTRUCTION IN COUNTRY VILLAGES.

BY GEORGE BURDER.

To which is added to each Sermon, a Short Prayer, with some General Prayers for Families, Schools, &c., at the end of the work.

COMPLETE IN ONE VOLUME, OCTAVO.

These sermons, which are characterized by a beautiful simplicity, the entire absence of controversy, and a true evangelical spirit, have gone through many and large editions, and been translated into several of the continental languages. "They have also been the honoured means not only of converting many individuals, but also of introducing the Gospel into districts, and even into parish churches, where before it was comparatively unknown."

"This work fully deserves the immortality it has attained."

This is a fine library edition of this invaluable work; and when we say that it should be found in the possession of every family, we only reiterate the sentiments and sincere wishes of all who take a deep interest in the eternal welfare of mankind.

FAMILY PRAYERS AND HYMNS,

ADAPTED TO FAMILY WORSHIP,

AND

TABLES FOR THE REGULAR READING OF THE SCRIPTURES.

By Rev. S. C. WINCHESTER, A. M.,

Late Pastor of the Sixth Presbyterian Church, Philadelphia; and the Presbyterian Church at Natchez, Miss.

One volume, 12mo.

SPLENDID LIBRARY EDITIONS.

ILLUSTRATED STANDARD POETS.

ELEGANTLY PRINTED, ON FINE PAPER, AND UNIFORM IN SIZE AND STYLE.

The following Editions of Standard British Poets are illustrated with numerous Steel Engravings, and may be had in all varieties of binding.

BYRON'S WORKS.

COMPLETE IN ONE VOLUME, OCTAVO.

INCLUDING ALL HIS SUPPRESSED AND ATTRIBUTED POEMS; WITH SIX BEAUTIFUL ENGRAVINGS.

This edition has been carefully compared with the recent London edition of Mr. Murray, and made complete by the addition of more than fifty pages of poems heretofore unpublished in England. Among these there are a number that have never appeared in any American edition; and the publishers believe they are warranted in saying that this is *the most complete edition of Lord Byron's Poetical Works* ever published in the United States.

The Poetical Works of Mrs. Hemans.

Complete in one volume, octavo; with seven beautiful Engravings.

This is a new and complete edition, with a splendid engraved likeness of Mrs. Hemans, on steel, and contains all the Poems in the last London and American editions. With a Critical Preface by Mr. Thatcher, of Boston.

"As no work in the English language can be commended with more confidence, it will argue bad taste in a female in this country to be without a complete edition of the writings of one who was an honour to her sex and to humanity, and whose productions, from first to last, contain no syllable calculated to call a blush to the cheek of modesty and virtue. There is, moreover, in Mrs. Hemans's poetry, a moral purity and a religious feeling which commend it, in an especial manner, to the discriminating reader. No parent or guardian will be under the necessity of imposing restrictions with regard to the free perusal of every production emanating from this gifted woman. There breathes throughout the whole a most eminent exemption from impropriety of thought or diction; and there is at times a pensiveness of tone, a winning sadness in her more serious compositions, which tells of a soul which has been lifted from the contemplation of terrestrial things, to divine communings with beings of a purer world."

MILTON, YOUNG, GRAY, BEATTIE, AND COLLINS'S POETICAL WORKS.

COMPLETE IN ONE VOLUME, OCTAVO.

WITH SIX BEAUTIFUL ENGRAVINGS.

Cowper and Thomson's Prose and Poetical Works.

COMPLETE IN ONE VOLUME, OCTAVO.

Including two hundred and fifty Letters, and sundry Poems of Cowper, never before published in this country; and of Thomson a new and interesting Memoir, and upwards of twenty new Poems, for the first time printed from his own Manuscripts, taken from a late Edition of the Aldine Poets, now publishing in London.

WITH SEVEN BEAUTIFUL ENGRAVINGS.

The distinguished Professor Silliman, speaking of this edition, observes: "I am as much gratified by the elegance and fine taste of your edition, as by the noble tribute of genius and moral excellence which these delightful authors have left for all future generations; and Cowper, especially, is not less conspicuous as a true Christian, moralist and teacher, than as a poet of great power and exquisite taste."

THE POETICAL WORKS OF ROGERS, CAMPBELL, MONTGOMERY, LAMB, AND KIRKE WHITE.

COMPLETE IN ONE VOLUME, OCTAVO.

WITH SIX BEAUTIFUL ENGRAVINGS.

The beauty, correctness, and convenience of this favourite edition of these standard authors are so well known, that it is scarcely necessary to add a word in its favour. It is only necessary to say, that the publishers have now issued an illustrated edition, which greatly enhances its former value The engravings are excellent and well selected. It is the best library edition extant.

CRABBE, HEBER, AND POLLOK'S POETICAL WORKS.

COMPLETE IN ONE VOLUME, OCTAVO.

WITH SIX BEAUTIFUL ENGRAVINGS.

A writer in the Boston Traveller holds the following language with reference to these valuable editions:—

"Mr. Editor:—I wish, without any idea of puffing, to say a word or two upon the 'Library of English Poets' that is now published at Philadelphia, by Lippincott, Grambo & Co. It is certainly, taking into consideration the elegant manner in which it is printed, and the reasonable price at which it is afforded to purchasers, the best edition of the modern British Poets that has ever been published in this country. Each volume is an octavo of about 500 pages, double columns, stereotyped, and accompanied with fine engravings and biographical sketches; and most of them are reprinted from Galignani's French edition. As to its value, we need only mention that it contains the entire works of Montgomery, Gray, Beattie, Collins, Byron, Cowper, Thomson, Milton, Young, Rogers, Campbell, Lamb, Hemans, Heber, Kirke White, Crabbe, the Miscellaneous Works of Goldsmith, and other masters of the lyre. The publishers are doing a great service by their publication, and their volumes are almost in as great demand as the fashionable novels of the day; and they deserve to be so: for they are certainly printed in a style superior to that in which we have before had the works of the English Poets."

No library can be considered complete without a copy of the above beautiful and cheap editions of the English Poets; and persons ordering all or any of them, will please say Lippincott, Grambo & Co.'s illustrated editions.

A COMPLETE

Dictionary of Poetical Quotations:

COMPRISING THE MOST EXCELLENT AND APPROPRIATE PASSAGES IN THE OLD BRITISH POETS; WITH CHOICE AND COPIOUS SELECTIONS FROM THE BEST MODERN BRITISH AND AMERICAN POETS.

EDITED BY SARAH JOSEPHA HALE.

As nightingales do upon glow-worms feed,
So poets live upon the living light
Of Nature and of Beauty.

Bailey's Festus.

Beautifully illustrated with Engravings. In one super-royal octavo volume, in various bindings.

The publishers extract, from the many highly complimentary notices of the above valuable and beautiful work, the following:

"We have at last a volume of Poetical Quotations worthy of the name. It contains nearly six hundred octavo pages, carefully and tastefully selected from all the home and foreign authors of celebrity. It is invaluable to a writer, while to the ordinary reader it presents every subject at a glance."—*Godey's Lady's Book.*

"The plan or idea of Mrs. Hale's work is felicitous. It is one for which her fine taste, her orderly habits of mind, and her long occupation with literature, has given her peculiar facilities; and thoroughly has she accomplished her task in the work before us."—*Sartain's Magazine.*

"It is a choice collection of poetical extracts from every English and American author worth perusing, from the days of Chaucer to the present time."—*Washington Union.*

"There is nothing negative about this work; it is *positively* good."—*Evening Bulletin.*

THE DIAMOND EDITION OF BYRON.

THE POETICAL WORKS OF LORD BYRON,

WITH A SKETCH OF HIS LIFE.

COMPLETE IN ONE NEAT DUODECIMO VOLUME, WITH STEEL PLATES.

The type of this edition is so perfect, and it is printed with so much care, on fine white paper, that it can be read with as much ease as most of the larger editions. This work is to be had in plain and superb binding, making a beautiful volume for a gift.

" *The Poetical Works of Lord Byron*, complete in one volume; published by L., G. & Co., Philadelphia. We hazard nothing in saying that, take it altogether, this is the most elegant work ever issued from the American press.

"'In a single volume, not larger than an ordinary duodecimo, the publishers have embraced the whole of Lord Byron's Poems, usually printed in ten or twelve volumes; and, what is more remarkable, have done it with a type so clear and distinct, that, notwithstanding its necessarily small size, it may be read with the utmost facility, even by failing eyes. The book is stereotyped; and never have we seen a finer specimen of that art. Everything about it is perfect—the paper, the printing, the binding, all correspond with each other; and it is embellished with two fine engravings, well worthy the companionship in which they are placed.

"'This will make a beautiful Christmas present.'

"We extract the above from Godey's Lady's Book. The notice itself, we are given to understand, is written by Mrs. Hale.

"We have to add our commendation in favour of this beautiful volume, a copy of which has been sent us by the publishers. The admirers of the noble bard will feel obliged to the enterprise which has prompted the publishers to dare a competition with the numerous editions of his works already in circulation; and we shall be surprised if this convenient travelling edition does not in a great degree supersede the use of the large octavo works, which have little advantage in size and openness of type, and are much inferior in the qualities of portability and lightness."—*Intelligencer.*

THE DIAMOND EDITION OF MOORE.

(CORRESPONDING WITH BYRON.)

THE POETICAL WORKS OF THOMAS MOORE,

COLLECTED BY HIMSELF.

COMPLETE IN ONE VOLUME.

This work is published uniform with Byron, from the last London edition, and is the most complete printed in the country.

THE DIAMOND EDITION OF SHAKSPEARE,

(COMPLETE IN ONE VOLUME,)

INCLUDING A SKETCH OF HIS LIFE.

UNIFORM WITH BYRON AND MOORE.

THE ABOVE WORKS CAN BE HAD IN SEVERAL VARIETIES OF BINDING.

GOLDSMITH'S ANIMATED NATURE.

IN TWO VOLUMES, OCTAVO.

BEAUTIFULLY ILLUSTRATED WITH 385 PLATES.

CONTAINING A HISTORY OF THE EARTH, ANIMALS, BIRDS, AND FISHES; FORMING THE MOST COMPLETE NATURAL HISTORY EVER PUBLISHED.

This is a work that should be in the library of every family, having been written by one of the most talented authors in the English language.

"Goldsmith can never be made obsolete while delicate genius, exquisite feeling, fine invention, the most harmonious metre, and the happiest diction, are at all valued."

BIGLAND'S NATURAL HISTORY

Of Animals, Birds, Fishes, Reptiles, and Insects. Illustrated with numerous and beautiful Engravings. By JOHN BIGLAND, author of a "View of the World," "Letters on Universal History," &c. Complete in 1 vol., 12mo.

THE POWER AND PROGRESS OF THE UNITED STATES.

THE UNITED STATES; Its Power and Progress.

BY GUILLAUME TELL POUSSIN,

LATE MINISTER OF THE REPUBLIC OF FRANCE TO THE UNITED STATES.

FIRST AMERICAN, FROM THE THIRD PARIS EDITION.

TRANSLATED FROM THE FRENCH BY EDMOND L. DU BARRY, M. D.,

SURGEON U. S. NAVY.

In one large octavo volume.

SCHOOLCRAFT'S GREAT NATIONAL WORK ON THE INDIAN TRIBES OF THE UNITED STATES.

WITH BEAUTIFUL AND ACCURATE COLOURED ILLUSTRATIONS.

HISTORICAL AND STATISTICAL INFORMATION

RESPECTING THE

HISTORY, CONDITION AND PROSPECTS

OF THE

Indian Tribes of the United States.

COLLECTED AND PREPARED UNDER THE DIRECTION OF THE BUREAU OF INDIAN AFFAIRS, PER ACT OF MARCH 3, 1847,

BY HENRY R. SCHOOLCRAFT, LL.D.

ILLUSTRATED BY S. EASTMAN, CAPT. U. S. A.

PUBLISHED BY AUTHORITY OF CONGRESS.

THE AMERICAN GARDENER'S CALENDAR,

ADAPTED TO THE CLIMATE AND SEASONS OF THE UNITED STATES.

Containing a complete account of all the work necessary to be done in the Kitchen Garden, Fruit Garden, Orchard, Vineyard, Nursery, Pleasure-Ground, Flower Garden, Green-house, Hot-house, and Forcing Frames, for every month in the year; with ample Practical Directions for performing the same.

Also, general as well as minute instructions for laying out or erecting each and every of the above departments, according to modern taste and the most approved plans; the Ornamental Planting of Pleasure Grounds, in the ancient and modern style; the cultivation of Thorn Quicks, and other plants suitable for Live Hedges, with the best methods of making them, &c. To which are annexe catalogues of Kitchen Garden Plants and Herbs; Aromatic, Pot, and Sweet Herbs; Medicinal Plants, and the most important Grapes, &c., used in rural economy; with the soil best adapted to their cultivation. Together with a copious Index to the body of the work.

BY BERNARD M'MAHON.

Tenth Edition, greatly improved. In one volume, octavo.

THE USEFUL AND THE BEAUTIFUL;

OR, DOMESTIC AND MORAL DUTIES NECESSARY TO SOCIAL HAPPINESS,

BEAUTIFULLY ILLUSTRATED.

16mo. square cloth. Price 50 and 75 cents.

THE FARMER'S AND PLANTER'S ENCYCLOPÆDIA.

The Farmer's and Planter's Encyclopædia of Rural Affairs.

BY CUTHBERT W. JOHNSON.

ADAPTED TO THE UNITED STATES BY GOUVERNEUR EMERSON.

Illustrated by seventeen beautiful Engravings of Cattle, Horses, Sheep, the varieties of Wheat Barley, Oats, Grasses, the Weeds of Agriculture, &c.; besides numerous Engravings on wood of the most important implements of Agriculture, &c.

This standard work contains the latest and best information upon all subjects connected with farming, and appertaining to the country; treating of the great crops of grain, hay, cotton, hemp, tobacco, rice, sugar, &c. &c.; of horses and mules; of cattle, with minute particulars relating to cheese and butter-making; of fowls, including a description of capon-making, with drawings of the instruments employed; of bees, and the Russian and other systems of managing bees and constructing hives. Long articles on the uses and preparation of bones, lime, guano, and all sorts of animal, mineral, and vegetable substances employed as manures. Descriptions of the most approved ploughs, harrows, threshers, and every other agricultural machine and implement; of fruit and shade trees, forest trees, and shrubs; of weeds, and all kinds of flies, and destructive worms and insects, and the best means of getting rid of them; together with a thousand other matters relating to rural life, about which information is so constantly desired by all residents of the country.

IN ONE LARGE OCTAVO VOLUME.

MASON'S FARRIER—FARMERS' EDITION.

Price, 62 cents.

THE PRACTICAL FARRIER, FOR FARMERS:

COMPRISING A GENERAL DESCRIPTION OF THE NOBLE AND USEFUL ANIMAL,

THE HORSE;

WITH MODES OF MANAGEMENT IN ALL CASES, AND TREATMENT IN DISEASE.

TO WHICH IS ADDED,

A PRIZE ESSAY ON MULES; AND AN APPENDIX,

Containing Recipes for Diseases of Horses, Oxen, Cows, Calves, Sheep, Dogs, Swine, &c. &c.

BY RICHARD MASON, M.D.,

Formerly of Surry County, Virginia.

In one volume, 12mo.; bound in cloth gilt.

MASON'S FARRIER AND STUD-BOOK—NEW EDITION.

THE GENTLEMAN'S NEW POCKET FARRIER:

COMPRISING A GENERAL DESCRIPTION OF THE NOBLE AND USEFUL ANIMAL,

THE HORSE;

WITH MODES OF MANAGEMENT IN ALL CASES, AND TREATMENT IN DISEASE.

BY RICHARD MASON, M.D.,

Formerly of Surry County, Virginia.

To which is added, A PRIZE ESSAY ON MULES; and AN APPENDIX, containing Recipes for Diseases of Horses, Oxen, Cows, Calves, Sheep, Dogs, Swine, &c. &c.; with Annals of the Turf, American Stud-Book, Rules for Training, Racing, &c

WITH A SUPPLEMENT,

Comprising an Essay on Domestic Animals, especially the Horse; with Remarks on Treatment and Breeding; together with Trotting and Racing Tables, showing the best time on record at one two, three and four mile heats; Pedigrees of Winning Horses, since 1839, and of the most celebrated Stallions and Mares; with useful Calving and Lambing Tables. By J. S. SKINNER, Editor now of the Farmer's Library, New York, &c. &c.

HINDS'S FARRIERY AND STUD-BOOK—NEW EDITION.

FARRIERY,

TAUGHT ON A NEW AND EASY PLAN:

BEING

A Treatise on the Diseases and Accidents of the Horse;

With Instructions to the Shoeing Smith, Farrier, and Groom; preceded by a Popular Description of the Animal Functions in Health, and how these are to be restored when disordered.

BY JOHN HINDS, VETERINARY SURGEON.

With considerable Additions and Improvements, particularly adapted to this country,

BY THOMAS M. SMITH,

Veterinary Surgeon, and Member of the London Veterinary Medical Society.

WITH A SUPPLEMENT, BY J. S. SKINNER.

The publishers have received numerous flattering notices of the great practical value of these works. The distinguished editor of the American Farmer, speaking of them, observes:—"We cannot too highly recommend these books, and therefore advise every owner of a horse to obtain them."

"There are receipts in those books that show how *Founder* may be cured, and the traveller pursue his journey the next day, by giving a *tablespoonful of alum*. This was got from Dr. P. Thornton, of Montpelier, Rappahannock county, Virginia, as founded on his own observation in several cases."

"The constant demand for Mason's and Hinds's Farrier has induced the publishers, Messrs. Lippincott, Grambo & Co., to put forth new editions, with a 'Supplement' of 100 pages, by J. S. Skinner, Esq. We should have sought to render an acceptable service to our agricultural readers, by giving a chapter from the Supplement, 'On the Relations between Man and the Domestic Animals, especially the Horse, and the Obligations they impose;' or the one on 'The Form of Animals;' but that either one of them would overrun the space here allotted to such subjects."

"Lists of Medicines, and other articles which ought to be at hand about every training and livery stable, and every Farmer's and Breeder's establishment, will be found in these valuable works."

TO CARPENTERS AND MECHANICS.

Just Published.

A NEW AND IMPROVED EDITION OF

THE CARPENTER'S NEW GUIDE,

BEING A COMPLETE BOOK OF LINES FOR

ARPENTRY AND JOINERY;

Treating fully on Practical Geometry, Saffit's Brick and Plaster Groins, Niches of every description, Sky-lights, Lines for Roofs and Domes; with a great variety of Designs for Roofs, Trussed Girders, Floors, Domes, Bridges, &c., Angle Bars for Shop Fronts, &c., and Raking Mouldings.

ALSO,

Additional Plans for various Stair-Cases, with the Lines for producing the Face and Falling Moulds never before published, and greatly superior to those given in a former edition of this work.

BY WILLIAM JOHNSON, ARCHITECT,

OF PHILADELPHIA.

The whole founded on true Geometrical Principles; the Theory and Practice well explained and fully exemplified, on eighty-three copper plates, including some Observations and Calculations on the Strength of Timber.

BY PETER NICHOLSON,

Author of "The Carpenter and Joiner's Assistant," "The Student's Instructor to the Five Orders," &c.

Thirteenth Edition. One volume, 4to., well bound.

A DICTIONARY OF SELECT AND POPULAR QUOTATIONS,

WHICH ARE IN DAILY USE.

TAKEN FROM THE LATIN, FRENCH, GREEK, SPANISH AND ITALIAN LANGUAGES.

Together with a copious Collection of Law Maxims and Law Terms, translated into English, with Illustrations, Historical and Idiomatic.

NEW AMERICAN EDITION, CORRECTED, WITH ADDITIONS.

One volume, 12mo.

This volume comprises a copious collection of legal and other terms which are in common use, with English translations and historical illustrations; and we should judge its author had surely een to a great "Feast of Languages," and stole all the scraps. A work of this character should have an extensive sale, as it entirely obviates a serious difficulty in which most readers are involved by the frequent occurrence of Latin, Greek, and French passages, which we suppose are introduced by authors for a mere show of learning—a difficulty very perplexing to readers in general. This "Dictionary of Quotations," concerning which too much cannot be said in its favour, effectually removes the difficulty, and gives the reader an advantage over the author; for we believe a majority are themselves ignorant of the meaning of the terms they employ. Very few truly learned authors will insult their readers by introducing Latin or French quotations in their writings, when "plain English" will do as well; but we will not enlarge on this point.

If the book is useful to those unacquainted with other languages, it is no less valuable to the classically educated as a book of reference, and answers all the purposes of a Lexicon—indeed, on many accounts, it is better. It saves the trouble of tumbling over the larger volumes, to which every one, and especially those engaged in the legal profession, are very often subjected. It should have a place in every library in the country.

RUSCHENBERGER'S NATURAL HISTORY,

COMPLETE, WITH NEW GLOSSARY.

The Elements of Natural History,

EMBRACING ZOOLOGY, BOTANY AND GEOLOGY:

FOR SCHOOLS, COLLEGES AND FAMILIES.

BY W. S. W. RUSCHENBERGER, M. D.

IN TWO VOLUMES.

WITH NEARLY ONE THOUSAND ILLUSTRATIONS, AND A COPIOUS GLOSSARY.

Vol. I. contains *Vertebrate Animals.* Vol. II. contains *Intervertebrate Animals, Botany, and Geology.*

A Beautiful and Valuable Presentation Book.

THE POET'S OFFERING.

EDITED BY MRS. HALE.

With a Portrait of the Editress, a Splendid Illuminated Title-Page, and Twelve Beautiful Engravings by Sartain. Bound in rich Turkey Morocco, and Extra Cloth, Gilt Edge.

To those who wish to make a present that will never lose its value, this will be found the most desirable Gift-Book ever published.

"We commend it to all who desire to present a friend with a volume not only very beautiful, but of solid intrinsic value."—*Washington Union.*

"A perfect treasury of the thoughts and fancies of the best English and American Poets. The paper and printing are beautiful, and the binding rich, elegant, and substantial; the most sensible and attractive of all the elegant gift-books we have seen."—*Evening Bulletin.*

"The publishers deserve the thanks of the public for so happy a thought, so well executed. The engravings are by the best artists, and the other portions of the work correspond in elegance."—*Public Ledger.*

"There is no book of selections so diversified and appropriate within our knowledge."—*Pennsylv'n.*

"It is one of the most valuable as well as elegant books ever published in this country."—*Godey's Lady's Book.*

"It is the most beautiful and the most useful offering ever bestowed on the public. No individual of literary taste will venture to be without it."—*The City Item.*

THE YOUNG DOMINICAN;
OR, THE MYSTERIES OF THE INQUISITION,

AND OTHER SECRET SOCIETIES OF SPAIN.

BY M. V. DE FEREAL.

WITH HISTORICAL NOTES, BY M. MANUEL DE CUENDIAS

TRANSLATED FROM THE FRENCH.

ILLUSTRATED WITH TWENTY SPLENDID ENGRAVINGS BY FRENCH ARTISTS

One volume, octavo.

SAY'S POLITICAL ECONOMY.

A TREATISE ON POLITICAL ECONOMY;
Or, The Production, Distribution and Consumption of Wealth.

BY JEAN BAPTISTE SAY.

FIFTH AMERICAN EDITION, WITH ADDITIONAL NOTES,

BY C. C. BIDDLE, Esq.

In one volume, octavo.

It would be beneficial to our country if all those who are aspiring to office, were required by their constituents to be familiar with the pages of Say.

The distinguished biographer of the author, in noticing this work, observes: "Happily for science he commenced that study which forms the basis of his admirable Treatise on *Political Economy*; a work which not only improved under his hand with every successive edition, but has been translated into most of the European languages."

The Editor of the North American Review, speaking of Say, observes, that "he is the most popular, and perhaps the most able writer on Political Economy, since the time of Smith."

LAURENCE STERNE'S WORKS,

WITH A LIFE OF THE AUTHOR:

WRITTEN BY HIMSELF.

WITH SEVEN BEAUTIFUL ILLUSTRATIONS, ENGRAVED BY GILBERT AND GIHON, FROM DESIGNS BY DARLEY.

One volume, octavo; cloth, gilt.

To commend or to criticise Sterne's Works, in this age of the world, would be all "wasteful and extravagant excess." Uncle Toby—Corporal Trim—the Widow—Le Fevre—Poor Maria—the Captive—even the Dead Ass,—this is all we have to say of Sterne; and in the memory of these characters, histories, and sketches, a thousand follies and worse than follies are forgotten. The volume is a very handsome one.

THE MEXICAN WAR AND ITS HEROES,

BEING

A COMPLETE HISTORY OF THE MEXICAN WAR,

EMBRACING ALL THE OPERATIONS UNDER GENERALS TAYLOR AND SCOTT.

WITH A BIOGRAPHY OF THE OFFICERS.

ALSO,

AN ACCOUNT OF THE CONQUEST OF CALIFORNIA AND NEW MEXICO,

Under Gen. Kearny Cols. Doniphan and Fremont. Together with Numerous Anecdotes of the War, and Personal Adventures of the Officers. Illustrated with Accurate Portraits, and other Beautiful Engravings.

In one volume, 12mo.

NEW AND COMPLETE COOK-BOOK.

THE PRACTICAL COOK-BOOK,

CONTAINING UPWARDS OF

ONE THOUSAND RECEIPTS,

Consisting of Directions for Selecting, Preparing, and Cooking all kinds of Meats, Fish, Poultry, and Game; Soups, Broths, Vegetables, and Salads. Also, for making all kinds of Plain and Fancy Breads, Pastes, Puddings, Cakes, Creams, Ices, Jellies, Preserves, Marmalades, &c. &c. &c. Together with various Miscellaneous Recipes, and numerous Preparations for Invalids.

BY MRS. BLISS.

In one volume, 12mo.

The City Merchant; or, The Mysterious Failure.

BY J. B. JONES,

AUTHOR OF "WILD WESTERN SCENES," "THE WESTERN MERCHANT," &c.

ILLUSTRATED WITH TEN ENGRAVINGS.

In one volume, 12mo.

CALIFORNIA AND OREGON;

OR, SIGHTS IN THE GOLD REGION, AND SCENES BY THE WAY.

BY THEODORE T. JOHNSON.

WITH NOTES, BY HON. SAMUEL R. THURSTON,

Delegate to Congress from that Territory.

With numerous Plates and Maps.

AUNT PHILLIS'S CABIN;

OR, SOUTHERN LIFE AS IT IS.

BY MRS. MARY H. EASTMAN.

PRICE, 50 AND 75 CENTS.

This volume presents a picture of Southern Life, taken at different points of view from the one occupied by the authoress of "*Uncle Tom's Cabin.*" The writer, being a native of the South, is familiar with the many varied aspects assumed by domestic servitude in that sunny region, and therefore feels competent to give pictures of "Southern Life, as it is."

Pledged to no clique or party, and free from the pressure of any and all extraneous influences, she has written her book with a view to its truthfulness; and the public at the North, as well as at the South, will find in "Aunt Phillis's Cabin" not the distorted picture of an interested painter, but the faithful transcript of a Daguerreotypist.

WHAT IS CHURCH HISTORY?

A VINDICATION OF THE IDEA OF HISTORICAL DEVELOPMENTS

BY PHILIP SCHAF.

TRANSLATED FROM THE GERMAN.

In one volume, 12mo.

DODD'S LECTURES.

DISCOURSES TO YOUNG MEN.

ILLUSTRATED BY NUMEROUS HIGHLY INTERESTING ANECDOTES.

BY WILLIAM DODD, LL. D.,

CHAPLAIN IN ORDINARY TO HIS MAJESTY GEORGE THE THIRD.

FIRST AMERICAN EDITION, WITH ENGRAVINGS.

One volume, 18mo.

THE IRIS:

AN ORIGINAL SOUVENIR.

With Contributions from the First Writers in the Country.

EDITED BY PROF. JOHN S. HART.

With Splendid Illuminations and Steel Engravings. Bound in Turkey Morocco and rich Papier Mache Binding.

IN ONE VOLUME, OCTAVO.

Its contents are entirely original. Among the contributors are names well known in the republic of letters; such as Mr. Boker, Mr. Stoddard, Prof. Moffat, Edith May, Mrs. Sigourney, Caroline May, Mrs. Kinney, Mrs. Butler, Mrs. Pease, Mrs. Swift, Mr. Van Bibber, Rev. Charles T. Brooks, Mrs. Dorr, Erastus W. Ellsworth, Miss E. W. Barnes, Mrs. Williams, Mary Young, Dr. Gardette, Alice Carey, Phebe Carey, Augusta Browne, Hamilton Browne, Caroline Eustis, Margaret Junkin, Maria J. B. Browne, Miss Starr, Mrs. Brotherson, Kate Campbell, &c.

Gems from the Sacred Mine;

OR, HOLY THOUGHTS UPON SACRED SUBJECTS.

BY CLERGYMEN OF THE EPISCOPAL CHURCH.

EDITED BY THOMAS WYATT, A. M.

In one volume, 12mo.

WITH SEVEN BEAUTIFUL STEEL ENGRAVINGS.

The contents of this work are chiefly by clergymen of the Episcopal Church. Among the contributors will be found the names of the Right Rev. Bishop Potter, Bishop Hopkins, Bishop Smith, Bishop Johns, and Bishop Doane; and the Rev. Drs. H. V. D. Johns, Coleman, and Butler; Rev. G. T. Bedell, M'Cabe, Ogilsby, &c. The illustrations are rich and exquisitely wrought engravings upon the following subjects:—"Samuel before Eli," "Peter and John healing the Lame Man," "The Resurrection of Christ," "Joseph sold by his Brethren," "The Tables of the Law," "Christ's Agony in the Garden," and "The Flight into Egypt." These subjects, with many others in prose and verse, are ably treated throughout the work.

ANCIENT CHRISTIANITY EXEMPLIFIED,

In the Private, Domestic, Social, and Civil Life of the Primitive Christians, and in the Original Institutions, Offices, Ordinances, and Rites of the Church.

BY REV. LYMAN COLEMAN, D. D.

In one volume 8vo. Price $2 50.

PRICE FIFTY CENTS.

NOTES

ON

UNCLE TOM'S CABIN:

BEING

A LOGICAL ANSWER

TO ITS

ALLEGATIONS AND INFERENCES

AGAINST

SLAVERY AS AN INSTITUTION.

WITH A SUPPLEMENTARY NOTE ON THE KEY, AND AN APPENDIX OF AUTHORITIES.

BY THE

REV. E. J. STEARNS, A. M.,

LATE PROFESSOR IN ST. JOHN'S COLLEGE, ANNAPOLIS, MD.

PHILADELPHIA:
LIPPINCOTT, GRAMBO, & CO.,
No. 14 NORTH FOURTH STREET.
1853.

In Press,

A NEW AND COMPLETE

GAZETTEER OF THE UNITED STATES.

It will furnish the fullest and most recent information respecting the Geography, Statistics, and present state of improvement, of every part of this great Republic, particularly of

TEXAS, CALIFORNIA, OREGON, NEW MEXICO,

&c. The work will be issued as soon as the complete official returns of the present Census are received.

THE ABOVE WORK WILL BE FOLLOWED BY

A UNIVERSAL GAZETTEER, OR GEOGRAPHICAL DICTIONARY,

of the most complete and comprehensive character. It will be compiled from the best English, French, and German authorities, and will be published the moment that the returns of the present census of Europe can be obtained.

History of the Mormons of Utah,

THEIR DOMESTIC POLITY AND THEOLOGY,

BY J. W. GUNNISON,

U. S. Corps Topographical Engineers.

WITH ILLUSTRATIONS, IN ONE VOLUME DEMI-OCTAVO.

PRICE FIFTY CENTS.

REPORT OF A GEOLOGICAL SURVEY

OF

WISCONSIN, IOWA, AND MINNESOTA,

AND INCIDENTALLY OF

A PORTION OF NEBRASKA TERRITORY,

MADE UNDER INSTRUCTIONS FROM THE U. S. TREASURY DEPARTMENT,

BY DAVID DALE OWEN,

United States' Geologist.

WITH OVER 150 ILLUSTRATIONS ON STEEL AND WOOD.

Two volumes, quarto. Price Ten Dollars.

MERCHANTS' MEMORANDUM BOOK,

CONTAINING LISTS OF ALL GOODS PURCHASED BY COUNTRY MERCHANTS, &c

One volume, 18mo., Leather cover. Price, 50 cents.

ARTHUR'S
New Juvenile Library.

BEAUTIFULLY ILLUSTRATED.

1. WHO IS GREATEST? and other Stories.
2. WHO ARE HAPPIEST? and other Stories.
3. THE POOR WOOD-CUTTER, and other Stories.
4. MAGGY'S BABY, and other Stories.
5. MR. HAVEN'T-GOT-TIME AND MR. DON'T-BE-IN-A-HURRY.
6. THE PEACEMAKERS.
7. UNCLE BEN'S NEW-YEAR'S GIFT, and other Stories.
8. THE WOUNDED BOY, and other Stories.
9. THE LOST CHILDREN, and other Stories.
10. OUR HARRY, and other Poems and Stories.
11. THE LAST PENNY, and other Stories.
12. PIERRE, THE ORGAN BOY, and other Stories.

EACH VOLUME IS ILLUSTRATED WITH

ENGRAVINGS FROM ORIGINAL DESIGNS BY CROOME,

And are sold together or separately.

TRUTHS ILLUSTRATED BY GREAT AUTHORS.

A DICTIONARY OF OVER FOUR THOUSAND AIDS TO REFLECTION—QUOTATIONS OF MAXIMS, METAPHORS, COUNSELS, CAUTIONS, APHORISMS, PROVERBS, &c. &c., IN PROSE AND VERSE;

COMPILED FROM SHAKSPEARE, AND OTHER GREAT WRITERS, FROM THE EARLIEST AGES TO THE PRESENT TIME.

A new edition, with American additions and revisions.

LIBRARY EDITION OF SHAKSPEARE.

(LARGE TYPE.)

THE DRAMATIC WORKS OF WILLIAM SHAKSPEARE,

WITH A LIFE OF THE POET,

AND NOTES ORIGINAL AND SELECTED, TOGETHER WITH A COPIOUS GLOSSARY.

4 VOLUMES OCTAVO.

STYLES OF BINDING:

Cloth, extra	$6 00
Library style	7 00
Half-Turkey morocco	9 00
Half-calf and Turkey, antique style	12 00
Full calf and Turkey, antique style	15 00

www.ingramcontent.com/pod-product-compliance
Lightning Source LLC
LaVergne TN
LVHW020211110826
845151LV00003B/673

* 9 7 8 1 4 2 5 5 3 4 3 4 9 *